FROM CHIEFS TO LANDLORDS

FROM CHIEFS TO LANDLORDS

Social and Economic Change in the Western
Highlands and Islands, c.1493–1820

Robert A. Dodgshon

Edinburgh University Press

© Robert A. Dodgshon, 1998

Transferred to digital print 2006

Edinburgh University Press
22 George Square, Edinburgh

Typeset in Monotype Plantin Light
by Norman Tilley Graphics, and
printed and bound in Great Britain
CPI Antony Rowe, Eastbourne

A CIP record for this book is available
from the British Library

ISBN-10 0 7486 1034 0
ISBN-13 9 7807 4861 034 1

The right of Robert A. Dodgshon
to be identified as author of this work
has been asserted in accordance with the
Copyright, Designs and Patents Act 1988.

Contents

List of Figures and Tables

Preface

Archival and library work for this book has been carried out over a number of years and has involved help from a large number of people. However, I am particularly grateful to the staff of the Scottish Record Office for their considerable help and patience over many years of this and other projects; to the staff of the National Register of Archives; the staff of the National Library of Scotland, particularly in the Map Room; to His Grace, the Duke of Argyll for his kindness in allowing access to the Campbell of Argyll Papers at Inveraray Castle; to Alistair Campbell of Airds, chief executive of the Clan Campbell and archivist at Inveraray, for his considerable help and time in arranging access to the Argyll Papers at Inveraray on a number of occasions and guiding me through the archives; to John MacLeod of MacLeod for his kindness in allowing me access to the MacLeod of Dunvegan Papers at Dunvegan; to Donald Stewart, the archivist at Dunvegan, for his help during my visits; to Mr R. Macdonald Parker of the Clan Donald Trust and staff at the Clan Donald Centre, Armadale, Skye for access to the Lord Macdonald Papers; to the Dowager Countess Cawdor for her kindness in allowing me access to the Campbell of Cawdor Papers at Cawdor Castle; and to the Lady Jean Fforde for her kindness in allowing me access to the Arran Papers at the Brodick Estate Office, Brodick. Finally, over the years, I have received much help with Scottish material from the staff of my own university library and the National Library of Wales here at Aberystwyth, to whom I would like to express my thanks.

The research for the book was greatly facilitated by research grants from the British Academy and my own university's Research Fund. The latter stages of the archival work involved, together with the drafting of the book, were carried out during research leave in 1995–6. I am extremely grateful to

Professor Kenneth O. Morgan, vice-chancellor of UWA, for granting me this research leave.

Finally, I would like to express my thanks to Nicola Carr at Edinburgh University Press for her help and support for the book, and to Mairi Robinson for all her help in preparing the final manuscript for publication.

Robert A. Dodgshon

List of Abbreviations

APS   Acts of Parliament of Scotland
CDC/MP   Clan Donald Centre, Lord Macdonald Papers
DC/MDP   Dunvegan Castle, MacLeod of Dunvegan Papers
ERS   Exchequer Rolls of Scotland
IC/AP   Inveraray Castle, Argyll Papers
NLS   National Library of Scotland
NRA(S)   National Register of Archives (Scotland)
OSA   The Statistical Account of Scotland
RPC   Register of the Privy Council of Scotland
SRO   Scottish Record Office

Introduction

Despite the amount that has been written on the history of the western Highlands and Islands, our understanding of how the region's society, economy and settlement developed is surprisingly uneven. Thanks to a growing amount of archaeological field-work and excavation and, for later centuries, toponymic work, there is now a well-established debate on the changing character of society, economy and settlement during the millennium or so from late prehistory down to, and including, the Viking colonisation of the ninth and tenth centuries AD.[1] Coming forward into more recent times, a range of detailed regional and systematic studies has left us with an informed grasp of how most aspects of society, economy and settlement have changed from the late eighteenth century down to the present day. However, by comparison, there has been much less debate over what was happening to society, economy and settlement during the period in between, that is, over the medieval and early modern periods from the Viking settlements down to the mid-eighteenth century.

Their wider political context is well understood, especially from the late medieval period onwards[2] but, on other matters concerning society, economy and settlement, there has been much less progress. Clan histories, real and fictitious, are a freely available source for social history, but they describe only a narrow section of society. Beneath the leading families portrayed by such clan genealogies, much lies hidden. Indeed, it would be true to say that we have barely begun to define what everyday life was like for the ordinary kinsman or farmer who actually worked the land, even for the two or three centuries that stretch back beyond the mid-eighteenth century. We know relatively little about how their families and communities were constituted or how they fitted into the wider structure of the clan system.[3] We know even less about what is arguably the most basic economic institution of the region,

1

namely, the farming township. Fundamental questions about its tenurial
and agrarian character over the medieval and early modern periods remain
unanswered. We also have scant knowledge about how its strategies of output were linked to the wider needs of the estate economy. Some of these
questions have been successfully explored in the context of the late eighteenth and early nineteenth centuries, but by this stage, the gradual clearance
of townships for sheep and the reorganisation of others into crofting townships were effectively bringing the history of the traditional township to an
end.[4] In fact, even for this eve-of-change period, there are still serious gaps
in our understanding. Once our perspective is pushed back beyond the mid-
eighteenth century, these gaps increase. Indeed, to date, only a small handful
of studies have attempted to explore some of the key questions bearing on
society, economy and settlement during the two or three centuries prior to
the mid-eighteenth century.[5]

The prime difficulty that we face is that whilst appropriate documentary
data is reasonably abundant from the mid–late eighteenth century onwards,
it thins significantly as we work back into the seventeenth century and fades
dramatically once we get to the sixteenth century. By the fifteenth century
and beyond, relevant data is so scarce as to make it unlikely that we will ever
be able to reach meaningful conclusions about Highland communities and
their economy using conventional historical sources. Most of our insights
about such themes are likely to come from the spade of the archaeologist.
Clearly, it is important that we acknowledge these basic data problems and
the constraints which they impose on what we can say. However, it is also
important to acknowledge that we are still far from exploiting the full potential of the material that is available for the period between the sixteenth and
eighteenth centuries. Indeed, even for the relatively data-rich eighteenth
century, there is material still to be analysed and fresh questions to be asked
of it. More serious, so long as our studies concentrate so much on the
evidence for the eighteenth and nineteenth centuries, it will leave us with an
overly static view of traditional Highland society and its economy. We need
to draw on available sixteenth- and seventeenth-century data and to set it
in comparison with eighteenth century material so as to create a deeper
perspective on the trends and changes already in progress prior to the more
dramatic, largescale changes of the late eighteenth and nineteenth centuries.

This book addresses these problems by looking at the changing character
of society and economy in the western Highlands and Islands of Scotland
from c.1493 down to 1820. Its primary concern is with the broad institutional forms, trends and processes rather than individual events and situations. In particular, the discussion will explore how two broad institutional
forms evolved and interacted with each other over the period c.1493–1820.
The first is represented by the system of ideology and behaviour that clan
chiefs had developed around themselves by the outset of the period under
review, a system which subsequently underwent a profound adjustment,
c.1493–1820, as chiefs were slowly forced to think and act more as landlords.

The second is represented by the ordinary farming community and its complex of subsistence needs and resource strategies, needs and strategies that shifted significantly, c.1493–1820, in response to their changing circumstances and to changes in the wider estate economy.

The study's chronological starting point of c.1493 coincides with the collapse of the Lordship of the Isles and its forfeiture to the Scottish Crown. The Lordship was a powerful and complex territorial lordship that covered a significant part of the region, embracing the southern Hebrides and parts of the mainland, mainly in Argyll. Though the Hebrides were formally ceded by Norway to the Scottish Crown in 1266, the emergence of the Lordship of the Isles in the mid-fourteenth century provided the southern Hebrides and parts of the mainland with a renewed independence of mind and a sense of political identity that amounted to a kingdom within a kingdom.[6] Having exercised such political self-will, its collapse inevitably had far-reaching political implications for the region.

Yet for all its political significance, it would be wrong to overstress c.1493 as a decisive or marked watershed in the social and economic development of the region. Rather, the choice of c.1493 as the study's starting point is determined more by the fact that this is when more specific social and economic data starts to become available for the region, albeit in fragmented form. The handful of charters available prior to c.1493 shed only a dim light on how society and economy were organised.[7] By the sixteenth century, we start to get a broadening range of material, from estate rentals and accounts to bonds of manrent. For the first time, it becomes possible to take a bottom-up approach to the character of local society and economy, to glimpse clan structures, communities and farming townships. However fragmented or limited such data might be, it enables us to open up a debate about the institutional character of Highland society and economy as they appear in the sixteenth and seventeenth centuries.

The terminal date for the study has been formally set at 1820 but its real terminal point is the disappearance of the broad institutional structures and processes around which the study is based. The clan system, and with it the whole notion of a chiefly economy, was already in decline by the early seventeenth century. Its decline, though, was a prolonged affair. Even after the defeat of the Jacobite cause at Culloden in 1746, there are still aspects of management on some estates that owed more to the values implicit in the clan system than to any cold or detached reading of market needs, despite the fact that many traditional estates faced acute financial difficulties throughout the seventeenth and eighteenth centuries.[8] By the end of the eighteenth century, though, the management policies of even the most conservative estate had become dominated by the opportunities of the marketplace and the need to maximise estate income. The farming township survived intact for longer. Its demise began when townships were cleared to make way for sheep, a conversion that was underway in parts of the southern Highlands by the 1750s and which spread northwards and westwards, reaching townships beyond the Great Glen by the 1790s.[9] By this point, however, another source of change was beginning to transform townships, with landlords reorganising runrig townships into crofting townships either *in situ* or, where clearance had taken place, on wholly new sites. Individual or even small clusters of two or three crofts had long existed attached to runrig townships, or to activities like milling or brewing. The creation of townships composed wholly of crofts, though, was new. Like the spread of sheep farming, the creation of these crofting townships continued long into the nineteenth century, especially in parts of the Hebrides.[10] However, we can take 1820 as the broad point at which the balance between a landscape dominated by runrig townships finally gave way to one dominated by sheep farms and crofting townships, the switch being hastened by the falling prices and economic problems that followed the ending of the Napoleonic Wars in 1815.

By nature, peasant communities are usually seen as timeless, unchanging societies, locked into tradition and time-honoured routines of survival. For most, their horizon of needs was immediate and pressing. The traditional peasant communities that existed in the western Highlands and Islands prior to 1820 were no exception to this rule. Indeed, there has long been a temptation to regard the patterns evident in the region prior to the Clearances or the formation of crofting townships as archaic, embodying institutional forms that had matured, Methuselah-like, over many centuries. Indeed, basic components of the traditional township economy, like outfield, have been labelled by some as prehistoric. In a sense, there is something ahistorical if not anti-historical in such a view, for it supposes that the character of such communities changed little across vast periods of time, at least at a grass-roots level. To put it another way, they are seen as having no experience of change, or history. Of course, such a view has also had another effect. It has enabled us to conveniently assume that what we see in the late eighteenth century on the eve of change could serve as an image of the region for the darker, less recorded centuries that stretched back beyond the eighteenth century.

This book will wholeheartedly reject such a view. In its place, it argues for a society and economy that was in a state of continual movement and adjustment, c.1493–1820. Not only did the basic relationship between the estate economy and the township economy, together with that between chiefs and kinsmen, slowly shift, but a case can be made out for a strategy of resource use that depended more on flexibility and adjustment than on conservatism. Furthermore, it argues that when we first begin to glimpse the region soon after c.1493, it may have been in the process of adjusting to a more fundamental qualitative change in its organisation, one that had developed over the late medieval period and whose impact on the basic institutional forms of the region must caution us against easy assumptions over how much continuity occurred between the medieval and early modern periods. Whilst this may mean abandoning some very cherished assumptions about the time-honoured nature of traditions in the region, it does so by putting back in their place what is a richer, more varied experience of change and the past.

NOTES

1. The sort of debate and insight being generated on late prehistoric settlement and landscapes is well illustrated by studies like Armit, 'Broch landscapes in the Western Isles'; Armit (ed.), *Beyond the Brochs*; Armit, *The Later Prehistory of the Western Isles*; Parker Pearson, Sharples and Mulville, 'Brochs and iron age society; a reappraisal'. The extent and vigour of the debate over Scandinavian settlement in the region is well conveyed by Nicolaisen, 'Norse settlement in the Northern and Western Isles'. Crawford, *Scandinavian Scotland*; Fellows-Jensen, 'Viking settlement in the Northern and Western Isles'; Andersen, 'Norse settlement in the Hebrides'.

2. Background reviews of the region's political history are provided by Duncan and Brown, 'Argyll and the Isles in the earlier Middle Ages', pp. 192–220; Barrow, 'The Highlands in the lifetime of Robert the Bruce'; Macinnes, 'Civil wars, interregnum and Scottish Gaeldom'; Macinnes, *Clanship, Commerce and the House of Stuart, 1603–1788*. An overview of the region's sources is provided by Barrow, 'The Sources for the history of the Highlands in the middle ages'. Extended comment on seventeenth-century sources is also provided by Shaw, *The Northern and Western Islands of Scotland*, especially pp. 7–13.

3. The kind of social and cultural history that is possible is well shown by Leneman, *Living in Atholl, 1685–1785*; Macpherson, 'An old Highland genealogy and the making of a Scottish clan'. For the period from the mid-eighteenth century onwards, see the fine studies by Withers, *Gaelic Scotland*; Devine, *Clanship to Crofter's War*.

4. A key introductory text to society and economy in the western Highlands and Islands after 1750 is Gray, *The Highland Economy 1750–1850*. Also valuable are Youngson, *After the Forty-Five*; Smith, *Jacobite Estates of the Forty-Five*. More thematic, but essential for any understanding of the region's rural society and its dynamics, is Devine, *The Great Highland Potato Famine*.

5. Three studies are particularly significant, see Shaw, *The Northern and Western Islands*; Wormald, *Lords and Men*; and, recently published, Macinnes, *Clanship, Commerce and the House of Stuart, 1603–1788*. Though largely concerned with the Lowlands, Whyte's study, *Agriculture and Society in Seventeenth Century Scotland* also provides comment on Highland conditions.

6. A review of the Lordship is provided by Munro, 'The Lordship of the Isles'; Bannerman, 'The Lordship of the Isles'; Grant, 'Scotland's celtic fringe in the late middle ages'.

7. A sample of the pre-1493 documentation available is provided by Lamont, 'The Islay charter of 1408'.

8. This is well shown by Shaw, *The Northern and Western Islands of Scotland*, pp. 43–6.

9. The most authoritative survey of the clearances is Richards' *A History of the Highland Clearances*.

10. Hunter, *The Making of the Crofting Community* is the starting point for any understanding of crofting. Valuable insights are also provided by geographical studies of crofting, such as Moisley, *Uig: A Hebridean Parish*; Caird, *Park: A Geographical Study of a Lewis Crofting District*; Caird, 'The creation of crofts and new settlement patterns in the Highlands and islands of Scotland', pp. 67–75; Turnock, 'Crofting in Lochaber'; Turnock, 'North Morar'; Storrie, 'Landholdings and settlement evolution', pp. 138–61.

1 The Western Highlands and Islands in Context, c.1493–1820

We can only begin to appreciate the character of society and economy in the western Highlands and Islands, c.1493–1820, by seeing them in the context of the region's physical setting. In particular, we need to establish how basic institutional forms coped with the environmental limitations and opportunities of the region. Across all aspects of Highland life, the environment is not just a setting but an active partner, one that in places can be accommodating and benign but in other places, unyielding and utterly uncompromising. Whilst there are patently other factors to be taken on board when analysing the constitutive character of Highland society and economy, few play such a part in the understanding of so many different aspects. For this reason, the ecology of society and economy, the way in which their basic institutional forms fitted in with the region's resource base and its problems, will form a recurrent theme throughout the study.

A VIEW FROM THE TOP DOWN: CLANS, CHIEFS AND TERRITORIES

A prime feature of Highland society for most of the period, c.1493–1820, was the role played by the organisation of society around clans and their chiefs. Admittedly, the period witnessed the gradual decline of the clan system in a functional if not an affective sense, a decline that quickened after the Statutes of Iona (1609) and progressed rapidly after the '45. However, enough of its characteristics and values survived even after the '45 for us to be able to see the changing role of clans and their chiefs as a unifying theme for the period as a whole.

The importance of the clan system, and the reason why it can be regarded as a system, lies in the multi-dimensional character of clans and their chiefs.

They were more than just communities bonded by, and stratified through, kin ties – real or assumed – under the leadership of a clan chief.[1] In the first place, we cannot conceive of clans in purely social terms. Their bonds of kinship were only sustained as meaningful when and where members of a clan had possession of land, either as owners or tenants. This underlying principle of clan formation was embodied in the saying that a clan without land was a broken clan. In other words, as well as being structured around kin-based communities, the identity and position of a clan was also given meaning through their strategic control over landholding and its potential resources. This control over landholding also provided the more powerful clans with the nucleus of a territory across which they could exercise a socio-political role. In effect, clans and their alliance structures defined the political geography of the region. Just as a clan without land was a broken clan, so also was it said that a man without a clan was a broken man. To be part of the established order of the region, you needed to be affiliated to an established clan. Even when central government began tentatively to extend its authority into the region, it tended to do so through the forms and framework offered by the clan system.

That clans were integrated through real or assumed ties of kinship, developed kin-based networks of landholding and formed the foundation of socio-political order within the region are well-worked themes in the literature. However, they are not sufficient in themselves to complete a definition of the Highland clan system. Clans and their chiefs were also associated with a distinct ideology of behaviour. The central features of this behaviour were displays of feasting and feuding. Feasting involved the extravagant consumption of vast quantities of food at chiefly feasts that could go on for days, with entertainment being provided by pipers, harpists, storytellers and clan historians. Feuding was no less an endemic feature of clan relations. In clan histories, they are typified by feuds that went on for decades and by the recounting of slaughter committed during particular raids and skirmishes. Less widely appreciated is the extent to which feuding, like feasting, was also food-centred, with inter-clan raids destroying standing crops, setting fire to grain stores and stealing cattle or whatever could walk for itself. In effect, feuding can be seen as a means of diminishing the capacity of rival clans for feasting whilst enhancing one's own capacity. As forms of behaviour, both feasting and feuding were also linked to a chief's capacity to gather in food rents or renders, with each forming part of what, ultimately, was a single circuit of food flows. This food circuit can be seen as part of a wider chief-focused system of exchange within the clan system, one that enabled chiefs not only to establish their position through display, but also, to convert food into prestige goods, such as body armour, and to contract more favourable marriage alliances (see Figure 1.1). Like the very constitution of clans as communities of kinsmen, what ultimately underpinned this exchange system was the chief's ability to secure his control over land and to fill it with his own kinsmen or those of allied clans.

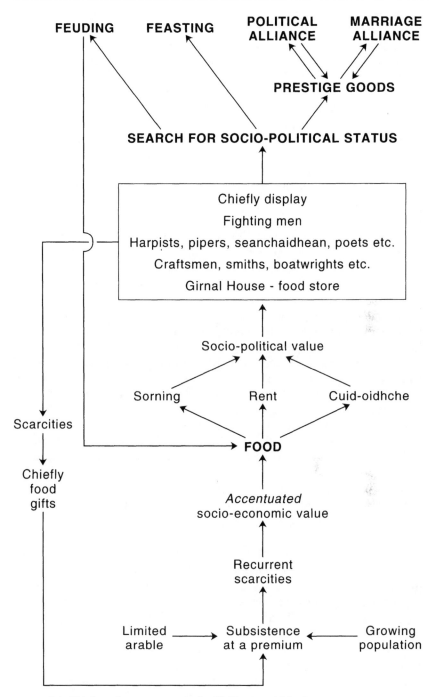

FIGURE 1.1. Chiefly exchange systems in the Highlands and Islands
Source: Reprinted from Dodgshon, 'Modelling Highland chiefdoms', p. 108.

If we are to establish a full understanding of the clan system, each of these different dimensions of its character must be explored in detail. To this end, subsequent chapters will explore, first, the constitutive role of kinship in the formation of clans and how it enabled chiefs to extend socio-political control over a defined territory; second, the success of a chief in uplifting food rents and renders, that is, in establishing an estate economy; and third, how chiefs incorporated these rents into a wider exchange system driven by different forms of chiefly consumption and display. Before subjecting the clan system to this sort of systematic analysis, though, we need to consider how it was affected by the physical character of the Highlands and Islands.

Chiefly systems of socio-political control and landholding were once widespread throughout Britain. What distinguished those in the Highlands and Islands is the way in which they survived as active social forms down into the early modern period. Arguably, this late survival was due more to nega- tive rather than positive factors. Seen from the vantage point of the Lowlands and an emergent state system based on feudal principles, the western High- lands and Islands offered a poor bargain. Its costs of integration via a fully- developed system of feudalism would have been high whilst its rewards, or what could be extracted from the soil, would not have covered these costs. The early penetration of the Anglo-Normans into the eastern and southern edges of the Highlands, with the implantation of families like the Morays, Chisholms and Stewarts, was enough to provide a strong buffer against clans positioned more deeply within the region.[2] In time, the Crown also worked to assert its authority over those clans whose territory lay deep within the heart of the Highlands, but it did so more slowly and by forcing local chiefs to acknowledge the Crown as their superior and to hold land from it by charter grant, though some displacements did take place. For this reason alone, we can expect some degree of continuity even after the granting of Crown charters. The Macdonalds of Keppoch, a clan holding land in the Braes of Keppoch, were reportedly the last family 'to hold by *duchas*', that is, 'without sheep-skin' or charter, though their claim was really an attempt to challenge the Crown grant of their lands to the Mackintoshes in the fifteenth century.[3] The same process also engulfed the Hebrides once control over them had been ceded from Norway to the Scottish king by the Treaty of Perth (1266), though it was not until after the collapse of the Lordship of the Isles in 1493 that the Crown acted to have individual Hebridean chiefs hold land from it by charter.[4] As one Hebridean chief reputedly said after visiting Edinburgh to acknowledge the Crown as his superior, whereas he had previously held his land on the edge of his sword, he now held it on the skin of a sheep.[5]

In character, the initial penetration of Crown authority into the region introduced a superficial rather than all-embracing form of feudalism, em- placing a capstone of Crown authority over a pattern of landholding that, in many areas, did not immediately change. Unlike in other frontier areas of Anglo-Norman feudalism, no attempt was made to secure the region through what we can describe as the conventional forms and institutions of military feudalism. The military ties and obligations exercised by chiefs, the means by which they secured socio-political control within their respective territories, owed as much to the traditional values of the clan system as to feudalism. Where a chief, like Campbell of Argyll, granted out blocks of land to his 'vassals', the grants were to kinsmen and served only to define new parts or branches of the clan rather than to replace the values involved with new ones rooted wholly in feudal service.[6] Even when chiefs extended their networks of alliance through bonds of friendship and manrent, this did not involve any explicit exchange of land in return for the pledges of mutual support.[7] This meant that whilst the region appeared outwardly tied to the Crown, inwardly or beneath the level of those who held by Crown charter, many chiefs continued to operate in their own self-interest, upholding values and institutions that dealt as much with kinsmen as with vassals and which had more to do with the immediate needs of their clan than with the wider needs of Crown feudalism. In short, a distinction needs to be drawn between the Crown's formal assumption of authority over the area and its reality on the ground. Indeed, it is worth noting that even after the collapse of the Lordship of the Isles and the re-granting of estates by Crown charter, the region experienced a period of extreme turbulence as the Crown moved slowly and uncertainly to replace the control previously exercised by the Lordship.[8]

Had the region offered more, both in terms of an easier terrain for fighting in or for moving across, as well as a more productive resource base, we might have expected the Crown to have pressed its close authority sooner and more vigorously. In the event, its relative standoffishness allowed power structures developed around Highland chiefs and their clans to continue as the prime focus of authority. Indeed, the Crown even used the clan system, co-opting chiefs like Campbell of Argyll, to serve its needs in the region through devices and institutions that had more to do with the clan system than with the normal procedures and processes of central government. Significantly, the success of families like the Campbells of Argyll in administering their greatly enlarged territories, as well as the growth of marketing with all its significance for estate income, have been linked to the emergence of better, more defined routeways over the sixteenth and seventeenth centuries.[9] Later, after the '45, when the government pressed its authority over the region in the firmest possible way, it is significant that it did so through a network of new roads, built by General Wade, and a programme of economic reform through the agency of the Board of Trustees for the Annexed Estates.[10] Between them, these two instruments of change addressed what had long been the problem of the region when seen from the standpoint of central government, a central government that was even more removed after the Act of Union (1707): namely, the difficulties of movement within the region and the worth of its economic product or what could be extracted from it.

Of course, these perceptions of the region's isolation and the difficulties of travel within it are entirely relative. For communities that see themselves as part of a local and largely self-contained socio-political structure and which, as with Adam Smith's portrayal of the traditional Highland farmer in his *Wealth of Nations*, work to satisfy all their own needs by being 'butcher, baker and brewer for his own family',[11] questions about their isolation prompt the reply, 'isolated from what?'. Every family functioned as 'a Kind of independent Colony'.[12] Location was not an issue. When we look at patterns of Highland settlement prior to the nineteenth century, especially at those in the more remote parts of the western Highlands and Islands, what stands out is not so much the sheer scale or density of settlement but the extent of its dispersal, filling out every possible niche. By the time plans and surveys become available, settlement had found its way into most localities and onto most islands that had any potential. We can appreciate this latter point by looking at the islands that fringed the 'mainland' of the outer Hebrides. Despite their size and difficulty of access during the winter months, many were heavily settled and cultivated. Even down into this century, mainland settlements like those of Smearsary in Moidart were routinely accessed by sea rather than by land. The survival of communities on such sites cannot be rationalised by treating them as remote or isolated settlements surviving on the edge of a much larger and wider system *and as handicapped by that fact*, but by seeing them as sufficient unto themselves or as communities that functioned within a relatively localised network of relations. Such sites only become remote when the pressures of modernity forced them into the framework of a national economic system.

When we look at the geography of the larger clans, they faced the task of holding together townships and communities scattered across the most difficult and broken terrain. No Lowland estate, for instance, faced the integration problems that were part and parcel of managing the territory controlled by MacLeod of Dunvegan. As well as controlling most of the islands that lay between North Uist and Harris like Pabbay, Ensay and Berneray and those that lay along the western edges of Harris like Taransay and Scarpa, or far out into the Atlantic in the case of St Kilda, MacLeod of Dunvegan also held the 'mainland' of Harris itself, including the very rugged terrain of the Forest. Across the Minch, on Skye, he also held Vaternish, Duirinish, Minginish and Bracadale. Though positioned around MacLeod's base at Dunvegan, even these Skye districts contained some physically isolated sites, such as the small string of townships that lay on the Minch-side of Minginish like Ramasaig and Lorgill, both well-settled townships in the eighteenth century. If positioned strategically on the high ground of south Harris, it would have been possible on a good day to see a high proportion of MacLeod's sprawling territory. Yet such a territory would have been difficult to integrate via any routinised system of estate management given the high costs and practical problems of communication between its parts in a pre-modern age. Altogether, MacLeod's total holding was vast. Like other extensive Highland estates, though, its size was hardly meaningful when its gross income barely matched that of a small-to-middling estate in the Low-lands. In such circumstances, locally-evolved systems of power which bound space through kinship would have provided a form of territorial bonding that outweighed questions of whether movement had economic costs that made it unprofitable. Rather was such a territory to be seen in terms of social space, movement through which was calculated via a different notion of cost.

This last point can be linked to another aspect of clans and how they related to the difficult broken topography of the region. Clans drew meaning not just from the presence of kin-ties, real or assumed, but from the fact that they were rooted in, and sustained through, their emplacement within particular areas. Clans needed space or territory if they were to have any sort of existence. So too, of course, did other traditional social systems, like those based on the feudal control of land. Feudalism established control over land through vertically defined ties between a lord and his vassal, the former offering protection and land in return for military service from the latter. Likewise, at the base of the social hierarchy, those who worked the soil were given land in return for labour service. But whilst, in practice, territorial lords turned their fiefs into hereditary holdings, a basic principle of feudalism was that all land was held ultimately from the Crown and passed back to it on the death of a vassal. What mattered to feudalism, first and foremost, was the constant renewal of the Crown's superiority over all men and all land, and the pledge of service given in return for grants of jurisdiction or land, not the continuity of particular families in particular fiefs or holdings. The resource demands of military and economic feudalism also need to be noted. Whether through the demands made in support of knightly service, or the demands made by a system of demesne production, feudalism was very much a system that operated best in fertile, arable areas. When it came up against environments like those of the western Highlands and Islands, the balance between profits and losses worked against it.

Yet by the time we see it in any detail, west Highland and Hebridean land-holding had been penetrated by some feudal principles, with chiefs holding their land from the Scottish Crown and letting it out to tenants in return for various dues, renders and even labour services. However, despite its hybridised character, such a system still retained features that distinguished it from a pure feudal system. In the first place, what mattered to a successful clan was how it used its leading branches to secure ongoing control over land at a managerial or tacksmen's level. Of course, we could put this another way and say that they became leading branches because they had a strategic role in helping a clan to extend and control its territory. Kinship ties and land became confused into a single scheme of social order, with the continuity of particular families in particular districts being synonymous with the con-tinuity of the clan itself. For part of a clan to secure control over a territory, whatever that territory's worth in resource terms, was to secure the basis for a new branch of the clan because it provided the clan with an extension to its social space. This topological transformation of territory into a form of social space is demonstrated by the way leading members of a clan were identified by the name of the district in which they lived, so they appear as, say, Campbell of Airds or Macdonald of Keppoch.[13] The implications of this point are simple. The clan system needs to be seen as having powerful space-filling tendencies, with clans constantly seeking to expand their social space. Driven as much by this social concept of space, as much as by the economic needs of the system, such expansion could place a value on even low-output environments. This willingness to exploit environments with low and un-certain levels of output was further helped by the fact that it lacked the heavy demands that military feudalism and demesne production placed on re-source needs, though a number of estates could and did levy quite substantial demands for the maintenance of chiefly households and what were called 'fighting men'. Whilst written rather late in the history of the clan system, there is much to learn from those eighteenth century travellers who, like Captain Burt, noted the dignity of Highlanders even in the most squalid of circumstances: their capital, and prime resource, was their pedigree.[14] Like-wise, a belief in the status of their clan, despite the realities of their ecological niche, lay behind the scorn reputedly shown to the Macneils of Barra for 'their Poverty and Pride'.[15]

There is another dimension to the ecology of clans, one that takes us to the very heart of their organisation as social systems. It concerns the role played by their exchange system in sustaining an ideology of behaviour and display (see Figure 1.1). This is an aspect that has been widely debated in the archaeological and anthropological literature on chiefdoms. Two basic fea-tures about their exchange systems are stressed. The first is its instrumental meaning. Chiefs gather in basic produce, including food, from their kinsmen. This primary circuit of flow into chiefly centres acts as tribute, underpinning the chief's central and ordinating position within the chiefdom. However, it is a flow which has its counterflow, with chiefs redistributing food and other resources in times of need. This collecting in and redistribution of food during times of need is seen by many writers as enabling chiefs to offer their kinsmen an insurance against risk, particularly in environments where re-current scarcities were present.[16] By any yardstick, traditional communities in the western Highlands and Islands faced a range of risk-laden environ-ments. Some of these risks will be outlined below. What matters here is to note that the type of redistributive exchange system which developed around the Highland clan system would have provided some insurance against such risks and, for that reason, is likely to have been a factor in their late survival within the region.

As well as providing a form of social storage against disaster, the food and other resources which chiefs accumulated were used in other ways. In particular, we find many chiefs using what they gathered in via the exchange system to generate secondary circuits of exchange. Part could be used to support craftsmen and the making of prestige goods, goods which only chiefs or the senior members of a clan had access to. These prestige goods could then be used to support exchange flows with other chiefs, or favourable marriage settlements with them. Likewise, the accumulation of food and other resources could be used to sustain different forms of chiefly display, including bouts of feasting and feuding. Where chiefdoms existed in risk-laden environments, so that scarcities were a recurrent feature of life, the conspicuous consumption of food via bouts of chiefly feasting and its destruction or theft via feuding must have had a powerful ideological value. They symbolise the ability of the clan, in the figure of its chief, to overcome such problems. Given the frequency of dearth in the western Highlands and Islands, with a crop failure reputedly once every three years, the ideological value that could be exploited by a chief's command over food resources would have been considerable. This comes across even at a general level. The Steward of the Southern Isles, for instance, was described by Martin Martin (1700) as a great man simply because of the large amount of food which he gathered in as rent,[17] a comment that is only meaningful if we take on board the immediate and primary value attached to food in a world in which subsistence could not be taken for granted and food storage was problematic. Likewise, it is not without significance that one of Rob Roy's supposed crimes was to steal from the girnal houses of the Buchanan chief and the Duke of Lennox. In a society racked with scarcity, the very existence of a girnal house could be a very potent symbol of a chief's position. Clearly, any analysis of Highland clans and their chiefs must look closely at this aspect of the problem.

Most conceptual reviews of chiefdoms stress their innate instability as systems. In a detailed review of Polynesian chiefdoms, Kirch suggested a cyclical switching between simple and complex chiefdoms.[18] When we look at their character, we can understand why. Clans competed with each other for land and tribute. One clan's gain was another's loss. Status gained through feasting and feuding could be converted into favourable marriage alliances and further expansion, again at another clan's expense. In short, the competitive nature of chiefly systems made the eruption and subsequent collapse of complex alliance structures a commonplace occurrence. In the case of the western Highlands and Islands, though any instability that arose from the working out of what we can call the dynamics of the clan system, and with it the territorial displacement of one clan by another, was compounded by the growing penetration of Crown authority into the region and its support for some clans at the expense of others.

A VIEW FROM THE BOTTOM UP: TOWNSHIPS AND THEIR RESOURCE STRATEGIES

That the environment posed special problems for farming communities in the western Highlands and Islands needs no special pleading. However, a number of background points need to be drawn out about how their organisation, economies and resource strategies reflected the limitations and

TABLE 1.1. Total arable acreage in the western Highlands and Islands, c.1800

	Total acreage	Arable	Arable as % of total
Tiree 1768	16555	8240	50
Barrisdale 1771	16335	101	0.6
Harris 1772	97170	6359	6.5
Assynt1774	105606	2586	2.4
Coigach 1775	60871	700	1.1
Glenelg 1775	25033	1367	5.4
Coll 1794	13766	4451	32.3
Ardnamurchan 1804–5	55818	3482	6.2
Sunart 1804–5	54135	1725	3.2
Benbecula 1805	17134	5595	32.6
S. Uist 1805	53709	12721	23.6
Macdonald Est/Skye 1810	206266	14618	7
Lewis 1817	172565	13268	7.6
Barra 1820–1	27810	4940	17.7
Eigg 1824	7128	1178	16.5
Canna/Sanday 1824	2838	578	20.3

Sources: SRO, Seaforth Papers GD46/17/46, Contents of the Island of Lewis, Extracted from Mr. Chapman's Books of the Plans of Lewis, 1817; DC/MDP, 1/466/22 Contents of the Mainland of Harris and Adjacent Islands 1772; ibid., 1/380/29 Glenelg Survey; SRO, RHP 1039, Plan of the Island of Benbecula, 1805; NLS, Survey of South Uist by William Bald, 1805; SRO RHP 5990/1–4 Eastern Part of the Island of Skye, 1810, surveyed by John Bell; SRO, Clanranald Papers GD201/5/1235/1, Particulars of Sale – Egg, Canna and Sanday, 1824; SRO, RHP 3368, Plan of the Island of Coll, 1794, Surveyed by George Langlands; IC/AP, V65, Contents of the Different Farms of Tiree, by James Turnbull, 1768; SRO, RHP 72 Ardnamurchan and Sunart, the Property of Sir James Riddell, 1806 and AF49/1 Survey of Ardnamurchan and Sunart; SRO, Forfeited Estates, E741 Barrisdale – Reports Concerning Farms 1771, by William Morison; SRO, Forfeited Estates, E746/189, Plans of Farms of Coigach, 1775, by William Morison; NLS Sutherland Papers, 313/3583; Adam (ed.) *Home's Survey of Assynt*, 1774; *NSA*, XIV(1845), p. 210. All acreages in Scots acres.

opportunities posed by their setting. Even when arable cultivation in the region was at its peak c.1800, it is unlikely that it exceeded 10 per cent of the region's land surface (see Table 1.1). Physically, there were four limiting factors on arable. First, there were the obvious problems of topography, with a high proportion of the region's land surface being too high, exposed and rugged for cultivation. Second, many soils were too acidic, though this could be alleviated in those coastal areas where calcium-rich sand was available. Third, even on low ground, rock outcrops or thin soils made cultivation a difficult affair, though considerable efforts were made to overcome such problems. Fourth, the climate of the region was not always conducive to cultivation, with wet springs and summers, short growing seasons and strong winds all being frequent. When estate surveys and accounts become available during the eighteenth and early nineteenth centuries, they are replete with reports of the adverse effect which weather was having on ploughing and harvesting.[19]

The primary way in which these various environmental factors combined to affect settlement and farming was through their close and tight-reined impact on the geography of settlement. If we look at the overall pattern of settlement in the eighteenth century, it can best be described as widespread, with well-settled townships to be found as much along inland glens and straths as on the coast or Hebridean islands. It was only from the late eighteenth century onwards that settlement along the interior glens and straths on the mainland was thinned by the Clearances, and that settlement along the western seaboard or out on the islands was both intensified and concentrated through the creation of crofting townships.[20] Before this geographical restructuring, it is true to say that all areas, especially the interior parts of the mainland, had a far wider pattern of farming settlement than is to be found today.

When we look more closely at individual areas, the pattern of settlement appears as an opportunistic adaptation to local circumstances. Admittedly, if we look at some of the earliest estate plans for mainland areas like those for Glenelg (1772)[21] or for islands like Islay (1748)[22] and Coll (1794),[23] they show all land, both hill pasture and arable, as largely divided up between individual townships so that the entire landscape would have appeared occupied by them. However, in each case, the area of intensive occupation, or arable and winterings, was actually much more limited, with by far the greatest proportion of land being exploited as hill grazing. Indeed, on most estates, the formal definition of townships is recorded on early surveys simply as the land (arable plus winterings) enclosed by their head-or outer-dyke (see Figures 1.2 and 1.3). The vast areas of open hill or mountain pasture that lay beyond this dyke were technically shared between townships, though it is obvious that some sectoring between township groups did exist, using cairns as a marker.[24] It was only over the late seventeenth and eighteenth centuries, as grazings acquired more and more value through the marketing of stock, that many estates moved to formally differentiate grazings between townships, dyking areas whose use by particular townships had previously been fenced off only by scattered cairns or the force of tradition. In some cases, documentary sources allow us to see this process of privatising the common grazings actually in progress.[25]

In terms of their potential for cultivation, local ground conditions in the western Highland and Islands are extremely varied with the core of many townships comprising a veritable mosaic of different sites. Few townships had the benefit of extended or uniform conditions suitable for tillage. Along inland glens and straths, where townships were strung out in linear fashion along the lower slopes and valley-floor bottoms, arable might form reasonably continuous if narrow and irregular blocks. Some of the raised beaches that lay along the western coasts both of the mainland and the Western Isles provided similar conditions. Occasionally, local circumstances worked to the advantage of farmers. On the western side of south Uist, the presence of broad belts of machair that has been both naturally and artificially mixed

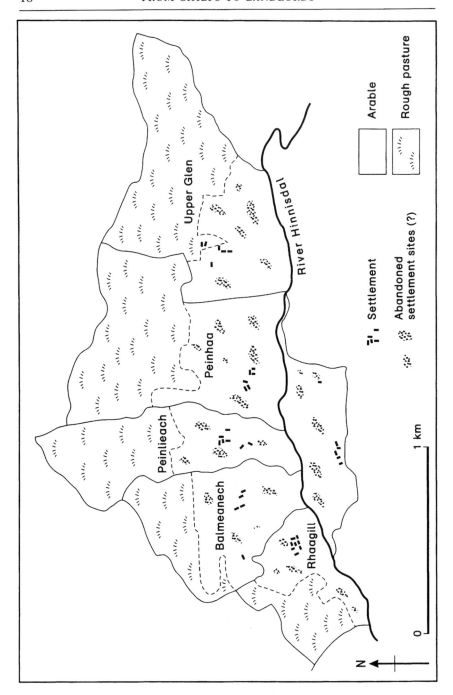

FIGURE 1.2. Townships in Glen Hinnisdal, Skye, 1766
Source: Based on SRO, RHP5993, Plan of Parishes of Portree and Uig, by M. Stobie, 1766.

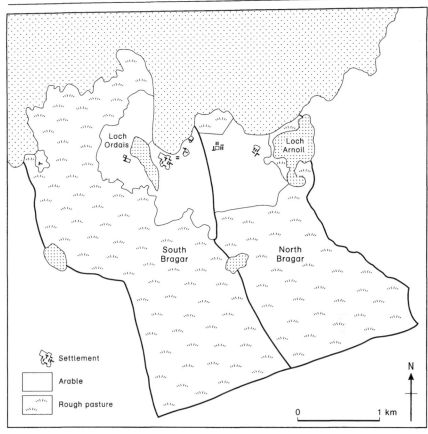

FIGURE 1.3. North and South Bragar, Lewis, 1817
Source: Based on NLS, A. Gibb's plan of Lewis, 1817, original in Western Isles Library service, Stornoway. Gibb's map was based on a survey by G. Chapman, 1807–8.

with local peat soils has produced an extensive strip of easily worked soil, but inland, it soon gives way to *gearraidh* or poorly drained peaty soils whose surface is broken by rock outcrops and lochans. On Tiree, a 1768 estate plan suggests that large areas of its sandy and easily-worked soils were laid out under impressively regular and continuous fields of arable.[26] Both in the extent of its arable and the relative tidiness of its fields, though, such a landscape was exceptional for the western Highlands and Islands. More usually, arable comprised irregularly sized and shaped patches of arable, whose surface was broken by areas or channels of poor drainage and by rock outcrops, with small detached outliers of arable adding to the fretted nature of its layout. Even in areas like the Trotternish district of Skye, where soils derived from the local volcanic rocks provide a particularly fertile soil, settlement tends only to fringe the peninsula, except where glens like that of Hinnisdal provided an opportunity for pushing a finger of settlement inland (see Figure 1.2). Further, despite the fertility its soils, there were still many Trotternish townships in which arable was broken and irregular in character.[27] In the southern Hebrides, Islay easily justified Storrie's description of it as the 'Hebridean exception'.[28] Its farming townships were to be found as much across the interior (such as around Loch Finlaggan) as around the coast but, when we consider the cropping data, the amount in cultivation was clearly restricted and many of its townships must have possessed broken rather than continuous arable.[29] Away from these fertile islands and areas, the character of arable becomes even more restricted in extent and broken in layout. In Assynt, or on the so-called 'mainland' of Harris, we are faced with highly disaggregated patches of cultivation that occupied the 'intricacies among the craggs'[30] or were made up 'of the smallest portion imaginable sometimes capable of growing only two or three potatoes'.[31] Indeed, surveys capture the broken nature of arable by having a special category called 'grassy arable' or 'arable with grass'.[32]

I have dwelt on the broad pattern of settlement and its environmental setting at some length because it has a bearing on three connected themes concerning how Highland society exploited its resource base. In a region like the western Highlands and Islands, the difference between what could or could not be cultivated was easily defined at the extremes, but in between lay a broad zone of land whose potential was less clearly defined. The problem was not simply about the physical attributes of such land, nor really about its pure economic worth, but about its social value. By this I mean that around many townships lay extensive amounts of land which, if sufficient labour was applied to preparing it, could produce a crop. Given the labour invested, such a crop might not have been economic if its costs were set against its market or exchange price. However, the food gained would still have had a use value to those who produced it. To a degree, we can expect means and needs to have worked together, with the increased labour abundance brought about by phases of population growth sustaining the labour intensiveness needed to expand arable. In other words, there were sound reasons why, when needs pressed and sufficient labour was available, we might expect the broad fringe of marginal land that surrounded the nucleus of many townships to be cultivated, with labour being used to offset its physical disadvantages. This social re-valuation could occur irrespective of any re-valuation that might have come about through climatic change. Seen in this way, the limits to cultivation were as much social as physical or economic.

We need to see the problem in terms of an opportunity slope, up which communities - if given the right social circumstances – were prepared to push cultivation. To reach a full understanding of the problem, therefore, we need not only to establish how communities pushed cultivation up this opportunity slope, but also to establish the social context in which they were prepared to do so. Seen in this way, patterns of production and their associated techniques may have been different under a chiefly system of production compared to those which prevailed under a system dominated by the needs of market production. Likewise, production and techniques may have been different during phases of high population pressure compared with phases of low population pressure.

ENVIRONMENTAL RISKS AND IMPACTS

For farmers, the western Highlands and Islands was a risk-laden environment. Even within the context of what, overall, might appear as a normal season, extreme climatic events, including gales, storms, floods and blizzards, were all capable of devastating crops and stock in a matter of hours. On a larger or longer timescale, poor seasons, especially when two or more ran in succession, could have an equally devastating effect on a regional scale. Cold, wet summers could leave farmers with a harvest barely sufficient to match the seed used, whilst long, hard winters could thin herds and flocks dramatically if little shelter was available, or could make it difficult to sow crops until well into the normal growing season.

We can glimpse the effect of such events and seasons through estate documentation. Occasionally, entries give the impression that the damage involved was localised. For instance, a 1696 entry in accounts for Campbell of Glenorchy's estate noted the township of Stronmilochan, at the head of Loch Awe, as paying ten bolls of oatmeal and ten bolls of bear meal 'to ye Girnall' together with 'ye number of sixty eight bolls Blasted oats qch would neither make meal nor feed'.[33] The following year, the tenants of Kilninver in Netherlorne were given an ease of meal due to what the estate described as an 'illness of the year singular to themselves'.[34] Likewise, when 'the greatest part' of the tenants on Luing and Seil 'lost half their corn' in 1793, it appears to have been a loss confined to that area alone.[35]

Not surprisingly, estate documentation is fuller when a poor season or succession of poor seasons led not just to problems over the payment of rent but to a major subsistence crisis. Though the estate did not yet see them as part of a wider problem, the difficulties facing the tenants of Stronmilochan and Kilninver in 1696 and 1697 occurred at the outset of a longer run of bad seasons known as King William's lean years, 1696–1703. Indeed, even by 1697, the estate was forced to take special measures to ensure all its tenants in Glenorchy and Netherlorne had a sufficient supply of grain.[36] Elsewhere, the effect of such a long run of poor seasons was manifest through the high turnover of tenants and the number of vacant possessions. Thus, an analysis of townships on Islay compiled by the Campbells of Cawdor for the period, 1703–07, shows a significant number of townships experienced short-term changes in occupancy,[37] whilst a surprising number had portions or shares described as lying 'waste'. Indeed, townships like Kelsay and Kilneave were described as lying entirely 'waste' for the first two or three years of the survey.[38] In all probability, what the survey shows, and possibly the reason why it was compiled, is the disruption to the occupation of townships caused by the succession of bad seasons, 1696–1703.

Later in the eighteenth century, the surges of emigration out of the Highlands and Islands which have been documented for the early 1740s[39] and
between 1770 and 1772[40] both co-incided with a short run of very poor
seasons. In the case of the latter, a letter dated 1772 and written to MacLeod
of Dunvegan about his tenants in Duirinish and Waternish told him that
'most part of the Inhabitants are already ruined by ye loss of yr Cattle … and
to add to yr Calamity, having nothing to eat or sow in ye Ground if the frost
and frequent snows would permit them'.[41] 'Never,' wrote one of MacLeod's
tenants, 'was a calamity so universal, wtout sowing wtout bread to support
Nature, wtout money or credit'.[42]

Of course, in a region like the western Highlands and Islands, some parts
were more prone to poor seasons than other. Thus, bad seasons were said
to be a recurrent feature of Coigach, 'because of the frequency of rains, to
which the Western Coasts is exposed'.[43] Faced with putting a value on them,
valuations could be quite blunt about the risks of farming particular sites.
Grigadale in Ardnamurchan, a coastal site, was said to be 'exposed to Sea
Blasts from all points But the East',[44] By comparison, the problem affecting
Kenkroch in Glenorchy was that it was 'high & exposed', so that it was
subject 'to severe and frequent losses in their sheep'.[45] As largescale sheep
farming began to replace runrig townships over the late eighteenth century,
and farmers began to stock the hills more exclusively with sheep, the problems of exposure were felt more acutely. High exposed farms faced other
problems. Many of the early sheep farms in areas like Sutherland suffered a
'prodigious loss of stock by death' not just from exposure and storms, but
also 'by foxes and eagles',[46] the latter risk being broadened by some commentators to include the threat that also came from wild cats, polecats and
weasels.[47] Part of the problem was that the clearances shifted stock management from a system based on shielings, in which balanced flocks and herds
were looked after closely by fairly large numbers of men, women and children
during summer, to an extensive system based on the management of large
flocks tended by a few isolated shepherds. Some commentators were also of
the view that the disarming act passed after the '45 inhibited farmers from
dealing with the predators that could decimate a flock.[48]

Arguably, the scale of risks and crises facing the farming community may
have fluxed in step with the pressure exerted on resources by population.
During times of population growth, when local communities pressed harder
on their resources, the environmental risks were increased. An obvious way
in which the pressure of numbers may have affected environment was
through the expansion of cultivation onto sites whose disturbance brought
increased risk of erosion. The extent to which cultivation rigs were pushed
high up hill-sides greatly increased prevailing rates of soil erosion. Its potential effect was not lost on contemporary observers. When John Blackadder
surveyed Lord Macdonald's estate on Skye in 1799/1800, he found that the
arable of one township 'lies so much upon the sides of Hills that the soil is in
a great degree carried off by the surface water'.[49] The problem was exacer-

bated by the fact that many rigs or lazy-beds involved a considerable amount of surface disturbance and worse, tended to run with the slope not across it, providing a natural gully for surface flow.

The disturbance of steep slopes, though, was only part of the problem. For many Highland farmers, valley ground or haugh land provided attractive but high-risk opportunities for the expansion of cultivation. But many must have found, like farmers in Glenshyra (Argyll), that where they ploughed one year, they were able to catch salmon the next as flooding re- arranged river channels.[50] This problem was especially acute in the central and northern Highlands. A glimpse of the problems faced by farmers who ploughed too close to highly braided river channels is conveyed by sources for the Cromartie and Sutherland estates, both of which had property that suffered acutely from this problem. Talking generally about the problem in a report drawn up in 1756, Francis Grant reported that the 'Water of Strath Achal in Coygach is an instance of this sort it has done so much Dammage covered with Gravel and taken away so much good Land that the Tenent will not be able to pay his Rent'.[51] The lessons though, were not learnt. By 1772, a letter from Langwell to the east reported that 'the River has done prodigious hurt this autumn & has covered three acres of the best arrable ground with stones and cut out a new channell ... the Rivers are very prejudiciall in most of our narrow Highland Glens more so in this place and Redorch'.[52] On the Sutherland estate, similar problems were experienced both in the straths and in Assynt. A tack for Carnachy in Strathnaver acknowledged that it was 'remarkably exposed to dammage by the Water of Naver' and agreed compensation to the tenant 'in case of any Extraordinary Devestation'.[53] Similar concerns can be found in Assynt tacks like those for townships along the Water of Evelichs[54] as well as in Ardnamurchan.[55]

Measured in terms of the scale of damage involved, the human impact on sand dunes or machair also formed a major problem for many of the townships that were sited along the western seaboard and in the Hebrides. The interactions involved were complex. The unstable nature of sand-dune areas meant that even without human interference, considerable and damaging sand blows could occur. This is well brought out in recent work on their ecology.[56] However, during phases of population pressure, excess use of the resources provided by sand dune areas (for example machair grazing, shell sand as manure, turf and bent) could greatly increase the risk of serious sand blows. It is impossible to say how much human interference with machair areas contributed to the major sand blows that caused devestation to many Hebridean townships, such as those of 1697.[57] However, contemporaries were in no doubt over its contribution to the recurrence of the problem in the eighteenth century. A survey of Tiree in 1768 listed some of the main contributory factors. They ranged from actually cultivating machair to over-grazing it, from pulling bent for ropes and baskets to collecting plants for dye.[58] On the island's Reef, an additional factor was 'the Custom of diging the soil of the Reeff to build Sheil Houses'.[59]

The risks were considerable. The 1768 survey for Tiree reported over 1624 acres of blown sand on the island.[60] As a problem, it was especially acute on the north coasts, with losses to arable reported in the townships of Cladichchrosan, Badewilline, Keylepol, Quiyeish and Kelis.[61] In the Outer Hebrides, a survey of Harris in 1772 reported that 'the Sand Drift has made great encroachments upon the Land' in the south west, with 'a great space Where many people still alive have reaped crops of grain'.[62] On the islands between Harris and North Uist, over 300 acres of 'the best Arable and pasture Land in the island of Pabbay' was reported as lost to sand, reducing its assessment from 10 to 7 pennylands in early eighteenth-century rentals, whilst, much later in the century, it was reported that 'about 300 acres of the best land on the Island of Bernera are entirely blown up with sand'.[63] Parts of South Uist were also said to be 'much empayned and destroyed be the sands ovir-blowing and bureing habitable lands' during the early eighteenth century.[64] Though storms were the trigger for devastation, over-ploughing was contributory. As on North Uist, where islands like Balshare and Kirkibost and townships like Sollas had 'suffered badly' from sand-blows, the risks could be lessened by 'prohibiting the Tenants from loosening the soil, either by ploughing or any other mode of culture within reach of the sand drift'.[65] Such advice was not necessarily taken by tenants for the fairly large township of Illeray on Balshare was devastated by sandblows during a mid-nineteenth-century storm, some of its former fields and even house plat-forms now lying isolated by tidal inlets to the north and west of the township's settlement nucleus.[66] Estates could also restrict the harvesting of resources like bent and shell sand.[67] In Ardnamurchan, the planting of stakes was also tried as a remedial measure. Whatever measures were taken, though, the risks involved could not be entirely eradicated.[68]

A major problem facing many communities was that Highland soils suf-fered from heavy leaching, acidity and stoniness or shallowness. In addition to using livestock manure, communities could combat these problems by applying a wide range of supplementary manures, such as peat, turf, shell sand and seaweed.[69] A consequence of their heavy use was that many essentially mineral soils were turned into rich organic soils, whilst many thin marginal soils or wet acid soils were turned into more workable soils.[70] Whilst the use of some manurial transfers, like seaweed, produced a beneficial but transient effect on soils, others produced a long-term environmental impact. In particular, the extensive use of peat, turf and shell sand as manurial supplements left many townships with patches of soil that can be described as anthropogenic. Hebridean islands like the Uists gained enormously from this mixing of shell sand and peat. In effect, they were extending what had been mixed naturally, with shell sand that had been blown inland over peat being mixed to form belts of easily-worked soil. As need arose, communities expended much effort in mixing the two soils themselves. Despite local regulations issued in 1825 forbidding any sort of practice that might cause sand blows, a valuation of North Uist a few years later boasted how shell sand could bring 'hundreds of acres of waste land annually into cultivation'.[71] Generations of local farmers had already proved the point.

Elsewhere, transfers of peat and organic soils were widely used on the mainland. On Campbell of Glenorchy's estate in Perthshire, a barony court reference of 1621 actually required tenants to transfer a quantity of soil each year 'for the guiding of each merkland'.[72] Regular transfers of soil from mosses were reported on the island of Lismore during the sixteenth century for 'guidis the teillit earth thairwith',[73] though later sources suggest the type of soil involved may have been clay marl.[74] It seems to have been commonplace across the Firth of Lorne in Ardnamurchan and Sunart for a survey of the estate in 1807 argued for its abolition, local tenants mixing it with livestock dung to make muck fail.[75] Other estates were moving to abolish the practice by the early nineteenth century. Tacks issued for farms on the Sutherland estate by the 1800s prohibited tenants from taking 'midden earth' either from pasture or unimproved grounds.[76]

Transfers of turf were also used to increase the organic content of soils, either directly or indirectly. In the case of the latter, turf used initially to build house walls, dykes, folds and roofs was subsequently recycled as manure. Yet whilst having a positive effect on arable, the largescale cutting of turf also had a detrimental effect on pasture ground. If we quantify the amount locked up in turf-and-stone dykes and walls, as well as that added directly to soil, then the negative impact on surrounding pastures must have been considerable. Many landowners became particularly anxious to prevent tenants from cutting green pastures. When the Barony Court of Menzies and Rannoch moved to control the cutting of turf in 1727, it was because the 'pasture grounds and fauldingis within the head dykes of Apinadull are very much damaged by the tennentis and possessoris ther casting of fewall and divott within the saidis head dykes'.[77] Its 'detrimental' effect on 'some of my best landis' was given as the reason why the duke of Argyll moved to ban the practice on Tiree in 1750.[78] Articles of Set issued for Lewis in 1795 likewise curbed its practice on 'green or swarded ground'.[79] In time, the use of turf for building houses, walls and dykes, much of which eventually found its way on to arable, was either forbidden or discouraged. Management clauses issued to tenants on the Macdonald estate on Skye and North Uist in the early 1820s prevented them from building 'enclosures made of earth or turf'. Yet in 1829, an estate report was still able to recommend to Lord Macdonald that he 'in no instance approve of the erection of Turf Dikes, so common in the country'.[80] An equally equivocal view was taken by the Sutherland estate when addressing the problem of turf cut for muck fail. Though it inserted clauses in Assynt tacks during the early nineteenth century binding tenants to 'preserve the green and the pasture ground' and 'not to suffer any part of the ground set to be tirred or Cut for feal' it did allow it on payment of five shillings for each load of turf or pasture cut.[81] Seen overall, the scale of turf used had a far-reaching effect on the quality of hill-grazing, particularly on that which fringed the arable nucleus of townships. Indeed, in the western isles, so much turf was harvested that many areas adjacent to townships were skinned or reduced to bare rock.[82]

Being a geologically old landscape, it is tempting to regard the physical character of the western Highlands and Islands as providing society with a stable setting. In reality, this was far from being the case. Quite apart from the way long-term shifts of climate must have altered the geography of production, and the way extremes of weather created periodic crises of output, there were other ways in which it was a risk-laden environment for the farmer. In an environment in which cultivable land was scarce, the temptation to cultivate haugh lands that were subject to regular floodings, hillslopes that could be swept bare by catastrophic downpours or machair land that, once opened by the spade or plough, was at risk of massive and destructive sand-blows was ever present. Yet however risk-laden the environment, ultimately, the real source of flux lay in the changing social and economic values through which society exploited the region. Seen c.1493, it was the physical character of the region, together with the tactical problems which it posed for invading armies and the limited rewards which its poor resource base offered in return, which had delayed, and continued to delay, its full incorporation into the wider Scottish realm. Yet whilst acknowledging these problems, some form of socio-political integration was possible even before c.1493. The Lordship of the Isles and the power exercised by the Norse kings demonstrate this. However, any sort of integration, regional or local, required solutions that coped effectively with its physical character. Arguably, the local or indigenous power structures represented by chiefdoms or clans was such a solution, albeit not the only one. Kinship provided a means by which the region's physical topography was ideologically transformed into a social topography whose peaks and troughs, distances and opportunities, were perceived and valued differently. Each clan's search for socio-political status through control over land meant that it was prepared to compete vigorously for territories and spaces of all kinds, even marginal or isolated ones. Further, each clan's search for status through displays of feasting and feuding meant that each had a vested interest in packing their estates with numbers, that is, in building as intensive an economic base as local resources would allow. Ties of kinship, real or assumed, provided the ideological cloak under which all kinsmen, from the lowliest cottar to the grandest chief, were enjoined in the search for status. In these circumstances, we cannot be surprised if relatively poor, marginal environments were transformed by heavy investments of labour, as if, to use a phrase of one commentator, 'labour had no value'.[83] By establishing subsistence at any price, the ordinary tenant secured his own position within a social as well as a physical landscape. By producing a surplus, indeed, by prioritising the chief's share, they ensured the survival of that landscape and the values that were embodied in the figure of their chief and his household men.

Yet if the clan system can be seen as providing an ecological solution, one that coped well with the opportunities of the region, it did not insure against change. As the region was drawn more and more under the rule of central authority, and as its economy was subjected to the pressures and demands of a market economy, the coherence of the clan system and its economy was gradually undermined. In its place, there emerged two contrasting and conflicting systems of production. As their political role was curbed and as their ideology of behaviour was transformed, and as the region was penetrated by market forces, chiefs became landlords. In the process, they had to cope with a different perception of the region, one which imposed an economics of distance and comparative advantage on their estates. The outcome was a growing evaluation of estate resources in purely economic terms and a gradual shift towards commercial stock production, a move that began with an emphasis on cattle production within both the estate and township economy. Chiefs, though, had to live with the consequences of past solutions. Many estates carried large numbers of tenants whose farm economies continued to be locked into subsistence strategies based on arable. As population grew, the demands of subsistence grew. For the subsistence sector, the limitations of environment continued to be overcome by throwing labour at the problem, ring-fencing the needs of subsistence against the increasingly intrusive realities of the marketplace. We cannot understand the changes that took place over the period between the sixteenth and eighteenth centuries if we do not understand how these two strategies of resource use evolved out of the ideology of the clan system and how they increasingly came into conflict by the mid-eighteenth century.

NOTES

1. Descriptions of the structure of a Highland clan are provided by Macpherson, 'An old Highland genealogy and the evolution of a Scottish clan'; Fox, 'Lineage cells and regional definition', pp. 111–15; Withers, *Gaelic Scotland*, pp. 76–7; Macinnes, *Clanship, Commerce and the House of Stuart, 1603–1788*, pp. 2–14.
2. Barrow, *The Anglo-Norman Era in Scottish History*, pp. 67–70.
3. Lang (ed.), *The Highlands of Scotland in 1750*, appendix, p. 166.
4. Nicholson, *Scotland: the Later Middle Ages*, p. 544.
5. SRO, Clanranald Papers, GD201/1/361, Genealogy of Clanranald. The conflicting ideology surrounding sword- and charter-land is well brought out by Grant in his *Independence and Nationhood: Scotland 1306–1469*, p. 212.
6. Cregeen, 'The changing role of the house of Argyll and the Highlands', p. 155.
7. Wormald, *Lords and Men in Scotland* reprints the details of many bonds of friendship and their more feudal version, bonds of manrent, and provides a review of their character; see especially Chapter 5.
8. Nicholson, *Scotland: The Later Middle Ages*, p. 544.
9. The growth of these better, more defined routes is discussed in Dawson, 'The origins of the Road to the Isles'.
10. A good summary of the work of the Forfeited Estates Commissioners is provided by Smith, *Jacobite Estates of the Forty-Five*, especially Chapters 4–8.
11. Smith, *Wealth of Nations*, i, p. 19.

12. SRO, RH2/8/24, John Blackadder's Description and Valuation of Lord Macdonald's Estate in Sky and North Uist, 1799/1800.

13. A good summary of how major clans were segmented through territory is provided by Fox, 'Lineage cells and regional definition', pp. 102–7.

14. *Burt's Letters from the North of Scotland*, ii, p. 148.

15. Lang (ed.), *The Highlands of Scotland in 1750*, p. 43.

16. This theme is well developed in studies like Halstead and O'Shea, 'A friend in need is a friend indeed', pp. 92–9.

17. Martin, *Western Islands*, p. 98.

18. Kirch, 'Polynesian prehistory: cultural adaptation in an island ecosystem'.

19. Good examples occur in NLS, Sutherland Papers, DEP313/1025, Assynt Factors and Sutherland Ground Officers 1823–1826, including the references in 1823 to April being 'colder and stormier than usual', July having 'incessant rain' and September being 'unusually stormy'.

20. A good overview is provided by Caird and Moisley, 'The Outer Hebrides', pp. 374–90.

21. DC/MDP, 1/380/29 (RHP 2307/1–2), Glenelg Survey.

22. Storrie, *Islay: Biography of an Island*, pp. 68–71.

23. SRO, RHP3368 Isle of Coll, 1794, by George Langlands.

24. Evidence for the sectoring of common pastures comes across from CDC/MP, GD2212/3695/2, Memorial of the Abuses in the present Management of Macdonald's estate 1733; GD221/4182, Minute of Meeting with Tacksmen respecting Commonty, 1801. See also the fine review in Bil, *The Shieling*, pp. 126–54, and the map of shieling areas in Barrisdale provided by Whittington, 'The field Systems of Scotland', p. 568.

25. References to such divisions being carried out in Skye are provided in CDC/MP, GD221/4208/1, Memorandum Lord Macdonald to his Chamberlain, 1806; GD221/4182, Minute of Meeting with the Tacksmen, 1801. The latter talks about it being advisable 'to divide the Commons in such a manner as to give each farm its own proprtion'. See also the discussion in Bil, *The Shieling*, pp. 151–4.

26. SRO, RHP 8826–1, Plan of Tiree. The sort of regularly-shaped arable plots shown on the Tiree map compare with those mapped by Moisley in townships on North Uist; see Moisley, 'Some Hebridean field systems', pp. 31 and 33.

27. Fine maps of northern Skye, including Trotternish, were produced by Mathew Stobie in 1764–6, see CDC/MP, RHP5991–3.

28. Storrie, 'Islay: a Hebridean exception'.

29. Cropping data is provided by Smith (ed.), *The Book of Islay*, appendix, Rental for 1722.

30. Johnson, *Journey to the Western Islands of Scotland*, p. 79.

31. NLS, Sutherland Papers, DEP313/1047, Reports on Sutherland, 1833. See also comments in *OSA*, x, p. 352.

32. The problems of measuring arable where it was interjected with grass are shown by NLS, Plan of Harris, 1803–4, by William Bald.

33. Breadalbane Muniments, GD112/93/3/5, Barcaldine his Accounts of Charge & Discharge with his Instructions 1696.

34. SRO, Campbell of Barcaldine Muniments, GD170/629/61, Letter, 4 March 1697.

35. SRO, Breadalbane Muniments, GD112/12/1/5/48, Report on the State of Netherlorne, 1795. Nearby, a petition by the tenants of Barbreck and Lochow documents another localised disaster. The petition reported 'losses by a storm' of 'no less than 40 bolls of meal'. It went on to ask 'for allowance, according to custom of the country'; see SRO, GD112/10/1/3/56, Breadalbane Muniments, Petition to Earl of Breadalbane, 23 April 1733.

36. SRO, Campbell of Barcaldine Muniments, GD170/629, Letter, 22 March 1697.

37. Cawdor Castle, Cawdor Papers, Bundle 721, Rent of Ilay for the years 1703, 1704, 1705, 1706 and 1707.
38. Ibid. The whole of Kelsay was set in 1706 and 1707. Half of Kilneave was set between 1704 and 1706 and the whole of the township in 1707. The problems which the Campbells of Cawdor had in setting land may well have been because tenants were not just reduced in circumstances or capital, but found labour scarce. On this, it is worth noting that Martin Martin reported how the recent years of scarcity had affected corn output badly and went on to say that 'many of the poor People have died by Famine', Martin, *Western Islands*, p. 14. Comparable information on the effects of the bad winter of 1744–5 is provided by Cregeen. He estimated that something like one half of the tenants around Inveraray and Loch Awe were left insolvent by it, whilst 26 out of 90 townships on Mull were waste or expected to be waste either in part or wholly by Whitsunday 1747. See Cregeen, 'Tacksmen and their successors', p. 127. The events before and after Culloden, of course, also left some farms waste by 1746.
39. Adam, 'The Highland emigration of 1770'.
40. Adam, 'The causes of the Highland emigrations, 1783–1803', pp. 73–89.
41. DC/MDP, 4/304/1, Letter, 28 April 1772.
42. Ibid., 4/304/2, Macleod of Ulinish State of Sky 1772. For wider comment on poor seasons, see Whyte, *Agriculture and Society*, p. 11; Smout, 'Famine and Famine Relief', pp. 21–31.
43. SRO, Forfeited Papers, E729, Report from Captain John Forbes Factor upon the Annexed estate of Lovat and Cromarty, 1755.
44. SRO, AF49/2A, Valuation of the Estate of Ardnamurchan and Sunart Property of Sir James Riddell by Alexander Low, 1807.
45. SRO, Breadalbane Muniments, GD112/16/13/4/9, Report relative to Sundry Farms belonging to the Rt. Hon. Earl of Breadalbane, 1810.
46. NLS, Sutherland Papers, DEP313/993, Misc. Estate Management Papers 1808–1816.
47. *Farmer's Magazine*, iv, p. 50.
48. Walker, especially, drew attention to how the 1746 disarming act affected the ability of sheep farmers and others to control predators like foxes and eagles; see McKay (ed.), *Walker's Report on the Hebrides*, 79, pp. 158–9.
49. SRO, RH2/8/24, John Blackadder's Description and Valuation of Lord Macdonald's Estates of Sky and North Uist, 1799 and 1800.
50. Macfarlane (ed.), *Geographical Collections*, ii, p. 146. Flooding was also a problem on rivers further east in Perthshire; see SRO, John Macgregor Collection, GD50/135, Barony Court Books – Menzies and Rannoch, 25 April 1678.
51. SRO, Forfeited Papers, E729/7 Report of Francis Grant, 1756.
52. SRO, Forfeited Papers, E746/79/10 Letter *ex* Simon Mackenzie of Langwell, 1772.
53. NLS, Sutherland Papers, DEP313/3160/15 tack of Carnachy.
54. Ibid., 313/3160/18 Assynt tacks.
55. SRO, Breadalbane Muniments, GD112/10/1/4/68, Copy Articles and Regulations Agreed Betwixt James Riddell Esq and Donald Campbell, 1774.
56. Whittington and Ritchie, *Flandrian Environmental Evolution of North East Benbecula and Southern Grimsay*.
57. McKay (ed.), *Walker's Report on the Hebrides*, p. 13.
58. IC/AP, RHP8826/2, General Description of the Island of Tiriy, 1768, by James Turnbull.
59. Ibid., V65, Remarks on the Island of Tiry, 1771.
60. Ibid., RHP8826/2, General Description of the Island of Tiriy, 1768, by James Turnbull.
61. IC/AP, V65 Content of the Different Farms … Turnbull 1768.

62. DC/MDP, 1/466/24 Description of Harris 29 Feb. 1772.
63. Ibid.
64. Innes and Buchan (eds), *Origines Parochiales Scotiae*, i, p. 368.
65. CDC/MP, 221/5914, Valuation of North Uist per Neil Maclean, 1830. On Lewis, the solution was seen as the prohibition of tenants from pulling up bent or rue; see SRO, Seaforth Muniments, GD46/1/277, Article and Conditions for Lett of Lewis, 1795.
66. In 1718, it was one of the largest townships in North Uist, with 11 tenants; see Forfeited Estates Papers, E656/1, Judiciall Rental of North Uist, 1718.
67. SRO, GD46/1/278, Articles of set for Lewis, 1795.
68. SRO, AF49/2A Valuation of the Estate of Ardnamurchan and Sunart Property of Sir John Riddell 1807. Other examples of damage on the mainland being caused by sand blows can be found in NLS, Sutherland Papers, DEP313/3164, Tacks Duchess Elizabeth, 1787–1801, Scheme of Sett of Assynt, 1766.
69. Dodgshon, 'The ecological basis of Highland peasant farming'; Dodgshon and Olsson, 'Productivity and nutrient use'.
70. Davidson and Simpson, 'Deep top soil formation in Orkney'.
71. SRO, Clanranald Papers, GD201/1235/9, Particulars of the Estate of Clanranald, 1829.
72. Innes (ed.), *The Black Book of Taymouth*, p. 355.
73. Skene, *Celtic Scotland*, iii, p. 435.
74. SRO, Breadalbane Muniments, GD112/16/10/2/1, Report James Campbell, 1728
75. SRO, AF49/2A, Valuation of the Estate of Ardnamuchan and Sunart, Property of Sir James Riddell, 1807, section on 'Articles of Lease for the Management of Arable Land'.
76. See, for example, NLS, Sutherland Papers, DEP313/1000, Expired leases for Assynt, 1812, Tack for Little Assynt, Cromount, Coulin, Camore and Unapool, 1819.
77. SRO, John Macgregor Collection, GD50/136/1, Barony Court Books of Menzeis and Rannoch, vol. IV, 1727–1739, Weem, 1727.
78. IC/AP, V65, Instructions for the Chamberlain of Tyrie, 23 Oct. 1750.
79. SRO, Seaforth Muniments, GD46/1/278, Articles of Sett for Lewis, 1795. Similar restrictions were imposed through tacks for North Uist, see CDC/MP, GD221/4289/2, Lease of Balliloch and Sponish, 1825, attached regulations, no. XXVI.
80. CDC/MP, GD221/121 Report on Lord Macdonald's Estate on Skye 1829; ibid., 221/5913.
81. NLS, Sutherland Papers, DEP313/1000, Expired Leases for Assynt.
82. Darling, *West Highland Survey*, pp. 272–8.
83. Macculloch, *Western Highlands and Islands*, iv, p. 118.

2 Chiefs, Kinsmen and Territories

Seen in c.1493, the western Highlands and Islands was a region in which kinship still mattered to the organisation of society. Though links established through one's mother or wife had some role in fashioning kinship structures, the most potent and active source of kinship affiliation was that established through one's father, brothers or male cousins. In its workings, Highland society was more an agnatic than a cognatic society.[1] A person's status in society, his access to resources and his political orientation, together with the legal controls which bound his behaviour, were all affected to a greater or lesser degree by his kin-ties, more particularly those on the male side. These ties were based on broad clan groupings whose unity as kin groups was focused around the figure of a chief, the latter being a member of the branch or *sliochd* that was closest in descent to the original ancestor-founder of the clan. In practice, the larger clans could form fairly complex hierarchies, with each major segment having its own chief whose rank position in relation to the chief of the clan *in toto* was carefully defined in genealogies.

Prior to the sixteenth century, the Highlands was not alone in being a kin-based society. Other parts of Scotland were dominated by the power and influence of extended family groups under the figure of a chief.[2] As in the Highlands and Islands, the rise and fall of a chief effectively signalled the rise or fall of his kinsmen. Though the western Highlands and Islands were more comprehensively shaped by the clan system and through it, more profoundly shaped by the institutions and values of a kin-based society, these same institutions and values were present outside of the Highlands.[3] Yet just as Barrow has argued against drawing too sharp a line between the character of Highland and Lowland society over the medieval period,[4] so also must we be cautious about how we define their differences after 1493. Areas like the Borders continued to be associated with kin groups for much of the sixteenth

31

century. When parliament discussed the problem of disorder caused by broken men and caterans in 1587, its legislation bound Border chiefs as much as Highland chiefs with responsibility for controlling them.[5] In this and other respects, the Highlands cannot be neatly isolated as a wholly distinct society. However, to recap on the point which I made in the previous chapter, we cannot ignore the way in which the physical problems of the region, the difficulties of movement for soldiers as well as for government officers, retarded its easy incorporation into the Scottish state. Seen in this way, what really distinguishes the western Highlands and Islands when seen over the period c.1493–1820 is the way in which it conserved the institutions and values of a kin-based society for longer, not the fact that it had such institutions and values uniquely to itself.

The clan system poses a range of questions. First and foremost, we need to consider the way in which it provided a socio-political framework for the region. Second, we need to look at how the geography of particular clans and the territories which they controlled fluxed during the period c.1493–1820, with some gaining and others losing ground. Third, and linked closely to the previous question, the different strategies by which clans were able to expand both as regards their kinsmen or clan members and their territories need to be explored, as also does the negative impact which this expansion had on less successful clans. Fourth, and a question that takes us to the very root of the problem, we need to ask how clans were bound together and, in particular, to clarify the precise role played by kinship in the organisation and functioning of clans. As will be shown, this is easier to answer when we take a top-down approach to clan structure by looking at the senior families or branches of a clan than when we take a bottom-up approach and ask how the ordinary peasant farmer fitted into the equation of kinship that bound clans together. For the latter, there were different ways of expressing identity, of which using a clan name was but one. Fifth and finally, no understanding of the clan system would be complete without highlighting the different ways in which it changed over the period, c.1493–1820.

THE ORGANISATION OF TERRITORY THROUGH SOCIETY

It has been said that pre-state systems organised territory through society, whereas state systems organised society through territory.[6] In the former, territory drew its political structure and identity from the tribal kingships, chiefdoms and clans that happened to occupy it. In the latter, jurisdiction was organised through fixed territorial units of lordship and authority, so that a community's identity and its place within the political structure derived from the territory in which it was located. For a substantial part of the period under review, the western Highlands and Islands fits more easily into the former type of system than into the latter. Where the authority of central government was weak or spread thinly, order was provided by the authority which chiefs exercised over their clans. The Crown itself recognised this fact. Not only did it work through the clan system by co-opting some chiefs to its cause, but it also tried to control lawlessness in the more difficult areas by holding chiefs responsible for their kinsmen or those who carried their name.[7] So long as chiefs and their clans shaped political order in this way, their geography served as a mapping of socio-political order. To a degree, this had the effect of reducing the dynamics of socio-political order to the struggle over land. As a successful clan expanded its control over land through all the different devices available (i.e. Crown favour, marriage alliances, feuding, cattle dealing), and as it implanted such windfalls with loyal kinsmen or friends, its sphere of socio-political space expanded in step. Significantly, when the Council of the Isles met at Finlaggan, it was first and foremost a meeting of chiefs, not a meeting of representatives from different districts.[8] The latter mattered only in so far as the communities or families who inhabited them mattered.

Considered more closely, the clan system structured space in a number of different ways. Few clans fitted the stereotype of a small, relatively independent clan whose chief held a localised or compact estate and was able to let out land to his close kinsmen who, in turn, sublet land to those who worked the soil. Despite the importance of territory to the constitutive character of clans, the one rarely fitted the other comfortably. There was too much flux surrounding chiefdoms and their clans for this to be the case. As a result, chiefs had to cope with either an excess of land relative to their followers or a deficiency.

In the case of the former, chiefs who built up extensive territories did so in one of two ways. First, a chief could work to secure an overarching control over new territories by creating what we can call canopy clans. These were usually represented by those clans whose chiefs acquired large amounts of land quickly. Control over such territories was secured by various strategies. In some cases, chiefs granted out blocks of land to their younger sons or to the most senior cadet branches of the clan, *uachdaran*, establishing them as their vassals. In other cases, they rented out large districts to cadet branches, with senior members serving as tacksmen, or *fir-tasca*.[9] By its very nature, such a process meant that the physical topography underlying a chiefdom was overlaid by a social topography, with cadet branches being established 'in an ever-widening circle around the original barony', with each progressively more removed in terms both of kinship and of physical proximity from their chief.[10] Once in place, such cadet branches proceeded to fill their territories with kinsmen by a process of downward genealogical emplacement. Such a process, though, was invariably a partial, incomplete affair, with non-kinsmen being just as likely to be granted land as kinsmen, simply because, where large amounts of land were being secured, compromises had to be made.

The second way in which chiefs projected control out over large territories was by supplementing the use of actual kin-ties by forging alliances with lesser clans through bonds of manrent or friendship that established com-

mon cause between them.[11] Though a contractual arrangement and, therefore, an instrument which threatened to expand a kin-society beyond itself,
such alliances were 'the most effective method of complementing and adding
to the kin group, and imposing on those who were not of the lord's kin the
obligations which bound those that were'.[12] In their effect, they fostered more
composite or aggregate clan systems, with a chief exercising control over a
territory through the use of senior members of his own clan and through
alliances with lesser chiefs and tacksmen from other clans.

When seen as a source of territorial control, the clan system clearly contained serious inconsistencies. A tenant's chief was not always his landlord,
either because some chiefs did not have direct control over enough land to
provide for all their followers. For Macinnes, the discrepancy between what
the senior lineages of a clan had direct control over, their *oighreach*, and the
land which their ordinary kinsmen occupied, their *duthchas*, was a recurrent
source of feuding between clans, particularly where the former was smaller
than the latter.[13]

CLANS AND COMPETITION: HOW CLANS SUCCEEDED

Yet for all the instability generated by this imbalance between a clan's needs
and its resources, a greater source of disequilibrium was the competitive
character of chiefdoms and clans as social forms. By nature, chiefs strove to
increase the status of themselves and their clan, to place themselves at the
centre of an expanding hierarchy of kin-ties and alliances. For all chiefs, the
cornerstone for any enhancement of status was the social and geographical
extension of their authority by securing control, directly or indirectly, over
extra resources of land. The converse, of course, was that those who lost land
also lost status, being ultimately reduced to the status of a 'broken clan' or a
clan without land. Any survey of the western Highlands and Islands between
the sixteenth and eighteenth centuries reveals considerable fluxes of this
sort. The growing penetration of Crown authority and the favour which it
bestowed on particular clans was an increasing source of this flux. However,
we need to appreciate that even without the disequilibrium caused by the
initial penetration of Crown authority, the competitive nature of the clan
system was more than capable of generating its own sources of disequilibria.

Chiefs who wanted to position themselves at the centre of a new eruption
of status and power could draw on a range of tactics to do so. First, and perhaps foremost in the early development of clans, was the use of physical
violence. When clans refer to how they held land prior to the introduction of
charter grants, they describe it not just as *duthchas*, but as land held by the
sword.[14] Though less important after c.1493 than before, the chiefly use of
different forms of coercion still had a place. However, it was used more as a
support for other tactics than as a sole means of establishing a right of claim
to land. Thus, when the earl of Argyll acquired MacLean of Duart's estate
covering part of Mull, Tiree, the two ends of Coll and Morvern, he did so as

principal creditor to Sir Allan MacLean, having purchased a heritable bond for MacLean's debts. His claim, though, counted for little until the earl invaded Mull, supported by his senior cadet branches in 1674. Armed resistance, in fact, continued down to 1678–80.[15]

More generally, the use of force to secure a claim on land tended to work itself out through the feud. Thus, whilst the earl of Argyll's acquisition of the MacLean estate gave him possession of most of Morvern, his actual possession still had to be demonstrated. Though he tried to rid its tenancies of those opposed to the change of landlord, his efforts and those of his tacksmen initially failed. Sustained arson attacks, thefts and cattle maiming by the Camerons meant that it was impossible to set the land to anyone except a Cameron even as late as the 1720s and 30s.[16]

Claims and counter-claims on land lay behind feuds elsewhere. The long-running feud between the Campbells of Glenorchy and the Macgregors had its roots in Glenorchy's acquisition of lands formerly held by the Macgregors.[17] When we see tacks such as that issued in 1588 to Donald and Dougall McTarlichis for the two merkland of Glenevarn, the one merkland of Elir and the half merkland of Glenkatillie in Lorne on condition that 'they enter in deidlie Feid with the Clan gregoure … making slaughter upone theme and thair adherentis',[18] we can hardly doubt the link between claims on land and the use of violence to secure that claim even though Lorne had hardly been part of the Macgregors' patrimony.

Another longstanding device by which chiefs extended their control was through various forms of alliance. The oldest form of alliance was that based on marriage. However, an observation by Wormald is worth noting. Whilst it was seen as providing a link between kin-groups, 'the marriage contract was the weakest form of alliance'.[19] In practice, when the interests of allied kin groups conflicted, that based on marriage was the most easily fractured. Yet despite this cautionary note, the very fact that chiefs developed their marriage alliances along clear tactical lines suggests that such alliances were perceived as serving wider interests. Amongst the larger clans, for instance, the Campbells of Argyll tended to marry their sons into the leading families of Scotland and their daughters into Highland families.[20] A comparable strategy, albeit at a more localised scale, featured in the early growth of the Clan Macpherson, with sons marrying out but daughters marrying within the clan.[21] Such a strategy as regards sons clearly served to draw extra re-sources and ties into the clan, whereas that regarding daughters was served to conserve what was already held. When we add the degree to which High-land chiefs remarried, with many having two or three wives over their life-time, and some, like the Campbells of Glenorchy, sometimes having more, it is easy to appreciate the potential number of connections provided by such alliances. Bonds of friendship, maintenance and manrent provided chiefs with another form of alliance. Their role in extending the effective as well as the affective bounds of kinship have been studied by Wormald. 'They made their bonds', she wrote, 'to become as kinsmen to one another'.[22] Because they did not take a standardised form, it is difficult to draw a clear distinction between bonds of friendship, maintenance and manrent. However, bonds of friendship were the simpler. They established common cause between two families, each behaving towards the other as if they were kin and doing so, as one put it, through 'all hazards of disgrace and infamy'.[23] Some bonds leave no doubt that they embraced the whole kin of the main parties involved: thus, a bond drawn up in 1587 pledged 'mutual support' between Donald Gorme and 'the whole kin of the Clan Donald' and Lauchlan McIntosche of Dunachtane and 'the kin of Clanchattane'.[24] In some cases, this mutuality was seen as extending to land. When Alex. MacIain MacAlister of Glengarry agreed a bond of friendship with Ewan Allanson of Lochiel in 1521, they pledged 'to lease land to each other if they obtained it'.[25] Bonds of manrent were a more feudalised form, with chiefs or lords variously offering protection and maintenance in return for counsel, active military support and payments of calp. Again, though fifteenth-century bonds of manrent are less explicit than sixteenth-century bonds in actually saying so, they generally covered individuals plus their kin. In the Highlands, it was the Campbells of Glenorchy, most notably, the sixth and seventh lairds, Colin and Duncan, who made most use of such bonds to extend and secure their position, though that said, many involved fairly small tenants.[26] Bonds of one sort or another continue down into the eighteenth century. As late as 1727, Ronald McAllane MacEane of Castellwirrie obtained a contract from Sir Donald Macdonald of Sleatt whereby the latter gave him protection 'as becomes a loving and kind chief and superior'.[27]

The use of the sword and various forms of alliance were longstanding devices by which chiefs could boost their position, both socially and geographically. Over the period c.1493–1820, new devices became available. The resurgent efforts of the Crown to 'civilise' the region, particularly the far west, enabled some clans, most notably the Campbells of Argyll, to gain new territorial opportunities and resources by serving as Crown agents in what became 'the daunting of the west'. As the power of the Macdonalds gradually waned in the years following the collapse of the Lordship of the Isles, it was the Campbells of Argyll who gained at their expense. On the mainland, they acquired Knapdale in 1493 and later, in 1607, Kintyre. With their seizure of MacLean lands in the late seventeenth century, the earl pushed his vast territory out into the Hebrides, acquiring parts of Mull, Tiree and the two ends of Coll.

A wholly new source of flux for Highland chiefs and their clans over the period c.1493–1820 was one that confronted them with wholly new values. More and more chiefs were drawn slowly into the orbit of a money economy, and forced to suffer its burdens as well as its rewards. Over the sixteenth and seventeenth centuries, some built a fairly elaborate network of debt around themselves. Individuals borrowed freely. Others stood as cautioners. The willingness with which they lent to each other or acted as cautioner – often without adequate security – suggests that this emergent debt network had functions that were political as much as financial, and that it was concerned as much to cement social dependencies as with rates of return. Even by the mid-seventeenth century, some were heavily burdened with debt and though the feuing and wadsetting of land provided a temporary relief, it did not stave off their insolvency.[28] By the second half of the seventeenth century, major shifts in clan geography were being precipitated by debt. The earl of Argyll's takeover of the MacLean estate followed Sir Allan MacLean's inability to redeem an heritable bond for debt. The adventitious movement by Mackenzie of Seaforth into Lewis over the mid-seventeenth century was triggered by MacLeod of Lewis' debt. The same as with the earl of Argyll's grip on Mull, Mackenzie's grip on Lewis was very effective in squeezing out local MacLeod tenants, including what the Crown regarded as some of the most lawless families in the Hebrides.[29] The cause of the MacLeod's misfortune was hardly a characteristic of the clan system, but the way in which their displacement was implemented owed much to its norms. Crown rentals drawn up in the early eighteenth century, when the Mackenzies themselves were at loggerheads with the Crown following the 1715 rebellion, show a fair proportion of townships held by Mackenzie tacksmen.[30]

THE CHANGING GEOGRAPHY OF CLANS c. 1493–1820

The combined effect of these various strategies was to bring about profound shifts in the geography of clans, c. 1493–1820. By far the most important shift was that involving clans that had comprised the federacy of the Lordship of the Isles. In time, the MacIans' control of Ardnamurchan, the MacLeans of Mull, Tiree, and Morvern, and the grip of the Macdonalds of Dunnyveg on Knapdale, Kintyre and Islay were all undermined. With the exception certainly of Morvern and to a lesser extent of Islay, the collapse of chiefly control in each case was marked by a progressive displacement of their kinsmen as major tacksmen and tenants. Using published rentals for the early sixteenth century, McKerral has drawn attention to the fact that no Macdonald occurs in the rental available for Kintyre (1505) and only one Macdonald is actually mentioned in the rental for Islay (1507).[31] The apparent absence of Macdonalds, or rather the apparent failure to use the Macdonald clan name so soon after the collapse of the Lordship, may denote caution or discretion rather than the disappearance of its clansmen at a tacksmen level, but even if this was the case, it would still signal to us just how conditions had changed for them. The clan that gained most from the Macdonalds' contraction of territory was the Campbells, with the Campbells of Argyll securing Knapdale (1493), Kintyre (1607), parts of Mull, Morvern, and Tiree (1678–80), and the Campbells of Cawdor ultimately securing command of Islay (1615).

The collapse of the Lordship of the Isles and the gradual expansion of the Campbells make for an interesting comparison. Analyses of chiefdoms in the anthropological and archaeological literature have always stressed the volatile nature of their structures and alliances, complex hierarchical chiefdoms forming and collapsing freely to the extent that chiefly systems of power experienced regular, cyclical shifts between simple and complex forms.[32] In this respect, the rise and eventual collapse of the Lordship of the Isles conformed to type. Though it would be wrong to cross-match anthropological concept and fact too closely in the western Highlands and Islands, the extent to which clans in the region warred with each other over the sixteenth century would be consistent with the anarchy and intense competition that follows the collapse of all complex chiefdoms.[33] To succeed as a complex hierarchical clan in the Highlands no less than elsewhere, alliances had to endure. In this respect, it is worth repeating Cowan's conclusions on why the Macdonalds failed and the Campbells succeeded in their place over the sixteenth and seventeenth centuries: the former, he argued, failed to contain their internal feuds whilst the latter succeeded in so doing.[34]

As a clan, the Campbells of Argyll descended from Colin Campbell, Macailein Mor, who held the Barony of Loch Awe during the late fourteenth century. Following the award of an earldom to Colin Campbell in 1457, the headquarters of the clan, or the Campbells of Argyll as they had now become, was switched to Inveraray. As part of their strategy of expansion, successive Campbell chiefs endowed younger sons with land, enabling them to establish a network of cadet branches allied to the earl as vassals and kinsmen. Among them were the Campbells of Glenorchy, a branch already firmly established by the mid-fifteenth century. Their rapid social and territorial growth as a branch of the Clan Campbell made effective use of all the devices available to would-be successful chiefs. The first laird of Glenorchy, Colin Campbell, was given the 80 merkland of Glenorchy and the 27 merkland of Innerynan in Lochaw in 1432 by his father, the then Campbell of Lochawe. Establishing what became a family feature, the first laird married four times, gaining territorial advantage through each of them. His second wife, Janet Stewart, was the daughter of William Stewart of Lorne. Her tocher gude gave Glenorchy the 18 merkland of the Braes of Lorne. When she died, he acquired the entire superiority over Lorne. The first laird's son, Sir Duncan Campbell, continued this expansion, acquiring tacks for Crown land in Breadalbane, a strategically significant toehold, and the 12 merkland of Cranduich. In addition, he acquired the 60 merkland of Glenlyon and the 8 merkland of Glenquerch by the time he died at Flodden (1513). The fifth Laird, John, added the 12 merkland of Ardbeich, but it was his brother, Colin, the sixth laird, who did most to recover the momentum of growth. Colin Campbell, self-described as 'the blakest hand in all the land',[35] acquired the extensive lands of Breadalbane (including both North and South Lochtayside), the 20 merkland of Auchlyne, Easter Ardehyllie and Dowinche. His son Duncan was equally active during his 48 years as laird (1583–1631), adding new land in Strathtay and Atholl. By the time his grandson Robert became the ninth laird in 1640, the opportunities for continued expansion by traditional means had diminished. Indeed, both

Duncan and his grandson probably handicapped rather benefited their cause by their impressive rates of breeding. The seventh laird (1583–1631) married twice and had a grand total of nine sons and eight daughters. Altogether, he paid out 130,000 merks in tocher-gude for his eight daughters and two sisters. The ninth laird, Robert (1640–53) married only once. In addition to eight sons, he had nine daughters, for whom he paid a total of 42,000 merks as tocher-gude for the seven daughters who married.[36] One of his sons, John the younger, became the first earl of Breadalbane (1677).[37]

Rival chiefs and their kinsmen paid the price for the rise of the Campbells of Glenorchy. Most notable amongst them were the Macgregors. As a clan, the Macgregors had emerged in the fourteenth century, but even by the fifteenth century their claims on land were being over-ridden by those of the Campbells. What became core territory for the Campbells (i.e. Glenorchy itself, Glenstrathfalloch, Rannoch) was all claimed as territory, *duthchas*, by the Macgregors.[38] The tangle of claim and counter-claim found its expression in years of feuding between the two clans. The upper hand lay with the Campbells. The more the MacGregors resorted to feud, the more they lost ground as landholders. The sixth laird of Glenorchy was especially successful in trying to marginalise them, turning what had been a private feud between the two clans into a breach of Crown authority. 'He was ane great Justiciar, all his tyme', wrote one clan genealogist, 'throch the quhilk he sustenit the deidly feid of the Clan Gregour ane long space'.[39]

In the western isles, the MacLeods of Lewis were another clan whose over-use of feud worked against them. The western isles generally had long been an unsettled region. In part, this may have been due to the simple fact that it was divided by a frontier, with clans bound into the Lordship of the Isles occupying the southern part of the Outer Hebrides and parts of Skye confronting those in the northern part of the Outer Hebrides and in other parts of Skye who were not. Rivalry between branches of the Macdonalds and the MacLeods was endemic, whilst segments of the latter, like the MacLeods of Lewis, compounded the problem with internal conflict. Such was their threat to the order embodied in the state that by the end of the sixteenth century, the Scottish Crown saw the problem of the west not in terms of reaching an accommodation with clans like the Macleods of Lewis but of 'extirpating them'.[40] Following the failure of chiefs from Lewis, Harris, Dunvegan and Glenelg to present their deeds to the Crown in Edinburgh when requested, the Crown seized the opportunity to re-set the region in terms more conducive to its goals. Because of its acutely unsettled conditions, with active feuds in progress between rival families as well as between rival clans, the immediate focus of the Crown's efforts was Lewis. The core solution adopted was to civilise it by introducing lowland values and enterprise. The two attempts to settle Lowlanders, the so-called Fife Adventurers, failed, the second in a bloodbath in 1607 when Neil MacLeod answered the Crown in terms that had become his hallmark. Though MacLeod retreated to the west of the island, his cause was doomed. By 1615, the Crown had shifted its support, and the character of its solution, from the Adventurers to Mackenzie of Kintail. The strengthening of the latter's position was completed when, in 1623, barely eight years after taking charge of Lewis, he was raised to the title of earl of Seaforth. Perhaps more attuned to the values at issue, he took firm control of the island, displacing MacLeod tacksmen where appropriate and eventually introducing Mackenzies in their place.[41] The role of the Crown in the re-setting of Lewis owed nothing to the values of the clan system, but the eventual solution had the effect of simply replacing one clan with another.

Not all clans established themselves as landowners. It was possible for smaller clans to thrive as tacksmen and tenants on estates belonging to the chiefs of other clans. Macpherson has provided a detailed study of how such a clan could establish itself in a study of the clan Macpherson, 1400–1700. Though its leading families had become wadsetters and feuars by the seventeenth century, their initial success was as tenants on land owned by the earls of Huntly and Moray and the lairds of Mackintosh.[42] Though its chief, Macpherson of Cluny, obtained a lease for a large estate, most of the clan's growth centred around individual families seizing their own opportunities and gaining tacks through favourable marriage arrangements and successful cattle dealing.[43] As with larger clans, marriage was a calculated affair. A critical part of the clan's strategy of expansion was its high proportion of endogamous marriages, both in the sense of marriage within the clan and within particular lineages, especially the *Sliochd Iain*. As with some of the larger clans, there was a tendency for the men of the leading *sliochdan* to marry into other landed families but for women to marry within.[44]

CLANS AND KINSHIP: A TOP-DOWN VIEW

In essence, clans were groups who perceived themselves as bound together by ties of kinship. When we probe this ideological belief in a unity based on kinship further, we find that the structural and constitutive character of clans was invariably a more complex affair. To understand this complexity, we need to distinguish between, on the one hand, those ties that were seen as determinate and which were used to give structure and identity to clans and, on the other, those that were more associative or generalised. In practice, this means distinguishing those that bound the leading families or branches of a clan together from those that bound the ordinary tenant or sub-tenant into the clan. So long as the former were used to structure primary control over the basic resources of violence and subsistence, the assumption was fostered that all must be related by kin. The bonds of alliance that emerged around the edge of clans, with chiefs and others pledging to behave towards each other 'as if they were kin', simply brought the contextual force of this ideology out into the open, placing it on a contractual footing. In short, prior to the penetration and acceptance of Crown authority and the assertion of its jursidictions, we are dealing with a society in which the only effective form of order and identity was that offered by ties of kinship, real or otherwise.

If we look more closely at the ties of kin that bound leading families, all clans took their identity from an ancestor founder. Thus, when Reginald the son of Somerled died around 1207, his extensive territories in Kintyre and the southern Hebrides were divided between his two sons, Angus and Ruairidh, the former acquiring Kintyre and Islay, the latter Arran and Bute. The former founded the clan Donald and the latter the clan MacRuairidh. On the mainland, the fourteenth-century Colin Campbell who held the barony of Loch Awe became the first MacCailein Mor, founder of the Clan Campbell. Tradition has it that the MacLeods descended from an individual of Danish origin, Leod, who conquered Lewis and Harris in the thirteenth century and who later acquired parts of Skye in settlement of his wife's dowry. It was Leod's two sons, Siol Torquil and Siol Tormod, who established the MacLeods of Lewis and the MacLeods of Harris and Skye respectively. In time, such clans evolved through a process of segmentation, with new branches, lineages or *sliochdan*, being formed, each ranked according to their genealogical distance from the ancestor founder of the clan.[45] However, we miss the point if we see clans in purely social or affinal terms. *Sliochdan* only came into being when land was available, their founder being granted land as a vassal or as a tacksman by the clan chief. Such land provided the social space which a branch needed before it could flourish. This was acknowledged in the way the chiefs of such branches were identified through their place affiliation. As Dr Johnson put it, the 'chief of a clan is addressed by the name. The laird of Dunvegan is called MacLeod, but other gentlemen of the same name are denominated by the place where they reside, as Raasa or Talisker'.[46]

Geography worked in other ways. Access to land mattered in the formation and preservation of the ties of a *sliochd*, but so too did mere proximity. For Wormald, it was a powerful contributory factor, with geographic unity and neighbourhood being 'of far more relevance to the recognition of kinship than the mere fact of being related by blood'.[47] A clan's structure, then, was not its full genealogy, but a statement about how particular individuals and branches had responded to a whole variety of opportunities and circumstances. Its formation was not an exercise in the creation of a social network pure and simple, but one which necessarily worked to extend such a network through social space, with genealogy being mapped into the landscape.

CLANS AND KINSHIP: A BOTTOM-UP APPROACH

Recorded clan genealogies tend to deal only with the ties that bound the senior families or branches of a clan. The majority of clansmen find no direct mention in them, so that their place within the clan's overall kinship structure can be elusive. Lifting the veil of assumption that the clan system had placed over such individuals and asking whether they were bound into the system through genuine or putative ties of kin poses a fundamental problem. What makes this a difficult question to answer is the fact that the ordinary High-lander could build up his identity by using different co-ordinates. First, there was that derived through his patronymic, or *sloinneadh*, an identity gained through the link with his father and grandfather. Thus, a tack for Five Penny Borve on Lewis in 1781 set the township to 15 tenants, amongst whom were John MacInish vic Coil, Angus MacCurichie vic Roy, Donald MacEan vic Inish and John MacGillychallum vic Gillyffadrick.[48] Occasionally, a person might acknowledge his identity back across three generations, to his great-grandfather. For example, a 1665 list of tenants in the Barony Court Book for Rannoch listed a Donald McGreigour VcKondrchie VcEane in the township of Kinlochar,[49] whilst a 1698 list of tenants in the Barony Court Book for Menzies refers to a Donald mcPhadrick VcEnduy VcEan in the township of Dounan.[50] The tack issued in 1781 for Five Penny Borve in Lewis meanwhile also included a Donald MacCoil vic Ean vic Coil amongst its 15 tenants.[51] Though by no means unusual, such four-generational patronymics appear the exception in sixteenth-, seventeenth- and eighteenth-century sources. As a rule, it was sufficient to be identified through one's father and grandfather.

Being identified through one's lateral relations provided a second but less frequently used source of identity, with lists noting a person by their first name then orientating them by reference to the fact they were the brother or cousin of someone.[52] In most cases, this was simply a form of shorthand, but in a few cases, it suggests that the social identity of the person in question was in some sense contingent on their brother or cousin. Adding a third source of identity was the use of epithets. These were in common usage. Some were purely descriptive, but others may be classificatory. In this latter category, I would include some instances of epithets like *more/beg* (great/little), *dubh, duie* (black, dark), and *ruaidh, roy* (red). By a classificatory function, I mean that they helped to identify a person not in a descriptive sense – so that someone described as *mor* or *ruaidh* was not necessarily big or red in a physical sense – but through categorical opposition.[53] Finally, at a fourth and much broader level, a person could identify himself through his membership of a clan by using a clan name, i.e. MacDonald, MacGregor. In many instances, it is possible to find individuals setting these personal and group forms of identity together, so we find them referred to as Duncan McNachtan alias MacAllan,[54] or Dougall McDonald, alias McEan vic Coull.[55]

There is a tacit assumption in some sources that these personal and group forms of identity were consistent with each other, the one being a close-focus version of the other, to be used where and when they were more appropriate. If we take the two main sources of identity, patronymics and clan names, we might expect the former to be used within the framework of the local community and the latter to be used in dealings with the world beyond. Yet when we survey their actual patterns of use, no simple or clear-cut rules emerge. If we take rentals, a source focused on the close-knit and familiar community of the township, we might expect a preponderance of patronymics. In fact, when we take an overview of rentals c.1493–1820, they display no such preference. Rentals deal variously in both patronymics and clan names. Yet there is a case for suggesting that behind the apparent variation, some logic may exist. Amongst the fine array of sixteenth-century rentals for estates in the southern Hebrides and parts of the mainland, the general form was to identify individuals through their clan name. As they were drawn up on behalf of the Crown and dealt mostly with tacksmen, this is hardly surprising. In the case of Kintyre and Islay, we can actually make a comparison between rentals compiled in 1506 and 1541. Whilst they show shifts in who held what and a tendency for the amount of land set to become smaller, the use of clan names was prevalent at both dates. However, by way of a cautionary note and in the case of the 1541 rental especially, it is not always clear whether the clerks who drew up the rental were not inclined to treat some patronymics as if they were clan names.[56] The style used in the 1541 rental for Ardnamurchan seems caught between the two forms, with patronymics seemingly being combined with the clan name MacKane.[57] The rental drawn up in the same year for Tiree shows little evidence of patronymics being used amongst its tackholders, but nor does it suggest any uniform use of a dominant clan name.[58] However, as with rentals for other estates, when more detailed rentals for the island become available, they show a free use of patronymics to identify tenants. A very full rental of 1662, for instance, when the island was still held by Sir Allan MacLean, shows as many tenants identifying themselves through their patronymic as through a clan name.[59] A less detailed rental drawn up in 1674, though, mentions few names, and most of those that it does are McNeills acting as tacksmen.[60] The good series of rentals for Harris and the Skye portions of the MacLeod of Dunvegan estate over the late seventeenth century are comparable with those for Tiree. Where tacksmen existed, the rental invariably identifies the tenant by a clan name but where townships were divided amongst a group of tenants, patronymics were just as likely to be used as clan names. Interestingly, there seems a much greater use of patronymics on the fertile islands that lay around the southern edge of Harris than in the less fertile townships on the mainland of Harris.[61] In some cases, such as on the island of Ensay, it is the smaller tenants who used patronymics.[62] That such differences may be chance is suggested by a comparison of the Harris rental for 1686 and 1688, with Ensay tenants being identified in the one by their patronymic and in the other by their clan name.[63] Yet in the right circumstances, such a distinction could make a powerful point. Thus, the 1718 rental for the Seaforth estate shows much greater use of patronymics to identify tenants on Lewis, some large tenants excepted, whereas tenants in Kintail and Lochalsh are uniformly depicted as Murchisons and MacRaes.[64] It may be that, as on Harris, some of the numerous lesser tenants of Lewis felt patronymics more appropriate, but there is also the possibility that they were making a point about Mackenzie of Kintail's lordship over Lewis.

Certainly, the Murchisons and Macraes were just as disposed to use patronymics in the right circumstances. When faced with court action in 1721, the kinsmen of the Macrae clan, almost to a man, used their patronymics to identify themselves before an Inverness-shire court enquiring into an ambush at Ath Nam Muileach. Most, in fact, were the same tenants who, in the 1718 rental of the Seaforth estate, were identified by their clan name. Whereas 48 out of the 69 tenants listed in the 1718 rental used the clan name of Macrae, 45 out of the 72 listed in the court record of 1721 used their patronymic.[65] They were surely making their ideological differences with central authority plain by doing so.

The circumstances under which patronymics and clan names were used has a bearing on the question of precisely how they were related. The stock assumption has always been that the two forms were related in that one captured a person's immediate linkages and the other, those of his more distant ancestors. Yet there is a reasonable case for arguing that the two forms of identity were not only different in principle but could stand in conflict to each other. The use of patronymics denotes a society in which a person's position was defined through descent. It can be rooted in a society organised around descent groups and in which vital social processes like the inheritance of property, the blood feud and marriage alliances were mediated through such groups. By the sixteenth century, the basis for these processes had weakened to the extent that we cannot speak of multi-generational kinship groups being constituted in any fixed or normative way though, as Wormald has shown, there were still customs in force that hinted at what once might have been.[66] Highland clans were still arranged into lineages and, to a degree, these still had a behavioural function, but they did not draw their force of meaning from their allodial possession of land in the way that they might once have done.[67]

This presumed erosion of the descent group as a focus of customary rights, and the corresponding rise of feudal and contractual rights attached to individuals, does not mean that kinship lost meaning. What we are faced with is more a change in structure than values, a shift of rights and social control from the lineage to individuals and chiefs. Socio-political order at the wider community level was still fashioned around kinship but the structures that now existed were more loosely defined and potentially much larger than the closed, normatively defined lineages that may have prevailed back in the medieval period, more capable of negotiation and of responding to circumstances.

What is clear is that when detailed sources become available over the sixteenth century, most Highland 'landowners' held their land by Crown charter[68] whilst the vast majority of Highlanders who held land beneath them – the tacksmen, tenants, cottars and so on – did so by tack, verbal agreement or were simply tenants at will, holding land directly from the landowner or his tacksmen. However, we miss the essential point if we see such tenures as representing landlord–tenant agreements, pure and simple. Although undoubtedly a dilution of earlier allodial rights held by lineage groups, most tacksmen and many of the leading tenants under them believed that their status as kinsmen gave them a prior claim to clan holdings and that their chiefs were chiefs not landlords. This was no empty claim. Tenants on Eigg, faced with MacLeod of Talisker as their tacksman, claimed to have a right to their holdings because they were kinsmen of Clanranald.[69] In fact, so strong were the assumptions underpinning this expected favour towards kinsmen that many Highlanders saw themselves as having a customary right to the hereditary possession of their holding, a right known as *duthchas*, though the term kindness is sometimes used in a similar way.

These are irritatingly elusive terms to define. At times, they appear a right so tangible that tenants actually bargained with them, as when a John McPherson renounced, temporarily, his 'douchtous' and 'kindness' in a third part of Blarogie beg (Inverness-shire).[70] At other times, they come across as rather vague concepts, called upon by clansmen only in generalised terms. Part of the problem is that by their very character, rights like those of *duthchas* were antithetical to being prescribed or redacted, with some tenants report-edly refusing to accept written leases precisely because it undermined their customary but unwritten rights to their holdings.[71] This uncertainty over whether clansmen had tangible rights to a share of clan territory raises many questions about how the chief's superiority had been constituted prior to the feudalisation of tenures, and makes for an interesting comparison with East African chiefdoms where, as in some Scottish sources, chiefs were seen as being a guardian rather than the absolute owner of the clan's territory.[72] Certainly, if we accept Macinnes's suggestion that the gross territory settled by each clan was their *duthchas*, 'over which the fine were trustees',[73] then it would suggest that the claims of the clan at large did have some force of meaning when set beside those of their chief. Particularly intriguing in this respect is the 1541 reference to the various townships held by Alane McClane that made up Tresenis in Mull and which, in a note added to the list, were 'callet the sepe namet Lanvallanaill, extending [to] xxll land of auld extent'.[74] The term 'sepe' as used here may well have been equivalent to the Irish term 'sept' which was used to describe the territories allocated between the different branches or septs of a clan.[75] Such a singular reference hints (but no more than that) at the possibility that some clans may have experienced an organised division of territory between their various branches, or septs, a division that suggests each may have had claims to part of the whole.

In practice, the idea that families had the *duthchas* of a particular holding, even if it was no more than a claim on the favour of their chief, would have fostered a descent-focused notion of entitlement. If perfectly developed, sons inherited their father's tenure. Such rights were sometimes embodied in tacks such as when John Makcounquhy Roy Vc Coull and his two sons, Alan McEan Vic Conoquhy Roy Vc Coull and Ewin McEan Vc Conoquhy Roy, were collectively granted a tack of Barcalton, Corrieblicaik and Firlochane and Glentindill in 1576,[76] or when the two merkland of Inverynan Wester was set in 1675 'to Allane Makconoquhy Vc Corquidill whom failing to Lauchlan McAllane Vc Conoquhuy Vc Corquidill his eldest son and failing him to Duncan McAllane Vc Conoquhy Vc Corquidill his Brother german'.[77] If we examine rentals which list more than just the tacksman, there is ample proof of close kin living within the same township or nearby. For example, a rental of 1678 for the Reay estate lists an Alex. McAngus vic Allan, John McAngus vic Allan, Neal McAngus vic Allan and Hugh McAngus vic Allan in the adjacent townships of Lettermoir, Torrandarrow, Achowlogart and Rhean-leadain respectively.[78] Likewise, the John mcCoil vic Coil vic Ewn who occupied Booness (Arisaig) in 1699, along with a John mcEan vic Innis, was recorded in a rental of 1718 as John mcCoull, along with John McEan, and becomes the 'old mcCoulle their father' noted after Angus McEachine, John McEachine, Donald McEachine, Ewine McEachine and Dugald 'his [=Ewine's] brother' in a court listing drawn up in 1739. The remaining two occupiers, another John McEachine and another Donald McEachine could well be the John McEan mentioned in the 1718 rental and his son.[79] In such circumstances, it is easy to see how patronymics would serve to position a person within the local community and establish his right of access to a share in its resources. To a degree, we are faced with conditions similar to those which Fox has documented for Tory island, across the North Channel from Kintyre. There, individuals traced their descent from the person who first established their family occupation of a holding. In some cases, it could foster an awareness of descent that spanned five or six generations even though only one or two were used in everyday situations,[80] a depth that would make it equal to the Highland *clann*.[81] In effect, they constituted loosely coupled descent groups that drew their meaning from the way they helped to control access to land. When we come across a Roderick MacEan vic Coil vic Conochie vic Inish reaching back across five generations to identify himself in a tack of 1778 for North Bragar (Lewis), it is difficult to resist the con-clusion that even when surrounded by 20 other tenants, he was expressing the depth, or continuity, of his agnatic ties to the land as much as to his forebears.[82]

Yet whilst there is a comparison to be drawn with communities like those of Tory Island, it is doubtful whether the typical Highland family could boast such a continuous occupation of particular holdings, c.1493–1820, despite the prevalence of claims to *duthchas* and kindness. Arguably, the generally unsettled nature of society, the problems caused by feuding and recurrent subsistence crises worked against long-term continuity in occupation. Mention has already been made of the significant number of townships recorded as lying waste or uninhabited in a rental drawn up for MacLean of Duart's Mull estate in 1674, that is, in the year when the earl of Argyll first claimed control of the estate.[83] Mention has also been made of how, when estates changed hands in this way, it was common for the new holders to secure their position by offering tacks for whole townships and even groups of townships to loyal kinsmen who, in turn, brought in members of their own family as under-tenants. In other words, switches of ownership often signalled largescale switches of tenancies.[84] In some cases, as when Campbell of Inverawe was given the tack of Aros and Morenish on Mull in 1696, tacksmen were bound 'to remove such of the gentlemen of the name of McLean as are at present tennents and possessors of the island as hereafter he shall be directed'.[85] The scale of disruption that could be caused by such drastic actions is well brought out by the case involving the wholesale eviction of tenants, mostly MacLauchlans, from the islands of Shuna, Luing, Torosay and Seil in 1669.[86]

Clearly, these evictions were moments of great and exceptional disruption, but even where we have the opportunity for looking at the 'normal' process of tenant succession, it suggests no great stability from one generation to another. A series of Crown rentals for Kintyre enable us to track patterns of tenurial occupation for south Kintyre from 1502 down to 1605, that is, from soon after the collapse of the Lordship down to the eve of the estates's takeover by the earl of Argyll. Significantly, no family appears to maintain its possession across all four rentals.[87] Of course, after 1605, Kintyre saw even more drastic change, as its new holder, the earl of Argyll, brought in kinsmen and Lowland lairds.[88] The nature of the changes involved are well shown by the fortunes of Angus Makconneill. In the 1596 rental for north Kintyre, he was listed as holding a string of ten townships in north Kintyre amounting to 23 merklands which he had acquired from the laird of Barskymming. By the time of the 1605 rental though, when they had passed from Angus Makconneill into Crown hands, all ten townships are recorded as 'waist'. Clearly, the tenants of these townships suffered as much as Makconneill from the unsettled conditions of the region.[89] One of the more interesting sets of data bearing on the continuity of tenant occupation consists of a short run of rentals for Tiree compiled when the earl of Argyll took possession of the island. The rentals take a backward glance and compile a list of occupation for 1662, that is, before the change of ownership. They suggest that a significant amount of land already lay waste or unoccupied.[90] The conclusion we must reach is that whatever the impact caused by changes in ownership, they were not the only reasons for breaks in the family occupation of land.

Elsewhere, a sequence of late seventeenth- and early eighteenth-century lists detailing all males over 14 years provides us with even fuller information for Rannoch, since it covers not just tacksmen but also under-tenants and cottars. Admittedly, Rannoch was a notoriously unstable area. Indeed, its problems of social control were the very reason for the lists being compiled. However, its problems in this respect were not entirely unique. Other areas shared such problems. As Table 2.1 shows, even an analysis of tenant occupiers over a short period, 1735–43, shows that whilst the same family groups, mostly ex-Macgregors, maintained their presence in the area as a whole, there was a constant turnover in the occupants of individual townships. In fact, if we add comments from other sections of the barony-court records, there appears no guarantee that those attached to particular town-

TABLE 2.1. Turnover of tenants in Rannoch townships, 1735–43

	1735	1739	1743
Kilchonan	8	4 (4)	4 (5)
Cregannon	5	2 (2)	0 (4)
Ardlarich	7	3 (3)	2 (6)
Aulich	7	5 (3)	5 (5)
Kinnachlachlar	4	2 (1)	2 (5)
Dunan	5	4 (2)	2 (1)
Annat	2	1 (1)	1 (1)
Crasanour	5	2 (2)	0 (4)

Sources: SRO, John MacGregor Collection, GD50/156, Lists of inhabitants for 1735, 1739 and 1745.

ships actually resided there all year round. Its inhabitants were regularly accused of sorning, that is, forcing food and hospitality out of other tenants.[91]

Given the importance which the sustained occupation of land had for any sort of descent system,[92] it is difficult to see how areas like Rannoch could have engendered a community in which relatively deep kin structures (i.e. lineages or *sliochdan, clann*) emerged comparable to those identified for the Clan Chattan in Badenoch.[93] In a sense, we are faced with a paradox. The very processes that enabled local kin groups to deepen into large, territorial clans also introduced, through the constant rivalry between clans, a potential source of discontinuity, a means for servering the link between kin groups and their *duthchas*. Once we appreciate the extent of this rivalry, then it follows that the relationship between the sort of shallow descent groups embodied in patronymics and the wider concept of the clan cannot be taken for granted.

Much can also be learnt from establishing how clan names were used in relation to patronymics. In practice, most individuals identified themselves through a clan name as well as a patronymic. Where this was done simultaneously, the clan name was either affixed to (e.g. Donald mcAllester McKane[94]) or set beside the patronymic as an alias (e.g. John Macdonald alias mcEan vic Inish,[95] Dougall McEan alias McDugall[96] or Dougall Macdonald alias McEan vic Coull.[97] The question that needs to be answered is whether these forms of identity were linked agnatically in the sense that one was merely a more specific form of the other, tied through a relationship that was inclusive and immutable, or whether their link was essentially ideological so that what determined how one was bound into the other was not the biological fact of kinship *sensu stricto*, but a nexus of shared interests and behaviour which, at the margins or in the right circumstances, could cut across kinship ties, acknowledging putative as well as real kinship ties. We can find contemporary sources that describe clans as composed of kinsmen, as with a 1587 reference to 'the whole kin of Clan Donald and the kin of Clanchattane',[98] but others qualify the point by talking about those who bear the same name, as in a bond of 1672 between the Marquis of Huntly and Duncan McPherson of Cluny which talked of the latter as 'cheifs of the name of Mcpherson' and responsible for 'those of his name wherever they dwelt'.[99] In fact, given the way in which the geography of many clans was in a continual state of flux, it is to be doubted whether any but the smallest and most localised segment of a clan could claim a genuine unity of kinship.

Writing in 1930, Grant pointed out how the inhabitants of Duthil parish (Strathspey) appear in a list of 1537 as comprised of different kin groups but as being mostly Grants in one drawn up a few year later.[100] Her further point about Fraser of Lovat offering a boll of meal to any one taking his name squares neatly with a society in which subsistence was at a premium.[101] By far the most publicised instance of a clansmen changing their clan name concerns the MacGregors. In 1603, after decades of feuding, use of their name was proscribed. Though restored in 1661, this proved only a temporary reprieve, for proscription was re-imposed in 1693. We can assess the impact of such legislation by tracing the identity of particular families through successive township lists for Rannoch. Clan affiliation, it seems, was a matter of prevailing political realities. Thus, in 1660, we find a reference to a John Dowe McGillespik in the township of Ardlarich. In 1664, just after the lifting of proscription, he is re-listed by that name along with his son, Archibald. In 1672, though, some time after the proscription had been lifted, the son now emerged as Archibald Roy McGregor. The son maintained this identity in the listing of 1683 but, in 1695, he had re-oriented himself as Archibald Menzies. Finally, in 1698, he is still referred to as Arch. Menzies but his son appears as 'Duncan Menzeis leat McGrigor'.[102] A number of such name shifts can be pieced together with the Rannoch lists. Their potential complexity is drawn together for us by a reference in the 1698 list for Ardlarich to 'Dod. Menzeis alias McWilliam leat McGrigor.[103]

It is easy to see the MacGregors as a special case. Yet whilst we can grasp the obvious impact which the restrictions on even small gatherings must have had on the clan's behaviour, it is difficult to see how a change in name could alter the fact of kinship unless clans were seen as a generalised kinship structures which, in the right circumstances, could add or drop members through the mere expediency of using or discarding a clan name. After all, having abandoned their clan name, the MacGregors did not simply restrict themselves to using only their patronymics, they adopted new clan names so that Duncan McGregor became Duncan Menzies just as his more infamous kinsman Rob Roy became 'Rob roy Campbell alias McGregor'.[104] Probably what was distinct about the MacGregors was not their change of clan name but the fact that it was forced on them by Crown authority. Just as an expanding clan could underwrite its external alliance with another clan by forging putative links, or through 'the gentle' and seemingly widespread 'art of pedigree faking' as Sellar calls it,[105] so also, could a clan contrive to grow internally by absorbing members at its base through a comparable process of tie-faking. For most individuals, adopting a clan name enabled them to draw on the favour and support of a chief. However, it could also be used to challenge authority. When Cregeen tells us that all 45 inhabitants in the township of Innimore in Morvern labelled themselves as Camerons, it is unlikely that they were but their solidarity made a point to the then land-owner of the township, the earl of Argyll.[106]

By its very nature, a kin-based society transformed physical space into a social space, one that was identified through and structured by the groups or clans that occupied it. For the Highlands, the tidiness of this sort of socially constructed space would need to be qualified to allow for those situations in which tenants held land from landowners who were not their chief. However, even allowing for these potential unconformities, the geography of clans and chiefly power would still have contoured the landscape in a way that was no less dramatic in the physiography of its peaks and troughs, in its islands and peninsulas, than the actual landscape. In so far as chiefs worked to build status through their control over land and its product, and through various forms of conspicuous consumption, this geography provides an essential lead in to any understanding of the chiefly economy and chiefly patterns of display behaviour.

NOTES

1. Wormald, *Lords and Men*, p. 79.
2. Grant, *Independence and Nationhood*, pp. 203–4.
3. See, for example, Wormald, 'Bloodfeud, kindred and government'; Brown, *Bloodfeud in Scotland*, p. 7.
4. Barrow, 'The lost Gaidhealtachd of medieval Scotland', pp. 67–79.
5. *APS*, iii, 1567–1592, pp. 456–7.
6. Sahlins, *Tribesmen*, p. 5.
7. *APS*, iv, 1593, 11 Sept., p. 40. It is worth adding here Macinnes's point that 'protection' was the 'primary value' of clanship; see Macinnes, *Clanship, Commerce and the House of Stuart, 1603–1788*, p. 2
8. Munro, *Monro's Western Isles*, pp. 103–10.
9. Cregeen, 'Tacksmen and their successors'; Macinnes, 'Crown, clans and fine', p. 33; Withers, *Gaelic Scotland: the Transformation of a Culture Region*, pp. 210–16; Shaw, *The Northern and Western Islands*, pp. 53–8.
10. Cregeen, 'The changing role of the house of Argyll', p. 155.
11. SRO, John MacGregor Collection, GD50/103, John MacGregor Collection, 50/103, Clan Gregor Genealogies.
12. Wormald, *Lords and Men*, p. 76
13. Macinnes, 'Crown, clans and fine', p. 31.
14. Lang (ed.), *The Highlands of Scotland in 1750*, p. 93.
15. Cregeen, 'Tacksmen and their successors', p. 96.
16. Cregeen, 'The changing role of the house of Argyll', p. 160; Cregeen, 'Tacksmen and their successors', p. 98.
17. The expansive claims of the early Macgregors are well made in SRO, John MacGregor Collection, GD50/93, Genealogy of 'Mac Gregor anciently Mor'.
18. Innes (ed.), *The Black Book of Taymouth*, pp. 416–7. See also Wormald, *Lords and Men*, p. 208.

19. Ibid., p. 79. See also Macinnes, *Clanship, Commerce and the House of Stuart, 1603–1788*, p. 9.
20. Cregeen, 'The changing role of the house of Argyll', p. 155.
21. Macpherson, 'An old Highland genealogy', pp. 18–20.
22. Wormald, *Lords and Men*, p. 76.
23. SRO, John MacGregor Collection, GD50/103, Clan Gregor Genealogies.
24. SRO, Clan Donald Trust, RH4/90/19/2, Extract Contract betw. Donald Gorme of Slaite and Lauchlan McIntosche, 1587.
25. MacDonald and MacDonald, *The Clan MacDonald*, iii, p. 377.
26. Wormald, *Lords and Men*, pp. 205–49.
27. CDC/MP, RH19/8, Extr. Contract betwe. Sir Donald Macdonald of Sleat and Ronald McAllane of Sleat, 1727. Further comment on bonds of manrent can be found in Macinnes, *Clanship, Commerce and the House of Stuart, 1603–1788*, pp. 8–14.
28. MacLeod (ed.), *The Book of Dunvegan*, i, pp. 161–80; Shaw, *The Northern and Western Islands*, pp. 43–6, Bangor-Jones, 'Mackenzie families'.
29. Mackenzie, *History of the Outer Hebrides*, pp. 236–65.
30. Macphail (ed.), *Highland Papers*, ii, especially p. 313.
31. McKerral, 'The Tacksman and his holding', p. 19.
32. Kirch, 'Polynesian prehistory: cultural adaptation in an island ecosystems', pp. 339–48.
33. Nicholson, *Scotland: the Later Middle Ages*, p. 548 talks about 'the unusual chaos in the west highlands and the Isles throughout the sixteenth century whenever (and it was more usual than unusual) the Crown was afflicted by minorities or other distractions'.
34. Cowan, 'Clanship, kinship and the Campbell acquisition of Islay', p. 157.
35. SRO, Breadalbane Muniments, GD112/22/2, 1599–1610 Inventory of Furniture.
36. Based on SRO, John MacGregor Collection, GD50/28, Genealogy – Clan Campbell of Glenurquhay; GD112/75/1–10, Writs, Campbells of Glenorchy.
37. All data for this review of the Campbells of Glenorchy has been drawn from SRO, John MacGregor Collection, GD50/28, Genealogy – Clan Campbell of Glenurquhay.
38. SRO, John MacGregor Collection, GD50/93, Genealogy of 'Mac Gregor anciently Mor'.
39. Ibid., GD50/28, Genealogy – Clan Campbell of Glenurquhay
40. Brown (ed.) *RPC, vii, AD 1605–1606*, pp. 360–2.
41. A full discussion of the Fife Adventurers is provided by Mackenzie, *History of the Outer Hebrides*, pp. 242–65.
42. Macpherson, 'An old highland genealogy', pp. 8 and 11–13.
43. Ibid., pp. 6–23.
44. Ibid., pp. 17–21; Macpherson, 'Migration fields in a traditional Highland community', pp. 1–14.
45. Fox, 'Lineage cells and regional definition', pp. 95–119 provides a review of how Highland clans were structured.
46. Johnson, *Journey to the Western Islands of Scotland*, p. 153. The enduring link between place and identity is well shown by Macinnes's reference to the fifteenth-century movement of a Campbell sept from Glassary to the Braes of Lochaber, where they adopted the name MacGlasserich; see Macinnes, *Clanship, Commerce and the House of Stuart, 1603–1788*, p. 4.
47. Wormald, *Lords and Men*, p. 82.
48. SRO, Seaforth Muniments, GD46/1/212, Old Leases 1765–1781.
49. SRO, John MacGregor Collection, GD50/136/1, vol. 1.
50. Ibid., GD50/136/1, vol. 2.

51. SRO, Seaforth Muniments, GD46/1/212, Old Leases, 1765–1781.

52. Good examples are provided by MacRae, *History of Clan MacRae*, pp. 423–5.

53. Dodgshon, 'Symbolic classification', pp. 74–5.

54. SRO, John MacGregor Collection, GD50/136/1, vol. 1.

55. SRO, Clanranald Papers, GD201/5/1257/1, Rental of the Estate of Moydart, 1718.

56. Burnett (ed.), *ERS, xii, AD 1502–1507*, pp. 625–41, 704–9; McNeill (ed.), *ERS, xvii, AD 1537–1542*, pp. 625–33. A 1543 rental for Kintyre is also available amongst the Argyll papers. It shows no significant changes in rent or its composition, but references to tenants 'labourand ye said ground with thair awin gudis at the nixt martyness' suggests that, as other sources also suggest, some tenants had occupied their land under some form of steelbow tenure, see IC/AP, N.E.11 vol. 1543–1610, Rentall of Kintyre 1543.

57. Ibid., pp. 622–4 and 643–5.

58. Ibid., p. 647.

59. IC/AP, Rental of Tiree for 1662, Box 2531.

60. Macphail (ed.), *Highland Papers*, iii, pp. 288–93.

61. See e.g. DC/MDP, 2/487/12, March, 1688, Ane Account of … rents of Harries at Martinmass 1687.

62. Ibid.

63. DC/MDP, 2/487/10 Rents of the Lands of Haries 1686; DC/MDP, 2/487/12, March 1688, Ane Account of … rents of Harries at Martinmass 1687.

64. Macphail (ed.), *Highland Papers*, ii, pp. 313–39.

65. MacRae, *Clan MacRae*, pp. 376–8.

66. Wormald, 'Bloodfeud, kindred and government'.

67. Charles-Edwards, *Early Irish and Welsh Kinship*, pp. 21–73, 226–303.

68. I use the word 'most' here because in one or two sources, one can glimpse claims to the contrary. For instance, in the 1541 Crown rental for Mull printed in McNeill (ed.), *ERS, xvii, AD 1537–1542*, p. 622, it was noted that 'Insula de Gommetry allegit perteining to McLane in heretag'. In case there is any doubt as to what 'in heretag' meant, the 1541 rental for Islay contained the 'Memorandum' that 'the Landis of Foreland ar acclamit be hector McClane in heretage. The Landis of Lek pertenis to the Kingis grace', p. 641. Clearly, 'in heretage' was to be distinguished from 'the Kingis grace'.

69. SRO, Clanranald Papers, GD201/5/1257/3, Rental for Eigg, 1718.

70. SRO, Macpherson of Cluny Papers, GD80/162, Contract 1683. See also Macpherson, 'An old Highland genealogy', p. 12; Gregory and Skene (eds), *Collectanea de Rebus Albanicis*, p. 161, reprints a petition by Islay tenants, dated 1613, in which they complain about exactions which will force them to 'leave thair kyndly habitatiounis rowmes and possessionis', a phrase which suggest that whatever else it might mean, the phrase 'kyndly habitatiounis' was linked to a continuity of occupation.

71. Lang (ed.), *The Highlands of Scotland in 1750*, p. 93, says how 'throughout all Lochaber and the adjacent wild Countries, the farms have been always given to the cadets of the Lesser Families that are the Heads of Tribes, which they possess for Ages without any lease, and look upon them as their right of Inheritance … These People have often Refused to take a written Lease thinking that by so doing, they give up their right of possession.' See also Withers, *Gaelic Scotland*, p. 214.

72. Shipton, 'Strips and patches', pp. 616–17; Mair, *Primitive Government*, pp. 173–4; Jamieson (ed.), *Burt's Letters from the North of Scotland*, ii, p. 177.

73. MacInnes, 'Crown, clans and fine', p. 34; Macinnes, *Clanship, Commerce, and the House of Stuart, 1603–1788*, pp. 5–6; Withers, *Gaelic Scotland*, pp. 77–8. In view of the chronology adopted in this book, it is worth noting that Macinnes,

Clanship, Commerce and the House of Stuart, 1603–1788, p. 233, argues that the concept of *duthchas* as a 'heritable trusteeship' by the clan elite or *fine* was only finally abandoned by the *fine* in favour of heritable title, *oighreachd*, after the '45.

74. McNeill (ed.), *ERS, xvii, AD 1537–1542*, p. 643. See also ibid., p. 622.
75. Duffy, 'The territorial organisation of Gaelic landownership'.
76. SRO, John MacGregor Collection, GD50/29, Extracts by MacGregor from original compilation of mss relating to Campbell of Glenurchay.
77. Ibid.
78. Mackay, *The Book of Mackay*, pp. 471–5.
79. SRO, Clanranald Papers, GD201/1/362/3, The Sett of Arasack for the Year 1699; GD201/5/1257/5, Rental of Clanranald's Estate in South Uist 1718; GD201/1/227A, Minutes of the Baron Court at Borrodill, Arisaig, 1739. Further examples are provided by Shaw, *The Northern and Western Islands*, p. 70.
80. Fox, *The Tory Islanders*, p. 122.
81. Macpherson, 'An old Highland genealogy', pp. 1–2.
82. SRO, Seaforth Papers, GD46/1/212, Old Leases, 1765–1781. An example of a six-generation patronymic, the deepest found by the author, is provided by a grant of the brewseat at Annat in Argyll to 'Gillemeachnell McEwne VcGillechallan VcEwne VcUnche VcGillemechaell'; see SRO, Campbell of Barcaldine Muniments, GD1700/44/159/5, Charter by Duncane Stewart of Appyne.
83. Macphail (ed.), *Highland Papers*, ii, pp. 273–83; Macphail (ed.), *Highland Papers*, iii, pp. 73–85.
84. Particularly good examples of this process are documented in Cregeen, 'The changing role of the house of Argyll', pp. 153–92.
85. Ibid., p. 97.
86. Macphail (ed.), *Highland Papers*, iv, pp. 221–4.
87. Burnett (ed.), *ERS, xii, AD 1502–1507*, pp. 698–701; Macphail (ed.), *Highland Papers*, iii, pp. 75–85.
88. Cregeen, 'Changing role of the house of Argyll', pp. 159–60.
89. Macphail (ed.), *Highland Papers*, iii, pp. 75 and 81.
90. IC/AP, V65, Rental of Tirie 1662 by Ardgour.
91. SRO, John MacGregor Collection, GD50/136/1, Barony Court Books Menzies and Rannoch, vol. 1622–93, 15 December 1686; GD50/136/1, 29 August 1700. Further comment on the question of tenant occupancy, one that gives greater stress to continuity, can be found in Shaw, *The Northern and Western Islands*, p. 70.
92. Cf. Leach, *Pul Eliya*, p. 11.
93. Macpherson, 'An old Highland genealogy'. Of course, it is possible that the Invereshie genealogy Book gives a more organised view of the Macgregor's clan structure than actually prevailed. A genealogy of the Macgregors is provided by SRO GD50/93 and 103. See also Brown (ed.), *RPC, vii, AD 1605–1606*, p. 82.
94. McNeill (ed.), *ERS, vii, AD 1537–1542*, pp. 622–4.
95. SRO, Clanranald Papers, GD201/5/1257/5, Rental of Clanranald's Estate in South Uist, 1718.
96. Ibid., GD201/5/1257/1, Rental of the Estate of Moydart, 1718.
97. Ibid.
98. SRO RH4/90/19/2.
99. SRO, Macpherson of Cluny Papers, GD80/89, Bond by Duncan McPherson of Cluny 1672.
100. Grant, *Social and Economic Development of Scotland*, p. 501.
101. Grant, *Highland Folk Ways*, p. 24, notes that, according to the Gartmore MS

(1747), adopting the clan name of a chief was standard practice where a person held land from him. It was 'custom of chiefs', the manuscript runs, to oblige 'all the farmers and crofters that got possessions on their grounds to take their name. In a generation or two it is believed that they really are of that name and this not only adds to the number of the clan and keeps it up, but superinduces the tie of kindred to the obligations and interest of the former'.

102. Based on SRO, John MacGregor Collection, GD50/136/1, Barony Court Books Menzies and Rannoch, vol. 1622–93; GD50/156, A List of the whole Tennentis men servantis above sexteine, Rannoch, available for various years including 1695, 1698, 1735, 1739 and 1745.

103 Ibid. A similar double identity is provided by Hugh alias Hucheon McIlle-speclarie alias McConneill, a tenant on Islay, see Smith (ed.), *The Book of Islay*, p. 94.

104. HMC, *Third Report*, p. 381.

105. Sellar, 'Highland Family Origins', pp. 103–16.

106. Cregeen, 'Changing role of the house of Argyll', p. 163.

3 The Nature of the Chiefly Economy

Many clan chiefs had control over vast areas or properties of land. As estates, these properties were amongst the largest in Britain. Of course, much of what they contained was low-value hill or mountain ground. The amount of land that could actually sustain a community was far more limited. When output was eventually directed at the marketplace, their relative isolation compounded the problems created by this low level of gross productivity. Such crude comparisons with estates elsewhere in Britain, though, are misleading. At the start of the period under review, c.1493, if not at the end, Highland landowners still saw themselves as chiefs rather than commercial landlords. Admittedly, most of the period is taken up by the transformation of one into the other, at first slowly, and then, by the mid-seventeenth century, rapidly, but we cannot begin to understand the strategies that helped shape the management of Highland estates during the sixteenth and seventeenth centuries except by seeing them in terms of how they served the chiefly economy.

Put simply, Highland chiefs saw themselves, first and foremost, as trying to maximise the social product of land rather than its cash returns, pure and simple. Chiefs no less than landlords were concerned to maximise the physical output, but whereas the latter tried to do so by reducing labour inputs, the former actually supported a system that allowed increased labour inputs. For chiefs, the more people involved in food production, the greater its social value, but for landlords, concerned with the profit left after costs had been removed from its market price, too much labour diminished the value of output. The reason why the increased labour value of food production increased its social value for chiefs lay in how they used their control over subsistence to build status. They did so in four inter-connected ways. First, the more tenants that could be settled by a chief, the more he could extend the number of his clansmen. Second, the more that could be settled, the more food could be gathered in as rent. Third, in a marginal environment, the more people that could be settled and the more pressure exerted on resources, the more a chief's control over food and subsistence acquired an ideological value. Fourth, the more food gathered in as rent by a chief, the more potential he had for translating it into status via various forms of display behaviour. Reduced to a strategy, these various sources of value meant chiefs had a vested interest in packing their estates, 'cultivating men as much as land' as some commentators put it, and in preserving the social value of rents by collecting them in kind rather than trying to realise what – under the conditions of the time – was their lesser market value. Only by appreciating these points of difference, can we make sense of the chiefly economy and its approach to land.

There is much to be gained from seeing the Highland economy over the sixteenth and seventeenth century in the context of the wider debate by anthropologists and archaeologists regarding chiefdoms and their redistributive exchange schemes.[1] What was given to chiefs by way of rents in kind and in the form of other renders was, in character, tribute, a gift that had the instrumental value of underpinning the chief's position. In consequence, those chiefs who acquired more rents in kind, whose girnal houses were always full, would have been seen as having greater status. For this reason, we first need to establish the character and scale of such rents if we are to understand how chiefs used them to sustain chiefly patterns of behaviour.

WHAT CAN HIGHLAND RENTALS TELL US?

Traditional societies are by nature conservative. The relationships, practices and routines of everyday life tend to be heavily value-laden and to be determined by custom, based on what has gone before, especially in matters dealing with land and the relationships between owner and occupier. If we examine Highland estate rentals as they become available from the sixteenth century onwards, it is easy to conclude that here too, we are faced with a customary society, one in which the nexus of dues and renders that bound tenants and landowners, clansmen and their chief, embodied longstanding obligations. As a broad generalisation, there can be no quibble with this. However, it cannot be the last word on the matter. Highland tenurial relationships were not static, locked timelessly into a particular form. When we glimpse such relationships through the earliest charters and rentals, or in those of the fifteenth and sixteenth centuries, there is evidence for supposing that some parts of the region were experiencing change and that this change was ongoing, as old forms were given a fresher face and new obligations were accreted to old ones. In character, what constituted rents appears as a complex bundle of dues and obligations, each with a different background. Moreover, when seen through the earliest rentals and other related sources, their character varies from one source to another and from one region to

another. If we look at early and mid-sixteenth-century Crown rentals covering those areas that formed part of the Lordship of the Isles, townships
appear set for a fixed, annual rent.[2] However, when we turn to other sources,
they suggest that the levying of fixed annual rents was a relatively recent
development, at least in the western parts of the region or those areas that
came under close Crown authority fairly late.

A key source with regard to this latter point is a late sixteenth-century
report on the Hebrides drawn up between 1577 and 1595.[3] Far from con-
firming that fixed, regular rents were in place across the region, this report
gives the impression that chiefs or landowners in most parts of the Hebrides
still relied on the *irregular* uptake of food renders in the form of *cuid oidhche*,
a longstanding render based on the obligation of tenants to provide hospitality for their chief or landowner and his household men. Significantly, the
scale of food involved more than matched that of later food rents. Thus, the
report notes that each merkland on Mull and Coll paid yearly '5 bollis beir,
8 bollis meill, 20 stanes of chese, 4 stanes of buttir, 4 mairtis, 8 wedderis, two
merk of silver, and twa dozen pultrie, by Cuddiche, quahanevir thair master
cummis to thame'.[4] Likewise, each merkland on the Uists 'payis 20 bolls
victuall, by all uther customes, maills, and oist silver, quhair thair is na certane
rentall'. It goes on to say that the 'customes of this Ile are splendit, and payit
at the Landlordis cumming to the Ile to his Cudicht'.[5]

The style of these entries, and others in the report, has considerable
bearing on how we might read the development of Highland rents. They
suggest that, when we first glimpse them through sixteenth-century rentals,
the food payments that appear at the heart of west Highland and Hebridean
rents may be rooted in the obligation of *cuid-oidhche*. Though *cuid-oidhche*
occurs in later sources alongside rent as an incidental obligation,[6] it appears
from this late sixteenth-century report to have formed the core of early food
renders. Certainly, given the scale of food that could be uplifted through
cuid-oidhche on a yearly basis, it is difficult to see how the food renders
recorded in early rentals can be anything other than those uplifted via *cuid-
oidhche* in a different guise, renders that were now gathered in rather than
consumed *in situ* as hospitality. Not surprisingly, when the food renders
uplifted through *cuid-oidhche* were considered from the vantage point of
the Lowlands, Highland chiefs were seen as collecting rents irregularly, an
irregularity that stemmed from the way in which the right of *cuid-oidhche* was
exercised.

Yet before seeing Highland and Hebridean food rents as rooted in earlier,
more irregular payments of food uplifted via the obligation of *cuid-oidhche*,
we need to consider how the Hebridean report drawn up between 1577 and
1595 relates to the Crown rentals available during the first half of the
sixteenth century for those parts of the south-west Highlands that had
previously been part of the Lordship of the Isles. Taken at face value, the two
sources appear to conflict, with the Crown rentals suggesting that food
renders were already being uplifted as part of a scheme of regular rents but

the late sixteenth-century Crown report describing all food renders as still uplifted in the form of *cuid-oidhche*, even in areas covered by the Crown rentals like Islay. In all probability, the late sixteenth-century report details the traditional form of food renders which tenants owed to their chief or landowner. By comparison, the early sixteenth-century rentals (1505 and 1541–2) show the Crown's attempt to turn such renders into regular food rents or, where conversions had occurred, their cash equivalent, during the two brief periods when it controlled the estates involved directly.

We can glean a number of clues about this change from the 1505 rental for North and South Kintyre, the earliest Hebridean rental available. By 1505, all Kintyre townships are depicted as owing a fixed annual rent but beyond this general point, there are three different types of entry in the rental. First, there are a small number of townships whose rent appears to consist of a cash payment equivalent to their merkland assessment, usually with the addition of one or two minor payments in kind, such as cain sheep. Thus, Glenherf, a three merkland township, was set for three merks of money rent, whilst Newklach, a one merkland township, was set for one merk, a cain mutton and a stone of victuals. Second, some were still set either entirely or largely for a rent in kind, with substantial payments of meal, cheese, malt and stock, the latter comprising marts, sheep or pigs. Where such townships owed a small cash payment, it constituted barely 10–15 per cent of their total rent. At Lossyd, a five-merkland township, for instance, the cash portion of its rent amounted to just 10 per cent of the total paid, the rest being made up of meal, cheese and stock. Third, a small cluster of townships, eight in all, paid a sizeable cash rent, but not one that exceeded the value of their merkland assessment. In addition, they also paid a modest amount of meal, cheese and stock, equivalent in value to about 20–25 per cent of their total rent. In each case, these payments of meal and cheese are labelled as *le coddocheich*.[7] Such variation suggests that – at the point when the rental was compiled – Kintyre rents were undergoing change, one that was affecting different areas and different townships at different rates. Logically, the baseline for this variation is represented by those townships which paid all, or virtually all, their rent as a payment in kind. Such payments probably represent the food renders initially uplifted in the form of *cuid-oidhche* converted into a regular rent payment. Other townships had moved away from this baseline by having all or part of their rent converted into a cash payment.

Such an interpretation, though, needs to confront two further questions. The first concerns the way that some townships appear to pay a cash rent equivalent to their merkland assessment, whilst others appear to pay a rent which, when their cash and food rents are combined, was significantly in excess of their assessment rating. One explanation for this would be to see some townships as having undergone the conversion or part-conversion to cash rents at different dates, with those experiencing a later shift bearing a higher cash rent simply because of inflation in the value of farm produce. Significantly, when we compare the cash rents levied in 1505 with those levied in 1541, all appear to have been increased by 50 per cent so that the cash portion of rents was seen as open to revision in step with market prices.

The second question raised by the assumption that the payment of rents entirely in kind represented the baseline for any changes that might be read from the 1505 rental concerns the references to the payment of *cuid-oidhche*. These references occur only in relation to a small number of townships, mainly located around Loch Kilkerran. They paid the bulk of their rents in cash but, in addition, also paid a significant amount of meal, cheese and stock, the latter being labelled as *le coddocheiche*. The problem is that the term *le coddocheiche* is not used in the case of those townships which paid most of their rents in kind even though such food rents may be rooted in the obligation of *cuid-oidhche*. The explanation for this discrepancy may lie in how those compiling the rental perceived food rents. Most of the food rents owed by Kintyre townships were now seen as marketable surplus rather than as the basis for supporting 'household men'. The extent to which the Crown levied cash rents in its 1505 rental is indicative of this. In these circumstances, Crown officers may have tried to preserve some food rents specifically for the maintenance of its local officers, hence its continued use of the term *le coddocheiche* to describe food renders owed by townships around Loch Kilkerran. By 1541, the use of the term had disappeared altogether, even though the townships involved still paid some food renders.

As an area penetrated by Crown authority sooner than other parts of the region covered by the early sixteenth-century Crown rentals, Kintyre may also have experienced the shift both to regular rents and to cash-based rents sooner. Certainly, if we take the 1505 and 1541–2 rentals at face value, Kintyre townships paid more of their rents in cash than elsewhere. All the signs are that the disappearance of *cuid-oidhche* in other parts of the region proceeded more slowly. The late sixteenth century report on the Hebrides suggests that even areas recorded as already paying regular rents by Crown rentals compiled earlier in the century, like Islay, were still seen as having a liability for food renders that was conceived in terms of *cuid-oidhche*.[8] Patently, the fact that the Crown rentals were compiled during very brief periods of Crown possession may give us a false sense of how far such areas had moved to a permanent state of regular rents. In the western isles, change appears to have worked itself out even more slowly. The Statutes of Iona (1609) found cause to ban chiefs like MacLaine of Lochbuie, the Captain of Clanranald and Donald Gorm of Sleat from the 'taking of cowdighis'.[9] In case this is seen as a reference to the practice of sorning, whereby those without right to hospitality forced food out of tenants, the Privy Council made its point clear. When Donald Gorm of Sleat and others re-appeared before it, they were required not only 'to foirbeare the taking of cowdighis and presentis from [their] tennentis' but also, to set their land for a 'certain constant and cleir dewtie' and not to exact any more than the 'cleir dewtie contenit in thair tak'.[10] Clearly, the conversion of one into the other had not yet taken place. Furthermore, the pressure for change was bound up with the assertion of Crown control over the region through the instrument of the Privy Council. In the circumstances, we cannot rule out the possibility that the earlier assertion of Crown control over lands that were formerly part of the Lordship of the Isles, like Islay and Morvern, may also have precipitated a shift towards regular rents.

THE NATURE OF RENTS

When we look more closely at the evidence for rents, the earliest rentals show landowners burdened their tenants with a diverse bundle of dues, renders and obligations. As already implied, some were deeply rooted payments, others recently introduced or modified. Altogether, we can divide the various dues, renders and obligations into four components: payments in kind including grain and stock, casualties, services, and cash.

Traditionally, the most important component of Highland 'rents' was the payment of victuals or food renders in the form of grain or meal and various types of livestock and livestock products. Throughout the Highlands and Islands, the two main types of grain payment were oat meal and bere. In character, the former is variously described as white meal, 'albe ferrine', negri ferrine', 'grocie ferrius', 'mediocrit ferrius', whilst the latter was paid in the form of either bere or malt.[11] In some cases, rentals might add extra conditions. On the Clanranald estate, a 1704 tack stipulated that the ten bolls of 'good and Sufficient Victuall' to be paid by the tenant of North and South Garrivaltos should be 'Such as grows upon the Ground of the said Lands'.[12] On Skye, meanwhile, MacLeod of Dunvegan insisted that all tacksmen had to pay their ferm meal in 'kylldryed & shelled Corn under forfeit of his Tack'.[13]

Table 3.1 summarises the amount of grain collected in as rent by various estates. Where appropriate and possible, it has been broken down into the amount paid by the different parts of the estate. As can be seen, the amounts involved were significant. Altogether, I want to draw out three general points about the character of such data. The first is that whereas payments in oat meal were well-nigh universal, those of bere or malt were not. The latter varied both between estates and within them. On the large estates, the policy appears to have been to extract bere only from select areas. On the Sutherland estate, vast quantities were paid in as rent down into the eighteenth century, but it was drawn mainly from the eastern coastal parishes. Likewise, on the Cromartie estate, areas like Strathpeffer paid substantial quantities but, not surprisingly, none was drawn from Coigach. The situation on Campbell of Glenorchy's estate was more complex. Areas like Netherlorne owed significant amounts, especially islands like Luing, Seil and Lismore, but the amounts involved became inconsequential as one moved eastwards into Glenorchy and to other interior parts of the estate. However, further east still, around Lochtayside, quite substantial amounts of bere were uplifted from a district like Lawers. Likewise, on MacLean of Duart's estate, considerably

TABLE 3.1. Sample rents in kind

	Meal	Bere	Malt	Cheese	Marts
North Kintyre (1541)	326 stones		4 chalder 13 bolls	239 stones	7
South Kintyre (1541)	992 stones		24 chalder 12 bolls	375 stones	45
Islay (1541)	598 stones			598 stones	79
Midward of Islay (1541)	1084 stones			44 stones	140
Rhinns of Islay (1541)	1010 stones			1010 stones	136
Jura (1541)	100 stones			100 stones	20
Colonsay (1541)	255 stones		1 chalder	255 stones	34
Aros, Mull (1541)	246 stones			246 stones	18
Tiree (1541)	653 stones	686 bolls			32
Ardnamurchan (1541)	705 stones			705 stones	13
Sunart (1541)	297 stones		3 chalder 13 bolls	297 stones	43
Morvern (1541)	525 stones			525 stones	42
Lewis (1577–95)	360 chalders				1160
Bernera (1577–95)	120 bolls				
Pabbay (1577–95)	60 bolls				
St Kilda (1577–95)	60 bolls				
Uist (1577–95)	2800 stones				
Trotterness (1577–95)	160 bolls		160 bolls		320
Mull (1577–95)	2400 bolls	1500 bolls		6000 stones	1200
Ulva (1577–95)	96 bolls	60 bolls		240 stones	48
Gometra (1577–95)	32 bolls	20 bolls		80 stones	16
Coll (1577–95)	240 bolls	150 bolls		600 stones	120
Islay (1577–95)	2160 bolls	1800 bolls		7200 stones	1260
Jura (1577–95)	180 bolls	150 bolls		600 stones	105
Colonsay (1577–95)	180 bolls	150 bolls		600 stones	105
Oronsay (1577–95)	24 bolls	20 bolls		80 stones	14
Gigha (1577–95)	180 bolls	150 bolls		600 stones	105

Sources: McNeill (ed.), *ERS*, xvii, *AD 1537–1542*, pp. 634–50; Skene, Celtic Scotland, iii, p. 429; Gregory and Skene (eds), *Collectanea de Rebus Albanicis*, pp. 173–7; Macpherson, *Glimpses*, pp. 503–13; Smith (ed.), *The Book of Islay*, pp. 487–90; DC/MDP, 2/485/26/3, Estate rental, 1724; NLS, Cromartie Papers, GD305/1/63, Rentals, 1612–1824.

more can be found collected as rent from Tiree than from townships on Mull. Yet if circumstances warranted it, even difficult, marginal areas could be pressed into producing bere or malt. The 1541 Crown rental for Sunart suggests that it may have been such an area, with sizeable quantities of 'grund malt' being paid by a number of townships as part of their rent. Collectively, the townships of Sunart yielded 3 chalders, 13 bolls, 2 firlots and 1 peck of malt.[14] Of added interest is the fact that those Sunart townships which paid malt appear to have done so as a surcharge over and above what they paid as the standard rent for townships rated as two-and-a-half merklands, each paying two marts, 25 stone of meal, 25 stone of cheese, and 12s 6d in money plus malt.

A second feature about grain payments that deserves notice concerns the question of how much it constituted as a proportion of total rent. To judge from the glosses that occur in rentals and accounts, and from the way rent was balanced, a number of estates(such as those of Campbell of Glenorchy, MacLeod of Dunvegan and Cromartie) appear to have drawn a distinction between stock farms and grain farms. I will argue later (see Chapter 7) that the basic needs of subsistence meant that when we look at townships in terms of their field economy, this distinction appears subdued. Nevertheless, when seen in terms of their rent liability, such a distinction appears to have mattered. On Tiree, an island renowned for its fertility, grain payments recorded in its 1541 rental represented on average 50–60 per cent of the value of the total rent paid.[15] By comparison, townships in the Ross of Mull that were recorded in a rental of the former lands of Iona Abbey were more suited to livestock production, grain forming less than 20 per cent in value of the total rent paid.[16]

A third aspect of grain rents concerns the vexed question of what proportion of a tenant's grain was actually handed over as rent. Whether more suited for grain or livestock, all Highland townships maintained some arable, so that what was paid as rent was potentially a charge against subsistence. The popular saying in Lowland Scotland that a tenant had one to sow, one to grow and one to pay the lord with suggests that even in more fertile areas, the margins within which the average tenant developed a subsistence strategy were fairly tight. Given the added problems of life in the Highlands, it would clearly further our understanding of these strategies if we could establish whether the proportion paid as rent was similar. One opportunity for doing so is provided by the practice on some estates of setting land in terms of how many bolls of sowing was allowed per unit of land assessment. In a region where arable was fragmented and uneven, and where only part of the surface might be cropped thanks to the use of lazybeds, treating the amount of arable being set in these terms had more precision than any acreage that might be implied by such assessments. By comparing such data with that on yields, we can derive a broad estimate of the total grain harvest yielded by a township and, by setting this gross yield down beside the amount paid as rent, we can gauge what proportion of the total crop was handed over as rent.

In the case of Tiree, the evidence enables us to probe the problem in the context of both the mid-sixteenth and mid-seventeenth centuries. Detailed seventeenth-century commentaries suggest that each tirunga on Tiree was sub-divided into a unit called the *mail*, or *malie*, with each tirunga comprising 48 *mails*.[17] In character, the *mail* would appear to have been either a unit of sowing, a unit of rent yield, or both. In terms of sowing, the seventeenth-century data suggests that each tirunga was customarily seen as sowing 48 bolls of oats and 24 bolls of bere.[18] When we look at the 1541 rental for the island, it reveals that at a time when no cash rents were levied, each tirunga paid 48.6 bolls of grain per year.[19] Clearly, there is a degree of symmetry between how townships were rated in *mails*, what they sowed in oats (1:1) and bere (1:0.5), and what they paid as rent (1:1). When broken down, grain rents in 1541 comprised 42 bolls of bere and 40 stones of meal (=6.6 bolls). If we assume a return on seed of c.4× for bere and 3× for oats (see p. 220), then it suggests that the island paid c.40–45 per cent of its bere crop as rent but barely 5 per cent of its oat crop. However, we cannot assume that a boll of grain produced a boll of meal. In all probability, to produce a boll of meal required 1–1.25 bolls of bere and as much as 1.5–2 bolls of oats.[20] Seen in these terms, the amount of crop paid as rent may well have been as much as 40–55 per cent of the harvested crop in the case of bere and c.7.5–10 per cent in the case of oats. By the time detailed rentals are available for the mid-seventeenth century (1652 and 1680), the amount of rent paid in meal had fallen, with each tirunga now paying only 32 bolls according to one source,[21] but 33.2 bolls according to another,[22] that is, approximately two-thirds of the 48.6 bolls paid per tirunga in 1541. The proportions of bere and oats had also altered. Assuming a return of c.4× for bere and a conversion ratio from grain to meal of 1–1.25:1, tenants now paid around 20–25 per cent of their total crop as rent, whilst if we assume a return of c.3× for oats and a conversion ratio for grain:meal of 1.5–2:1, then they paid between 13.5–18 per cent of their oat crop. In other words, the amount of bere paid as rent may have fallen significantly, whilst the amount of oats paid may have risen.

In the case of Campbell of Glenorchy's estate, a similar analysis can be carried out for parts of Netherlorne using early eighteenth century data. It suggests that townships paid between 20–50 per cent of their bere crop as rent, the overall average being 30 per cent, whilst they paid from just under 10 per cent to over 25 per cent of their oat crop, the average being 15.6 per cent.[23] As on Tiree, the estate appears more interested in what it could uplift from the bere than the oat crop. The estate's use of steelbow tenure enables us to carry out similar calculations for townships in the interior parts of the estate during the late sixteenth and early seventeenth centuries. By such a tenure, the estate provided tenants with seed, stock and 'strenth silver' as working capital.[24] The township of Acherye, for instance, a six merk land, had 40 bolls of steelbow oats and 200 merks Scots of 'strenth money' in 1697.[25] Generally speaking, early rentals for the estate, such as those compiled during the late sixteenth and early seventeenth centuries and covering a limited number of townships in Glenorchy and Breadalbane, suggest that steelbow townships could pay twice as much oats in rent as they received in steelbow seed.[26] If we work from the assumption that oats gave a threefold return on seed, then it is clear from such data that these townships owed about 33 per cent of their oat crop for the replacement of steelbow seed, paid another 33 per cent as rent, and were left with 33 per cent for subsistence. In some cases, their margins may have been even tighter. The township of Acheryre, for instance, paid 48 bolls of oat meal as part of its rent so unless its gross yield was a little higher than a threefold return on seed, the proportion which it paid as rent may have been higher than 33 per cent when we allow for how much grain was needed to produce 48 bolls of meal.[27] In addition to these payments of oat grain and meal, a few of the townships also paid bere as part of their rent, but the amounts involved were very small. Most appear to have been given a firlot, or a firlot and one peck of seed, and to have paid a boll in rent or its cash equivalent, suggesting little could have been left for tenants.[28] The one cautionary note that might be entered against such figures concerns the precise nature of steelbow seed. In origin, it is likely that the seed given to tenants as steelbow represented the total amount sown. By the time we can compare what was being paid as steelbow with what was actually sown, though, it is clear that tenants had started to sow more, using their own resources of seed.[29] In other words, whilst steelbow seed may once have represented the total amount sown, we cannot assume that this necessarily remained the case down into the late seventeenth and early eighteenth centuries.

In addition to the grain paid as rent, tenants were also required to pay grain as teind and multures. For fertile areas, the gross amount paid as teind could be significant. Muckairn parish in Argyll, for instance, paid 99 bolls of meal as teinds during the late seventeenth century,[30] whilst the parishes of Kilmichael and Kilneuair in Glassary paid 265 bolls of victual meal.[31] By comparison, the amount paid as multure was modest. This was largely because prior to the eighteenth century, mills were unevenly scattered in the western Highlands and Islands. A large estate like Campbell of Glenorchy's Breadalbane estate had mills in all its districts or officiaries,[32] but generally, mills became significantly fewer in number as one moved northwards and westwards through the region. Tiree, for instance, only had one mill serving the entire island prior to 1700.[33]

Most Highland townships had rent bundles that involved livestock as well as grain. The most onerous form was undoubtedly that of marts, or cattle (Table 3.1). As a broad generalisation, their recorded payment in kind is more evident in sixteenth-century rentals than in those of the seventeenth and more evident in those of the seventeenth than in those of the eighteenth century. However, even when still paid in kind, it does not appear to have been a burden on all townships. To judge from sixteenth-century data, all townships on Islay and Tiree paid significant numbers of marts. Those of

Islay had the greatest burden, at least according to the report on the Hebrides compiled between 1577 and 1595. Each merkland 'payis yeirlie three mairtis and ane half', whilst each township rated as two-and-a-half merklands also paid 'of Gersum at Beltane four ky with calf'.[34] On Tiree, meanwhile, each 'Quarter' of a tirunga, equal to one and a half merkland, paid a 'martinmas cow' and a 'whit sunday cow & calfe'.[35] Whereas all townships on islands like Islay and Tiree were burdened with marts in a fairly systematic way, the pattern elsewhere suggests marts were a more uneven payment by the time rentals become available. A livestock district like Ardnamurchan, for instance, appears to have paid only modest numbers according to the Crown rental of 1541. Altogether, only seven of its townships paid marts, rendering two each.[36] Like the bere payments made by some of the townships in Sunart, these marts appear as surcharge over and above what they paid as rent relative to other townships with similar assessments. A detailed rental for Skye, a MacLeod of Dunvegan rental dating from 1724, suggests that there too, only select townships were burdened with marts, though this selectivity may be accounted for by the general differences noted above between the data for the sixteenth and seventeenth centuries.[37] On the interior parts of Campbell of Glenorchy's estate, a 1620 rental of livestock shows that only six townships in Glenorchy and fourteen in the East and West Ends of Lochtayside paid marts, whereas all six townships in Lochaw paid marts, the estate collecting in the modest total of 35 marts a year.[38] In the 1671 rental of Morvern, no marts are recorded but, between them, its townships paid 29 veals.[39] Veals were also featured elsewhere, such as amongst payments on the Campbell of Duntroon estate in Argyll.[40] On many estates, adding to the burden of marts was the payment of cattle (along with horses) as herezeld. Even as late as 1727, 'all the Tennants of Breadalbane' were 'oblidged to pay Herezelds ... at their Death'.[41]

An important component of rents in kind, even in arable areas, was the payments made up of butter and cheese (Table 3.1). Generally speaking, payments in butter were confined to particular districts, presumably those seen as specialist livestock districts, whereas payments in cheese were far more widespread. Indeed, most townships paid cheese in greater or lesser amounts. On Islay, for instance, every merkland paid 20 stones of cheese, but none had any liability for butter.[42] Cheese, but not butter, was also a standard payment from all townships in Ardnamurchan, Sunart and Morvern in the Crown rental of 1541.[43] As a cautionary note though, the same rental recorded that Tiree townships only paid cheese, but later sources suggest the each *mail* also paid a quart of butter, making 48 quarts per tirunga.[44] More so than with the payment of marts, payments of butter and cheese can be used to identify townships that clearly specialised as stock or dairy farms. According to its 1541 rental, for instance, Kintyre had a number of townships that paid quite substantial amounts of cheese relative to other townships, such as Killonane, Kinlocha, Mauchrumore and Carska.[45] Local differentials were also apparent in areas like Harris suggesting that some townships there may also have had a distinct role within the wider estate economy.[46]

A feature about payments in cheese and butter is that whilst some are listed as rent, pure and simple, others are described as part of the 'casualties' or 'customs' owed by a township or, more revealingly, its 'old casualties'. Though the terms 'presents' and 'casualties' are used in some rentals as a catchall,[47] and are even treated in some rentals as alternate ways of describing the same payment,[48] other rentals draw a clear distinction between them.[49] In some cases, the items paid as 'presents' are also further described as 'yuil and pace', or 'beltane and allhallows', or simply 'goodwill' presents. In character, such payments represent a layer of dues and renders that may take us back deep into the medieval period, serving not just as part of the burdens that were attached to the possession of land but as an acknowledgement of the goodwill that clansmen implicitly owed to their chief or landowner and the gifts which they were bound to provide. In content, most payments of casualties and presents involved livestock or livestock products. A typical definition of 'casualties' on many estates was the payment of one stone of cheese, one quart of Butter and one wedder by townships in Moydart as 'the Customs or presents'.[50] The veals paid by townships in the 1671 rental for Morvern and listed as part of their 'Zuill and Pace presents', though, were fairly exceptional.[51] Most only involved payments of cheese and wedders. Where recorded systematically, the payment of wedders rarely involved more than four wedders per township, and most averaged only one or two. On the Breadalbane estate, they are listed as a standard 'Beltane' and 'Allhallows' presents, or as 'grassum' wedders, payable by virtually all townships across the estate.[52] Though goats were present on Breadalbane estate, none were paid either as rent or presents, though one or two townships in Breadalbane itself, paid 'swyne'.[53] Swine were also an exceptional payment on the MacLeod of Dunvegan estate on Skye, the tacksmen of Roag in Duirinish having to pay 4 swine or 16 marks each in lieu.[54] An early reference to the payment of swine by the townships of Kildallage, Knokquhyrk, and Achaquhone also occurs in the 1505 rental for Kintyre.[55]

Presents, customs and casualties could be a diverse basket of payments. As well as cheese, butter and wedders, they could include poultry including cocks, eggs, 'fedd kidds', 'kyndis tallow', whisky and linen.[56] The payments of poultry are particularly interesting for the simple hen appears to have been steeped in an aura of custom that begs many questions. On the MacLeod estate in Harris, poultry were tagged as 'flying customes',[57] whilst on other estates, they appear variously as 'reik hens'[58] or 'kain hens'.[59] The term 'reik' draws on a symbolism that links back to a Kintyre charter of c.1200, which required a penny to be paid by each house from which smoke issued, for a 'reik hen' was simply a hen from each house from which smoke issued.[60] The term kain or cain was equally archaic, being linked to a burden of hospitality that appears in the earliest documents.[61] It appears in rentals as a payment of hens usually with a corresponding payment of eggs. Even as late as 1795, tenants on the Seaforth estate in Lewis were still required to pay 'kain fowl and eggs, as in time past'.[62] In Islay, townships not only paid hens but also geese. Though some townships, like Coole and Ballynaby, might have taken advantage of the wild geese that winter around sites like Loch Gurm, the uniform levy of geese across the island suggests that early rentals were dealing solely with domesticated geese.[63]

On a number of estates, what was paid under headings like casualties was defined in a fixed, proportionate way. On Tiree, they embraced wedders, poultry and horse corn and were set as three-and-a-half merks worth from each *male*.[64] Some rentals record casualties as converted into cash payments under the heading of 'broch money'.[65] A rental of 1674 for Aros in Mull set 'the casualties of a penny-land, viz. four quarts, butter, four stones of cheese, four wedders, four stones of victual',[66] whilst in Netherlorne, a marginal gloss in a 1698 rental declared 'each markland laboured payes of small casualties 6 poultrie 6 doz. of eggs 2 loads of straw and 13 loads of peats'.[67]

This last example leads us to the question of whether labour services formed part of the relationship between landowners and tenants, or chiefs and their kinsmen, in the Highlands. Tenants in Netherlorne, like those on the Breadalbane estate generally, bore standard obligations of 'arrage & carriage [according] to use & want',[68] but the burdens elsewhere on the estate included 30 loads of peat for each merkland.[69] Glenure's lands on Lismore required tenants to cart 200 loads of peat, 4 loads of candle fir plus six days work for a man and a horse.[70] On Jura, a number of townships (i.e. Knockcrom, Keill, Craikaig) were required to 'perform 34 days service of one Man & 4 days service of a Man + horse'.[71]

As well as carting, such broadly defined services could involve the 'feudal' burdens of ploughing and harvesting. All the tenants in Netherlorne, for example, owed services in 'Hay Time, and Harvest'.[72] Occasionally, we are able to glimpse the diverse range of services that could be called upon by landowners. When Murdo McCaskill took a tack for the two pennylands of Peinmore on the Macleod Estate in Skye, he was required to deliver 'one hundred and twenty loads of Peats casting and Leading thereof to the house of Dunveggan or six pennies Scots as the price of each load thereof and perform three days service in very quarter of a year and thatching of houses or Six Shillings Scots for every days absence or Refusall'.[73] In case such burdens are seen as the downside for tenants living too close to the chiefly centre, tenants for townships as far away as Ramasaig, on the far side of Macleod's Tables, were required to provide peat for Dunvegan.[74] Some services were specific to local circumstances, such as those Assynt tacks which required tenants carry out services to the salmon fishing, amongst which were the maintenance of cruives and dams on the Water of Naver.[75] The tenant for Alphen and Unapool was not only charged with services to the salmon fishing but acted, for a fee, as the runner between farms in Assynt and Dunrobin 'when on estate business'.[76] Though services were increasingly converted rather than drawn in kind by the eighteenth century, there were still estates where the option of conversion was not given. The Seaforth estate, for instance, offered tenants no chance of conversion when it enacted a demand for six days service a year from each tenant on Lewis in 'articles of sett' issued in the early nineteenth century.[77] Indeed, a list of services extracted from his tenants by Campbell of Barcaldine and drawn up for James Riddell when he took over the Ardnamurchan and Sunart estate gives the impression that Riddell was looking to use them as a guide, even if it meant introducing them for the first time. In character, they were fairly wide-ranging and onerous, with '3 Days for laying out of fulzie 3 Days to Cuting winning and Leading his Masters Peats – 2 Days shearing – 1 Days Leading of Corn – 1 Days cuting Hay – and 1 Days Thatching' being only some of a fairly long list of Barcaldine's services, though it added that 'at all these works the master gives meat'.[78]

The cash component of rents is sometimes labelled in rentals as forming a townships's silver duty or mails. With only a few notable exceptions,[79] most townships appear even in the earliest available rentals as paying some form of cash rent. Taking an overview of such payments, there is something very old and yet very modern about them. The mails or silver duty that lie at the core of these payments appear longstanding. Yet such an assumption is not without its problems. In the first place, if we take the sixteenth-century Crown rentals available for former areas of the Lordship of the Isles as our point of reference, there is a distinct uniformity about the level of cash payments involved within each district. Thus, in the Aros district of Mull, the townships of Laidbeg, Lettermoir, and Drumfyne are each rated as a 16s 8d land, and each has the same cash liability, or 6s 8d of silver duty, whilst Tron is rated as a 8s 4d land and was liable for 3s 4d of silver duty.[80] Likewise, townships in Ardnamurchan like Aherhill, Lawga, Ardslegingis and Bordblege are all rated as two-and-a-half merklands and each was rated as liable for 12s 6d of silver duty.[81] On Islay, each merk land bore a duty of two merks of silver according to one late sixteenth century source[82] whilst, despite the absence of cash rents in its 1541 rental, each tirunga on Tiree was later described as carrying a silver duty of twenty merks or 160 pounds.[83]

Such payments clearly appear to have been levied according to a standard scheme of values within each district, without regard to the variations that must have existed in the resource mix of each township. Either such townships preserved old payments with a remarkable degree of conservatism or the payments involved had not long been imposed. Seen in relation to areas like Tiree, where townships only paid rents in kind when first seen in the Crown rentals for 1541 but where a cash portion had appeared by 1652, the balance of evidence favours the conclusion that regular cash payments – as opposed to occasional fiscal levies – were a relatively recent innovation. The most likely explanation for their appearance lies in the efforts of the Crown to assert its authority following the collapse of the Lordship of the Isles. However modest in its scale, adding a regular cash component to local rents would have made a powerful ideological point, for it not only directly burdened tenants with a form of rent associated more with the demands of the Crown than with local chiefs, but also it would have had the effect of forcing the township economy into the marketing of produce in order to meet such cash rents.

Seen over the sixteenth and seventeenth centuries, these early payments of mails or silver duty were soon supplemented by other cash payments. By far the greatest proportion of these extra cash payments stemmed from the conversion of rents in kind. The sixteenth-century Crown rentals provide clear evidence for this process. Faced with the task of moving and marketing large quantities of mostly poor-quality grain from the Highlands, it allowed tenants the option of buying their produce back. A note appended to the 1541 Crown rental for Morvern actually states that 'all the martis, cheis and mele ar sauld for silver to the tennantis of the ground as Kintyre is'.[84] Some of the rentals, such as those for Tiree, record the sale price for each stone of meal and bere after stating how much grain tenants paid.[85] There would have been good reasons why the Crown did not want to cart produce like meal out of the region. Arguably, it was more significant when Highland chiefs decided that they too, preferred rents in cash rather than kind.

A further source of cash payments in early rentals came from absolute increases in rent. Because of their customary nature, and the preponderance of payments in kind, it was difficult for landowners to force an absolute increase in rents paid in kind. Where such increases can be detected, they invariably involved extra cash payments. A rental covering land formerly belonging to Iona Abbey and granted by James VI to MacLean of Duart in 1587–8 shows various townships in the Ross of Mull together with a handful on Islay and Tiree as having an *eik* in rent, or an augmentation, that was calculated entirely in cash.[86] Significantly, the rental suggests that the entire rent of these townships had previously been computed as rent payments in kind, though the charter does give each payment a cash equivalent. In a sense, therefore, the eik now being added was the first payment exclusively in cash. By the time of a rental drawn up for Tiree in 1652, and detailing rent as it 'was use to be paid to the Laird of McLean', each of the 960 *mails* into which the island was divided now paid 5 merks of money plus their victual rents.[87] The most likely explanation would seem to be that such cash payments were formed by converting part of the former grain rents into cash equivalent.[88] In fact, when we look at the level of grain payments still being made, they suggest that grain payments had fallen by one third compared with the figures given in the 1541 rental.[89]

A widespread form of due was the payment of *grassum*, or *gersum* as it was called in some sources. Defined strictly, *grassum* was a fine paid on entry to a holding. One or two early sources suggest it may originally have been a payment in stock,[90] but by the time it starts to occur widely in seventeenth- and early eighteenth-century sources, it had become a cash payment. In practice, it appears as a flexible payment, one that lay outside of the constraints surrounding customary rents. For this reason, it formed an attractive means by which landowners could raise more revenue for a holding. A memorandum drawn up for the Macdonald estate on Skye, c.1730, lays out the occasion if not the logic behind its imposition. It suggested to Sir Alexander Macdonald that when setting his land, he should ascertain 'the nature quality & Extent of the Ground as well such part of it as is fit for tillage as what is only fit for pasturage should be examined & thereafter the Rent to be accordingly stated wt.out Respect to qt. it paid formerly or in case that method of doeing proves difficult then in place of Raiseing the Rent, to oblige the tennant to pay such a Grassum corresponding to the Difference betwn. the Real value & the old Tack duty, & in proportion to the years of the Tack'.[91] In some cases, the notion of grassum worked as a crude principle of favour, with a tack for Hoill in Trotternish being set to seven tenants with 'a grassum for preferring them to this present tack'.[92]

By the early eighteenth century, the levying of grassums was reported on many estates. On the MacLeod of Dunvegan estate on Skye, late seventeenth-century rentals make no mention of it, but eighteenth-century rentals make frequent reference to 'grassum or Entry money'[93] and in one or two cases, such as in a gloss on the entry for Strond in a 1724 rental for Harris, we can actually see it being imposed for the first time.[94] In other cases, rentals appear to distinguish clearly between 'grassum' and the 'augmentation' of the rent.[95] One particularly valuable source is a dispute regarding MacLeod's lands in Glenelg and dated 1733. The documentation produced talked about the tenants paying 'every fifth year a Years Duty & sometimes more of Grassum or Entry Mony Attour the ordinary yearly rent'.[96] On the mainland, grassums were reported as paid by townships in Coigach 'Every five years', the total for the district amounting to 8000 merks.[97] Free use of grassums was also made on the Breadalbane estates in both Argyllshire and Perthshire by the early eighteenth century. In some cases, 'a considerable grassum' was paid 'besides the augmentation',[98] whilst in at least one source, the use of grassums appears to have been restricted to particular parts of the estate.[99]

THE INCOME OF CHIEFLY ESTATES: CASE STUDIES

The scale of estate income derived by landowners can best be gauged by examining particular examples. Data has been compiled for four estates: the former lands of the Lordship of the Isles (Islay and Kintyre); Tiree before and after its acquisition by the earls of Argyll; the MacLeod of Dunvegan estates on Skye and Harris; and finally, the Campbell of Glenorchy's estate in Argyllshire and Perthshire. Each offers a different perspective on what landowners typically derived from their land and on the way in which these patterns of chiefly income altered over the sixteenth and seventeenth centuries.

Systematic data is available for Kintyre and Islay from the early sixteenth century onwards, soon after the Lordship had collapsed. That for Kintyre starts with a detailed rental drawn up in 1505[100] and that for Islay with a rental of 1506.[101] As already mentioned, these rentals were drawn up when Kintyre and Islay (along with other mainland areas like Ardnamurchan and Sunart and other islands like Colonsay and Tiree) passed into the hands of the Crown and, for a brief time, were managed directly by it. To restate a point already made, there may be ways in which the compilation of these rentals by the Crown embodied changes in practice. Their concern to state conversion values may be one sign of that change. Nor were these conversion values simply a means of computing the cash value of rent yields for the sake of making up the accounts for, as again already noted, tenants in Morvern and Kintyre were reported to have bought their food rents back from the Crown in the 1541 rental. Yet whilst acknowledging that Crown possession introduced a different appreciation of the problem through its concern to put a market value on produce, it did not in any way suppress rents in kind but continued to record them as the basis for calculating each township's rent liability. In the case of Islay, the generalised way in which the 1507 rental deals with the cash rent yield of the island can be compared with the 1541 rental, in which all townships still have a carefully defined burden of rents in kind.[102] Clearly, the use of cash conversions in the sixteenth-century Crown rentals did not signal the final replacement of rents in kind with cash, only what their value meant in the Crown's accounts.

Altogether, the Kintyre data has been drawn from rentals for 1505, 1541, and 1664,[103] whilst that for Islay has been drawn from rentals for 1541, 1614 and 1686.[104] Taking an overview of the 1505 rental for Kintyre, together with the 1541 rentals for both Kintyre and Islay, two main conclusions stand out. The first is the extent to which some rents appear to be systematically derived within each district, with townships carrying the same proportionate share of rent for each unit of assessment. On Islay especially, what each township paid in respect of cash, meal, cheese, marts, wedders, and poultry was proportioned to their merkland assessment.[105] A similar case can be made for North and South Kintyre but there, as explained earlier, some variations had emerged in respect of cash payments made per merkland but they are not random variations. Altogether, the overall impression is of a pattern of rent burden that has been imposed in a systematic way rather than built up through the individual resource mix of each township.[106]

The second conclusion concerns the different kinds of rent gathered in from Islay and Kintyre. In aggregate, far more silver mail was raised from North and South Kintyre than from Islay, largely because the 'paper' conversion of food rents appears to have been more advanced, even by 1505. Possibly bound up with this last point, Islay paid a substantially greater number of marts than either North and South Kintyre, as well as substantially more meal, cheese, wedders and poultry. Though individual townships in Kintyre paid sizeable quantities of cheese, the overall output from North and South Kintyre combined was barely 30 per cent of Islay's rent yield in cheese. Similarly, their combined yield in meal was only just over one half that of Islay. However, this was balanced by the large amounts of malt paid by townships in Kintyre, especially those of South Kintyre, a form of payment surprisingly absent from the 1541 rental for Islay. Altogether, the impression gained is that beyond their basic flows of meal and cheese, Islay was prized for its stock and Kintyre for its malt.

In the case of Islay, we can bring our perspective forward by using rentals for 1614 and 1686. The comparison between 1541 and 1614 is particularly revealing. It suggests that far from being a period when food rents were gradually eroded, they actually increased. As well as a modest rise in silver rents, there also took place a significant rise in the payments of meal, cheese, marts and poultry, each being raised by about one third. We can only speculate as to why this increase took place. The late sixteenth century was a time of gathering price inflation, but the fact that so much of the rental increase was loaded onto payments in kind suggests this was a real or absolute increase in the island's rent yield. Part of the answer might also lie in a petition submitted in 1613 by the Crown tenants of Islay to the Privy Council complaining that 'SIR RANALD McSORLE KNYCHT and his officearis and servandis in his name have begun to impost upoun theme verie havy burdynis exactionis and impositionis'.[107] One aspect of the complaint dealt with extra dues being levied on all livestock grazing the common waste, and gives the impression that Ranald McSorle, alias Macdonald, may have squeezed tenants for as much as he could exact during his very short lease of the island following the death of his brother in 1611. It is possibly in this context that we need to see some of the general inflation of Islay's rents in kind between 1541 and 1614.

The second case study, or Tiree, is first recorded for us in the 1541 Rental of the Isles. Subsequent rental data is available on a township-by-township basis for 1652[108] and 1680.[109] As with other districts covered by the 1541 rental, the allocation of rent between townships is proportional to their land assessment. In fact, the Tiree portion of the rental makes the systematic allocation of rent absolutely clear, declaring that 'everie sex mark land peyis yeirlie xlii bollis beir lx stanis [meal] ii martis, and for ane of the foirsaidis martis everie sex mark land thair is fyve furlotis of beir to be defalkit to the tennentis, and sua ilk sex mark land peis yerly xl bollis iii furlotis beir'.[110] As the rental list itself confirms, no silver duty or money rent was levied in its own right though all payments in kind, with the exception of bere, were given a conversion value. The failure to declare a conversion price for bere possibly meant that it was actually gathered in as grain. Like Kintyre, Tiree was renowned for its fertility, being known as *terra ethica* and as 'McConnell's girnal',[111] and like Kintyre, its rental income was marked by substantial payments of bere. When grossed up, they were by far the most valued item of rent, amounting to 840 bolls. Its payments of meal, though, were more modest by comparison with Kintyre or Islay. Surprisingly, the 1541 rental makes no mention of any payments of either cheese or butter, despite the fame of the island's rich machair pastures and the claim that cows grazed on them gave three milkings a day.[112] It is possible that they were regarded as

TABLE 3.2. Tiree rents, 1541–1768

	Sown (bolls)	Oats (bolls)	Bere (bolls)
1541	960	924	840
1662	960	790	1148
1680	1174	1447	1071
1768	1070	1115	1914

Sources: McNeill (ed.), ERS, xvii, AD 1537–1542, pp. 647–8; Argyll Papers, Inveraray Castle, Memorandum of the Rentall of Tiree, 1662; ibid., 3531, Rental of Tirie, 1680; ibid., V65, List of Inhabitants … 1768.

'casualties' and, for that reason, not mentioned by the 1541 rental. Later rentals certainly confirm they were paid as casualties.[113]

Comparison between the 1541 rental and that compiled to show the state of rent when Sir Allane MacLean held the island in 1652 reveal a number changes. Cash rents now appear, with each tirunga carrying a money rent of 160 lib,[114] a figure based on each *mail* (of which there were 48 in a tirunga) paying five merks.[115] Casualties are now specified, amounting to payments of 12 stones of cheese, 12 quarts of butter, 16 wedders and 48 hens per tirunga.[116] The grain payments were now set as 'bear meall malt equallie',[117] and proportioned so that 'every quarter of the Tirung is worth – 60 stane of victual wherof 20 stane meall 20 bear and 20 stane malt', an amount which burdened each *mail* with five stone of victual.[118] Overall, the amount of grain paid as rent had declined since 1541, to 743 bolls compared with 960 bolls.[119] Furthermore, when we break these grain payments down, whilst the amount paid in the form of bere or malt had declined sharply that paid in the form of meal had actually doubled (see Table 3.2). As I will argue in Chapter 4, these shifts between bere, malt and meal could well reflect the impact of the Statutes of Iona (1609) on the nature of the chiefly economy.

The third case study is provided by the MacLeod of Dunvegan estate covering parts of north-west and western Skye and Harris. Though its rentals have not the time-depth of those for Islay, Kintyre and Tiree, the first not being available until the 1680s, they are available as a remarkably detailed series for the next century or so and have the further interest of covering some of the smaller islands that surround Harris. That for 1724, including a breakdown of its data for the various parts of the estate, is summarised in Table 3.3. Overall, it discloses a significant cash component together with a fairly standard package of renders in kind, though by 1724 some of the latter were being uplifted as cash payments. Overall, what was paid in kind, including those items that were now assessed wholly in cash such as the teinds, amounted to just under 40 per cent of the total rent. Clearly, the switch into cash rents had already made significant progress by 1724, though how much of this was brought about by levying extra cash rents or by converting some of the existing rents in kind is difficult to say. The way the rental itemises the converted cash value of marts and teinds, without

TABLE 3.3. MacLeod of Dunvegan estate, 1724: rents

	Money rent	Cess money	Teinds money	Mart money	Victual half meal and bear bolls	Butter and cheese stones	Wedders	Horse corn money	Hens money	Total Scots money	Sterling money
Duirinish	2711.6.8	168.3.4	471.0.0	96.6.8	55	81	57	61.0.0	53.2.0	4092.5.4	340.19.7
Waternish	1636.13.4	154.6.8	304.0.0	100.13.4	91.5	95	81	37.16.0	41.6.8	3063.3.4	255.4.11
Bracadale	2122.6.8	196.0.0	483.0.0	144.0.0	74.5	119	62	57.0.0	37.16.0	3720.2.8	309.19.8
Minginish	1611.6.8	136.0.0	353.6.8	72.0.0	88.5	104.5	92	55.0.0	39.12.0	3085.12.0	257.2.2
Harris	2711.10.0	109.10.0	495.13.4	29.13.4	45	74	50	0	0		

Sources: DC/MDP, 2/485/26/3, Estate rental, 1724 (original version reportedly lost, but available as a typed copy). The main rental used was originally dated in the typed version as 1664; see MacLeod (ed.), *The Book of Dunvegan*, i, pp. 270–1. However, comparison with the rent and occupiers given in other rentals for 1724 confirms that it should be re-dated as 1724.

recording the number of animals or bolls involved, suggests it may have been concerned to distinguish such payments from that part of the rent which was seen as cash *ab origine*. In terms of payments in kind, the main components were those of victual, which the rental defines as half meal and half bere, and dairy produce, which it breaks down equally between butter and cheese. As with the Macdonald estate on Skye, payments were also made of horse corn.[120] Finally, a noteworthy feature of the rental is the sheer number of hens debited as rent. Altogether, the rental values them as 161 lib 16s 8d. Calculated at 3/- a dozen, a figure used by the rental itself, this represents a supposed render from the estate of 12945 hens!

The 1724 rental enables us to balance the payments made by the different parts of the estate: Duirinish, Waternish, Bracadale, Minginish and Harris (see Table 3.3). The most revealing feature of such a comparison concerns the differences between, on the one hand, Waternish, Minginish and Harris and, on the other, Duirinish and Bracadale. The former were liable for payments in kind that comprised a greater portion of their total rents compared to the latter. Further, though Duirinish and Bracadale paid more rent *in toto* than either Waternish, Minginish and Harris, the latter were bound to supply more victuals and dairy produce both in absolute terms and as a proportion of their respective rents. Waternish paid 60 per cent more victuals than Durinish even though its overall rent was one third less. As with Kintyre and Islay, the estate had clearly allocated different roles to different parts of the estate.

The availability of a succession of rentals for the MacLeod of Dunvegan estate over the late seventeenth and early eighteenth centuries provides an opportunity for exploring not just the general trend of rents but their short-term variability. By their very nature, food rents were subject to the vagaries of weather and other crises. In circumstances like those of the western isles, we can expect tenants to have faced recurrent problems over meeting their rent demands. Two areas have been selected for comment: Harris and Waternish. The first detailed for Harris is available in 1680. Thereafter, a series of rentals are available at regular intervals. The pattern of rent yielded by its townships confirm what later surveys indicate, that the small islands that lay around the southern edge of Harris were far more productive in terms of arable than the mainland townships. This comes across from their rental obligations, with the islands of Pabbay and Ensay providing between them nearly 60 per cent of all the grain extracted as rent from the Harris portion of the estate. Nearby Bernera also provided MacLeod with substantial amounts of grain as teind. In fact, helped by these islands, Harris could boast a higher level of grain rents than any other part of the estate, Waternish included. The low-lying, easily-worked soils of Pabbay, Ensay and Bernera no doubt helped it into this position, but it still says a great deal about the prevailing locational economics of the area that these relatively small islands could be treated as a 'breadbasket' for the estate. Seen through the fine sequence of late seventeenth-century and early eighteenth-century rentals, what stands out about rent payments of Harris is their short-term variability. The estate was never faced with a regular flow of food rents. Both victuals and payments of butter and cheese rise to a peak in the closing years of the seventeenth century, then fall back sharply. By the 1720s and 30s, though, former levels had been recovered and surpassed. In fact, cash rents only displaced rents in kind on Harris during the second half of the eighteenth century. As in Harris, what the estate collected in by way of both grain and cash rents in Waternish fell away towards 1700 owing to poor harvests, the estate's accounts constantly referring to tenants having 'rests' of rent. By 1711, the amount of grain gathered in by the estate had started to recover and by 1717–18 was almost 100 per cent greater than those for years like 1707, but then, by the 1720s, it had started to fall back as all payments in kind were converted and as cash rents began a steady and sustained rise. Yet that said, the estate actually increased the number of marts from Waternish over the early eighteenth century, presumably in response to the rising market for stock.[121]

At its maximum extent, Campbell of Glenorchy's Breadalbane estate covered an extensive territory stretching from some of the inshore islands along the Argyllshire coast (i.e. Seil, Luing), across both the Netherlorne and the Braes of Lorne, to Lochaw, Glenorchy and Breadalbane, but with extensions beyond into Strathfillan, Dull and Weems. As an estate, it offers what is easily one of the finest rental series available for a Highland estate, detailing rents on a fairly regular basis from the late sixteenth century onwards. Naturally, their coverage reflects the growth of the estate, with townships in core areas like Lochaw, Glenorchy and Breadalbane having the longest series. In character, the rentals are amongst the most detailed and most systematic available, with grain and livestock records being maintained together with a separate record of those payments made as Beltane and Allhallows presents. They are also amongst the most interesting in terms of the styles used, enabling us to build a picture of just how varied the traditional Highland landscape may have been as regards the forms and practices of tenure used.

Overall, the estate drew a clear distinction between what it saw as arable townships and what it saw as grass rooms and bowhouses,[122] the latter being farms used by the estate to manage the stock which it gathered in as rent. Their distinction, though, was relative rather than absolute. Even grass rooms were required to provide some victual rents in the form of oat-meal and bere, a uniformity of expectation that may owe something to the duty of support that all clansmen were obliged to provide for their chief and lord. However, beyond this basic flow of meal, grass rooms were clearly part of a well-organised estate-managed system of livestock production, one that is first evident in rentals drawn up for the estate in 1582 and 1594. What the rentals show is the constant interflow between estate and tenant as regards stock. The extent to which stock appear divided between what belonged to the estate and what belonged to the tenant gives the impression that under steelbow, tenants were effectively herding stock on the estate's behalf.[123] More so than other Highland estates, Campbell of Glenorchy's estate appears to have designed a system that not only yielded livestock to it by way of rent, but enabled it to use its tenants to co-ordinate a complex estate-wide system of production on its behalf, with the number of stock on each farm being maintained by means of a 'scoir stik'.[124] What had been gathered in by the estate as 'gersum wedders' or 'gersum kye' in one part of the estate were moved to the bowhouses in other parts.

Just as grass rooms were not exclusively devoted to livestock production, so also were arable townships not exclusively devoted to arable production. They too, were required to pay small quantities of wedders and marts as part of their rent. However, the main component of their rent was the payment of meal and bere. As on MacLeod of Dunvegan's estate, islands like Seil and Luing, together with low-ground farms in Netherlorne, paid proportionately large amounts of grain rent. In 1665 Luing alone paid 279 bolls of meal and 53 bolls of bere.[125] Interior parts of the estate, such as the townships around Lochtayside or adjacent districts, also paid substantial amounts of rent in grain and did so until well into the eighteenth century. However, when we look closely at the pattern of payments, the main burden appears to have fallen on select districts. A 1733 rental shows small amounts of bere and meal from areas like Ardtalnaig, Morinish, Carwhin, Crannich, but none from Glenlyon, Fernan, Glendochart, Strathfillan, Killin or Glenlochy. By comparison, significant amounts of both bere and meal were paid by townships in Lawers and from the East End of Lochtay.[126] Generally, rentals only record the core payments made by tenants, not the wider range of casualties that might be bound up with tenures. Occasionally, we are able to glimpse the latter, such as in a 1670 rental for Campbell of Glenorchy's estate (see Table 3.4). With its mix of meal, bere, wedders, geese, swine, whisky, nuts, fruit and cloth, it captures the wide range of payments in kind that could bind tenants and their landowners within the framework of the traditional estate economy.

In character, rents in kind formed part of an economy of direct consumption. In an environment in which poor harvests meant 'not scarcity, but emptiness',[127] having command over a surplus provided a powerful ideological weapon in the search for chiefly status. Though craftsmen of various sorts were given rent-free or discounted holdings, there are no indications that Highland chiefs used the food which they gathered to support such craftsmen directly. Instead, we need to see food rents as providing the basis for a primary circuit of consumption, enabling chiefs to support kinsmen and tenants in times of crisis, to support household men or the chief's retinue, to sustain display of feasting and feuding, and to build alliances through marriage and bonds of manrent with other chiefs and their families. As I have shown, food rents were already being converted into cash payments by the time the first rentals are available in the sixteenth century. Yet though

TABLE 3.4. Breadalbane estate: summary of rent, 1670

Silver Mails	£1236 14 08
Girsum 1670	£293 06 08
Blak Mairt Silver	£20 08 00
Meal	10 chalder 15 bolls 1 firlot 1 peck 1 lippie
Bear	8 chalder 8 bolls 111 firlots
Fed swyn	11
Wedders	52
Butter	xxv quarts 1 pint
Geese	32
Capons	vi dozen 10 wt
Poultry	viii dozen and a half dozen
Fed kids	viii
Lambs	xiii
Aquavitae	1 gallon
Tallow	iiii stone
Socking	viii els
Girding	xl els
Nuts	i firlot
Apples & pears	1000 wt
Also militia money and loads of peat	

Sources: SRO, Breadalbane Muniments, GD112/9/24, Rentals of Breadalbane 1669–78, 1670 rental.

seen only as change transformed it, reconstructing the nature of the so-called chiefly economy provides us with two basic insights. First, the broad range of food gathered in via *cuid-oidhche* or as rent and, in particular, the gathering in of large amounts of grain imposed a template on the township economy which was to dominate its character long after such rents had been converted into cash. Second, the scale of food rents involved meant that when change came, landowners were well placed to redirect output towards markets.

NOTES

1. See, for example, Kirch, *The Evolution of Polynesian Chiefdoms*, pp. 160–8; Sahlins, *Tribesmen*, pp. 81–95; Dalton (ed.), *Primitive, Archaic and Modern Economies*, pp. 9–15.
2. McNeill (ed.), *ERS, xvii, AD1537–1542*, pp. 611–50.
3. Skene, *Celtic Scotland*, iii, pp. 428–40.
4. Ibid., p. 435.
5. Ibid., p. 430.
6. It is, in fact, mentioned in the Napier Commission's report in 1884 as a surviving payment, irritating to tenants but one of no great consequence, see *Report of the Commissioners of Inquiry*, p. 993.
7. Burnett (ed.), *ERS, xii, AD1502–1507*, pp. 698–701.
8. Skene, *Celtic Scotland*, iii, pp. 437–8.
9. Masson (ed.), *RPC, ix, 1610–1613*, pp. 26–30. It is worth adding that the Islay charter of 1408 granting various townships to Brian Vicar Mackay required

him to pay 'yearly, four cows fit for killing for my house', see Lamont, 'The Islay charter of 1408', p. 165.

10. Masson (ed.), *RPC, x, 1613–1616*, pp. 778–9. See also pp. 773–6.
11. Part of the difference between white meal or albi ferrine and negri ferrine lay not just in the difference between the use of black and grey oats, but also, in the way graddaning, or the burning away of the chaff, could produce a black meal.
12. SRO, Forfeited Estates, E744/1, Judicial Rental of the Estate of Clanranald, 1748.
13. DC/MDP, 2/8 Acts of Court, 29 April 1735.
14. See McNeill (ed.), *ERS, xvii, AD1537–1542*, pp. 624 and 650.
15. Ibid., pp. 647–8.
16. Gregory and Skene (eds.), *Collectanea de Rebus Albanicis*, pp. 173–7.
17. IC/AP, Box 2531, Memorandum anent Tiric; ibid., Mcmorandum of the Rentall of the east end of Tirii, 1662.
18. Ibid., Box 251, Rentall of Tiry, what it payed in the year :52 and in all the years thereafter, compiled 1675.
19. McNeill (ed.), *ERS, vii, AD1537–1542*, pp. 647–8.
20. Examples of grain conversions at a grain:meal ratio of c.1.5–2:1 are provided by SRO, Forfeited Estates, E729/9/1 Menzies' Report, 1768; *OSA*, XIV, pp. 141 and 303; McKay (ed.), *Walker's Report on the Hebrides*, p. 76.
21. IC/AP, Box 2531, Memorandum anent Tirie.
22. Ibid., Memorandum of the Rentall of the east end of Tirii, 1662.
23. The figures given are based on data abstracted from SRO, Breadalbane Muniments, GD112/9/22, Rental of Lands belonging to Lord Neill Campbell in Loyng, Seill and Netherlorne 1665. Similar analyses, and producing similar results, can be carried out for the three townships held by Glenure on Lismore, see ibid., GD112/16/10/2/1, Report James Campbell 1728, which provides data on both sowing and rent yield. For comparison, a later 1753 source shows all three townships (Killean, Ballygrundel and Auchnacrosk) as paying even more grain as rent, see SRO, Campbell of Barcaldine Muniments, GD170/420/1/1, Rental of Glenure's Lands in Lismore, 1753.
24. 'Strenth silver' can be defined as that which made up what was deemed sufficient for the management of the farm, in effect, bringing it up to strength.
25. SRO, Breadalbane Muniments, GD112/9/3/3/7, Rentall of the Estate of the Earle of Breadalbane's estate in Argyleshire, 1697.
26. Ibid., GD112/9/7, Rental of Breadalbane, 1600, provides examples like Botuary Mor whose two tenants were each given 7 bolls 2 furlots of oat seed and each had to pay 15 bolls of oats as part of their rent. Likewise, the two tenants of Botuary beg were each given 7 bolls of oat seed and each had to pay 14 bolls of oats as part of their rent. The later 1620 rental, ibid., GD112/9/9, provides examples like Arribeane whose four tenants were each given 2 bolls of seed for sowing and they each had to pay 4 bolls as rent.
27. Ibid., GD112/9/3/3/7, Rentall of the Earl of Breadalbane's Estate in Argyleshire, 1697.
28. Examples are provided ibid., GD112/9/7, Rental of Breadalbane, 1600; ibid., GD112/9/9 Rentall of Bestiall for Breadalbane estate 1620. Despite its title, this rental also has good data on the amount of seed provided under steelbow and the grain paid as rent.
29. Usually, steelbow tenure is explained as a way of overcoming the tenant's lack of capital, but it had the extra advantage for the Highlands of attaching the chief's authority to stock and crop as they stood in the field. A simple definition of steelbow is provided by Innes, *Scotch Legal Antiquities*, p. 245. Elsewhere, steelbow can be documented for the Sutherland estate, at least in respect of cattle, see NLS, DEP313/2133, Sutherland estate rental, 1724. At the opposite

end of the Highlands, it existed on the Campbell of Duntroon estate, see SRO, Campbell of Duntroon Muniments, GD116/1/188, Rental of the Lands of James Campbell of Oib, 1749.

30. Cawdor Castle, Cawdor Papers, Bundle 655, Statement of Charge and Discharge for Muckairn priory Lands (dated on cover to 1710 but figures refer to 1691–1692).

31. IC/AP, B/4/14, Accnts and Rentals 1696–1704, Rentall of the Haill Teinds of the said Parroches of Kilmichael and Kilnewar in Glasrie. Substantial payments of teind meal are also recorded ibid., Bundle 2694, Abbreviat of the Report by the Commissioners appointed to enquire into the state of the teinds ... in Kintire, 1719.

32. The larger vertical mills, together with their associated crofts, are carefully recorded by early rentals. Those that existed on the Breadalbane estate in the late seventeenth century are, for example, clearly indicated in SRO, Breadalbane Muniments, GD112/9/5/6/3, Compts of Money Rent and Victual for the Breadalbane Estate 1684.

33. IC/AP, RHP8826/2, A General description of the Island of Tiriy, Surveyed 1768 by James Turnbull. Turnbull not only reports that Tiree had only one mill, at Crossapoll, but says that it was 'at present not in proper repair'.

34. Skene, *Celtic Scotland*, iii, pp. 437–8.

35. IC/AP, Box 2531, Memorandum anent Tirie.

36. McNeill (ed.), *ERS, vii, AD1537–1542*, pp. 643–4.

37. DC/MDP, 2/485/26/3, Judiciall Rental of the Baronies of Durinish, Waternish, Bracadale and Mingnish, 1724.

38. SRO, Breadalbane Muniments, GD112/9/9 Rental of Bestial, 1620. The same pattern is repeated in earlier rentals, e.g. GD112/9/7, Rental of Breadalbane Estate 1600–1602.

39. Macphail (ed.), *Highland Papers*, iii, pp. 285–8.

40. SRO, Campbell of Duntroon Muniments, GD1161/117, Ane Just Rental of the Lands of Kilfinkan and others, 1687.

41. SRO, Breadalbane Muniments, GD112/9/43 Rental of Estate of Breadalbane ... 1736, includes report on soumes of each Merk lands, 1727. See also DC/MDP, 2/494, List of tenants who have paid heriot, or 'herezeld horse'.

42. Skene, *Celtic Scotland*, iii, p. 438.

43. McNeill (ed.), *ERS, vii, AD1537–1542*, pp. 622–5, 643–5 and 648–9.

44. IC/AP, Box 2531, Memorandum anent Tirie.

45. McNeill (ed.), *ERS, vii, AD1537–1542*, pp. 630–1.

46. The main differences evident in Harris concern the extent to which the smaller islands like Pabbay and Ensay paid substantial rents in kind (meal, cheese and butter) compared with the mainland townships, and the extent to which some of the mainland townships paid relatively more in butter and cheese than in meal, see DC/MDP, 2/487/14, Rental of Harris, 1697.

47. See, for example, IC/AP, Rental of Kintyre, 1720.

48. SRO, Clanranald Papers, GD201/5/1257/2, Rental of Arasaik, 1718.

49. Macphail (ed.), *Highland Papers*, ii, pp. 285–88.

50. SRO, Clanranald Papers, GD201/5/1257/1, Rental for Moydart, 1718.

51. Macphail (ed.), *Highland Papers*, iii, p. 288.

52. SRO, Breadalbane Muniments, GD112/9/9 Rental of Livestock, 1616–20 records 248 collected in 1620. See also GD112/9/5/17, Accompt of the wedders east end of Lochtay, 1674–6; GD112/9/35 Rental Book of Netherlorne, 1693–1704 has reference to 'present wedders'.

53. SRO, Breadalbane Muniments, GD112/9/24, Rental of Breadalbane, 1669–78.

54. DC/MDP, 2/490/8 Rental of Duirinish, 27 July 1724.

55. Burnett (ed.), *ERS, xii, AD1502–1507*, p. 699.

56. SRO, Campbell of Barcaldine Muniments, GD170/420/1/1 Rental of Glenure's lands in Lismore 1753; Campbell of Barcaldine Muniments, GD170/420/1/2, Jottings of Glenure's rental, 1753; GD112/9/24/ Rentall of Breadalbane, 1669–78.
57. DC/MDP, 1/382/3 Letter Will. Fraser to Sir George Strickland, 1772.
58. SRO, Breadalbane Muniments, GD112/9/5/8/17, Rental of Botuassimmore, 1722.
59. Early rental references to cain as a due occurs in rentals for Kintyre, dated 1505, Burnett (ed.), *ERS, xii, AD1502–1507*, pp. 698–703.
60. Innes and Buchan (ed.), *Origines Parochiales Scotiae*, vol. 2, p. 2. An example of the term's use occurs in SRO, John McGregor Collection, GD50/19, Book of the proceedings of the Baron Baile Courts of the Robertsons of Lude from the year 1621 to 1806, 7 March 1738. By the early modern period, though, the term was used more in the eastern than western Highlands, see, for example, SRO, Huntly Muniments, GD312/30/3 Tack 1723 betw. Earl of Huntly and Thomas Cromar setting … Drumdounan, which refers to a 'reek hen for every reeking house upon ye Ground'.
61. McKerral, 'The tacksman and his holding', p. 15.
62. SRO, Seaforth Papers, GD46/1/278, Articles of Set and Regulations for the Tenants of Land in Lewis. See also DC/MDP, 2/487/31 Rental of Harris, 1754.
63. Smith (ed.), *The Book of Islay*, appendix iii, pp. 486–90, rental summaries for 1542 and 1614.
64. IC/AP, Box 2531, Memorandum of the Rentaill of the east end of Tirii, 1662; ibid., Box 2531 Memorandum anent Tirii.
65. Ibid., Rental for Kintyre, 1720. See also SRO, Breadalbane Muniments, GD112/9/5/17/23 Breadalbane Rental 1678; Smith (ed.), *The Book of Islay*, p. 408.
66. Macphail (ed.), *Highland Papers*, ii, p. 273.
67. SRO, Breadalbane Muniments, GD112//9/35 Rentall Book of Netherlorne, 1693–1704.
68. SRO, Campbell of Barcaldine Muniments, GD170/420/1/2 Jottings of Rental of Baruamuch, 1753.
69. SRO, Breadalbane Muniments, GD112/9/43 Rental of the Estate of Breadalbane, 1736.
70. SRO, Campbell of Barcaldine Muniments, GD170/420/1/2, Jottings of Glenure's rental 1753.
71. SRO, Campbell of Jura, GD64/1/86/7, Rentall of Archibald Campbell Jura estate, 1764.
72. SRO, Breadalbane Muniments, GD112/9/3/3/20, Rental of the Earl of Breadalbane's estate in Argyllshire 1795.
73. DC/MDP, 2/19, Tack to Murdo McCaskill, 1754. A similar tack for issued for Bearnsdale, 2/21, with the extra burden of servicing the mill.
74. Ibid., 2/61, Tack for Ramasaig, 1769.
75. NLS, Sutherland Papers, DEP313/3160/12 Tack for town and lands of Rhinovie, Achinlachy and Achnaburn, 1765. See also DEP313/3161/2 Tack for Upper and Lower Achumore and Little Assint, 1765.
76. Ibid., DEP 313/3161/22, Tack for Alphen and Unapool, 1765.
77. SRO Seaforth Papers, GD46/1/278, Printed articles and regulations for the tenants in Lewis, N.D. See also ibid., GD46/1/277, Articles and Conditions for Lett of Lewis, 1795.
78. NLS, ADV. 29.1.1, vii, Copy of the Last Discharge by James Campbell to the tenants of Ardnamurchan 1725. A good discussion of services on Lismore is provided by Shaw, *The Northern and Western Islands*, p. 52.
79. There were townships in both Tiree and Sunart that appeared to pay only

rents in kind, 1541, see McNeill (ed.), *ERS, vii, AD1537–1542*, pp. 614–15 and 628.
80. Ibid., pp. 621–2.
81. Ibid., pp. 622–3.
82. Skene, *Celtic Scotland*, iii, p. 438.
83. IC/AP, Box 2531, Memorandum anent Tirie.
84. McNeill (ed.), *ERS, xvii, AD1537–1542*, p. 646.
85. Ibid., pp. 647–8.
86. Gregory and Skene (eds.), *Collectanea de Rebus Albanicis*, pp. 172–9.
87. IC/AP, Box 494, Letter 1 June 1681, dealing with Tiree Rental.
88. bid., Box 251, Rentall of Tiry, what is payed in :52, and in all years thereafter, compiled 1675.
89. This statement is based on a comparison between McNeill (ed.), *ERS, viii, AD1537–1542*, p. 650 and IC/AP, Box 2531, Memorandum anent Tirie.
90. Skene, *Celtic Scotland*, iii, p. 438.
91. CDC/MP, GD221/3695/4. For instances of such a principle being applied, see GD221/4277/5/3 Tack for Killivaxter, Peinmuch, Kite, Feall, Quirtolan and Peianrichrannan, 1734.
92. Ibid., GD221/4277/6/1.
93. DC/MDP, 2/61 Tack betwn. Normand MacLeod and Neill Mckinnon 1769.
94. Ibid., 2/487/19. Rental of Harris, 1724.
95. Ibid., 2/487/31 Rental of Harris, 1754; ibid., 2/493/9/3 Sky Augmentation & Grassums as settled by the Laird of MacLeod, 1754.
96. Ibid., 1/380/2, Copie of Excheqr. Order & Affidavits . . . Normand MacLeod, 1733.
97. SRO, Cromartie Papers, GD305/1/63 Rentals 1612–1824, no. 141, A General Rental of Ld. Cromartie's Estate, 1735.
98. SRO, Breadalbane Muniments, GD 112/9/5/8/26 Remarks on the property lands of Breadalbane, 1722.
99. Ibid., GD112/9/5/8/12 Estimate of the Grassums of the Property Lands in Breadalbane 1721.
100. Burnett (ed.), *ERS, xii, AD1502–1507*, pp. 698–703.
101. Ibid., p. 709.
102. McNeill (ed.), *ERS, vii, AD1537–1542*, pp. 611–13 and 615–20.
103. Ibid., 625–33; Burnett (ed.), *ERS, xii, AD1502–1507*, pp. 698–703; the 1664 rental is listed in Macphail (ed.), *Highland Papers*, iii, pp. 72–85.
104. The 1614 and 1686 rentals for Islay are listed in Smith (ed.), *The Book of Islay*, appendix.
105. On Islay, for instance, townships rated as two and a half merkland in the 1541 rental paid 4 marts, 4 wedders, 10s. of silver, 30 stone of cheese, 30 stone of meal, 4 geese and 4 fowl; see McNeill (ed.), *ERS, vii, AD1537–1542*, pp. 612–13 and 615–20.
106. The uniformity was also stressed by Lamont, 'Old land denominations and old extent in Islay', part i, pp. 188–9.
107. Gregory and Skene (eds.), *Collectanea de Rebus Albanicis*, pp. 160–1.
108. IC/AP, Box 251, Rentall of Tiry, what is payed in :52, and in all years thereafter, compiled 1675.
109. IC/AP, Box 2531, Rentall of Tirie, 1680.
110. McNeill (ed.), *ERS, xvii, AD1537–1542*, p. 648.
111. The term *terra ethica* was reportedly given to Tiree by the monks of Iona abbey. Its description as 'McConnell's girnal' is noted by Skene, *Celtic Scotland*, iii, p. 437. The reference to McConnell's girnell' is interesting. It compares with a reference to 'Lapis Makconeile' which Innes thought was an error for McCoull or McDougall, the old Lords of Lorne who controlled a territory embracing

Lorne, Mull, Coll, Tiree and Jura; see Gregory and Skene (eds), *Collectanea de Rebus Albanicis*, p. 172.

112. Skene, *Celtic Scotland*, iii, p. 437.

113. IC/AP, Box 2531, Memorandum anent Tirie.

114. Ibid.

115. Ibid., Bundle 494, Letter 1 June 1681 dealing with Tiree rental.

116. Ibid, Box 2531, Memorandum anent Tirie.

117. Ibid., Rental of Tirie by Ardgour, 1662.

118. Ibid., Box 2531, Memorandum anent Tirie. The breakdown is repeated in Bundle 494, Letter, 1 June 1681, dealing with Tiree rental and as it 'was in use to be paid to the Laird of McLean'.

119. McNeill (ed.), *ERS, xvii, AD1537–1542*, p. 648; IC/AP, Rental of Tiry, what it payed in the year :52 and in all yeares therafter, 1675; IC/AP, Rental of Tirie by Ardgour, 1662.

120. Instances of horse corn being paid are provided by DC/MDP, 2/491/8, Rentall of the Barrony of Minginish, 1744; CDC/MP, GD221/118, Judicial Rental of the Macdonald Estates in the Isle of Skye, 1733.

121. Discussion based on DC/MDP, 2/487/14, Rental of Harris 1694; ibid., 2/487/15, Rentall of ye Lands of Mack Leod His pairt of Harish 1698; ibid., 2/487/18, Rentall of Mackleods Land in the Haries as it was sett to the Tenants 1703; ibid., 2/485/6, Rental of Skye estate, 1683; ibid., 2/485/7, Rental for Skye estate, 1684; ibid., 2/485/9, Vaternish Rents of Crop and yeare 1685; ibid., 2/485/14, Rentall of MacLeod's estate, 1709; ibid., 2/493/1; Judiciall rental of the Baronie of Vaternish, 1724; ibid., 2/485/6–8, 11–16 and 21–2, 'The rests of Crope and yeare', 1683–5, 1706–11 and 1717–18.

122. The 1594 rental for the Breadalbane estate which Innes published in 1855 describes all the farms listed as bowhouses, including Auchinchgalden, Aribeane, Barren, Pitmatik, Bray of Balloch, Killin and port of Glennorquhaye. See Innes (ed.), *The Black Book of Taymouth*, pp. 287–96. Elsewhere, bowhouses and 'bowing' are well described in a 1623 contract amongst the Campbell of Cawdor Papers, see Innes (ed.), *The Book of Cawdor*, pp. 262–3 and 334. The role of bowhouses on the Sutherland estate is explained by a memorial on the duties of Captain Ross, 1725, which said that he was charged with 'Stocking on ye Severall Bows' where he was required to distinguish between milk cows and yield cattle, and to compute the yearly produce of butter and cheese, as well as the 'Cattle yearly Received from ye Tennents in payment of their Rents, and putt upon ye severall Mains', NLS, DEP313/649/19, Memorial anent Captaine Ross, 1725.

123. Innes (ed.), *The Black Book of Taymouth*, pp. 268–99, provides references to the movement of stock, including 'gressume kye' and 'gressume wedderis', in and out of townships, i.e. pp. 272–3, as well as references to animals that were in the tenant's 'awin hand', p. 274. References occur to stock being moved in from Glenorchy and Breadalbane, and also from Menteith such as those delivered to a tenant in half of Boithworny 'efter the compt making of martis that come out of Menteith', p. 280.

124. Ibid., p. 276.

125. SRO, Breadalbane Muniments, GD112/9/22, Rental of lands belonging to Lord Neill Campbell, in Loyng, Seill and Neitherlorne, 1665.

126. Ibid., GD112/9/5/10/2 Rental of Breadalbane, 1733. Altogether Lawers yielded 123 bolls of meal and 114 bolls of bere, whilst East End yielded 123 bolls of meal and 119 bolls of bere.

127. Johnson, *Journey to the Western Islands of Scotland*, p. 137.

4 Patterns of Chiefly Display and Behaviour

If we can speak of the clan *system* as a distinct form of social order, one that survived after c.1493 then, arguably, its core consists of the patterns of display and behaviour that were developed around the chiefly control over land and its resources. Three basic types of chiefly display need to be considered: feasting, feuding, and the various forms of redistributive exchange that centred on chiefs. These various forms of display were not confined to the western Highlands and Islands, but they lasted longer there and acquired a particular intensity through the way in which they built on the region's problems of environment and the difficulties which it posed for society and subsistence. Put simply, Highland chiefs exploited the scarcity value of food, adding a powerful ideological value to its basic use value. When we look closely at the different types of chiefly display, their common thread is the symbolism which they attach to food, either directly or indirectly. Whilst each has other aspects that also deserve to be examined, I want to give particular emphasis to this common thread.

THE CHIEFLY FEAST

The role played by food in chiefly displays of feasting is straightforward.[1] Many clans have traditions about the lavishness of their chiefs as hosts. When the son and heir to MacLeod of Dunvegan married the daughter of the Captain of Clanranald in 1613, the feast is said to have lasted six days, the chief's unbounded hospitality being marked by the fact that the guests were carried to bed each night![2] In fact, the MacLeods had an even more potent and enduring symbol of their chiefs' hospitality in the shape of MacLeod's Tables, the flat-topped mountains in front of Dunvegan castle. The implication of such a name was clear to all who stood before them. With a table this size, MacLeod had to be a great chief. The topography of the social and natural world stood in perfect conjunction. A similar attempt to use topography as a fairly direct metaphor for hospitality is provided by a MacGregor tradition. Despite their relative poverty of land and resources, the MacGregors made the boast that their chief entertained James IV for eight days in 1506 at Inchcalloun. When the king expressed his surprise at the size of Gregor Mor's retinue and extent of his hospitality, the MacGregor chief reportedly likened Loch Tay to his basin, 'sixteen mile long', large and unlimited.[3] Such traditions brought a number of different concepts into common focus, but at their centre was the belief that if their chief lived well then so did the clan. His capacity to host, to be prodigal, was confused with the clan's well-being. When the heir to the captaincy of Clanranald returned to South Uist after being fostered by the Frasers on the mainland, he was said to have expressed his surprise at the lavishness of the feast prepared for him, saying a few hens would do.[4] His comment so struck at the self-belief of the clan that it replaced him with his brother. Of course, once a chief's ability to host had become confused with the well-being of the clan at large, then it was inevitable that the chief's claim on resources took priority. Such a prioritis-ation certainly makes sense of the simple ritual whereby a member of McNeil of Barra's household would climb to the topmost turret of Kisimuil Castle after McNeil had finished each meal and would proclaim to the world that now McNeil had finished his meal, the rest of the world could start theirs. We even find the prioritisation of the chief's welfare creeping into agreements over land. Charters issued by the Lord of the Isles were reported to have begun with the words, that 'I Macdonald, sitting upon Dundonald give you right to your farm from this day till to-morrow, and every day thereafter, so long as you have food for the Great Macdonald of the Isles'.[5]

In practical terms, the capacity of a chief to feast depended largely, but not entirely, on what he consumed by way of *cuid-oidhche*, or what he accumu-lated in his girnal house and his bowhouses by way of food rents and stock. The directness of this link was appreciated by contemporaries. The late six-teenth-century report on the Hebrides informs us that Lewis 'paid 18 score chalders of victuall, 58 score of ky, 32 score of wedderis, and ane great quantitie of fisches, pultrie, and quhyte plaiding by thair Cuidichies, that is, feisting their master quhen he pleases to cum in the countrie, ilk ane thir nicht or twa nichtis about, according to thair land and labouring'.[6] Clearly, a chief's 'feisting' was founded on his tenant's obligation to provide hospitality for him and his retinue. That it was designed to support the chief and his retinue all year round is well brought out in the report's entry for Harris, which revealingly defines the food rents and casualties of the island not as a total yearly sum but as an obligation whereby it paid '3 bolls malt and 3 bolls meill for ilk day in the yeir, 40 mairtis and eight score wedderis, by customs, pultrie, meill, with oist silver'.[7]

Looking at the character of what was gathered in, basic items like oat meal, hens and cheese provided chiefs and their retinue with the staple of year-round subsistence, but the stuff of feasts depended on his ability to abstract other items from his followers. Cattle, veals, wedders, lambs, geese, hens, swine and fish were all featured in food rents and would have greatly extended a chief's capacity to host lavishly. However, as the review of food rents in Chapter 3 pointed out, not all districts were able to provide such renders. Wedders and lambs were the most widespread with hardly a township not providing some. The extraction of cattle was altogether more demanding, and usually paid only by the more fertile, productive townships, so that their slaughter in the cause of a feast must have been much more of a gesture. Significantly, the greatest number of cattle uplifted as rent was on Islay, the former base for what had been a powerful eruption of chiefly power, namely, the Lordship of the Isles. Amongst other items gathered in as rent on a more localised basis were veal, swine and geese, each of which would have made a significant addition to the table of a chief.

Chiefs could also draw on game. The hunting of game like deer and the catching of game fish like salmon were closely regulated, though unevenly so. On the mainland, areas like Rannoch offered much potential to chiefs like Campbell of Glenorchy, though the fact that MacGregors were widely settled in the townships that lay around it created problems. For the MacGregors, hunting the laird's deer was an easy gesture of defiance. Certainly, fines and banishment for hunting deer were a recurrent feature of the Barony Court proceedings for Rannoch.[8] To judge from Donald Monro's description of the Isles in 1549, the larger Hebridean islands also carried rich stocks of game. Mull had 'mony deiris and [verey] fair hunting game'.[9] He also provides a description of how 'infinit deir [were] slain' on Jura.[10] By comparison, his report on Harris was qualified. He describes northern Harris, the Forest, as having 'mony forrests, mony deir but not great of quantitie'.[11] Certainly, there were enough to attract poachers, as a 1658 bond binding two brothers not to poach MacLeod's deer on Harris demonstrates.[12] Indeed, Martin Martin offered an estimate of at least 2000 deer present in the Forest.[13] However, Monro's verdict is given some support by a survey drawn up in 1775, ahead of the sale of Harris, which avoids putting any value on its game potential though it does mention its yield of otter and seal skins.[14] On the mainland, the Forest of Fascich in Cromartie was said to contain 1500 deer when it was let to Donald Mackenzie in 1732 for £52. 10s plus 'a yearly Number of deer'.[15]

Not surprisingly, Monro also notes the abundance of salmon in many Hebridean rivers and lochs, such as on Skye, where the waters of 'Snersport', 'Sliggacham', 'Stratsnardill' and 'Linlagallan' were all noted as offering a 'gude tak of salmond'.[16] Usually, estates leased out salmon fishing, drawing in part of the catch as a rent,[17] but there is no hint of this in either MacLeod or Macdonald rentals for Skye.[18] By far the most organised Highland estate in respect of salmon fishing appears to have been that of Sutherland. Mid-eighteenth-century tacks for townships in Assynt bound tenants not to kill fish, and to maintain both the fish nets and cruive dams on prized rivers like the Water of Naver.[19] By the early nineteenth century, they also bound tenants to remove 'sportsmen' who did not have permission, which suggests that by then the business of game fishing had moved beyond being a preserve of chiefs and their table.[20] In the south of the Highlands, the Breadlabane estate drew a regular flow of salmon, as well as sizeable quantities of herring, from select tacks on its estate.[21]

PATTERNS OF CHIEFLY DISPLAY: FEUDING

Though feuding has strong associations with the Highland clans, it was an approach to justice and violence that needs to seen as practised throughout Scotland. In fact, in an analysis of feuding 1573–1610, when feuding across Scotland was at its height, Brown has shown that only 16 per cent of all feuds can be classed as Highland feuds.[22] He has also shown that in character, feuds 'included a whole range of relationships of conflict'.[23] The wide range of behaviour that needs to be included under feuding is particularly relevant to the Highlands. When we look at instances of feud, we find that they range from simple acts like cattle maiming to the outright slaughter of rival kinsmen and their families. However, as with feasting, I want to suggest that Highland feuding had a powerful sub-text. In a region where subsistence was at premium, the destruction or theft of a rival clan's food base made as powerful a statement as the slaughter of their clansmen. To steal their cattle and grain, or to lay waste their lands, was to enhance one's own capacity to host and support whilst diminishing that of one's rivals. In fact, when we explore typical Highland feuds, the struggle with food over food forms a prominent part of the story.[24]

The long-running feud between the Mackenzies of Kintail and Macdonalds of Glengarry was continually re-charged by the theft of each other's cattle and the wasting of each other's lands.[25] So too was the feud between the MacLeods and Macdonalds on Skye.[26] When Donald and Dougall McTarlichis were given their tack for land in Lorne in 1588, it stipulated that they not only enter 'in deidlie Feid with the Clan gregoure ... making slaughtir upon thame', but also that they 'continew ... unto the tyme the said Duncane Campbell of Glenurchay finds himself be oure trauellis and diligence satisfit with the slaughter we sall do and commit upone thame', suggesting that Glenorchy clearly saw the feud as a simple matter of slaughter or extermination.[27] The MacGregors for their part were interested as much in theft as in slaughter. When, in 1602, they raided Lennox, a raid that led to the proscription of their name, they not only murdered 80 Buchanans, but also were said to have stolen 600 cattle, 800 sheep and 280 horses, and wasted lands and byres.[28] Only a year or so before, they had also been accused of joining with members of both the Clan McRannalds and Clan Chattane in stealing 2700 cattle and 100 horses from Glenyla.[29] In a late instance of the feud reported in 1675, MacLaine of Lochbuie is said to have left all 32 inhabitants on one of the 'small islands' amongst the Garvellachs, including John McLauchlan of Kilbryde (Lunga), the tacksman, naked on the shore, having extingished all fires and having taken not only their clothes, but also their livestock.[30] The broader focus of the feud, the way in which it drew on symbols of resource wealth like cattle, is well brought out by Martin Martin. Writing in 1700, he described how clans in feud 'were obliged to bring by open force the Cattel they found in Lands they attack'd, or die in the Attempt'. In a phrase that takes us to the very heart of feuding as a form of mutual display as much as an instrument of justice, he goes on to say that being 'reciprocally us'd among them, [it] was not reputed Robbery, for the Damage which one Tribe sustain'd by the Essay of the Chieftain of another, was repair'd when their chieftain came in his turn'.[31]

The problem for clans heavily involved in the feud was that by the seventeenth century, it had become an uneven contest as clans like the Campbells of Glenorchy or Breadalbane used official acts of fire and commission to bolster their side of the argument. What had previously been a game played out by a set of rules, now became a case of one clan applying Crown law against another. Those still engaged in the feud by the seventeenth century were increasingly treated as thieves and broken men. This was the fate of the MacGregors. More and more, clans and groups like the MacGregors were marginalised by official opinion. Instead of a clan bidding for status by time-honoured methods, they were now seen as 'a desperate wicked crew of bandits ... pillageing and plundering the country people'.[32] Though increasingly pushed out of their tenancies, the MacGregors were said to assemble annually in a group of 200–300 on Rannoch for bouts of feasting and feuding, the two forms of display clearly helping to sustain each other.[33] Whereas Campbell of Glenorchy had responded to them in terms of the feud back in the sixteenth century, as the tack given to Ronald and Dougal McTarlich demonstrates, their response by the seventeenth-century was now to use judicial powers and the device of 'black mail'. Mid-seventeenth century rentals record tenants on the Breadalbane estate, such as in parts of Lochtayside and Ardenlonich, paying what was termed 'blak mairts' or their 'proportione of blak mairt',[34] a payment to maintain the watch against cattle thieving. As a proportion of the total though, such black mail formed a neglible amount, amounting to just over 1 per cent of the total silver and grassum money for 1670, and substantially less if one adds the value of payments in kind. However small in price, it brought a new meaning to the idea of the chief as an insurance against risk.

THE CHIEFLY RETINUE

Displays of feasting and feuding involved more than simply chiefs and their immediate family. The whole ritual of feasting could draw on a range of retainers: storytellers, clan historians and genealogists, *seanchaidhean*, pipers, harpists as well as those preparing the food, the brewers and the maltsters. The nineteenth MacLeod of Dunvegan was even said to keep a fool. All the major clans, especially those bidding for maximum status, maintained a full range of such retainers. Usually, the skills involved were passed down within particular families, with chiefs encouraging such a tradition by allowing them to have the hereditary possession of a holding on a rent-free basis. Many of the more distinguished families of clan historians, pipers, etc., are documented in their own right, performing their duties for particular clans across many generations and being renowned for such. Thus, living side by side in Kintyre were the MacMhuirichs and the MacIlschenochs, the former being the chief poets and the latter the chief harpists to the Lord of the Isles.[35] Likewise, the Macruaris were bards to the Macdonalds of Sleat, whilst the MacArthurs were pipers.[36] In fact, references to such families holding land in return for their services as clan historians or pipers are fairly common in available rentals. Thus, on the MacLean estate, the rental compiled in 1674 reported 'Phanmoir, possest be the harper, and pretends kyndnes therto for his services, and pays nothing'.[37] The earliest extant rental for the Clanranald estates, one compiled in 1718 shortly after it had been forfeited, reported Sterigerly in South Uist as held by a Donald McMoiry and that he 'has a liferent tack of Two pennie Land more worth p. annum sometyme Twenty pounds, & sometymes less which his predecessors & himself had from the family of Clanranald for Registring the Deeds & Genealogie of the family & making panegyrics etc yn Desyred'.[38] A subsequent rental of 1748 described Neil McMurich as having two pennyland in Stilligarry for being 'Chronologer and Poet Laurent'.[39] Another rental drawn up for South Uist, c.1718, talked generally about 'the lands possessed by heritable Falconers, Fowlers, Pipers and Foresters'.[40] Individuals like a clan's *seanchaidhean* had a vital role in celebrating how the chief and his ancestors had, through all the various forms of display behaviour, raised the status of the clan.

No less vital to both displays of feasting and feuding were a chief's fighting men. As a group, a chief's fighting men were fairly exclusive and restricted in number. Not all clansmen were expected to respond at the sign of the fiery cross. Usually, it was only the younger of his close kin and the younger members of the clan's leading cadet families who formed a clan's fighting men. In some sources it is clear that as a group they were professional fighting men, detached from the day to day farming life of the region, but wholly dependent on it for material support. In the description of the Hebrides written between 1577 and 1595, it was said that MacLeod of Lewis could raise 700 men 'by thame that labours the ground, of the quhilkis nane are chairgit or permittit to gang to ony oisting or weiris in all the hail Iles, but are commandit to remane at hame to labour the ground'.[41] The same source also talks about how 'ilk merk land' on Islay 'sustein daylie and yeirlie ane gentleman in meit and claith, quhilk dois na labour, but is haldin as ane of their masters household men, and man be sustenit and furneisit in all necessaris be the tennant, and he man be reddie to his maisters service and advis'.[42] Strong hints of a similar arrangement occur in a seventeenth-century memorandum on Tiree. A note appended to the document says that

'Tirie was want to quarter all the Gentlemen's men that waited on McLaane all winter, not under 80 or 100'.[43]

In origin, the imposition of such fighting men as a direct charge on townships probably had its origin in the chief's right of *cuid-oidhche*. In its full definition, the right of hospitality owed by clansmen to their chief was an obligation to support their chief and his household. Inevitably, what constituted his household was open to interpretation. The greater the chief, the greater his household. Tenants in Sleat on Skye were expected to provide 'samekle as thair maister may be able to spend being ane nicht (albeit he were 600 men in companie) on ilk merkland'.[44] A bond between John Campbell of Glenurchay and John Menzeis of Rorow in 1549 bound the latter to be 'reddy with mete and drynk and wther necessaris conwenand thairto [for] the said John Campbell his howsald and followaris' when they visited him.[45] Such a system, though, lent itself to abuse, particularly once chiefs or their household men began to treat it as a right of hospitality with or without the chief's presence. The instances cited in the previous paragraph fall into this category. As a variant though, it was easily corrupted into a practice whereby men on the edge of the chief's retinue could extract food from tenants, not just with or without his presence but with or without his permission.

The extraction of food and hospitality without proper right, or sorning as it was called, was a widespread abuse in the Highlands, one that became associated with broken men. As a clear usurpation of chiefly right, it is not surprising that we find it being used as an instrument of feud, with rival clans exploiting each other's tenants by sorning on them, as in the feud between Glengarry and Mackenzie.[46] Amongst the grievances listed by the tenants of Islay when they petitioned the King in 1613 was that 'they ar verie havelie oppreist troublit and wrackit be a nomber of ydill men, vagaboundis and sornaris who lyis upoun thame, consumis thair viveris and spoylis thame of thair goodis at thair pleasour'.[47] Elsewhere, chiefs like Campbell of Glenorchy can be found reaching agreements binding his vassals to maintain their territories free of sorning, 'as he does his own lands', in 1586.[48] The fact that we find similar agreements being reached well into the seventeenth century, though, suggests that there was no immediate solution to the problem. Even in 1636, an agreement between John and Donald MacLeod reminded the latter of how the Laws of the kingdom prohibited 'the former abuse of sorneing and cudeachis oppression' and bound them each 'to live upon oure awen meannes'.[49] By contrast, the Captain of Clanranald issued a tack for lands in Moydart in 1625 that still bound the tenant to provide 'ane nichtis meit or cuddyche to me my househauld and servandis'.[50]

PATTERNS OF CHIEFLY EXCHANGE AND THE
CONTROL OF PRESTIGE GOODS

Most anthropological or archaeological reviews of chiefdoms have stressed the extent to which chiefs underpin their position by the control of prestige items.[51] The term prestige can cover a range of goods and values. However, a standard item of value, one present in virtually all chiefly societies, is that of cattle. Through a combination of their fairly heavy resource demands, the fact that one can store them, the fact that, within the constraints set by available grazings, they can increase from year to year, and their role in feasting, cattle were a prized item of value and currency in the exchange system of traditional societies. This was the case in the western Highlands and Islands no less than in chiefly societies elsewhere.

The most telling indication of the role played by cattle within the exchange systems of Highland chiefs is the part which they played in marriage agreements. As in other kin- based societies, such marriage agreements were between families, not individuals. In content, they could could involve transfers of property, goods and cash, as a support to the marriage itself. The property element was given to the wife by her prospective husband's family, and could involve a gift of land, either as an outright transfer of property, a gift for life, or its rental income for life. The intent behind such transfers was to secure the independent support of the wife. Moving counter to them were payments of what were known as tocher-gude, or payments of bride-wealth given ostensibly to the groom's family as a supplement to the value of the bride but, by the time we see them, they were payments explicitly to the groom. A number of marriage agreements can be documented in which cattle served as the payment of tocher-gude, presumably because they were the most prized item of resource for any clansmen bidding for greater status. Thus, in 1613, a marriage agreement was drawn up between Rory MacLeod of Harris and the Captain of Clanranald, Donald MacAllane Vichean of Ilandtirim, in respect of the marriage between Rory MacLeod's daughter, Moire, and Clanranald's son, John of Moydart. As well as Clanranald settling the 20 pound land of Arrasyle on the couple, Rory MacLeod agreed to deliver to John Moydart 'in name of tochyr with ye said Moire nine score of gud and sufficient quick ky togidder with othir twentie ky incais the said John sall desyre thaime'.[52] In fact, John of Moydart later brokered a deal involving cattle, or '100 kine', as part of the tocher-gude to be paid when his own daughter, Catherine, married Gallean McNeill son and heir to Neill Mcneill of Barra. Unfortunately for Clanranald, it is documented for us by the dispute that arose when he failed to pay.[53] Such agreements continued down into the eighteenth century. In an 'antenuptial' contract drawn up in 1709 between Sorlie Nicolson, tacksman at Shuddar, and Christine Macdonald, daughter of Ronald Macdonald of Camiscross, whereby the said Ronald bound himself to deliver to Sorlie 'the number of thirty five cowes and five piece of horse with his said daughter in name of dote and tocher good as they ordinarily rune within the barronie of Staffin and Sleat'.[54] These and other marriage agreements involving cattle as payment for tocher-gude[55] can be regarded as the residual instances of a once-wider practice, one which drew on the special value or currency of cattle within a chiefly society. By the seventeenth century, and even by the late sixteenth century, most of the major landowners on the mainland were paying tocher-gude in the form of cash.[56]

In addition to using cattle, chiefs could draw on other types of prestige good. Though the marriage agreement of 1613 between Rory Macleod and the Captain of Clanranald also involved the payment by MacLeod of 'ane gaillay of twentie foure airis with her sailing and rowing gear gud and sufficient within ye spaice of ane yeir',[57] there are no other hints available from marriage settlements as to what also might have served as a prestige good. However, given their consumption of resource and their military value, it is difficult not to believe that weaponry, especially the two-handed claymore, and body armour, notably the light and highly-portable armour represented by the basinet, aketon and shoulder mail, were valued early on as chiefly items of exchange even though, as Steer and Bannerman have suggested, they were fairly basic in European terms.[58] The fact that some families were given land in return for their services as smiths and armourers suggests that chiefs must have had some control over the production of such weaponry and armour. Families or minor clans like the Gowans and McFederanes, for example, were noted as smiths and armourers. Groups of the latter were settled in Benderloch and were famous for their swords.[59] The role which such weaponry and armour may have played in patterns of chiefly display are possibly captured for us in the work of the late medieval school of monumental sculpture that flourished in Argyll, with individuals like Malcolm of Poltalloch being represented 'in the costume that they actually wore in life',[60] with basinet, aketon and shoulder mail and clutching the two-handed claymore. Logically, they were so depicted because these were symbols of status.

Steer and Bannerman argue that the title or service of a smith could cover other crafts, such as gold and silver-smiths. They suggest that the group of smiths commemorated by the monumental sculpture in the churches at Kilmory and Keills in Knapdale may have been gold and silver-smiths, perhaps in the service of the Lords of the Isles.[61] Certainly, there was at least one fifteenth-century Lord of the Isles, Angus Mor, who had a reputation as 'the generous dispenser of rings'.[62] For comparison, when the earl of Douglas visited the earl of Ross in Knapdale in 1453, bringing gifts of silver, silks and wine, the latter reciprocated with mantles and plaid rather than samples of the local silver or gold work.[63] When Gregor Mor entertained King James IV at Inchcalloun in 1506, he gave the King presents of venison and horses.[64] With the collapse of the Lordship of the Isles, it is unlikely that any subsequent chiefdom managed to surround itself with a wide range of skilled craftsmen, though we still find individuals being given holdings because they served a chief as boat-wright, mason or smith down to the early eighteenth century. Clanranald, for instance, still had tenants who claimed possession of their holdings because they were 'Boatwright or Carpenter to Clanranald' or 'for service as officer & mason' as well his genealogist and panegyrick-writer.[65]

PATTERNS OF CHIEFLY EXCHANGE: TACKSMEN
AND CLANSMEN

Just as chiefs enhanced their status by conspicuous displays of hospitality and by using gift exchange to further their alliances, so also could they bind their followers more closely to them by using their resource base to dispense favour and support. Beyond their household and fighting men, and beyond the specialist craftsmen or those with specialist roles who were given holdings 'by way of a gift', there lay the tacksmen and the ordinary clansmen. In many ways, it was how chiefs treated these individuals that distinguished the clan system from other forms of social order. The stock image of clans stresses the close bond between chief and kinsmen, with chiefs extending favour to all tenants in times of crisis and generally establishing a bond between them that had greater warmth and expectation than a purely feudal relationship. The initial character of this relationship is best seen within the framework of chiefly exchange systems, for prior to the intrusion of the market, the food rents gathered in by chiefs were entirely charged with a social value, to be expended on status building in a range of ways, from feasting to supporting kinsmen in need.

In fact, there is a case for arguing that the mutuality of the relationship between chief and clansmen, whether tacksmen or lesser tenant, their feeling of common welfare, is an aspect of the clan system that survived longer than other aspects of its character. We need to explore this at two levels. First, we need to examine the position of tacksmen and the claims which they could make on their chief. Second, we need to examine how and to what extent chiefs could show favour to the ordinary tenant on their estates.

By the time they appear in the revealing light of eighteenth-century data, tacksmen generally had a bad press. They are seen as parasitic, an unnecessary level of landholding between the landlord and his tenant, 'intercepting the advantage due to those above and beggaring those beneath'.[66] Certainly, the tacksman appeared to many commentators as an institution that required immediate attention and it is hardly surprising that we find its removal was a focus of early reform. On the Argyll Estate, Duncan Forbes of Culloden carried out a survey of the Argyll estate in 1737. His report recommended their comprehensive removal on the grounds that the estate could be reset at an advance of rent without surcharging the tenant, his clear assumption being that tacksmen were a cost without benefit that was best absorbed as extra rent by the chief.[67] In fact, there are hints that some advisers to the earl of Argyll were uneasy at the 'percentage' taken by tacksmen as early as 1683.[68] Though the most publicised, Culloden's case against the tacksmen of the Argyll estate was not the only attack on their position at this time. To the north, a memorandum that can be dated to 1733, dealing with the Macdonald's estate on Skye, reached similar conclusions. Describing them as the gentlemen tenants, it described how 'they generally squeeze a higher Rent from their Subtennents than they pay the Heretor, and always oppress

these subtennents with Services'.[69] One of most substantial write-ups of rent
by a tacksman that can be documented involved Raasay. In the late sixteenth
century, it was held of the Bishop of the Isles for 15 merks by Gillechallum
Raasay who sub-let it for 500 merks of rent.[70] Sub-tenants on MacLeod of
Dunvegan's Skye estate fared no better. A report on the estate's tacksmen
in 1769 talked about these under-tenants being 'often victimised by the
immediate superiors who burden them with the whole of the rent paid to the
laird'.[71]

The problem for tacksmen is that when seen in the eighteenth century,
they appeared anachronistic. Their socio-political role had faded leaving
them simply as an economic charge for services that were no longer rendered
or needed. The context in which they initially developed as a group probably
intended them to intercept rents in a substantial way, enabling them to live
like local or petty chiefs and to answer more easily to the chief's call for
military support.[72] To appreciate their predicament by the eighteenth
century, we need to draw the distinction between the nature of a landlord-
estate economy and a chiefly-estate economy. The former was designed to
maximise rental income by maximising surplus output and forcing it into
the marketplace. By contrast, chiefly-estate economies were organised to
consume as much as possible within the social framework of the estate, to
maximise food's social value, balancing that part which was fed into chiefly
systems of redistributive exchange with what they received in return. In these
circumstances, the fact that tacksmen were seen to consume part of what
they gathered in as rent would simply have served the wider cause of the clan,
establishing the status and well-being of the clan through conspicuous consumption. As close allies of the chief within a socio-political system, we can
also understand why tacksmen were shown considerable forbearance over
rents. Unlike landlord and tenants within a landlord-estate system, tacksmen
and chiefs within a chiefly-estate system shared the same ends. If his own
needs were secure, a chief had a vested interest in protecting the position of
those around him, from his senior kinsmen, usually his tacksmen, downwards. A 1681 report on how MacLean had rented out townships on Tiree
made the point that many tenants had reductions of rent and that one reason
for this had been his 'favour' towards the tenants involved.[73] The problem is
that when such forbearance was carried forward into the eighteenth century,
and viewed by would-be estate improvers and advisers, it appeared to be a
mismanagement of the estate's now single interest, to maximise cash incomes
for the landlord. Thus, the 1733 memorandum on Macdonald's Skye estate
noted that 'some of the tennents presume on their Relation to the Heretor or
some considerable man of the Clan etc., & without any pretense alleadged
keep their Rents in their own hands, or squander them away'.[74] When Dr
John Walker visited Islay in 1764, he found that 'some of the farms are lett
for four times the Rent payed by the original Tacksmen, and the whole, upon
an Average, are subsett for three times more Rent than is payed to the
Landlord',[75] but such an advantage may have had much to do with the length

of leases on which they held and the inflation of rents since they were initially set. Yet though tacksmen were now being hemmed in by the spread of new, less tolerant attitudes and, above all, by the growing indebtedness of traditional Highland chiefs and their need for raising more economic rents, many eighteenth-century observers were still aware of how the social values that surrounded tacksmen had shaped the estate economy. In a letter concerning the sale of Harris by MacLeod of Dunvegan in 1772, William Fraser, the lawyer handling the sale, wrote that estates in the Western Isles measured their success 'from the number of their followers – They gave Leases of their Lands to their younger Sons and other Connexions, and very seldom to any but their own name and Kindred The Tacksmen formed a kind of inferior Gentry in the Country and their rents were often little more than an acknowledgement to their Chief or head of their family – This was in particular the situation in Harries'. As an adviser on the sale, the point which he was making was that once sold out of the family and into a different system of values, it could be re-let at a great increase in rent.[76]

The extent to which chiefs showed goodwill towards their lesser tenants can best be pieced together from rentals and from accounts of charge and discharge. There were three broad kinds of circumstance in which chiefs might be expected to help tenants. First, individual holdings or tenants might have become impoverished. Second, it might be difficult for tenants to find the silver mail needed for a holding, especially in the more remote parts of the Highlands where scarcity of money was always a problem. Third, help would have been needed when communities suffered crises of production due to poor seasons or exceptional storms. In practice, these different reasons tended to run together. In a 1701 rental for Harris, for instance, the township of South Scarista is recorded as set to 'the old smith and his sone' but because of 'poverty', they had 'gotten down two bolls & 4 stones for ye year' whilst in South Coppinphoal, Neil McAskil was 'given down fyve merks of his monie rent & half a stane & half a wedder' due to his 'poverty'. When we turn to Northtown in Pabbay, we find a Kenneth McIllochallum 'forgiven' a quarter of a stone because of 'his poverty & the badness of the year'.[77] In fact, what stands out about an estate like that belonging to MacLeod of Dunvegan is that when we look at records of what was actually paid as opposed to what was owed in rent, we find a fairly extensive pattern of arrears or 'rests' as regards rents. In the case of Harris, lists of such 'rests' are available for a number of years across the 1680s and 90s. In some years, the lists are available for the entire estate, and clearly involved a high proportion of its occupiers.[78] In all probability, they reflect the endemic problems which tenants in the more remote and difficult parts of the Hebrides had in paying rent regularly during years when harvests were poor and money scarce.

The estate's response was to operate a form of give-and-take economics, though whether we see this as a practical response to circumstances or a reflection of a longstanding accommodation of tenurial problems is impossible to say. In fact, to judge from the amount of comment generated, eighteenth-century crises were serious affairs. A letter written in 1745 by the occupier of the fairly well-endowed township of Trumpan-more in Waternish complained to Macleod that 'your Cuntries were never in such a bad situation ... and suppose we all made use of our sowing seed (except a verie few) unless we will get a relief within a few days the most of us will perish for want of Bread etc'.[79] Barely 25 years later, problems had returned on such a scale that many tenants joined the flood of Highland emigration. Letters talked about 'inhabitants are already ruined by ye loss of yr cattle' and had 'nothing to eat or sow on ye ground',[80] about being 'wtout soweing wtout bread' and in 'deplorable condition', 'hundreds will starve',[81] and about 'the very lowe price of cattle, kelp and bade cropts with I am afraid a discontented people'.[82] Again, the expectation was that Macleod should respond. He did so by a programme of rent reductions to 'enable my Tenants to live comfortably on my Estate'.[83]

Because of their detail, the records available for Campbell of Glenorchy's estate provide a particularly rich archive of data on how traditional Highland estates responded to tenurial problems. It is especially forthcoming as regards data for the late 1690s, a period which saw the start of a succession of severe winters known as King William's lean years. These severe conditions had their greatest impact in north-east Scotland, where many died, but farming over a much wider areas was also affected. Occasional references in contemporary accounts, such as Martin Martin's reference to the severe difficulties which tenants on Lewis had recently experienced in paying their rents because of poor harvests, suggests that the region was certainly affected by weather conditions over the late 1690s.[84] Given its size and diversity, Campbell of Glenorchy's estate enables us to see whether the impact of such conditions varied regionally and whether the estate was able to use this diversity so as to offset areas of deficit with areas of surplus. If we work through the detailed rentals available for Netherlorne (including islands like Luing and Seil), and the commentaries which they provide, there are really relatively few signs of crisis. In the 1697 rental, for instance, the township of Barbreck was reported as 'short of the rest of their ferme throw the badness of their cropt'.[85] In fact, it paid only 17 bolls of meal compared with the 60 that it paid in normal years. Its problems continued, for the following year, 1698, it paid no victuals whatsoever.[86] Other townships, like Auchnasaul, Kilbride, Ardluing and Kilchattan were also given an 'ease' of victuals.[87] One or two other farms are described as waste. For example, part of Rarey was declared waste, whilst two and a half out of the six merklands of Barrachrail were waste.[88] Clearly, Netherlorne had some difficulties in meeting its victual obligations in the late 1690s. However, the scale of rebates and rests was still not as great as those of 1670, when more substantial payments of victual seem to have been rested by the estate.[89] In fact, despite its problems in the late 1690s, it was still able to produce over 400 bolls of victual as rent, most of which was sold on by the estate to the garrison at Inverlochy.[90]

If we move inland to areas of the estate like Glenorchy, and look at its rental

for a year like 1697, there are outwardly only a few signs of production problems. Some tenants appear to have difficulty paying their cash rents and a
small handful appear to be in receipt of meal from the estate. In character,
these inland areas were mostly organised around mixed farming systems.
Though more suited to stock, most tried to be self-sufficient in grain, producing what they needed for subsistence. However, as indicated in Chapter 3, many also paid oat meal and malt as rent, along with livestock.
However, compared with townships in the more fertile areas to the west, their
crop margins were tighter. Townships on the lower ground of Netherlorne
and on Lismore produced surpluses far beyond what was needed for subsistence so even severe fluctuations did not put subsistence at risk. By comparison, even modest fluctuations of output in areas like Glenorchy tended
to mean a serious cut in what was available for basic needs. In other words,
so long as inland townships of the estate carried substantial numbers of
people, and so long as they were still expected to yield meal and malt as rent
and to grow what they needed for subsistence, then any significant dip in
output created problems of subsistence. The real clue as to how such townships fared during the poor seasons experienced in the mid and late 1690s
comes not so much from rentals but from correspondence. One letter written
in 1698 talked about it being a 'badd yeir' for the 'braes' or hill districts of the
estate.[91] In fact, it was only one amongst a run of bad years. Letters written
over the 1690s by the earl of Breadalbane – as Campbell of Glenorchy had
now become – suggest that the estate played an active part in redistributing
meal both within Netherlorne[92] and between the low ground of Netherlorne
and Glenorchy[93] when need arose. In Glenorchy, the earl responded to the
crisis apparent by the spring of 1697 by proposing that a meeting be held of
'all the tenants in the country, at least a man out of every merk land ... and
propose to them a cast, how much every toun or every man will neid'.[94]
Though tenants were expected to pay for such meal, or to have it as a 'rest'
to be paid later,[95] the letters written by the earl show him more as a chief than
as landlord, accepting responsibility for his tenant's welfare. They also provide a fine example of how a chiefly economy could redistribute subsistence
between different parts of an estate during times of crisis. However, there
may have been more to the problem, as one or two of the earl's letters also
make clear. In one, he suggests that the tenants in Netherlorne were using the
crisis to ask for too great a rest of grain rents.[96] With prices so high, they had
much to gain from selling their grain at the high prices generated by the crisis.
Once the region had been penetrated by market activity, tenants no less than
chiefs could play to the markets or to the mutuality of their relation with
chiefs according to what maximised returns most.

When we look at some of the traditions that surround the history of clans and
their chiefs, they invariably contain accounts that elaborate on display
behaviour, such as their capacity for feasting, extravagant generosity or
sustained feuding. Likewise, when we look at the attempts made by central

government to control clans from the sixteenth century onwards, the curbs which they placed on different forms of display behaviour, notably feasting and feuding, had a central role. For all concerned, these chiefly forms of behaviour clearly lay at the heart of the system. For the present argument, though, chiefly forms of display behaviour mattered because they served to drive farm production, giving it goals that served to enhance the position of their chief and infusing relations of production with those between a chief and his kinsman. In thought if not in practice, most tenants, like those granted land by the Lord of the Isles, accepted that their first principle of production was to provide food for his table. Drawing on an ideology accepted by all, they confused the welfare of their chief and his capacity to feast as a symbol of their own status and well-being.

NOTES

1. For a wider discussion of the role of feasting in Gaelic society, see Simms, 'Guesting and feasting in Gaelic Ireland'.
2. MacDonald and MacDonald, *The Clan MacDonald*, iii, p. 119. For comparison, the feasts held at the inauguration of the Lords of the Isles was said to have lasted for a week, see Macphail, *Highland Papers*, i, p. 24.
3. SRO, John Macgregor Collection, GD50/93 Geneaology of MacGregor.
4. Logan, *The Scottish Gael*, i, p. 195. Other instances of feasting are provided by Macinnes, *Clanship, Commerce and the House of Stuart, 1603–1788*, p. 4.
5. Innes and Buchan (eds), *Origines Parochiales Scotiae*, ii, p. 26.
6. Skene, *Celtic Scotland*, iii, p. 429.
7. Ibid., p. 430.
8. The most infamous case was surely the one in which all the tenants in the Barony of Rannoch were accused of having 'crewallie and execrably killed and murdered 100 deer and more that cam out of the forest in tyme of the great Storm last', SRO, John Macgregor Collection, GD50/135, Barony Court Books – Menzies and Rannoch, 25 March 1684. Apart from the scale of the case, the interesting word here is the use of the term 'murdered'. For other examples, see 24 August 1669.
9. Munro, *Monro's Western Isles*, p. 61.
10. Ibid., pp. 49–50.
11. Ibid., p. 86.
12. DC/MDP, 1/445, Bond 3 June 1658 by Murdoch MacAngus vicDonald and Donald MacAngus vicDonald.
13. Martin, *Western Islands*, p. 35.
14. DC/MDP, 1/466/24, Description of Harris, 1772.
15. SRO, Cromartie Papers, GD305/143, Estimate of the value of the estate of Cromartie, 1752.
16. Martin, *Western Islands*, p. 68.
17. See, for example, MacDonald and MacDonald, *The Clan MacDonald*, iii, p. 136.
18. However, the MacDonald Estate did make some moves. See CDC/MP, 221/3695/4 Memorandm. c.1730s which notes that when 'Sir Alexr. is in the country that he mind to give orders about the fishing of salmond in the proper places, Either with Nets or Cruives'.
19. Examples are provided by NLS, Sutherland Papers, DEP313/3160 Tacks of Earl William Assynt, 1757–66, and 313/3161 Tacks of Assynt, 1765–6.
20. Ibid., DEP 313/1000, Expir'd leases for Assynt, 1812. The adjacent estate of

Cromarty received a sizeable yearly income from its control of the herring fishery in Lochbroom, equal to a third of the cash rents of Coigach; see SRO, GD305/ 1/63, Rentals, 1612–1824, no. 141, A General Rental of Ld cromartie's estate, 1735.

21. SRO, Breadalbane Muniments, GD112/9/3/3/6, Rental of the Earle of Breadal-bane Estate, etc his Old Estate in Argyleshire viz Glenurchay, Benderloch, Lochow-side 1697 records 60 salmon paid for Knochintigh. Ibid., GD112/9/40, Rental of Breadalbane Estate 1717–20, records 9 barrels of herring paid to the earl for Kilbride and Cullnacroa in Cowal and Lochfyneside.

22. Brown, *Bloodfeud in Scotland*, p. 277.

23. Ibid., p. 4.

24. Young, *Fighting with Food*.

25. Mackenzie, *History of the Clan Mackenzie*, p. 106. For other instances of cattle theft involving the Mackenzies of Kintail, see Masson (ed.), *RPC, vi, AD1599–1604*, pp. 184 and 459.

26. See, for example, MacLeod (ed.), *The Book of Dunvegan*, I, pp. 47–8 and 139–40.

27. Innes (ed.), *The Black Book of Taymouth*, pp. 416–17.

28. Masson (ed.), *RPC, vi, AD1599–1604*, p. 534.

29. Ibid., pp. 500–1.

30. IC/AP, B/4/46, Information of the Dammage and Loss Susteined by John McLauchlan, 18 Oct. 1675.

31. Martin, *Western Islands*, pp. 10–12. For further comment on the feud, see Macinnes, *Clanship, Commerce and the House of Stuart, 1603–1788*, pp. 37–46. His documentation of the feud between Ewen Cameron of Lochiel and Mackintosh of Torcastle which – as tradition had it – lasted for 'three hundred and sixty years' provides a fine illustration of how feuds were conducted, and why; ibid., pp. 40–2.

32. HMC, *Third report*, appendix, p. 382.

33. Ibid., p. 382; *OSA*, ii, p. 457.

34. i.e. SRO, GD112/9/24, Rentall of Breadalbane 1669–78.

35. Steer and Bannerman, *Late Medieval Monumental Sculpture*, p. 150.

36. MacDonald and MacDonald, *The Clan MacDonald*, iii, pp. 125–6.

37. Macphail (ed.), *Highland Papers*, i, p. 279. See also the reference to the six merk land of Revaig and Vuill possessed by Lauchlan McLean, 'possessed free from McLean this year, for service'.

38. SRO, Clanranald Papers, GD201/5/1257/5 Rental of Clanranalds Estate in South Uist, 1718.

39. SRO, Forfeited Estates, E744/1 Judicial rental of the Estate of Clanranald, 1748. For other examples, MacDonald and MacDonald, *The Clan MacDonald*, iii, pp. 125–9.

40. Ibid., E648/1/4 Abstract of the Real Estate of Ronald MacDonald holding of the Crown, S. Uist.

41. Skene, *Celtic Scotland*, iii, p. 429.

42. Ibid., p. 438.

43. IC/AP, Box 2531, Memorandum anent Tirie.

44. Skene, *Celtic Scotland*, iii, p. 432.

45. Innes (ed.), *The Black Book of Taymouth*, pp. 187–9. See also MacDonald and MacDonald, *The Clan MacDonald*, ii, p. 773; Burnett (ed.), *ERS, xii, AD1502–7*, pp. 698–700.

46. Mackenzie, *History of the Clan Mackenzie*, pp. 122–3.

47. Gregory and Skene (eds), *Collectanea de Rebus Albanicis*, p. 161.

48. Innes (ed.), *The Black Book of Taymouth*, pp. 237–9.

49. MacLeod (ed.), *The Book of Dunvegan*, i, p. 183.

50. MacDonald and MacDonald, *The Clan MacDonald*, ii, p. 775.

51. See, for example, the discussion in Bradley, *The Social Foundations of Prehistoric Britain*, especially pp. 96–127.
52. MacLeod (ed.), *The Book of Dunvegan*, i, pp. 52–4.
53. SRO, Clanranald Papers, GD201/1/277, Letters of Horning in favour of Gallean McNeill, 28 April 1653.
54. CDC, MacDonald Papers, GD221/5294/5, Antenuptial Contract of Marriage between Sorlie Nicolson … Christine MacDonald, 1709.
55. See, for example, Innes (ed.), *The Black Book of Taymouth*, pp. 187–9.
56. Examples of cash being used as tocher-gude abound in SRO, GD50/28 Genealogy – Campbell of Glenurquhay.
57. MacLeod (ed.), *The Book of Dunvegan*, i, pp. 52–4.
58. Steer and Bannerman, *Late Medieval Monumental Sculpture*, p. 27.
59. Ibid., pp. 144–6.
60. Ibid., p. 22.
61. Ibid., p. 145.
62. MacDonald and MacDonald, *The Clan MacDonald*, i, p. 443
63. Ibid., pp. 162 and 443.
64. SRO, John Macgregor Collection, GD50/93, Genealogy of 'Mac Gregor anciently Mor'.
65. SRO, Clanranald Papers, GD201/5/1257/1, Rental of Estate of Moydart, 1718, and GD201/5/1257/5, Rental of Clanranald's Estate in S. Uist, 1718.
66. Garnett, *Observations on a Tour through the Highlands*, i, p. 173.
67. Cregeen, 'Tacksmen and their successors', p. 116.
68. SRO, GD64, Campbell of Jura Papers, Minit of the Rent of the Isle of Jura, 1683. This rental notes land in the hands of Duncan Campbell, and then says 'which lands are sett … for fyve hundred merks albeit the tack bears six hundred merks'.
69. CDC/MP, GD221/3695/2, Memorandum of the Abuses in the Present Management of Macdonalds estate, 1733.
70. Skene, *Celtic Scotland*, iii, p. 433.
71. DC/MDP, 4/294, Report on tenure, 1769.
72. McKerral, 'The tacksman and his holding', p. 11.
73. IC/AP, Box 494, Letter, 1 June 1681, Dealing with Tiree rents.
74. CDC/MP, GD221/3695/2, Memorial of the Abuses in the Present Management of Macdonalds Estate 1733.
75. McKay (ed.), *Walker's Report on the Hebrides*, p. 101.
76. DC/MDP, 1/382, Copy of the Correspondence betwixt A. B. and Mr. Fraser regarding the sale of Harries, 6 Jan. 1772.
77. Ibid., 2/487/16.
78. Ibid., 2/484/10, The Rents of the lands of Sky for the cropt and Year 1686.
79. Ibid., 4/151, Letter, 12 May 1745.
80. Ibid., 4/304/1, Letter, 28 April 1772.
81. Ibid., 4/304/2, Letter, MacLeod of Ulinish, State of Sky, 1772.
82. Ibid., 1/466/23 Letter, 30 Jan. 1772.
83. Ibid., 2/485/44, Rental of Macleods Lands on Skye and Harris, 1771. See also 2/487/32, Rental of the Barony of Harris, 1778.
84. Martin, *Western Islands*, p. 2.
85. SRO, Breadalbane Muniments, GD112/9/35, Rentall Book of Netherlorne 1693–1704.
86. Ibid.
87. Ibid.
88. Ibid.
89. Ibid., GD112/9/22, Rental of the Lands belonging to Lord Neill Campbell in Loyng Seill and Netherlorne 1665.
90. Mention of the sale of meal to Inverlochy is mentioned in a number of letters

written by Breadalbane. See, for example, the reference to the sale of over 400 bolls in SRO, Campbell of Barcaldine Muniments, GD170/629/43 Letter, 5 Nov. 1694.

91. Ibid., GD170/612, Letter, 23 Feb. 1698.
92. Ibid., GD170/629/47, Letter, 23 Nov. 1695.
93. Ibid., GD170/629/64, Letter, 19 March 1697
94. Ibid., GD170/629/65, Letter, 22 March 1697.
95. Ibid. East from Glenorchy, barony court records for Weem show an 'Ease of fearm' or oat meal for crop, 1700, being granted to townships, whilst the maltster explained that he paid no rent that year because 'ther was no malt made that yeir by reason of the badness of the year and ill frosted stuff', SRO, John MacGregor Collection, GD50/35, Weem, 18 Jan. 1703.
96. Ibid., GD170/629/68, Letter, 26 March 1697.

5 The Transformation of Chiefs into Landlords

In this chapter, I want to explore the processes and pressures by which chiefs began to think and act as landlords. Even in the far west of the region, this is likely to have been a process under way by the sixteenth century. Highland chiefs and their tenants were encouraged to attend Lowland markets and were given protection when doing so, a policy clearly designed to expose them to new values.[1] It had its desired effect. When farmers on Islay petitioned the king in 1610 about recent restrictions introduced in Islay, Mull and other western isles that prevented them from attending Lowland markets, they made it clear that paying their rents now depended wholly on their ability to sell livestock.[2] Yet at the other end of the period under review, there is also a sense in which the process by which chiefs became landlords was still not finally complete even by 1820. Even deep into the nineteenth century, there were expectations about landlords who were still clan chiefs that went beyond the purely economic. In other words, their transformation into landlords needs to be seen as a gradual affair rather than something that happened dramatically or suddenly in the aftermath of defining events like Culloden. In this chapter, I want to draw out the pressures and processes that brought this gradual transformation about.

THE IMPACT OF GOVERNMENT POLICIES

Throughout the period under view, c.1493–1820, we find official attempts, local and regional, to curb what were seen as the excesses of the clan system. The forfeiture of the Lordship of the Isles in 1493 provided the Crown with an obvious opportunity for taking action, since it now acquired control over an area which had seemed beyond its political reach. It main concerns were that many parts of the region followed their own law and that its 'pepill ar

102

almaist gane wilde'.[3] Despite its efforts, there were no easy solutions. The fact that we find legislation more than a hundred years after the forfeiture of the Lordship still complaining about the region's lack of respect for Crown authority and about the 'evill dispositioun and barbaritie of ye peopill',[4] makes this abundantly clear. Even the 'daunting of the west', as the destruction of the Lordship and the gradual replacement or suppression of its deep-rooted loyalties became known, was to last into the eighteenth century. Yet for all the problems which it faced in applying its policies, the Crown had reached a very clear diagnosis of what the region's difficulties were and the policies by which they could be solved by the sixteenth century. Put simply, it saw the inter-connection between the uplifting of *cuid-oidhche* by chiefly retinues, including their fighting men, and the constant feuding between clans as the core problems whilst the encouragement of trade and the marketing of farm produce were seen as the solution.

Arguably, part of the Crown's initial response to the forfeiture of the Lordship may lie concealed in the sixteenth-century Crown rentals which it drew up for the various parts of the Lordship: that is, for North and South Kintyre, Islay, Jura, Colonsay, Tiree, South Uist, Ardnamurchan, Morvern and parts of Mull. As already argued in Chapter 3, it is unlikely that the Crown rentals simply recorded conditions of set as it found them. The very fact that the Crown took direct control over these areas, albeit for only two brief periods, provided it with an opportunity for changing how land was set, dispossessing those who were disloyal and redefining the nature of rents. As an opportunity for advancing Crown policy, it may have anticipated the confiscation of estates after both the '15 and '45 rebellions.[5]

Mention has already been of the clues which may help us here. The first is provided by the late sixteenth-century report on the Hebrides which appears to describe conditions that, in character, precede those depicted in the Crown rentals, with food renders being uplifted irregularly via the obligation of *cuid-oidhche*. Skene thought the late sixteenth-century report helped to prepare the way for the Statutes of Iona (1609), a set of enactments by the Privy Council that were directed at the region and its problems.[6] Given that a key part of these enactments was the Privy Council's attempt to force clan chiefs on Skye and in the western isles to shift away from *cuid-oidhche* into regular rents, we cannot rule out the possibility that Crown rentals available for the former lands of the Lordship of the Isles may, by their very compilation, have also served to regularise rents. Indeed, in so far as the late sixteenth-century report suggests that renders uplifted from islands like Islay and Mull still had the character of *cuid-oidhche*, the shift may have been a drawn-out affair despite what Crown rentals appear to tell us.

Just as the Crown may have used its brief control over lands within the former Lordship to further the spread of regular rents, so also it may have used its control to extend the cash component of rents. Certainly, it always regarded marketing as a means by which the values of the region could be redirected. The cash recorded in its rentals probably derived from two separate sources. First, there is the possibility that it may have used its temporary control to convert some of the food renders paid by townships into cash. Given the extent to which it sold produce back to the tenants 'on the ground',[7] the latter could have exercised some choice over which items were sold to raise cash and which were consumed on the farm. Second, there are indications that some cash obligations originated as such, being treated as extra rent, that is, as an eik or augmentation. The way some cash rents appear in the sixteenth-century Crown rentals as linked to a township's assessment may also be of interest in relation to this point. In principle, township assessments based on Old and, later, New Extent provided the basis for fiscal levies. At first, these were occasional levies but by the time of the Crown rentals for areas like Islay and Kintyre, the framework of assessments devised under New Extent was being used as the basis for the payment of regular rents. Indeed, in some cases, townships actually paid in cash an amount equal to their assessment. Given that New Extent was introduced into the area by the Crown, probably after the collapse of the Lordship in c.1493,[8] we cannot rule out the possibility that it was designed not only to further the spread of regular rents, but to introduce an extra cash component, one that symbolised the Crown's newly asserted superiority. In fact, a number of Hebridean sources refer to cash rents as 'Crown mails' as if they were rooted in dues or levies raised by the Crown.[9]

If what sixteenth-century Crown rentals can tell us about the Crown's early attempts to initiate change remains unclear, there can be no mistaking the Crown's intentions when we look at the legislation and court enactments directed at the region during the sixteenth century. The earliest sought to curb the problems created by sorning and feuding. In 1506, the King's commissioners issued a declaration that went to the very heart of the region's problems. It called upon all chiefs and estate holders to hold baillie courts where 'the best and worthiest persons of the cuntre' were expected to give up the names of 'all thevis, pikaris, and sornaris that oppress the cuntre and the pure commonys or that takis mete, drink, or ony uthir thing without payment, and the names of menslaaris that committis slaughter and common tulyeouris'.[10] It also required chiefs to 'caus all sornaris and oppressouris of the Kingis liegis within your boundis and all utheris idill persons that wirkis nocht nor has to leve apon of thair awin to be expellit ... or ellis caus thame to wirk and labour for thair leving'.[11] Though directed at sorners, that is, those who forced food out of tenants illegally or without right, it is difficult to see how this act could have been applied without also compromising the position of a chief's fighting men, especially where the latter were farmed out to townships so that the basis of their claim for hospitality was not always clear. This, of course, may have been part of its intention.

The process of applying the Crown authority, though, was a slow laborious affair. In 1585, the Scottish parliament passed a general act against sorning. The problem, and one recognised by the Act, was that apprehending 'notorious thevis brokin men and soirneris of clannis' carried costs which dissuaded many.[12] Not all chiefs could hope to benefit in the way that the earl of Argyll did when he was given the feu-ferms of Kintyre in return for his part in subduing the MacGregors.[13]

The Crown's efforts at the daunting of the west intensified towards the end of the century. Acknowledging that clansmen were not always tenants on the estates of their chief, an Act of 1593 made 'captains, chiefs and principals of all branches' responsible for those under their direction. The Act also recognised the essential complexity of clans and the fact that they were bound as much by 'pretence of blude' as by 'place of thair duelling'.[14] In 1597, Highland and Hebridean chiefs were called upon to present themselves and the titles which they had to their estates in Edinburgh by the following May.[15] The preamble to this order reveals much about the government's thinking towards the region, particularly its continuing concern over the way in which the unsettled socio-political conditions of the region prevented its full and proper economic development. This unsettled character was seen to 'not onlie frustat his maiestie of the yeirlie payment off his proper rentis and dew service' but meant that despite 'the fertillitie of ye ground', the region was reduced to being 'altogidder unproffitabill'.[16] Clearly, the Crown was as concerned with its economic as with its political integration into the wider state. Its perception of the region as fertile and productive recurs the following year in the legislation passed concerning the plantation of Lewis. Lewis was symptomatic of the wider problem. It was seen as occupied by barbarous people of an 'evill dispositioun', a people without religion. Not only did the branches of the dominant clan, the MacLeod of Lewis, fight with clans elsewhere, but they also fought amongst themselves. Worse, they were seen as 'violentlie possessing his hienes proper landis wtout payment of maill or gressum'.[17] The Crown based its solution on the introduction not just of new social values but of new economic values, hoping that it could introduce a greater commitment to trade and marketing by settling Lowlanders. In the event, the plantation was a disaster. Even before some had been slaughtered by the MacLeods, the Lowlanders involved had complained that reports of the island's fertility were exaggerated, and had negotiated a reduction in the feu duty to be paid, including a shift from farm produce to fish.[18] In the event, the Crown repaid in kind, ordering the 'extirpatioun' of those against it.[19]

No doubt spurred on by the failure of the Lewis plantation, the government returned to address what it perceived were the basic problems of the region. At a meeting held on Iona in 1609 between the Bishop of the Isles, acting as the king's commissioner, and various clan chiefs, a series of Statutes were issued that became known as the Statutes of Iona. We can only make sense of these Statutes, and their significance, if we grasp the importance of display behaviour like feuding and feasting to the ideology of the clan system. As well as binding chiefs to support and obey the ministers of the kirk, the Statutes set out to systematically undermine the practices which sustained feasting and feuding. Sorning, the forcing of food and clothing out of tenants in the name of *cuid-oidhche* by those who had no claim to it or by persons whom the Statutes labelled as 'idill belleis' was a particular target. Anyone 'found soirning, craving meit, drink, or ony uther geir fra the tennentis and inhabitantis thairof be way of conyie [cuddeachies] as they terme it, except for reasonable and sufficient payment ... salbe repute and haldin as thevis and intollerable oppressouris'.[20] Further, because the problem of sorning and feuding was bound up with the size of a chief's retinue and the number of fighting men that he could muster, the Statues limited the number of household men who could be maintained by them, specific chiefs being given a set number of servants which they were not allowed to exceed. Because it had contributed to 'the grite povertie of the said Ilis', restrictions were also placed on 'their extraordinair drinking of strong wynis and acquavitie brocht in amangis thame'. In a further Statute that was presumably directed at the occasion of feasting, 'vagaboundis, bairdis, juglouris, or suche lyke', including those 'pretending libertie to baird and flattir', were to be apprehended. A further Statute addressed the problem of feuds, reminding chiefs of the Act anent feuding passed in 1598.[21] The Statutes took the opportunity to refer to the 'monstrous deidlie feidis heirtofoir intertenyit within the saidis Yllis' and to note that the Act against feuding had not been observed. Re-stating the terms of the Act, it banned the carrying of hagbuts and pistols and forbade the shooting of deer, hares and fowl. Finally, the Statutes reminded all chiefs, or the 'principall of every clan', that they were answerable for every one of their kinsmen, friends and followers.

Like all legislation dealing with the Highlands and Islands, there needs to be a clear distinction drawn between intentions of the Statutes and their achievements. Within a few years, or in 1616, seven of the leading chiefs were bonded to appear annually before the Privy Council and to observe conditions that were mostly those of the Statutes of Iona re- stated, but there were some new conditions.[22] They were now to reside in a fixed place and to take the mains or home farm and to 'labour the same with thair awne goodis, to the effect they may be thairby exercised and eshew idilnes'.[23] The extent to which clan status had distinguished between those who laboured the fields and those who did not would have made this a most unwelcome condition for chiefs. They were also bound to let the remainder of their estates to tacksmen for a fixed rent, without the additional customs which they had imposed on their tenants.[24] As argued earlier, this probably served to transform the whole concept of what constituted rent, forcing chiefs, or at least those who had not already done so, to replace irregularly uplifted obligations of hospitality with a fixed and regular payment of rent. Further, the various chiefs were bound not to maintain more than one birling or galley and not to sorn on tenants when travelling through the Isles with it. This condition is especially interesting because it was the first official attack on sorning that involved chiefs themselves and, no less revealing, it now treated the uplifting of *cuid-oidhche* by chiefs as sorning whereas previous use of the term had been restricted to the illegal uplifting of foods and hospitality by broken or marginalised men, and by those around the edge of chiefly retinues. Finally, the Privy Council now extended its controls on drinking to 'tennentis and commonis', compelling chiefs 'to tak a strait ordour throughoute thair haill boundis that nane of thair tennentis or cuntry people by or drink ony wynis'.[25]

Taken collectively, the Statutes of Iona (1609) and what Mackenzie called their 'second edition' in 1616[26] addressed a root source of the Highland problem, that is, the practices and behaviour which sustained the ideology of the clan system. Such legislation had no sudden or dramatic effect in changing this ideology or the mind set of Highland clans. The way some later gathered round the Jacobite cause is proof of this. However, it did change the base conditions of the clan system in a way that is not readily appreciated. Moreover, it changed these conditions intentionally. From the moment it took over the estates of the Lordship and became directly involved in the region, the Crown appears to have worked at the general strategy of replacing the local chiefly consumption of produce with its marketing. The introduction of regular cash may have been one way in which it did this. Converting payments in kind to cash was another. Both forced tenants to market produce. When chiefs were forced to follow suit, it would have left them with cash in hand rather than a well-stocked girnal or bowhouse. Seen in this way, the appearance of such cash demands would have been a potent force in dissolving the ideology of the clan system. Yet at best, the Crown and its commissioners can only be credited with helping to start this process. What we also need to consider is how chiefs themselves slowly advanced the process.

CHIEFS, LANDLORDS AND MARKETS

As I have tried to show, the economics of production under the clan system were quite different from those which came to prevail once the Highlands and Islands had been penetrated by markets and their values. The former involved the production and consumption of food according to local needs, whilst the latter were geared to the demands and price structure of distant markets. The former carried with them no major locational disadvantage, whereas the latter patently burdened the region with all the problems of distance and cost. Put in its starkest form, the former were all about use values whilst the latter were all about exchange values. But there is a second point of difference that needs to be highlighted. So long as production was geared to a system of direct consumption, then townships throughout the region were burdened with demands that encouraged arable as much as livestock production. By contrast, a market system encouraged specialisation and, through its invisible hand and the principles of comparative advantage, created demands which sooner or later meant the replacement or downgrading of arable subsistence farming relative to the needs of stock production. Under the clan system, even areas best suited to stock production sustained heavy patterns of arable cropping and paid some of their rents in the form of meal or bere. Drawn into a market system, though, their cost structure worked against them in a plain and simple way. Once burdened with cash rents, and forced into the market to meet these cash needs, then the whole geography of opportunity and cost began a slow but progressive upheaval. This process began not with the clearances but with the first spread of regular cash rents, a process in place by the sixteenth century.

How quickly or slowly these pressures spread depended on the pace at which chiefly perceptions changed. To some degree they had only a limited choice in the matter. Once the consumption of food via chiefly patterns of display had been legislated against, then even the most recalcitrant chiefs were forced to confront the question of what to do with the vast quantities of food which they had previously gathered in as rent or uplifted in the form of *cuid-oidhche*. In principle, there were two ways in which they could transform their estate produce into a cash income. Either they could take responsibility for marketing produce themselves or they could switch to cash rents, transferring the burden onto tenants. The overall picture is that most appear to have adopted policies that involved a mix of both approaches.

Taken at face value, rentals, even the earliest ones, appear to suggest that chiefs followed the example set by the Crown and solved their problems by converting their rents in kind progressively into cash. Even when rentals still list rent in terms of the amount of produce owed by each tenant or by each merkland or pennyland, many also state the cash value of such produce. The overall impression conveyed is that rentals, and the system which they were trying to record, now dealt only in cash. In fact, such a simplistic reading may mislead. In many cases, such entries are simply computing the cash value of rents in kind, and not necessarily stating what the tenant had paid as cash in lieu of such rents. In a system in which everything now had to be accounted, or set down as charge and discharge, this was the only way in which estates could value the flow of produce through their accounts. In some cases, it also served to introduce a flexibility between the custom of paying rents in kind and the demands of the new cash economy. Usually, this worked to the advantage of the landowner enabling him or her to play the market by taking grain when its set value was lower than the market price and cash when it was higher.

On Campbell of Glenure's estate, for example, Campbell reserved to himself the right of whether food rents should be converted. In a 1758 rental for Portcharran, 18 bolls of meal were noted as paid by the tenant each year. This was 'payable to the Master or in his option £7 Scots for every 10 stone'. It then appended a further note saying 'The Masters always obliges the tennants to Pay in the Meal to his Girnal as he prefers it to the above converted price thereof'.[27] The tack issued by the Clanranald estate to Angus Macdonald for the townships of North and South Garrivaltos in 1704 went further, binding the tenant to pay 'either oat meall or Bear, or Eight merks Scotts for each Boll in the proprietor's option'.[28]

On MacLeod of Dunvegan's estate, rentals from the mid-seventeenth century onwards also record the cash value equivalent of rents in kind. What actually passed between tenants and MacLeod, though, appears to have varied. Some make it clear that items like marts had been converted.[29] However, acts of court issued in 1735 and dealing with tacksmen make it clear that tacksmen were still expected to pay their meal, butter and cheese 'with their own product & not whats made by their subtennants' and to pay their wedders 'wt their year old Fleeces'.[30] Mid-eighteenth-century tacks, such as that issued for Ulinish in 1754, contained the clause that 'it shall be in the option of the said Normand Macleod and his forsaids either to Exact the forsaids Mart, Victual, Wedders, Butter and Cheese & Horse corn in kind, and to have the same Delivered at Dunvegan, or the forsaid rexively yearly Converted prices thereof'.[31] For comparison, the Macdonald estate occupying the eastern side of Skye was being advised to have its casualties 'converted in the tenents tacks so as it may be at their Masters option to Demand either the Ipso Corporate or ye Converted prices'.[32]

The question of who gained from such flexibility was sometimes more complex. Part of the problem arose from the practice of debiting tenants with the cash equivalent if their harvest prevented them from paying rents in kind. During the poor harvests of the 1690s, when grain prices were high, there is more than a hint that tenants were using the excuse of poor harvests to pay less rent in the form of grain so that they could redirect more surplus to the market. Clearly, the values that were starting to affect landlord behaviour were also capable of influencing the decision-making of some of their tenants, even by the closing years of the seventeenth century.[33] Seen in the longer term, though, Campbell of Glenorchy's Breadalbane estate continued to draw large quantities of food rents from its Netherlorne farms throughout the eighteenth century. Yet to judge from a 1795 rental, the person who gained most was the earl's chamberlain for Netherlorne. Appended to the rental is a note to the effect that 'all the meal payable out of Netherlorn was formerly paid to the Chamberlain in Kind, The meal he received at the rate of nine stone one lippie for every Boll, and the Bear, about 5 Linlithgow firlots, This meal & bear he was charged with and accompted to the earl at the converted price of 12 shilling the boll of meal, 3/4 the Boll of Bear All this Meal & Bear he sold on his own acct at what it would bring, some times more & sometimes for less but always at considerable advantage and this & some other years it was worth double the converted price'.[34] By comparison, other landowners were much more concerned to maintain the link between the current market price of grain and what was actually debited against the rent of a township. Thus, even in the early eighteenth century, the Argyll estate issued an annual 'Decreet of Maills and Duties', fixing the current conversion prices for oatmeal and bere so that its factors in the various parts of the estate had less opportunity for exploiting any differential between a conversion value fixed relatively infrequently and the run of the market.[35] Yet this was not an absolute insurance against such profiteering for there were items like livestock that had no such fixed or standardised price. Some years later, the duke still felt it necessary to issue a warning to his factors or chamberlains that they must not 'deal in cattle or trade of any kind without giving me previous notice and having consent to the same. And if any profits are made in the course of their dealing with my tennants or otherways in executing their commissions of Chamberlaincy, I shall look upon it as a breach of the trust I have committed to them'. [36]

For Adam Smith, tenants invariably gained from rents in kind because it insured them against inflation.[37] Dr Johnson was also of this view. He mentioned how tenants on Coll had asked for their rents to be converted seven years earlier or in the early 1750s because, once converted into cash, they believed that they would be of the same value each year, an interpretation which Johnson, like Smith, rejected.[38] In fact, the real problem for such tenants, and the circumstances that they were probably trying to escape from, was the option of flexibility. *Contra* Smith, many tenants must have seen the value of their grain flux up and down, but if landowners exercised the option of cash or grain, they could have suffered just as much in the good years when landowners preserved their real value by taking their fixed cash equivalent and suffered in the bad years when landowners took the set grain payments despite the fact that such grain may have been valued well above its fixed price equivalent.

Another factor needs to be taken into account. When the Crown sold food rents back to its tenants in areas like Morvern,[39] such a move was probably prompted as much by its lack of interest in taking average-to-poor quality meal out of the region as by its desire to force tenants into the marketplace. However, in time, another powerful consideration entered the equation. Townships, especially those burdened with high tenant numbers or which were less well endowed in resource terms, could ill afford to hand over even part of their grain output as rent, especially if arable was scarce or insufficient for those dependent on it. To a degree, there may have been common cause between tenants and landowners on this matter. The poorer areas were the areas whose arable or grain output would have offered least potential for marketing, whilst at the same time, their tenants could least afford to have such grain taken out of the township economy. By switching rents into cash, thereby allowing such tenants to shift their rent burden into other less pressurised areas of the township economy, notably the livestock sector, landowners effectively gave them a subsistence bonus.

In fact, this became a common structural feature of Highland estates for the next two centuries, with the less fertile parts of the estates having cash rents, or the option of cash rents, but with grain rents being maintained from the more fertile areas. Relatively few townships or areas in the western Highlands and Islands produced grain in sufficient quantity and of sufficient quality to encourage estates to maintain their rents in meal and bere down into an age when the market price of grain determined its value to the estate. Once having a full girnal ceased to be a source of status, most estates began to convert grain payments into cash payments. Only where its quantity and quality allowed it to be marketed was it maintained. We can see this clearly on an estate like the Cromartie estate, with late seventeenth-century rentals for Coigach listing only cash rents whilst other parts of the estate, including Strathpeffer and New Tarbet, paid large amounts of meal, both oatmeal and bere, and continued to do so until well into the eighteenth century.[40] On Campbell of Glenorchy's Breadalbane estate, the large quantities paid by select arable townships in Netherlorne, including Luing and Seil, and in Lismore, continued down into the late eighteenth century.[41] Across in Perthshire, the estate was also drawing significant amounts of grain from districts like Lawers and the east end of Loch Tay well into the late eighteenth century, though most of the interior parts of the estate had ceased to pay grain in any quantity by then.[42] In more remote areas elsewhere, grain payments were being phased out over the seventeenth century. On the MacLeod of Dunvegan estate, grain payments from the Skye portion of the estate had become modest even by the time of the first estate rental in 1683.[43] The barony of Duirinish illustrates the early shift away from grain payments on the estate. By the time of the 1724 rental, only 13 of its 33 townships paid meal or grain and even then, all payments were given a cash equivalent as well as a calculation in bolls (1/2 meal and 1/2 bere), 55 bolls in all,[44] though the amount had risen slightly by the time of the 1744 rental.[45] By comparison, but very much against the wider trend for such islands, all townships on Harris (as well as St Kilda) were still listed as liable for rent payments in grain in a rental of 1754, with the islands of Berneray, Ensay, and Pabbay (Kirktown, Northtown and Linga) together paying 109 bolls, more than any other barony on the estate.[46]

On the Macdonald estate on Skye, its 1733 rental shows grain payments had become modest compared with the quantities that must once have burdened townships.[47] Further west, islands like South Uist show equally small quantities being extracted by the early eighteenth century, though it should be borne in mind that Clanranald was one of the last to introduce regular rents on his estate.[48] The experience of Tiree provides a particularly good illustration of how trends ultimately worked against rent payments in grain even on islands that were relatively productive (see Table 3.2). When seen in 1541, Tiree paid substantial amounts of bere as rent, with lesser amounts of oats. Over the sixteenth–eighteenth centuries, its payments of bere fell progressively, disappearing altogether between 1680 and 1768. Initially, the payments of oats increased slightly 1541–1662, but shrank again by 1680 and had disappeared altogether by 1768.

The dilemma for tenants in the less fertile parts of the region was that whilst they had a vested interest in the conversion of grain rents into cash because it left them with more grain in hand for subsistence, they were hardly better placed to provide cash in its place. They were forced to confront cash rents out of necessity not out of opportunity. Two responses were open to them. For areas capable of producing bere which however felt the handicap of distance from markets, one solution was to raise the value of their produce by processing it into whisky. By 1768, tenants on Tiree no longer paid bere, but with 50 distilleries on the island, they clearly fed a great deal of what they had continued to grow into whisky-making.[49] Despite the extent of whisky-making on Tiree, the duke of Argyll was not supportive of this as a solution to householding problems of his tenants, at least not when it avoided duty. In instructions for his chamberlain in Kintyre, where distilling was also wide-spread, he reported that his tenants 'have of late got into a most pernicious Custom of distilling their Barley privately into Whisky or acquavitie contrary to Law by which his Majesty's revenues is greatly hurt' and ordered his chamberlain to stop the practice.[50] On many Highland estates, the estab-lishment of changehouses, brewseats, etc., such as that set up at Snizort (Skye) on the MacLeod of Dunvegan estate in 1754, provided tenants with an outlet for bere and a source of cash.[51] This comes across in data for Jura, where a rental of 1764 shows substantial quantities of malt being delivered to the maltbarns at Lag and Taychorran by tenants from townships like Ardfernal.[52] Even on the Breadalbane estate, where tenants had easier access to markets, bere found its way to local changehouses. In a report drafted in 1722, the author complained that the 'benefitt of the Malt kiln of Killin is unaccountable considering that all the country bear that comes in to that kiln is kiln dryed before it be received from the tennents yrof they make but very sober malt except what is made to the brewer himself ... and to his favorits'.[53]

A still more widespread response to the problem of raising cash for rents was for tenants to market cattle. Seen from the standpoint of those living along the western Seaboard or out on the islands, the marketing of cattle had two clear advantages. First, they were not only a product that walked to market, but also, one whose condition could be improved by Lowland feeding. Second, marketing cattle allowed for a simple piece of factor substitution. It not only enabled tenants to raise that portion of their rent represented by 'silver mails' and the cash needed to cover the conversion value of grain rents, but it also enabled them to shift the burden of their rents from what was scarce, or arable, onto what was abundant, or grass. For the ordinary tenant, the marketing of cattle was a necessary piece of house-holding, an exchange of use values. Even when seen in the late eighteenth century, few would have seen marketing as an end in itself, a source of profit for the sake of profit.[54]

The same cannot be said of chiefs and landowners. Arguably, their values changed significantly between the sixteenth and eighteenth centuries. Initially, the cash demands made on them must have been a unwelcome intrusion into a system hardly geared for the generation of cash profits. The constraints progressively introduced over the sixteenth and early seventeenth centuries on the customary uses of food rents meant that vast quantities of food previously gathered in and consumed via the various forms of chiefly display were now surplus to such needs. Re-directing this surplus towards the marketplace posed the same difficulties for chiefs and landowners as it did for ordinary tenants. Those possessing estates that were well placed and fertile had every incentive to continue with grain rents, directing bere towards malt production and meal to the marketplace. However, as a solution, this still left large surpluses in those areas not so well placed. For chiefs and landowners, the willingness of tenants to buy back their meal rents or products like cheese and butter must have been a welcome solution in principle. I say in principle because such a solution did not do away with the problem of raising cash rents but simply shifted it to other items of the township economy.

Of all the traditional forms of rental income gathered in by chiefs and landowners, the most marketable were their marts or cattle. Of course, even within the chiefly economy, cattle were the most valued item of account. When faced with cash demands, chiefs, like their tenants, must also have seen them as the most marketable product. Indeed, in so far as we can recover details about the early history of cattle droving out of the Highlands and Islands, it was a trade in which chiefs and landowners played a critical supervisory role from the very beginning. The scale on which the Breadalbane estate appears to have been involved in cattle production over the closing decades of the sixteenth century suggests that it was regularly marketing stock by then. Furthermore, the way in which it organised livestock production around its bowhouse system and the extent to which these were used to orchestrate the movement of stock between different 'grass rooms' suggests that its marketing involvement had backward linkages that impinged on many tenants.[55] Certainly, some of the complaints that were being put to the Privy Council about cattle theft make it abundantly clear that chiefs, even in areas like Kintail, had already turned to the marketing of stock by the time the Statutes of Iona (1609) were enacted.[56]

More significantly, not only were chiefs and landowners engaged in marketing cattle themselves, but they appear to have provided the organisational means by which tenants could market their cattle, negotiating with Lowland dealers on their behalf. In 1641, for instance, the earl of Seaforth can be found agreeing with an Edinburgh dealer to have 300 cattle delivered by his tenants each year to Stornaway.[57] Likewise, just over half a century after his predecessor had been bound to abandon the traditional practices of a chief and to raise fixed and regular rents on his lands, the Captain of Clanranald can be found negotiating with cattle drovers over the sale 'of all the cows to be sold furth of his lands for the year 1677'. Such were the problems of cattle droving in the seventeenth century that all the risks were debited to Clanranald, with the drovers agreeing to drove them only from Strathfillane to Down in Menteith.[58] In some cases, estates used their bowhouses as the collection points, with tenants delivering cattle to them as a first stage in assembling droves. Tenants in Coigach, for instance, were required to deliver their cattle, including those paid in lieu of cash rents, to the two bowhouses maintained by the estate.[59] The Sutherland estate also had such a scheme but it can also be found organising droves locally rather than through its bowhouses. Early eighteenth century rentals for the Sutherland estate record tenants paying cattle in ones and twos into particular droves, the organisation of the drove seemingly being an estate-managed activity.[60]

The Cromartie estate's use of cattle as a substitute for cash rents was a feature of other estates. The duke of Argyll allowed chamberlains to buy cattle 'upon [his] account or taken in payment of rents' provided 'an exact account be kept both of the number and price'.[61] There are strong hints on the Clanranald estate on South Uist, albeit from the early eighteenth century, that it too accepted cattle as a form of internal currency for the estate. Rather scrappy notes of account for the early eighteenth century show tenants and others paying for their cash obligations with whatever stock were to hand, the estate setting a cash equivalent for each animal.[62] Its hints of an *ad hoc* economy between chief and clansmen, landowner and tenant is further supported by an interesting report by Zachary McAulay on how rents were paid on the earl of Seaforth's Lewis estate during the early eighteenth century. Again, it gives the impression that cattle were a general form of currency. Little of the money rent burdened on tenants was actually 'payed in cash. But in the monthes of October and November cowes were raised and slaughtered and the beefe sent to such mercats as the managers thought fit'.[63] McAulay's reference to the marketing of deadstock rather than livestock echoes a comment made by Walker about North Uist. There too, farmers exported some of their cattle as salted beef but he goes on to say that they were 'the refuse of their Cattle, which the Drovers will not take out of the Country, and which would not live through the Winter'.[64]

Of course, what the use of such 'money-stuff' indicates is that whilst the Highlands and islands had moved into a money-economy in terms of account-keeping, the reality was that few tenants, sub-tenants or cottagers actually had access to sufficient real money for transacting day-to-day business. Within the framework of the estate, the bartering of produce against liabilities was still necessary to make the system work. For the tenant, the shift was a subtle one. He or she previously paid produce in its own terms, whereas now they paid it against a set cash rent. The real change was in the way chiefs and landowners reckoned or accounted their rents, and in the way they interacted as a group with the wider world.

Arguably, the start of this critical change in the perception of chiefs and landowners first took place over the closing decades of the sixteenth and early decades of the seventeenth century, perhaps a little earlier for some and a little later for others. The problem for them was that the rising demands placed on them could not be shifted or offset in the way that it could with their tenants. The cash liabilities which increasingly burdened landowners over the sixteenth and seventeenth centuries had to be paid as such. There was no substitute for the cash payments involved. However, they could spread the burden. Through the wadsetting and feuing of land, they could involve the senior branches of the clan in the task of raising cash. On some estates, quite substantial amounts of land were involved,[65] including some of their best land.[66] In the long term, though, such a strategy worsened their position as the value of the loans involved were devalued in real terms. As chiefs and landowners became involved more and more with Lowland society, their expectations also changed. Even by the start of the sixteenth century, chiefs like Campbell of Glenorchy were paying huge amounts of cash in marriage settlements, a switch which must have altered the family's expectations of estate income in a quite dramatic way.[67] Visits to the Lowlands and to the continent gave them an appetite for fine clothes and furnishings, again boosting their need for cash. One of the stipulations of the Statutes of Iona (1609) was that the sons of Highland chiefs should be educated in the Lowlands. Previously many had been fostered through an arrangement that bred or cemented alliances, with cattle being used as payment.[68] The consequences of this change was that not only were future chiefs and chieftains now exposed to a different code of behaviour but they acquired new tastes. To judge from some reports, their taste for fine living spread to other senior clan members. When a memorial was drawn up about the Macdonald estate in the 1733, its author was clearly surprised at what tacksmen were spending on 'Brandy Tobacco & fine cloaths, which three articles cost them Incredible summs'.[69]

By this point, however, many of the larger estates – Campbell of Glenorchy, MacLeod of Dunvegan, Macdonald, Seaforth and Clanranald – were suffering severe financial problems. Almost without exception, we find the role of advisers becoming more prominent. Inevitably, their advice focused on how estates were being run and the need to raise more revenue from them. As Forbes of Culloden advised the duke of Argyll in 1737, one solution adopted was to cut out tacksmen and their percentage of estate income.[70] Another was to find ways of augmenting rents. The memorial cited above for the Macdonald estate explored this approach, looking for ways in which the estate could break out of customary forms of rent. Its solutions included setting land according to what it actually comprised in terms of arable and grass rather than in terms of pennylands, or using grassums to make up the difference between what was paid and what townships were actually worth. Another strategy was to cost everything, so that dues or obligations which had lain dormant for years were now accorded a conversion price.[71] A petition submitted to the earl of Breadalbane in 1722 by tenants occupying townships in Toyer provides us with the tenant's perspective on the problem. The tenants were basically complaining about the difficulties which they were experiencing in paying their grassums because their crop was 'very bad', but additionally, 'our casualities &c being now converted into money we can scarce promise to pay this years duty with cess, watch money, Ministers and School Masters stipend &c. And lastly we are now oblidged to buy our woods which [we] were not in used to do formerly And besides we are threatened with being fined for bygones which if exacted with the Grassums this bad year will undoubtedly reduce a great many of us to beggary'. To compound matters, they added, money was 'scarce with us'.[72]

On many estates, though, the real problem lay in the advancing price of stock, particularly in the decades that followed the Union (1707). Anxious to profit from it, many estates pressurised their rents over the middle decades of the eighteenth century. Some appear to have done so at a quicker rate than farmers could adjust. Whatever the reason, many commentators thought that, as on Lewis, landowners had 'screwed their Rents to an extravagant height'.[73] By the 1770s, though, poor harvests squeezed tenants from the opposite direction. As in the 1720s, the response was a spate of high outward migration.[74] Typically, on the MacLeod of Dunvegan estate, the general augmentation of rents over the middle decades of the century, coupled with the poor harvests of the early 1770s, left many tenants in crisis and unable to pay their rent. Though tenants appear to have been in difficulty across the estate, tenants in Glenelg displayed the greatest dissatisfaction, with some tacksmen emigrating to America and persuading their under-tenants to go with them.[75] In many ways, the crisis of the 1770s, coming after so many decades of steadily rising prices and rents, dramatically illustrated the risks and problems that would-be landlords now faced in responding to the run of markets but in their reaction, the tacksmen and tenants of Glenelg also highlight the contrasting ideologies that now prevailed between landlords and tenants in the region.

One particular strategy, and one which does much to reveal the landlord mentality that had emerged amongst Highland chiefs and landowners by the mid-eighteenth century, is the way many appear to have adopted an aggressive attitude towards the income that could be generated from thirlage and multures. The thirling of tenants to a mill and the payment of multures to the miller was a longstanding obligation. However, it was one unevenly exploited simply because the large vertical water mill was unevenly distributed, such mills becoming few and far between as one moved northwards and westwards across the region. Areas like Netherlorne, Glenorchy, Breadalbane, Knapdale and parts of Kintyre were all well provided with mills, certainly by the seventeenth century.[76] Elsewhere, though, for example in Coigach, Ardnamurchan and the Outer Hebrides, mills are notable by their absence from or their infrequency in rentals.[77] In these areas, the vast proportion of tenants used the small horizontal mill or the hand quern, at least for the meal that provided their subsistence. However, by the mid-eighteenth century, landowners across the region appear to have seized on the building of new mills as a lucrative source of extra cash and, despite the fact that such rights could not have been invoked in such areas before, we find tenants being forced to destroy their querns and to take their grain to the new mills. Its possible that landlords were encouraged into this more aggressive stance over mills not just because they saw it as a neglected opportunity, but because the switch out of grain rents into cash had produced a fundamental change in how grain was processed. So long as tenants paid large amounts of grain into estates as rent, then having a centrally sited mill to grind what became the chief's or landowner's grain may have been deemed sufficient.[78] With the conversion of such rents, tenants may have turned to farm-based solutions. In other words, the greater interest shown in mills by landowners may have been an attempt to recover control not to extend it.

Whatever the reason, estates built more mills over the eighteenth century. The Argyll estate, for instance, enacted regulations against querns from the 1730s onwards, forcing tenants to use existing mills or mills which it set about constructing.[79] The estate's efforts were not successful for even on Tiree, many tenants still used the quern according to a report of 1788, despite the fact that the number of mills had recently been increased from one to three, with the mill at Crossapoll (reportedly unreliable due to irregular water flow) being supplemented by new mills at Cornaig and Scarinish.[80] The earlier cited memorandum for the Macdonald estate on Skye also saw the virtue of mills in those areas where only the quern was used. The Skye portions of the estate had mills by the 1730s, though extensive areas like Kilmuir were served by only one mill.[81] The memorandum also recommended that 'mills be contriv'd on Uist', meaning north Uist.[82] It also recommended that tenants be obliged to use mills not querns.[83] On South Uist, a mill seems to have been erected at Howmore during the middle decades of the century. The pressure which the estate put on tenants to use the new mill at Howmore led to a prolonged dispute towards the close of the century. The documentation surrounding the dispute explained how the barony court had forbidden the use of querns and how the the miller himself had forcibly removed querns from some townships.[84] Most tenants also used querns on Lewis yet new regulations issued shortly after the turn of the century thirled tenants to the proprietor's mills 'whenever the proprietor shall erect one therein'.[85] The attention which estates gave to the replacement of querns with mills could of course be seen as an improvement. Yet given how much it burdened many smaller tenants with extra costs at a time when margins were being tightened, one can just as easily see it as an example of how many landowners, including traditional landowners, were under much more pressure by the mid-eighteenth century to think as landlords, maximising the rental income of their estates.

In fact, we can see this concerted pressure over milling as simply one of a number of ways in which landowners began to think and behave as landlords, putting in place strategies of management that maximised rental income. We can, for example, marshall a similar argument as regards distilling and brewing, and the efforts made by a number of estates over the eighteenth century to eradicate illicit distilling and to concentrate whisky and ale production at the growing number of official ale houses and changehouses that were erected by estates such as the Macdonald and Islay estates over the eighteenth century.[86] The growing interest in the commercial possibilities of kelp production from the 1750s onwards was another indication of how estates were now looking to exploit resources to the full. As Gray has shown, landlords acted to control production and marketing almost from the very beginning, reserving the right to cut kelp for the estate.[87] Its impact on estate income was as much indirect as direct. As kelp production boomed during the closing years of the eighteenth century, landlords in those areas where kelp production was well established (i.e. the Uists) began to rack-rent smallholdings, thereby forcing smallholders and cottars to raise extra cash through kelp-making. As with other areas of the estate economy, landowners were using the instrument of rent increases to drive change. When we put such strategies down beside other changes, we can see just how far landowners now thought as landlords, long before the sheep clearances provided a more dramatic indication of their changing values.

NOTES

1. For comment, see Macinnes, 'Crown, clans and fine', p. 43. An overview of the early cattle trade is also provided by Shaw, *The Northern and Western Islands*, pp. 155–7.
2. Masson (ed.), *RPC, x, AD1607–1610*, p. 757.
3. *APS*, ii, 249, c3.
4. *APS*, iv, June 29th, 1598, p. 161.
5. Smith, *Jacobite Estates of the Forty-Five*.
6. Skene, *Celtic Scotland*, iii, p. 440.
7. McNeill (ed.), *ERS, vii, AD1537–1542*, p. 644.
8. Lamont, 'The Islay charter of 1408', p. 182.
9. Examples are provided by CDC/MP, GD221/118 Judiciall Rental of the Macdonald Estates in the Isle of Skye, 1733.
10. Burnett (ed.), *ERS, xii, AD1502–7*, pp. 703–4.
11. Ibid., p. 704.
12. *APS*, iii, 1585.
13. *APS*, iv, 1607, p. 379.
14. *APS*, iv, 1593, p. 40.
15. *APS*, iv, 1597, p. 138.
16. *APS*, iv, 1597, p. 138.
17. *APS*, iv, 1598, p. 160.
18. *APS*, iv, 1600, p. 248; Mackenzie, *History of the Outer Hebrides*, pp. 171–235.
19. Brown (ed.), *RPC, vii, 1605–6*, pp. 360–2.
20. Masson (ed.), *RPC, ix, 1610–1613*, pp. 26–30. Macinnes rightly observes that legislating away so-called household men, or buannachan, was extremely difficult in practice, see Macinnes, *Clanship, Commerce and the House of Stuart, 1603–1788*, pp. 67–70.
21. *APS*, iv, 29 June 1598.
22. Masson (ed.), *RPC, x, 1613–1616*, pp. 773–81.
23. Ibid., p. 775. The term 'mains' does occur in the Highlands and Islands. Ormclete, on south Uist, was described as Clanranald's 'Mains or Lands about ye Mannour' but it was reported as 'waste' in 1718, see SRO, Clanranald papers, GD201/5/1257/5, Rental of Clandranald's Estate in South Uist, 1718.
24. Masson (ed.), *RPC, x, 1613–1616*, p. 775.
25. Ibid., p. 777.
26. Mackenzie, *History of the Outer Hebrides*, p. 278.
27. SRO, Campbell of Barcaldine Muniments, GD1170/420/1/6 Rental of Portcharran 1758.

28. SRO, Forfeited Estates, E744/1, Judiciall Rental of the Estate of Clanranald, 1748, Tack for the Ten Pennyland of North and South Garrivaltos.
29. DC/MDP, 2/485/26/3, Judiciall rentals of the Baronies of Durinish, Waternish, Bracadale and Minginish, 1664.
30. Ibid., 2/8, Acts of Court, April 29th, 1735, Conditions for Tacksmen.
31. Ibid., 2/16, Tack laird of Macleod to Alexander McLeod of Ulinish, 1754.
32. CDC/MP, GD221/3695/4, 'Memorandm. c.1730s.' For a different perspective on the process of conversion, see Shaw, *The Northern and Western Islands*, p. 67; Withers, *Gaelic Scotland*, pp. 207–10.
33. The kind of debate that must have taken place over how much meal should be paid by townships during times of scarcity, when townships had less surplus but prices were high, is shown by the letter written in 1697 by the earl of Breadalbane about the rests that should be allowed to the tenants of Netherlorne; SRO, Campbell of Barcaldine, GD170/629/68, Letter, 26 March 1697.
34. SRO, Breadalbane Muniments, GD112/9/3/3/20 Rental of the Earl of Breadalbane's estates in Argyllshire 1795.
35. IC/AP, Bundle 2532, Accompt of Charge and Discharge ... estate of Appin including Glencoe, 1715 and 1716.
36. Ibid., Instructions for Archibald Campbell ... Chamberlain of Tyrie, 10 Oct. 1748.
37. Smith, *Wealth of Nations*, i, p. 19.
38. Johnson, *Journey to the Western Islands*, p. 129.
39. McNeill (ed.), *ERS, vol. xvii, AD 1537–1542*, p. 644.
40. A good illustration of this is provided by SRO, Cromartie Papers, GD305/1/63, Rentals 1612–1824, no. 141, A General rental of Ld. Cromarties estate 1735.
41. SRO, Breadalbane Muniments, GD112/9/3/3/20, Rental of the Earl of Breadalbane's Estates in Argyleshire, 1795, shows Luing as still paying 260 bolls of meal and 41 bolls of bere, and Seil as paying 62 1/2 bolls of meal and 22 bolls of bere. For comparison, a rental of 1665 notes Luing as paying 279 bolls of meal and 53 bolls of bere.
42. Ibid., GD112/9/5/10/2, Rental of Breadalbane 1733.
43. DC/MDP, 2/485/6, Rental of the Skye estate in 1683. The Silver Rent ... for the Crop and yeare 1683.
44. Ibid., 2/485/26/3, Judiciall Rental of the Barony of Durinish, 1724; ibid., 2/490/9, Judiciall Rentall of the barronnie of Duirinish, 1724.
45. Ibid., 2/490/10, Rentall of the Barony of Duirinish, 1744.
46. Ibid., 2/48728 and 29, Rental of Harris, 1754.
47. CDC/MP, GD221/118, Judicial Rental of the Macdonald Estates in the Isle of Skye, 1733.
48. SRO, Clanranald Papers, GD201/5/1257/5, Rental of Clanranald's Estate in South Uist, 1718.
49. IC/AP, RHP 8826/2 A general description of the Island of Tiriy, Surveyed 1768, James Turnbull, copy also in SRO.
50. Ibid., Bundle 2530, Instructions His Grace the Duke of Argyll to David Campbell his Chamberlain of Kintyre 1761.
51. DC/MDP, 2/20, Tack to Ross for 'change at Snizort with the privilege of brewing malting vending and Distilling all sorts of Legal Spirits and Liquors thereon', 1754.
52. SRO, Campbell of Jura Papers, GD64/1/86/7, Rental of Archibald Campbell Jura Estate 1764.
53. SRO, Breadalbane Muniments, GD112/9/5/8/26, Remarks on the property of Breadalbane 1722.
54. I am conscious here that despite what has been written about peasant value systems by some anthropologists, nevertheless, some economic historians have

argued that the propensity to maximise self-interests, to work for maximum gain, is universal amongst such societies. See, for example, the recent review by A. Offner, 'Between the gift and the market: the economy of regard', pp. 450–76.

55. Innes (ed.), *The Black Book of Taymouth*, pp. 268–99.

56. Masson (ed.), *RPC, vi, 1599–1604*, p. 184 refers to cattle belonging to Mackenzie of Kintaill and one of his tenants being stolen whilst on the way to Glamis fair, 1600.

57. SRO, Clanranald Papers, GD201/1/54, Contract between earl of Seaforth and Edinburgh burgess, James Barnis, for 1500 Lewis kine, 1641.

58. SRO, Clanranald Papers, GD201/1/115, Contract between Donald Macdonald, Captain of Clanranald, and Alexander McMillane of Dunmore and Donald McNeill of Creif. For a discussion of how the early droving trade was organised on Islay, see Shaw, *The Northern and Western Islands*, pp. 155–7. See also Innes (ed.), *Book of Cawdor*, pp. 351–2.

59. SRO, Cromartie Papers, GD305/1/119, Acct of the Milk Cows uplifted from the tennents of Coigach at Beltane 1691 and given to a Bowmen.

60. NLS, Sutherland Papers, DEP 313/918, Rent book and tacks 1708–14 and 6494/21, Accompt Charge and Discharge Alexr. Gordon of Ardoch, 1724; ibid., 649/19, Memorial anent Captain Ross, 1724. A comparative instance of the estate raising a drove is provided amongst the Campbell of Cawdor papers. In 1689, Sir John Campbell of Cawdor wrote that 'I vill raise a drov on my own venture and give the tennents a resonable pryce', see Innes (ed.), *Book of Cawdor*, p. 378.

61. IC/AP, Instructions for Archibald Campbell ... Chamberlain of Tyrie, 10 Oct. 1748.

62. SRO, Clanranald Papers, GD201/1/115, Cattle receipts.

63. Mackenzie, *History of the Outer Hebrides*, p. 536. In a letter written by McAulay, 1722, he also reported 'acquavitae received in January for a considerable part of the money rent' for Lewis, SRO, Forfeited Estates, E655/26, Letters 1721–30. Good data and comment on the use of cattle as a 'money-stuff' is also provided by Gray, 'Economic welfare and money income in the Highlands, 1750–1850', pp. 51–3; Shaw, *The Northern and Western Islands*, pp. 115–6. Shaw makes fine use of testamentary evidence to establish the sort of stock and crop that some tenants possessed. She shows, ibid., pp. 116–17, that stock were by far the most valuable component by the seventeenth century.

64. McKay (ed.), *Walker's Report on the Hebrides*, p. 65.

65. Some estates feued or wadset sizeable portions of particular districts. Good examples are provided by Muckairn and the Braes of Lorne, see Cawdor Castle, Campbell of Cawdor Papers, Bundle 655, Rental of Muckairn, 1653; SRO, Breadalbane Papers, GD112/9/40, Rental of the Braes of Lorne, 1718. Work by Macinnes has provided a detailed analysis of the pattern of wadsetting and feuing in Argyllshire. His work is particularly valuable in showing not only the increasing rate of wadsetting and feuing over the seventeenth century, but in showing how grants of wadsets and feus occurred within the framework of the dominant clan, or clan Campbell, and were made largely to its leading members or the fine. The effect was to increase the number of small landowners, but not at the expense of the clan. Indeed, Macinnes suggests that it actually strengthened the cohesion of the clan. See Macinnes, 'Civil wars, inter-regnum and Scottish Gaeldom', pp. 58–69 but especially pp. 64–5; Macinnes, 'From clanship to commercial landlordism', pp. 170–85.

66. CDC/MP, GD221/3695/2, Memorial of the Abuses in the present Management of Macdonald's Estate, 1733. The memorial notes the favourable rates at which wadsetters had their land and describes them as 'having the best farms on the Estate'.

67. SRO, John Macgregor Collection, GD50/93. Genealogy of Campbell of Glenurchay.
68. Typical examples are provided by MacDonald and MacDonald, *The Clan MacDonald*, i, pp. 133–4; Mackenzie, *History of the Clan Mackenzie*, p. 119; Logan, *The Scottish Gael*, i, pp. 177–8. Usually, the foster child was given a herd of milk cattle whilst the foster parent had the produce as a reward, though they could also get land as well. Thus, Lauchlan McVcMartin, a tenant in Ballemenoch (Mull), 'declared himself' in 1678–9 to have 'another toune called Ormsaig quhich he hade in ferme for fostering Brolass sone and that the said roum is stocked with 40 head of catell belonging to the Chyld', IC/AP, B/4/46, Disarming of Mull, etc, in the winter of 1678–1679.
69. CDC/MP, GD221/3695/2, Memorial of the Abuses in the present Management of Macdonald's Estate, 1733.
70. Culloden was scathing about tacksmen on Tiree, referring to 'the tyranny of taxmen' (p. 88) and their 'unmerciful exactions' (p. 89); see Forbes of Culloden's Letter concerning the Duke of Argyll's estates in Tiree, Morvern and Tiree, 24 Sept., pp. 389–92. According to Cregeen, Culloden overstated the case against tacksmen. However, his own analyses show that before 1737, Tiree tacksmen received a money rent that was 30 per cent above the tack duty paid to the earl; Cregeen, 'Tacksmen and their successors', p. 101.
71. CDC/MP, GD221/3695/2, Memorial of the Abuses in the present Management of Macdonald's Estate, 1733.
72. SRO, Breadalbane Muniments, GD112/11/1/1/14, Petition for the Tennants of Toyer, etc., 1722.
73. Lang (ed.), *Highlands of Scotland in 1750*, p. 39. See also comments by Smith, *Wealth of Nations*, i, pp. 151 and 222; Johnson, *Journey to the Western Isles*, pp. 87 and 94. Johnson described Highland rents as 'raised with too much eagerness', p. 94.
74. Adam, 'The Highland Emigration of 1770', pp. 80–93.
75. DC/MDP, 22/105/1–2, Statement about Glenelg, 1776 and which tenants had left since leases were granted.
76. The general presence of mills on an estate like the Breadalbane estate even by the late seventeenth century is well shown by early rentals such as SRO, Breadalbane Muniments, GD112/9/33, Rental of the estate 1688, which records eight in the Perthshire portion of the estate. By 1736, 15 were recorded, ibid., GD112/9/44, rental of the Earl of Breadalbane's Estate in Perthshire, 1736. Where such mills existed, tenants were thirled to them as a matter of routine. Court by-laws re-inforced thirlage, such as that passed in 1683 binding all the tenants and cottars in 'the Lordshipe of Apinadull barrondrie of Menzies' not to send 'thaire grindable Cornes to any miller to be ground but that quhich they are thirled to (except it be in the caise of ane strait and being necissidet be reason of ane storme or ane great douth thaire own mill wanting water), see SRO, John MacGregor Collection, GD50/35, Barony Court Books – Menzies and Rannoch, 16 Jan. 1683.
77. A 1723 list of townships in Ardnamurchan and Sunart shows only one mill, or that at Achateny. See Murray of Stanhope, *True Interest*, appendix a. To judge from a rental of 1743, only one mill existed on MacLaine of Lochbuy's estate, see SRO, MacLaine of Lochbuie Papers, GD174/715, Rentall of the Estate of Lochbuy, 1743. Coigach reportedly had no mills in the 1750s, see SRO, Forfeited Estates, E746/151, General report on Estate of Cromarty, c.1755.
78. Though this may have been a factor, the balance of evidence suggests that the real problem was the absence of mills in the more remote areas. Certainly, there are ample signs that some of the mills being built were new mills designed to

replace the previous use of querns. See, for example, CDC/MP, GD221/3695/4, Memorandm, ND (probably 1730s).

79. IC/AP, Bundle 663, Instructions by His Grace, the Duke of Argyll ... to Mr. Campbell of Airds, factor of Morvern, 17 Feb. 1733.

80. SRO, RHP8826/2 A General description of the Island of Tiry, Surveyed by George Turnbull, 1768; IC/AP, Observations on Tirie by Minister McColl, 4 July 1788.

81. The mill for the Kilmuir district is referred to in tacks, see CDC/MP, 4277/5/3, Tack for Kilivaxter, Peinmuch, etc., 1734.

82. Ibid., GD221/3695/4, Memorandm. c.1730s.

83. Ibid.

84. SRO, Clanranald Papers, GD201/1/351/12, Report as to Sundry Matters in South Uist.

85. SRO, Seaforth Papers, GD46/1/278 Articles of Set and Regulations for the Tenants ... in Lewis. Attempts to control the use of querns was not confined to the Hebrides. Even in 1740, tenants on the Lude estate in Perthshire were warned against possessing querns, see SRO, John MacGregor Collection, GD50/159, Baron Baile Courtts of Robertson of Lude from the year 1621 to 1806, 9 Dec. 1740.

86. The scale of their growth is well shown by the 17 official changehouses reported on Islay in 1765, Smith (ed.), *The Book of Islay*, p. 483.

87. Gray, *The Highland Economy 1750–1850*, pp. 124–37. The role played by estates in marketing is well shown by an early memorandum for the Macdonald estate which talked about the efforts that should be made to sell its kelp in Newcastle, CDC/MP, GD221/3695/5, Memorandum Anent Sir Alexr. Macdonalds Affairs, 1739. The extent to which kelp production conflicted with the traditional use of seaweed for manure, even though each favoured different types of seaweed, is brought out by *OSA*, xiii, p. 330; SRO, AF49/2A, Valuation of the Estate of Ardnamurchan and Sunart, 1807.

6 The Farming Township and the Institutional Basis of Farming

The basic socio-economic unit in the farming landscape prior to the changes of the late eighteenth and early nineteenth centuries, the unit around which the life of the vast majority of society was organised, was the farming township. Yet despite being a core institution of the region, there is a case for arguing that its basic character has been misrepresented in the literature. Some have depicted it as a deep-rooted, archaic institution. With its runrig layout of landholding and communal ordering of farming practice, it has been seen as the focus for a complex web of old-established techniques and customs that were sustained, without change, generation after generation. For commentator after commentator, it symbolised the profound maturity of Highland culture and provided us with – to adapt Kenneth Jackson's phrase – 'a window on the Iron age'.[1] Descriptions of the township's physical appearance as an irregular amorphous cluster, merging imperceptibly into the environment around it, served to create the impression that it grew out of the landscape, a human landscape that could match the claims of its physical landscape to being one of the oldest landscapes of its type in Europe. James Loch was not alone when he noted in his report on Assynt, 1829, that 'coming suddenly near one of these little towns' at Clachtoll, they found the houses 'so low and so much of the colour of adjoining Rocks and the cultivation so scanty that it is not until one is close to them they distinguish them from the adjoining mountains'.[2]

Yet despite the range of support which it has received across the years, the classification of the Highland farming township as an archaic survival is based more on assumption than on hard and fast evidence. In particular, two interconnected ideas have been used to sustain it. First, it was assumed that the farming community embodied in the township was essentially the clan at work, just as feasting and feuding were the clan at play. To put this another

123

way, the farming township was seen as bonded by the same ties of kinship and amity as the wider clan, ties which provided it with its organising principles of equity and sharing. Once constituted in kinship terms, it became but a simple step to assume that runrig communities were devolved in a direct and uncomplicated way from early tribal or Iron age farming groups and their tribal possession of land.[3] A second assumption, again based on a misconception, was that the regular, even annual reallocation of land or strips between members of the farming or township community was driven by a socially based desire to maintain an absolute equality between all landholders as a matter of principle. Tenurial or agrarian reasons for reallocation were not considered.

Quite apart from sitting uncomfortably beside the evidence that is available to define the Highland farming township, these assumptions about the deep-rootedness of its basic institutional character have had the effect of closing the debate about its experience of change during the historic period. Questions which we should be posing about its character and how it responded to the many problems and pressures of change have not been posed, let alone answered. Though there is no Pandora's box of undiscovered data about farming townships which can answer these questions directly, there is sufficient for the period between the sixteenth and early nineteenth centuries for us to establish that the traditional farming township was neither a uniform nor a static form.

HOW WERE TOWNSHIPS CONSTITUTED?

The primary question that we need to ask of the farming township is how it was constituted. What defined the township in a unitary or corporeal sense? Was it first and foremost a socially based unit, defined simply as those who opted to farm as a group because of social ties, i.e. kinship? Alternatively, was it an economically based unit, defined by the mix of resources which individuals, living side by side, had brought into use together and whose exploitation was, for purely economic reasons, best seen as shared owing to the demands made by the maintenance of ploughteams and the like? Both these approaches provide us with a tenant's view of how townships were constituted, a view that stresses the advantages that tenants themselves may have derived from coming together as farming communities. As interpretations of the township, though, each could also have been affected by the patchiness of Highland resources, and the way arable was broken down into pockets or, at best, strips of cultivable valley ground or coastal soils. In such circumstances, the efforts of farmers would have been in some way circumscribed when there was pressure for growth, encouraging them to intensify the farming of what they already had or to share it more effectively, as much as to expand outwards onto less productive sites.

An alternative is to see the broad pattern of townships as shaped from above, either as a by-product of the need to break down territorial schemes of fiscal assessment so as to create a more localised unit of assessment for burdens and renders, or as a simple by-product of an estate's need to break down its gross resources into appropriate units of set. Of course, these two top-down forms of township order may be linked, with estates using local units of assessment as the basis for setting land or vice-versa. Again though, the patchwork nature of local resources may have been a contributory factor, helping to explain why townships in areas like the western side of South Uist or on Tiree extended to a whole tirunga, or the equivalent of 20 pennylands, whilst on the western fringe of the mainland, townships rated as only a pennyland were to be found.

Each of these perspectives can reveal something about the constitutive nature of townships but in the final analysis, any real understanding of their formative character lies not so much in trying to stress one factor at the expense of another but in asking how the different dimensions fitted together. To this end, I want to use this chapter to explore the notion of the township in its various guises: as a community, a working group, a unit of resource, a unit of assessment and a tenurial unit.

TOWNSHIPS AS COMMUNITIES

Townships appear, first and foremost, as small communities of landholders. In establishing the scale of these communities, we have to negotiate a number of problems, notably, the extent to which the presence of tacksmen concealed the true size of the farming community. The term 'tacksman' occurs freely in early rentals and refers to the individuals, often members of the chief's family or one of its cadet branches, who held a written lease or tack for a township or cluster of townships, or simply for a portion of a township. Even if the term 'tacksmen' may only extend back to the fairly late spread of written tacks or leases, the military and economic roles played by such locally dominant individuals must extend back further still.

In most cases, tacksmen are thought to have sub-let part of what they held to sub-tenants, usually without a written tack, so that a rental that simply lists tacksmen may conceal the true size of the farming community. The extent to which they do so is further complicated by the fact that the role of tacksmen was not stable. If we analyse sixteenth-century rentals for those areas that had formed part of the Lordship of the Isles, we find that it was common for tacksmen to hold clusters of townships (see Table 6.1). This is well shown by rentals for Kintyre. South Kintyre, especially, had a high proportion of townships held as part of a larger group. In 1505, 17 tenants held 68 townships between them out of the 94 listed, an average of four each, though some individuals, like Colin McKacherne, held significantly more than that figure. In 1541, the number of tacksmen holding more than one township had risen to 22 but their average holding had fallen to an average of only 3.77 townships each. Despite the smaller average size of these township clusters, though, they embraced a higher proportion of townships than in 1505. By

TABLE 6.1. Multiple tenant townships: sixteenth century

	Year	Number of townships	Number held by single tenants	Number of township clusters	Average cluster size	Number held by multiple tenants	Average number of multiple tenants per township
Ardnamurchan	1541	28	27	7	3.4	1	2
Morvern	1541	28	25	5	2.2	3	2
Aros	1541	10	6			4	2
Tiree	1541	22	8	0	0	14	3.5
Colonsay	1541	14	14	1	14	0	
Islay – Insula	1541	38	35	6	4	3	2
Islay – Mid Ward	1541	55	54	13	2.69	0	
Islay – Rhinns	1541	49	46	11	2.63	1	2
Jura	1541	11	11	1	11	0	
North Kintyre	1541	50	48	15	2.4	1	2
South Kintyre	1541	95	89	23	3.69	6	2.3
Breadalbane	1594	20	10			10	2.3
South Kintyre	1596	80	58	10	5.8	22	3.6

Sources: McNeill (ed.), ERS, xvii, AD 1537–1542, pp. 634–50; Innes (ed.), The Black Book of Taymouth, pp. 268–95.

1596, the trend towards more multiple township tacksmen had reversed itself. Now only ten tacksmen held more than one township, but the average number of townships involved had risen to 6.5 townships each. A similar pattern, at least for 1541, can be found in other areas that that once formed part of the Lordship. In Ardnamurchan, for instance, most of the 28 townships listed in its 1541 rental were held by tacksmen as part of a wider portfolio of townships, with seven tenants holding an average of 3.4 townships each.

Whilst we might suppose that most of these townships must have been further sub-divided between those who actually worked the land, early rental or tack data only acknowledges the existence of sub-tenants in exceptional circumstances. In fact, across all these sixteenth-century rentals, there are few indications of townships being shared between a community of farmers. Thus, on Islay, only four out of the 141 townships listed in its 1541 rental were recorded as shared between more than one tenant. Whatever else we can or cannot say from these rentals, all we really see through them are glimpses of a socio-political rather than an agrarian landscape. As regards those areas that formed part of the Lordship, the one exception to this generalisation was Tiree. Out of 22 townships recorded in its 1541 rental, 14 were held by more than one tenant, averaging 3.57 tenants each. Elsewhere, late sixteenth-century rentals for the Breadalbane estate also provide glimpses of multiple tenancies, with a number of townships covered by its rentals for 1582 and 1594 being held by two or three tenants.

When we set this sixteenth-century data besides that for the seventeenth and eighteenth centuries, restricting the eighteenth-century data to those rentals compiled prior to any clearances, we can discern two broad trends (see Table 6.2). First, the degree to which tacksmen were set clusters of townships had declined, but had not disappeared. Even in the early eighteenth century, we can still find individual tenants holding small clusters of townships in areas like Ardnamurchan.[4] In terms of the number of townships involved, though, the primary role for tacksmen by this point was as the tack-holders of single townships. On the Macdonald estate on Skye, for example, 66 out of the 99 townships listed in a rental of c.1718 were set to single tenants even though multiple tenancy was said to be widespread throughout the estate.[5] In Morvern, all but two townships were set to single tenants or tacksmen in a rental of 1755.[6] Arguably, this shift towards a more prescribed role for tacksmen reflects a long-term decline in their political role, a decline in place before landowners acted to remove tacksmen altogether in the eighteenth century.[7]

The second broad trend concerns what rentals can tell us about townships set directly to multiple tenants. As Table 6.2 shows, when compared to those available for the sixteenth century, rentals for the seventeenth and eighteenth centuries record significantly more townships as held by multiple tenants, with rentals for quite a number of areas now listing a majority of townships as held by multiple rather than by single tenants (for example the MacLean

TABLE 6.2. Multiple tenant townships: seventeenth–eighteenth centuries

	Year	Number of townships	Number held by single tenants	Number held by multiple tenants	Average number of multiple tenants per township
Breadalbane	1620	19	9	10	2.5
Islay	1633	194	129	63	3.5
South Kintyre	1636	83	6	77	4.45
North Kintyre	1636	33	2	31	5.15
Colonsay	1642	14	4	10	3.6
Tiree	1662	32	12	20	6.7
Muckairn	1653	13	9	4	3.5
Netherlorne	1667	15	2	13	5.3
Islay	1670	177	107	70	4.12
Morvern	1671	15	14	1	2
Reay	1671	66	16	50	4.06
Mull	1678	38	2	36	4.13
Ulva	1678	10	2	8	3.37
Gometra	1678	4	0	4	6
Lochbuie	1678	27	3	24	3.08
Duirinish	1683	16	10	6	7.6
Waternish	1683	11	5	6	5.8
Duirinish	1683	23	15	8	6.87
Breadalbane	1683	95	8	87	3.29
Waternish	1686	10	5	5	8.4
Islay	1686	237	148	85	3.56
Breadalbane	1688	153	68	85	3.02
Moydart	1692	13	7	6	2.33
Arisaig	1692	12	5	7	3.85
Arisaig	1699	14	9	5	2.6
Netherlorne	1704	35	9	26	4.73
Netherlorne	1709	34	10	24	4.29
Strathpeffer	1717	11	3	8	3.9
Kintail	1718	35	30	5	2
Lochalsh	1718	44	37	7	3
Lewis	1718	72	44	28	8.8
North Uist	1718	36	21	15	7.8
Lochowside	1718	8	2	6	3.1
South Uist	1718	30	13	17	4.9
Arisaig	1718	21	11	10	3.5
Moydart	1718	19	12	7	4.7
Eigg	1718	8	1	7	3.5
Trotterness	c.1718	99	63	36	4.62
South Uist	1721	14	7	8	10.1
Strathnaver	1724	27	19	8	3.5
Kildonan	1724	19	7	12	5.41
Minginish	1724	22	18	4	2

TABLE 6.2. Multiple tenant townships: seventeenth–eighteenth centuries *continued*

	Year	Number of townships	Number held by single tenants	Number held by multiple tenants	Average number of multiple tenants per township
Waternish	1724	18	9	9	7
Duirinish	1724	32	26	6	4.16
Bracadale	1724	22	20	2	4.5
Coigach	1725	19	10	9	0
Arnamurchan	1725	20	16	4	5
Netherlorne	1730	32	8	24	4.66
Ardtallanage	1736	20	4	16	3.31
East End of Lochtay	1736	36	13	23	3.78
Easter Ardownage	1736	12	3	9	3.11
Glendochart	1736	10	8	3	6.33
Glenlochay	1736	23	11	12	3
Morinish	1736	11	4	7	5.14
Finlarig & Tirarthur	1736	7	1	6	3.6
Carwhin	1736	8	2	6	3.5
Cranich	1736	5	1	4	4.75
Lawers	1736	18	3	15	3
Arisaig (Strath)	1739	12	0	12	5.5
Arisaig (Braes)	1739	13	0	13	3.8
Sanda	1749	10	1	9	3.11
Harris	1754	17	9	8	4.12
Morvern	1754	19	15	4	2
Coigach	1755	28	18	10	4.4
Barrisdale	1744	18	5	13	2.6
Strathpeffer	1755	18	10	8	4.75
Strathyre	1755	14	3	11	3.45
Struan	1755	40	5	35	5
Stratherrick	1755	31	31	0	0
Lovat	1755	52	25	27	4.2
North Uist	1764	40	25	15	11.5
Tiree	1768	34	3	30	7.51
Barrisdale	1771	14	2	12	2.6
Glenelg	1773	21	8	13	5.6
Assynt	1775	31	15	16	8.2
Harris	1778	14	6	8	4.2
Breadalbane	1780	196	48	148	3.66
Coigach	1785	33	15	18	4.5
Bracadale	1789	11	11	0	0
Minginish	1789	15	9	6	5.16
Glenelg	1789	21	9	12	5.3
Duirinish	1789	29	18	11	7.18
Waternish	1789	11	5	6	9.6
Minginish	1792	13	7	6	5.16

TABLE 6.2. Multiple tenant townships: seventeenth–eighteenth centuries *continued*

	Year	Number of townships	Number held by single tenants	Number held by multiple tenants	Average number of multiple tenants per township
Glenorchy	1794	44	28	15	2.8
Luing	1794	8	2	6	4.8
Netherlorne	1794	17	11	6	4.5
Lochowside	1794	9	4	5	2.8

Sources: Macphail (ed.), *Highland Papers*, iii, pp. 75–81; SRO, Breadalbane Muniments, GD112/9/9; ibid., GD112/9/3/3/3; ibid., GD112/9/5/17/7; ibid., GD112/9/35; ibid., GD112/9/1/3/48; ibid., GD112/9/43–44; ibid., GD112/9/54; ibid., GD112/9/3/3/20; Smith (ed.), *The Book of Islay*, appendix iii; IC/AP, Bundle 746; ibid., Box 2531; Cawdor Castle, Campbell of Cawdor Papers, Bundle 655; Macphail (ed.), *Highland Papers*, i, pp. 285–88; MacKay (ed.), *The Book of Mackay*, pp. 471–5; IC/AP, Bundle 1009; DC/MDP, 2/485/6; ibid., 2/487/2; ibid., 2/485/26/3; ibid., 2/487/31; ibid., 2/493/8; ibid., 2/485/44; ibid., 2/105/1–2; ibid., 2/487/32; ibid., 2/485/55; ibid., 2/485/59; IC/AP, V62; SRO, Clanranald Papers, GD201/1/362/3; SRO, Cromartie Papers, GD305/1/63/116; MacDonald and MacDonald, *The Clan MacDonald*, iii, pp. 659–62; Macphail (ed.), *Highland Papers*, ii, pp. 313–33; SRO, Forfeited Estates, E655/1/3; SRO, Clanranald Papers, GD201/5/1257/1–5; SRO, Forfeited Estates, E656/2/2; ibid., E648/4; NLS, Sutherland Papers, DEP313/2133; NLS, ADV 25.1.1; CDC/MP, GD221/118; SRO, Clanranald Papers, GD201/1/227A; SRO, Campbell of Sanda, GD92/173; Gaskell, *Morvern Transformed*, pp. 124–5; SRO, Forfeited Papers, E729/3; IC/AP, RHP8826/1–2; Adam (ed), *Home's Survey of Assynt*, pp. 71–88.

of Duart estate on Mull, 1678, and the Reay Estate, 1671). Yet arguably their increased number reflects a change in the way estates set land, and the growing practice of setting it directly to those who farmed the soil, as much a change in the number of townships actually occupied by multiple tenants. If we calculate the number of tenants involved, using data only for those townships which record the presence of multiple tenants, then the average number of tenants per township works out at 2.37 for the sixteenth, 4.36 for the seventeenth, 4.54 for the early eighteenth and 4.95 for the late eighteenth century. If the averages are weighted according to the number of townships, they work out at 3.9 for the seventeenth, 4.6 for the early eighteenth and 4.77 for the late eighteenth century (see Table 6.2). The sample size for the sixteenth century makes it difficult to draw any firm conclusions from the apparent increase between it and the average for the seventeenth century, but when the latter is compared with the eighteenth century, it suggests that a modest increase in numbers may have taken place.

We can analyse these trends in greater detail by looking at data for individual estates and areas. In the south-west Highlands, rentals for Kintyre enable us to bring the perspective offered by early and mid-sixteenth-century Crown rentals forward into the seventeenth and eighteenth centuries. In the case of North and South Kintyre, we have a succession of rentals and tenant lists covering the sixteenth and seventeenth centuries. If we concentrate on rentals alone, they suggest that tacksmen formed the principal feature of Kintyre's tenurial structure throughout, with only a handful of townships set directly to multiple tenants in 1505, 1541, 1544, 1596 and 1605 (see Table 6.2). Furthermore, more so than in other areas, it was common for tacksmen to control more than one township. As already mentioned above, the 1505 rental shows 17 tacksmen held more than one township in South Kintyre, their combined holding accounting for 68 out of the 94 townships listed. Just how much may be concealed by the operation of such a system, though, is well shown by a list drawn up c.1636. Though labelled as a list of 'tenants and inhabitants', its primary object was to list the stock carried by townships. Given that all the individuals mentioned had stock of some sort, the list can be taken as a statement of those who were involved in farming the land to a greater or lesser degree. As a document, it offers a quite different perspective from that of rentals. Out of 33 townships in North Kintyre, only two appear to have actually been farmed by individuals. The rest were in the hands of multiple 'occupiers', with an average of 5.15 'occupiers' per township. In the case of South Kintyre, only six out of its 83 townships were farmed by single tenants. The rest were shared by an average of 4.45 'occupiers'. In terms of status, though, these 'occupiers' involved not only tacksmen or main tenants, but those to whom they sub-let shares, plus crofters and cottars or cottagers, who were allowed to graze a few cows, sheep or goats, that is, all those who grazed stock on the township's pastures.

A feature of the earlier 1605 rental especially is the number of townships recorded as lying 'waist', a sign of the unsettled conditions in Kintyre by the early seventeenth century. In response, the peninsula was soon after planted with tenants from the south-west of Scotland.[8] Such a change may well have encouraged the switch from the setting of township groups to tacksmen to the system more evident in the seventeenth century in which tacksmen tended to be set individual townships rather than groups of townships. What the 1636 list helps us to appreciate, albeit only through differences in stock-holding, is that whilst some tacksmen may have sub-let large sections of their tack, there were others who could only have sub-let small portions.[9]

In addition to the 1541 rental noted earlier, tenant numbers on Islay are covered by rentals for 1633, 1670, 1686 and 1733 (see Table 6.2). Though they do not relate to an exactly matched or consistent sample of townships, they suggest that tenant numbers fluxed rather than remained stable over the seventeenth and early eighteenth centuries. The 1633 rental lists 194 townships, of which 129 (65.7 per cent) were held by single tenants or tacksmen. The 63 held by multiple tenants were held by an average of 3.5 tenants. In the 1670 rental, the proportion of single-tenant townships had fallen, involving only 107 townships (59.9 per cent) out of a total of 177 townships. Not only had the number of multiple tenant townships now increased, but also, the average number of tenants in them had risen to 4.1 tenants. Of the 237 separate townships recorded in the 1686 list, one was recorded as waste,

three as 'put to the laird's cattle' and 148 (62.4 per cent) were recorded as
set to tacksmen. Some tacksmen still held small groups of two or three townships and a fair proportion were reported as feued or wadset to them, more
than in 1670. Of the 85 recorded as set to more than one tenant, most
involved between two and six tenants, the overall average now being only
3.56 tenants: these figures include a number of townships whose tenancy
may have been set to fathers and sons, or to brothers. Keppallis, with ten
tenants, was exceptional. In the later 1722 rental, 172 townships are listed,
of which 102 (59.3 per cent) are recorded as held by a single tenant or
tacksman. Amongst those set to multiple tenants, there is a noticeably higher
average number of tenants per township (4.61) when compared with 1686,
especially in Kildalton parish and in Killarow and Kilmanie parish. Again,
whether this represents a real increase in the number of tenants per township,
or merely a change in the way occupiers were being recorded is difficult to
say, but as will be shown later there are grounds for believing that numbers
in some townships were expanding by the eighteenth century. However, as
the data for the seventeenth century also shows, any overall change evident
between 1686 and 1722 would not have been part of a sustained trend. We
need only look at the Campbell of Cawdor estate's own analysis of tenant
occupancy and vacant possessions on Islay between 1703 and 1707, following King William's lean years, 1696–1703, to appreciate this.[10]

Tiree has a particularly good sequence of rentals from 1541 onwards, with
detailed tenant lists for 1652 and 1680, that is, before and after the earl of
Argyll took over most of the island from MacLean of Duart. Whereas the
1541 rental for Tiree noted only two or three tenants per township, the later
seventeenth-century Tiree rentals disclose townships, such as Ballevullume,
in which as many as ten or more tenants were resident. Further, the average
number of tenants in townships set directly to multiple tenants had risen
quite sharply from 3.5 in 1541 to 6.7 tenants per township in 1652 (Table
6.2). Even seen simply in terms of tenants, these were sizeable townships.
Alongside them, though, around one third of Tiree townships were recorded
in the 1541, 1652 and 1680 rentals as held by single tenants. The rental
provides some indication of the dynamics surrounding these different types
of townships. Ballemartin, for instance, was described as 'used to be set to a
gentlemen but now in the hands of small tenants'. Shallim had seemingly
moved in the opposite direction, being 'now possessed by a gentleman'.[11]
This distinction between townships set to 'gentlemen' and townships set to
'small tenants' occurs in other entries. It suggests that more was involved than
simply setting land to a tacksman or directly to those who worked the land.
In fact, if we look at the 1680 rental for the island, one is struck by the extent
to which townships held by more than one tenant were not always evenly
divided between them. Some involved significant numbers of multiple
tenants, but were quite clearly dominated by one or two individuals. When
we move forward into the eighteenth century, detailed rentals are available
for a number of years. A landholding survey compiled for 1768 is especially

detailed and can be used as the basis for a comparison with earlier data. It shows that by then, not only were more townships set directly to multiple tenants, but the average number of tenants in each had risen still further to 7.5.[12]

As rentals become more freely available for other estates, they too, draw a distinction between townships set to single tacksmen and others set to directly to groups of tenants. In a few cases, there is the hint of a geographical component to this contrast. Irrespective of the disguise that could be thrown over it by the tacksmen system, early rentals for the Harris portion of the MacLeod of Dunvegan estate suggest a fairly predictable contrast between those mainland townships, with smaller, more restricted resources of arable, and the islands that lay around its south-western edges, which had much greater resources of arable. Generally speaking, the more arable a township possessed, the more tenants it possessed. The 1687 rental for Harris, for example, shows that the smaller townships were generally set to single tenants or, at most, to two or three tenants. Thus, on the mainland, we find townships like Luskentyre, Selebost and Borromor all set to a single tenant or tacksman.[13] Even the Two Scaristas, easily the largest townships on the mainland in terms of arable, were set to a single tenant, or Rorie Campbell, MacLeod's officer on Harris. The physically small townships that existed on islands like Scalpay and Taransay also carried few tenants, with Scalpay being held by two tenants, and Paible and Eye on Taransay also being held by two tenants and Raa by one. With the exception of Rodel, which, with its 19 tenants, was easily the largest township on Harris, most of the larger tenant groups recorded in the 1687 rental were located on islands like Pabbay and Ensay. On the former, Kirktown and Linga were set directly to eight and seven tenants, whilst Ensay was set to 11 tenants. Had the rental detailed how Sir Norman MacLeod sub-let his possession of Berneray, we would no doubt have found large townships there too, for it boasted over 1000 acres prior to the sandstorms of the late seventeenth century.[14] One further point worth noting about the Harris rentals is that their availability in fairly quick succession over the late seventeenth and early eighteenth centuries enables us to detect short-term changes. Where such a perspective is possible, it suggests a fairly regular but smallscale movement of tenants in and out of townships. We can see this best in regard to Pabbay. Despite its isolated position four to five miles out into the Atlantic, there was nothing fixed about tenant structures even during the late seventeenth century.[15]

Even before any switch into sheep farming and crofting, the tenurial structure of Harris appears to have shifted. When we come forward to rentals for the 1750s, 60s and 70s, we find only two townships recorded as carrying sizeable groups of tenants or 'in tenantry' as one rental puts it: Meikle (or North) Scarista and Kirktown of Pabbay.[16] In a list of tenants who had tacks from 1769 onwards, the former township had 14 listed tenants and the latter, eight.[17] For comparison, late seventeenth-century rentals list the former as held by a single tacksman.[18] In all probability, this apparent change represents the disappearance of the tacksmen rather than the appearance of a large community of tenants. In the case of other townships, the 1769 rental suggests an opposite trend. Ensay, for instance, was now held by a single tacksman, John Campbell, who was almost certainly the same John Campbell who held the adjacent island of Killegray with Strond and Luskentyre. Lingay and Northtown, along with St Kilda, were now held by Alexander Macleod as tacksman. A noteworthy feature of this particular rental is the number of tenancies listed as shared between either brothers, or fathers and sons, or cousins. Horgibost, for instance, was held by Dougald and John McAulay whilst eight of the 14 tenants listed for Meikle Scarista may have been related to one or more other tenants.

When we survey rentals for other parts of the MacLeod of Dunvegan estate, the distinction between townships held by a single tacksman and those set directly to groups of tenants is again evident (see Table 6.2). In Waternish, for instance, rentals from the late seventeenth century onwards always record townships like Halistra and Trumpanmore as held by multiple tenants whilst townships like Trumpanbeg and Bays were always recorded as held by a single tenant or tacksman. The earliest rental for Waternish, that for 1683, shows 6 out of the 11 townships listed as held by multiple tenants, with Halistra entered as held by 10 tenants and Trumpanmore by 7, whilst townships like Trumpanbeg were noted as held simply by a single tacksman, Donald MacAlister.[19] In rentals for 1684 and 1685, Trumpanmore was combined with its sister township, Trumpanbeg, with a total of 14 tenants in 1684 and 13 in 1685. However, rests of rent for these years show that only Donald MacAlister was liable for the rent of Trumpanbeg, the remaining tenants being attached to Trumpanmore.[20] A list of tenants for 1686 shows no basic change to this pattern. Trumpanbeg was noted as held by a single tacksman, Donald McAlister, whilst Trumpanmore was set down as held by 11 tenants.[21] This pattern of set continued into the eighteenth century. Townships like Trumpanbeg continued to be leased to a single tenant, whilst the same townships that had earlier been leased to multiple tenants, like Trumpanmore, continued to be held as such. In the detailed 1724 rental, 11 out of the 22 townships now listed for Waternish were held by multiple tenants. As in the 1683 rental, the largest were Halistra (15 tenants), Trumpanmore (12 tenants) and Gearie (10 tenants).[22] In 1754, Haldistra still carried 15 tenants but those in Trumpanmore and Gearie were down to eight tenants.[23] Data for Trumpanmore is not available over the late eighteenth century but that for Halistra suggests it maintained its position as the most crowded township in Waternish, its recorded number of tenants growing to 20 by 1792.[24] Significantly, a rental scheme drawn up in 1768 by the estate refers to townships like Halistra, Trumpanmore and Gearie as set to 'small tenants', suggesting that those recorded in rentals as set directly to multiple tenants were perceived as different.[25]

In many respects, the MacLeod of Dunvegan estate mirrors tenurial structures across the Hebrides at large. Once we get into the eighteenth century, available estate rentals enable us to take a broad cross-sectional view of the problem. The estates forfeited after the 1715 Jacobite rebellion had rentals compiled in 1718 or shortly after. Those for the Seaforth estate lands on Lewis, and in Kintail and Lochalsh, for the Macdonald lands on Skye and for the Clanranald estate lands on South Uist, Eigg, Rhum, Muck, Moydart and Arisaig are summarised in Table 6.2. As with the MacLeod of Dunvegan estate, they suggest a mixture of townships set to single tacksmen and townships set to multiple tenants. Again, as on the MacLeod of Dunvegan estate, some of the townships held by multiple tenants formed sizeable communities. This was especially true of the townships that lay strung out along the north-western coast of Lewis and of those that were located on the mix of machair and peat soils that lay along the western edge of both North and South Uist. Before assuming that these townships were more crowded than those elsewhere, we should bear in mind that late eighteenth-century survey data shows that those in North and South Uist especially were amongst the largest in the region, with arable acreages that were two or three times larger than those to be found on islands like Skye or in townships along the western edge of the mainland (Table 6.3). In other words, whilst they were larger socially, it does not automatically follow that they were more crowded with less arable per person than elsewhere.

Tenant numbers on Campbell of Glenorchy's estate can be reconstructed from the late sixteenth century onwards. The two earliest rentals, or those for 1582 and 1694, cover a small sample of townships in Glenorchy and Lochtayside. By the mid-seventeenth century, the coverage of the rentals is greatly broadened, embracing Netherlorne on the west and areas like Strathfillan on the east. Altogether, long-run data has been sampled for five main areas: Glenorchy, Lochtayside, Lochowside, the Braes of Lorne and Netherlorne, the latter including islands like Seil and Luing as well as the mainland portion of Netherlorne (see Table 6.2). What stands out about townships in the earliest rentals, all of which can be classed as pasture farms but which, even in the late sixteenth century, had modest arable acreages, is the high proportion of multiple tenant farms and the extent to which we are dealing with relatively small groups of tenants, few townships being occupied by more than three or four tenants. A 1683 rental illustrates these points well. Altogether, 83 out of the 95 townships listed in the rental were set directly to multiple tenants, the average being 3.29 tenants per township. However, there was a distinct tenurial geography to the estate by the 1680s. A list of tenant numbers drawn up in 1688 listed data for a much larger sample of townships, or 153, but the number of townships recorded as held by multiple tenants was still only 85, most of the townships in the new areas covered by the rental being held by single tenants.

Tabulating raw data from rentals is only part of the problem. We still have to decide on what exactly such data can tell us. The question of what can be said about single tenant townships, or townships set to a tacksman, revolves around the question of what they conceal. The standard assumption is that

TABLE 6.3. Arable per township

Barrisdale 1755	5.9
Kinloch 1755	15.9
Slisgarrow 1755	22.4
Coigach 1775	28
S. Lochtayside 1769	29.4
Fernan 1755	31.7
Strathyre 1755	36.5
N. Lochtayside 1769	46.6
Assynt 1772	55
Glenelg 1776	84
Sunart 1807	86
Ardnamurchan 1807	99.5
Macdonald Est. 1810	145
Arran 1772	103.8
Sanda 1789	113.5
Coll 1794	118
MacLeod Estate 1810	124.8
Kilmuir (Skye) 1799	135
Gigha 1747	137
Ness 1810	149
Tiree 1768	242
Harris 1772	278
Benbecula 1805	363
South Uist 1804	454

Sources: SRO, Seaforth Papers GD46/17/46, Contents of the Island of Lewis, Extracted from Mr. Chapman's Books of the Plans of Lewis, 1817; Dunvegan Castle, MacLeod of MacLeod Papers, 1/466/22 Contents of the Mainland of Harris and Adjacent Islands 1772; ibid., 1/380/29 Glenelg Survey; SRO, RHP 1039, Plan of the Island of Benbecula, 1805; NLS, Survey of South Uist by William Bald, 1805; SRO RHP 5990/1–4 Eastern Part of the Island of Skye, 1810, surveyed by John Bell; SRO, Clanranald Papers GD201/5/1235/1, Particulars of Sale – Egg, Canna and Sanday, 1824; SRO, RHP 3368, Plan of the Island of Coll, 1794, Surveyed by George Langlands; IC/AP, V65, Contents of the Different Farms of Tiree, by James Turnbull, 1768; SRO, RHP 72 Ardnamurchan and Sunart, the Property of Sir James Riddell, 1806 and AF49/1 Survey of Ardnamurchan and Sunart; SRO, Forfeited Estates, E741 Barrisdale – Reports Concerning Farms 1771, by William Morison; ibid., E746/189, Plans of Farms of Coigach, 1775, by William Morison; NLS Sutherland Papers, 313/3583 John Home's Survey of Assynt, 1774; *NSA*, XIV(1845), p. 210. All acreages in Scots acres.

tacksmen sub-let their townships to sub- or under-tenants, so that beneath them, we can expect to find 'normal' multiple-tenant or runrig townships. When, as in sixteenth-century Crown rentals, we see tacksmen holding clusters of townships, there can be little doubt that such townships were being sub-let to other tenants. In other words, such townships would have differed from other multiple tenant townships only in so far as they had an extra layer of landholding inserted into their tenurial structure, occupied by tacksmen. Certainly, when commentaries become more freely available over the eighteenth century, the stock criticism of tacksmen is that they had tenants beneath them whom they exploited, by extracting excessive rents or labour. Thus, rentals for townships in Coigach suggest only a few were held by multiple tenants, yet a report on the Cromarty estate drawn up in 1755 talked about the 'considerable Number of Sub-tennants, Maillers & Cottagers on this Estate, particularly in the Barony of Coygach'.[26]

As already suggested, though, we cannot ignore the fact that the role of tacksmen was subject to change. Though some areas need to be exempted from the generalisation, relatively few tacksmen had more than a handful of townships by the end of seventeenth century.[27] Indeed, some labelled as tacksmen in the rentals held only part of a single township. With their now diminished socio-political role, new opportunities were being adopted. Like chiefs, many were being drawn into a more commercial, cash-driven economy by the late seventeenth century. Macinnes has noted how tacksmen in Argyll were drawn more and more to commercial cattle production by the late seventeenth century.[28] Other strategies were also exploited, such as largescale bere and meal production. With these more commercial strategies may have come different tenurial structures. The possibility exists that some tacksmen were effectively gentleman farmers, farming the entire township, or a large proportion of it, in their own hands, using hired labour.

A limited amount of evidence exists for such an arrangement. Mention has already been made of how some tenants in areas like Kintyre and Tiree held a disproportionate share of townships, suggesting that their strategies of farming must have been quite different from those around them who farmed far smaller portions. The stocking lists for mid and north Argyll (1609) and for Kintyre (1636), with their listing of all tenants and inhabitants or occupiers, indicate that some townships were farmed by a single tenant or occupier and that others, though involving a number of occupiers with grazing-rights of some sort, appear to have been dominated by a single tenant.[29] Also relevant to this point is the way some references to tacksmen talk of them letting land not to sub-tenants but to cottars, a quite different sort of occupier normally asssociated with individuals who farmed small parcels in return for their labour.[30] Indeed, one contemporary comment asserted that, by definition, tacksmen kept most of the land in their own hands but let 'the skirts of the township' to cottars.[31] Assuming that some tacksmen were farming the land themselves may help enlarge on what was meant by the 1652 Tiree rental with its distinction between townships set to 'gentlemen' and those set to 'small tenants'. Indeed, the entry for the township of Hollife, held by the bailie, notes that he was not allowed to have 'sub-tenants'. Given that it was easily one of the largest townships on Tiree, equal to a tirunga, it could only have been worked with hired labour.[32] In fact, even where townships were set to fairly large numbers of tenants, imbalances could exist. According to the rental for 1652, the township of Caillig was set to 14 tenants, with four tenants holding over three-quarters of it and the rest holding barely enough to sow one or two bolls of grain.[33]

Establishing the existence of the various smallholders who helped to fill out the farming commmunity at Caillig is straightforward because they each were recorded in the rental, along with their respective shares in terms of *mails*. Elsewhere, those smallholders who held crofts were also recorded in rentals. Most of these crofts were tied to mills, brewseats, maltsters, black-smiths and the like. Some, though, appear to have been designed to provide more substantial tenants with a source of labour. Thus, in addition to those attached to mills and brewseats, the Breadalbane estate had quite a number of crofts located within the townships that lay along either side of Loch Tay. Extending to no more than an acre or so of arable, they were kept separate from the arable belonging to the main tenants of the township and were probably used as a source of labour by them.[34] A similar arrangement existed on Campbell of Glenure's estate on Lismore, with Killean and Achnackrosh each having a croft attached to them.[35] Being recorded in rentals, such crofts are easily detected. Less easily recorded are the cottars, cottagers and farm servants who had less formal agreements over what land they could sow but who were vital to the working of townships and to its character as a community, though some rentals, like that just mentioned for Glenure, or a 1730 rental analysis compiled by the Breadalbane estate for its Netherlorne portion, do sometimes specify the presence of cott-houses or cottars and confirm their significance.[36] The presence of all these groups means that whether townships appeared in rentals as held by a single tenant or a group of tenants, the reality on the ground would have been a small farming community.

Occasionally, sources enable us to go beyond the stark listing of tacksmen and tenants provided by rentals and to gauge the real scale of these communities. One of the most detailed consists of a series of lists of inhabitants for Rannoch covering the period from the mid-seventeenth century down to the mid-eighteenth century. Ostensibly designed to enable the court at Rannoch to keep a check on all males over 16, the lists provide some indication of the different types of person who made up the farming community in the Highlands, with tenants, cottars, servants and retired farmers all being listed (see Table 6.4).

Similar data is available for Tiree but only for one year. A detailed report drawn up in 1768 lists all the inhabitants to be found within each township, breaking them down into tenants and hinds, cottagers, men, women, boys and girls. The list provides us with a detailed indication of how the tenurial and wider social structure of Hebridean townships were linked. It confirms that some townships must have been farmed as single-tenant townships using hired labour, though the fact that the list was compiled after Duncan Forbes of Culloden's recommendation over the abolition of tacksmen limits the significance of this point. What stands out is that for virtually every township, there was a sizeable presence of cottagers together with a significant number of men and women who were 'neither tenants nor cottagers'. Overall, whilst the average number of tenants per townships worked out as 6.9, the total number of cottagers per township was exactly five (three men and two women each), whilst the average number of total inhabitants per

TABLE 6.4. Male inhabitants per township in Rannoch, 1660–1743

	1660	1664/5	1672	1683	1695	1698	1735	1739	1743
Ardlarich	12	10	6	11	17	14	12	13	19
Aulich	17	8	13	14	30	22	20		19
Camserachmore	5		10	10	7	13	13	13	15
Camserachbeg	7			11		5	12		20
Dounan	5	8	2	5	6	10	9	14	11
Kilchonan	6	3	4	11	8	7	9	14	21
Kinlochar	7	4	6	10	6	7	14	13	13
Learagan	8	6	6	7	14	6	5	4	
Liaran	6	6	6		10	19	10	6	8

Sources: SRO, John MacGregor Collection, GD50/156, Lists of inhabitants for 1660, 1683, 1692, 1695, 1698, 1735, 1739 and 1745; ibid., GD50/35, Barony Court Books – Menzies and Rannoch.

TABLE 6.5. Average number of inhabitants per township

	Persons per township	Families per township
Ardnamurchan (1723)	28.1	6.28
Sunart (1723)	19.75	3.35
Glenorchy (1730)		4.6
Coigach (1755)	40.9	5.9
Barrisdale (1755)	19.4	2.2
Tiree (1768)	49.2	
Assynt (1766)	40.9	
Assynt (1774)	40.9	8
Arran (Late 18th cent.)	39	8

Sources: Murray of Stanhope, *True Interest*, appendix; SRO, Breadalbane Muniments, GD112/16/12/3/1, Rentall of Glenorchy Shewing the present Rent … Holdings and Sowings, 1730; SRO, Forfeited Estates, E729/3, States of Various Farms 1755; IC/AP, V65, Contents of the Different Farms of Tiree, by James Turnbull, 1768; Adam (ed.), *Home's Survey of Assynt*, pp. 68–88; Brodick, Arran Estate Office, List of families and inhabitants, ND (assumed late eighteenth century).

township was 49.2. By any standards, the Tiree townships were large townships.[37] For comparison, a 1727 survey of Ardnamurchan shows an average number of inhabitants per township, including children, of only 29.9, whilst the same survey show the average number of inhabitants per township in Sunart was only 19.75.[38] If we set such figures beside an Ardnamurchan estate rental drawn up in 1725, it shows just how understated these farming communities might be when we are forced to see them through rentals. In the rental, only 36 tenants are listed. In the survey, the same townships carried a total of 957 people.[39] Similar late eighteenth-century data is available for both the Arran and Breadalbane estates. Again, when we calculate the average number of occupants per township (see Table 6.5), it shows how much rentals may conceal about the farming community in toto.

Relevant data on township occupancy for the MacLeod of Dunvegan estate is more restricted in character. However, it is still revealing. It consists of a listing of the men who were out 'in the service' during '45 and those who stayed at home. As with the data for Tiree, Ardnamurchan and Sunart, it sheds light on what may lie hidden in rentals. If we take two townships discussed earlier, Trumpanbeg and Trumpanmore, the former was noted in contemporary rentals as held by a single tenant, whilst the latter was held by multiple tenants. In the listing, the former had five men noted as 'in the service' and 11 who stayed at home, whilst the latter listed seven as in service and eight who stayed at home.[40] In some cases, such a listing can be used to prise open the clam-like nature of early sources, albeit just a little. To give an example, the northern tip of Waternish was occupied by the ten pennylands of Unish. From the late seventeenth century onwards, rentals record Unish as held by a single tacksman or ignored its existence altogether, even though it was the largest unit of assessment in Waternish, with a large and complex pattern of settlement at the tip of the peninsula plus a number of small outlying settlements along its western side about which successive rentals are absolutely silent. The '45 listing hints at what lies hidden, with five men recorded as 'in service' and eight as 'continuing at home'.[41]

TOWNSHIPS AS UNITS OF RESOURCE

In function, farming townships were units of resource exploitation. These units were turned into viable working units through the practical effort of communities, reclaiming, working and manuring the soil over many generations. For this reason, we would expect the pattern of local resource availability to have played a critical part in shaping the disposition of townships on the ground. Certainly when we take the earliest estate plans and look at the patchy, broken nature of arable and the marginality of so much hill or water-logged ground in the region, it is easy to see how the geography of environmental opportunity served to group or isolate, to align or constrain, to disperse or concentrate the layout of townships and their associated communities. Whatever else we can conclude about the human landscape of the western Highlands and Islands prior to the changes of the late eighteenth and early nineteenth centuries, it was one in which the composition of townships as regards their overall size and basic resources varied considerably from district to district if not between adjacent townships.

An indication of the broad differences that existed across the region as regards their actual composition and size can be gauged from survey data compiled over the late eighteenth and early nineteenth centuries. Most of these surveys were compiled in anticipation of change, but they serve to provide a last-minute glimpse of what traditional townships contained as regards resources. In aggregate, the surveys covers nearly a million acres and nearly 400 townships. If we see townships in terms of their arable resources (see Table 6.3), those that existed along the western seaboard and on inner Hebridean islands like Skye were the smallest, with townships only exceptionally having over 100 acres of arable. Though there were parts of the Hebrides that had townships whose arable acreage was equally modest, notably Lewis and Coll, there were also islands like Tiree, the Uists, and even Harris where the average size of township arable was much higher. On South Uist, township arable averaged 454 acres across the island, with some of the largest having over 800 acres. Even on Harris, visibly one of the most rugged of the Hebridean islands, townships had an average arable acreage per township of 278 acres according to a survey of 1772. This gross average, though, is deceptive, concealing the fact that mainland townships had very restricted arable acreages whilst townships on islands like Berneray, Pabbay, Killegray and Ensay, had large acreages. Simple averages hide a further difference between townships. In some cases, ground conditions allowed for a continuous, if irregularly-shaped, block of arable, whereas in other townships, arable was broken down into innumerable patches of arable by outcrops of rock, lochans, or waterlogged soil. Many surveys acknowledge this, devising categories of 'grass-arable' or, as on Harris, 'arable with the spade or pasture' in order to describe the intricately mixed land uses that prevailed on poor land.[42] Whatever else we conclude from the environmental setting of Highland townships, we cannot see it as conducive to any uniform or regular plan of layout. More so than in other any other environment in Britain, the basic realities of the farming landscape appear to have been pieced together in a very *ad hoc* and laborious way. Whilst it might be argued that the scattered, blocky nature of arable might have helped to bring farmers together into a community of effort, to focus their efforts around a few scattered sites, it could also be argued that its excessive scattering and fragmentation could have worked with equal effect in the opposite direction, creating a resource base more suited to the independent family than the community.

THE TOWNSHIP AS A WORKING COMMUNITY

It is a common supposition that open-field communities, runrig included, may derive their character from the fact that the farmers around whom they were organised *necessarily* shared the tasks of exploiting resources together, and that it is this need for sharing that generates their communal character. A range of evidence can be assembled on how runrig communities in the Highlands actually worked their land together, but as will be shown, there is little to suggest that this sharing underpinned runrig as a system of co-operative effort, despite references to them in some contemporary sources as 'club farms', such as in references to Cannisban, Galder and Coran in Glenelg.[43]

Some of the most interesting data is provided by those estates which operated a steelbow system of tenure, providing tenants with all the necessary farm gear, seed and stock needed to work the township. In a world of recurrent feuding, it is easy to see how such as arrangement might become essential if those tenants subjected to a repeated destruction of their byres and crops and to the theft of their stock were to maintain output. A primary feature of it was the organisation of townships around horsegangs or plough-teams, with tenants being responsible for portions of a horsegang. The Breadalbane estate used the horsegang system particularly on its more fertile townships in areas like Netherlorne, and in parts of Lochtayside.[44] Evidence for the use of horsegangs also exists for parts of Knapdale.[45]

Given the relatively small size of holdings held by Highland tenants, the idea that they clubbed together to work a plough has a superficial attraction as a basic explanation for the very existence of township organisation.[46] However, the horsegang system is limited in distribution. There is no mention of it on an island like Tiree, despite the fact that the island's arable was almost entirely ploughed.[47] More serious still, there are many parts of the region, especially in the Hebrides, where arable was largely dug with the spade or caschrom (see pp. 213–15).

There is a further dilemma confronting any attempt to link runrig to the sharing of labour tasks and resource exploitation. It is one which forces us to confront a misconception about runrig. When we recover detailed descriptions of how townships were worked, they suggest that far from being one and the same thing, the communal working of the land and runrig were not compatible concepts. Two descriptions, one for the Breadalbane estate lands in Netherlorne and the other, a description of late-surviving runrig townships in North Uist compiled by Alexander Carmichael and submitted to the Crofters Commission, can be used to make this point. The former is contained in a survey of Netherlorne compiled in 1785 as a preliminary step to a reorganisation of landholding in the area. Many local townships, he wrote, had eight tenants, who 'first plow the whole land, They then divide every field or spot of ground, which they Judge to be of equal quality into eight parts or shares and cast lots for what each is to occupy for that crop. After this, each sows his own share and reaps it again in harvest & so they go on year after year'.[48] On North Uist, where arable was largely spade- and caschrom-worked, Carmichael's description makes it clear that runrig tenants did not even work the soil together before dividing out the year's arable into strips between the various tenants, each tenant preparing the soil, seeding it, and harvesting the crop on their separate strips. In this and other sources, runrig refers to the holding of land in the form of intermixed strips, not to the communal working of land.[49] Indeed, compared to the communal working and exploitation of arable, runrig seems perversely concerned with upholding the private interests of each tenant, identifying his or her share on the ground. Seen in this way, it hardly denotes a system that had devolved from an archaic system of landholding, one whose guiding principles were those of communalism and common property. If anything, there is a case for completely inverting such a view and arguing that runrig appears as a system under which tenants valued private property, and persisted with such a idea despite having to co-operate with others in preparing the soil.

TOWNSHIPS AND THEIR FRAMEWORK OF ASSESSMENT

So far, I have limited the discussion to what we can call a bottom-up view of the problem, or the perspective offered by what actually existed on the ground and how it may have contributed to the formation and definition of townships. When we come to look at townships from the perspective of the estate, we are provided with a top-down perspective, one that appears detached from the day-to-day world of farming resources and routines. It is a perspective based on land assessments, or traditional units of land measure.

With the exception of those townships that came into existence late, most townships in the western Highlands and Islands possessed an assessment in either merklands, pennylands, tirungas (= ouncelands), davochs, mail-lands or quarterlands. Whether we see townships through sixteenth-, seventeenth-

or eighteenth-century rentals, assessments played a key role in the setting of land. Even in the eighteenth century, tacks are freely available that still refer to the ten-pennylands of this township or the four merkland of that township, and tenants are still set proportions that were measured in the same terms. Indeed, rentals or accounts may list a township's rent, without bothering to list its tenants, but they invariably include its assessment rating.[50] The unavoidable conclusion must be that assessments were still very much a functioning system down to the eighteenth century, functioning in the sense of being the basis by which land was proportioned and set and by which rent was calculated.

Yet this point acknowledged, there is also a fundamental problem about how Highland assessments were used. Though some appear to have been laid out in a fixed and measured way on the ground, 'per rectas divisas suas',[51] this does not come across from rentals or surveys as a prominent feature of their character in the way that it does for Lowland assessments. There may have been no general rule of practice, but some estates, especially in the parts of the south-western Highlands and Hebrides, defined what a township cultivated or farmed through the simple expediency of attaching a sowing and souming rate to each unit of assessment within a township.[52] This had the effect of allowing for the broken terrain, enabling tenants to respond to whatever local topographic circumstance presented itself. It also accommodated those cropping systems in which all arable was shifted on a grass-arable basis (see Chapter 7). In other cases, such as in Gairloch, estates expressed the actual capacity of townships in terms of how much stock they maintained, the assumption being that the number of stock which a township could roum, and the manure thereby produced, also determined how much arable it could sustain.[53] What I am suggesting here is that whilst west Highland and Hebridean townships had assessments, and whilst these assessments had a role in scaling how much a township could sow and soum, they do not appear to have been widely used to lay out townships, to meith and march them, in the same way as Lowland assessments.[54] Rather what lay within their head dyke, and what their assessments provided the basis for, first and foremost, was seen in terms of a capacity not an acreage.

This use of land assessments as a measure of capacity has a bearing on how west Highland and Hebridean assessments developed. Viewed overall, the distribution of the different types of assessment can be broken down into distinct but overlapping regional components. The most widespread unit of assessment used in the region was one variously known as the davoch, tirunga or ounceland. However, whilst examples of its use occur in the Hebrides,[55] its main area of use was on the mainland, such as in Badenoch,[56] Glenelg[57] and Assynt.[58] Much more widespread in the western Highlands and Islands was the pennyland, a much smaller unit than the davoch and one that was used freely on the mainland west of the Great Glen and in the central and northern Hebrides. As a unit, we find it being actively used down into the eighteenth century to set land in Sutherland, Cromartie, Lochalsh,

Glenelg, Morvern, Ardnamurchan and Sunart.[59] No references exist as to its use in Lewis rentals but it does occur in placenames (e.g. Five Penny Ness). Eighteenth-century rentals, though, do record its use in Harris, the Uists, Coll, Mull and throughout Skye.[60] Tiree had a pennyland rating at an island level, but only one instance of its use at a township level has been found.[61] Many other parts of the Hebrides also had a district or island-based assessment in pennylands, one whose use suggests that pennyland assessments was probably first devised at this level. One further feature about pennylands is their apparently elastic or flexible nature, with some rentals distinguishing between 'great' and 'little' or 'single' and 'double' pennylands, such as in a 1743 rental for Sleat in Skye,[62] or in a 1756 statement of the rent of Ballivannich in South Uist.[63] Such usage may possibly have been an attempt to distinguish between land that was ploughed and land that was worked with the spade or caschrom in the form of lazy-beds,[64] a type of cultivation that left the land between the ridges uncultivated. An equally valid explanation, though, might be to see 'double pennylands' as merklands by another name, for some areas operated a system in which a merkland equalled a pennyland (=single), or just over a pennyland, and others a system in which merklands equalled two pennylands (=double).[65]

As a form of assessment, merklands overlapped with pennylands in parts of both the Inner and Outer Hebrides. The late sixteenth century report drawn up for the Hebrides gives virtually every Hebridean island a total merkland assessment.[66] However, their use to assess townships was limited to the central and southern Hebridean islands, like Coll, Islay, Colonsay and Jura, and only in sixteenth-century Crown rentals.[67] On the mainland, merklands were used to assess townships in both North and South Kintyre, parts of Knapdale and on Campbell of Glenorchy's estate, from Netherlorne and the Braes of Lorne to Breadalbane.[68] Sixteenth-century Crown rentals for Ardnamurchan, Sunart and Morvern also assign merkland assessments to all townships, though later sources deal solely in pennylands.[69]

In addition to these widely used forms of assessment, one or two areas had more individual forms. Though it is not used in sixteenth-century Crown rentals for the island, the main system of assessment used in Tiree rentals was one based on *mails*, with both townships and tenants being set in terms of *mail*-lands (=rent-bearing lands) down into the eighteenth century. A late seventeenth-century memorandum provides the code by which these *mail*-lands were linked to wider systems of assessment. The entire island, it declared, was rated as 20 tirungas or ouncelands. Each tirunga was equal to six merklands, or 48 mails, or 20 pennylands. Hinting at yet another variant of the system is a calculation of rent on the basis of what each quarter of the tirunga paid.[70] Away from Tiree, other references to *mail*-lands occur in eighteenth century rentals for Netherlorne,[71] whilst in a mid-eighteenth century rental for Canna, the island is assessed as 50 *mail*-lands.[72] With its three townships being 16, 16 and 18 *mail*-lands respectively, it is possible that Canna's *mail*-lands were roughly of the same value as those for Tiree, for together its three townships are almost equivalent to the Tiree *tirunga* of 48 *mails*.

Islay too, had individual forms of assessment: the cowland and quarterland in addition to the merkland. As forms of assessment, these were discussed at length by McKerral[73] and Lamont.[74] Both agree on the basic assumption that soon after the Crown first acquired the Hebrides by the Treaty of Perth, 1266, Alexander III (1249–86) imposed an 'Extent' on Islay. However, they differ over what should be regarded as the 'Old' and what should be regarded as the later 'New Extent'. Whereas McKerral favoured the system based on quarters and eighths that appears in sources from the late fifteenth century onwards, in which the Quarter is equated with 33/4d or two-and-a-half merklands, as the 'Old' form of extent, Lamont opted for a different interpretation. The true 'Old Extent', he argued was a smaller unit, possibly equal to six cowlands or 20/-. Further, the transition from 'Old' to 'New', or the adjustment of Islay to a '33/4d to the Quarterland' system, probably took place soon after Islay was forfeited to the Crown in 1493.[75] He suggested that when the Crown took over the Lordship in 1493, it found 'no properly organised system for the levying of Crown dues'. The person appointed as bailie of Islay, MacIan of Ardnamurchan, 'probably had to re- create a system for distributing the burden over the lands in detail',[76] one which imposed a regimented system of '33/4d to the Quarter'. Prior to this, Lamont sees Islay as organised around an older mixed system based on merklands, poundlands and cowlands, cowlands being a unit which rendered a cow and which worked out at a quarter of the merkland and a sixth of the poundland.[77] Patently, Lamont's argument links in directly with my earlier discussion over the introduction of regular rents, with New Extent possibly facilitating their introduction.

Lamont, like McKerral, makes two further points whose wider significance needs to be drawn out. The first is that there seems to be a lack of correspondence between what was being imposed through the Crown and its agent, MacIan of Ardnamurchan, and the assessments actually used on the ground, with townships appearing grouped under their merkland assessments in Crown rentals but subsequent estate rentals for Islay still using older forms of assessment. In fact, he suggests that on Islay, it was not until the eighteenth century that the two really came together.[78] The second is that when seen through late fifteenth- or sixteenth-century Crown charters and rentals, the assessment of townships in terms of quarters, or their merkland equivalents, appears to have a striking uniformity, the hallmarks of a system imposed from the top downwards without too much regard for on-the-ground arrangements.[79] It is important to appreciate that both these points have a wider context of meaning. The use of an assessment system in early Crown rentals that appears to be different from that actually used by estates to set townships was a feature of other parts of the former Lordship, i.e. Jura, Kintyre, Ardnamurchan, Morvern, Coll, Tiree and South Uist.[80] Further, though there are exceptions, these same Crown rentals and charters suggest that townships in some of these former Lordship areas, such as on Jura and Coll, or in Kintyre, Ardnamurchan and Sunart, also bore impressively uniform levels of assessment, not just in terms of the merklands used in Crown rentals but in terms of the pennylands used in subsequent estate rentals. On Coll, for instance, all townships were rated at two and a half merklands or five pennylands. The same rate of assessment was used on Jura, and for the majority of townships in Ardamurchan and Sunart.[81] In Kintyre, many townships were rated at four merklands. On Tiree, townships were rated as six, three or one-and-a-half merklands depending on whether they were a tirunga, a half or a quarter of a tirunga.[82] In subsequent rentals, use of the merkland was abandoned not for the pennyland but for the *mail*, a choice which may have been connected to the fact that Tiree merklands did not have a simple relationship to the pennyland, with 3.33 pennylands equalling a merkland compared with two pennylands elsewhere.[83]

Because he found discrepancies between the old and new forms of assessment, Lamont considered the possibility that when the Crown imposed its *new* pattern of assessments on Islay townships, it may have actually altered the layout of townships in the process, squeezing townships into its procrustean scheme by adding land to some townships and taking it away from others. Having considered this possibility, though, Lamont ruled it out. The change involved was a paper change, altering the rental definition but not the layout of townships.[84] However, there is a case for arguing that Lamont had narrowed the question too much, being primarily concerned with identifying the type of land assessment used when Alexander III first introduced an 'Extent' in the late thirteenth century and that used when, subsequently, a new 'Extent' was imposed after the Crown took direct control of the Lordship in 1493. Equally important is the question of whether such changes also involved a change in the precise nature or meaning of assessment.

We can best answer this last question by seeing it in terms of the region at large. There is a general belief that some 'land' assessments take us back deep into the early medieval period. For Lamont, the basal layer of Highland and Hebridean assessments, at least in the south-west, was the cowland and merkland. Others see the basal layer as formed by the tirungas and pennylands introduced by the Scandinavians. Recently, Easson has put forward a strong case for seeing the tirunga, with its 20 pennylands, as based on the 20-house unit of Dalriada and, therefore, as pre-Viking in origin.[85] I have no disagreement with the basic thrust of what Easson concludes, but I think that we need to be absolutely clear about what is being dated. That some form of early assessment existed and that it may have provided the metrological basis for later forms cannot be doubted. However, it does not follow that, from the very beginning, such assessments formed an assessment of land *sensu stricto*. In all probability, early assessments were initially based on the person or, as Easson argued, the house. In such a form, it could easily have been used as the basis for renders, military service or taxation. Its adaptation to land would only have come about when such burdens became bound up with the conditions on which land was held. The most logical point for such a switch was when landholding became feudalised and rulers began to territorialise rights and obligations.[86]

These changes are not visble to us in any direct way, but all the signs are that the region was feudalised slowly and unevenly. Just how slowly and unevenly is disclosed by the sixteenth-century evidence. The coexistence of different types of assessment, the need to introduce a wholly new system of Extent following the collapse of the Lordship in 1493, the systematic patterning of assessments, the way standard assessments appear to embrace pairs or groups of townships, the absence of regular rents in many parts of the region, the way in which the food renders uplifted via *cuid-oidhche* appear, initially, to have been the dominant form of rent and, finally, the widespread claims of *duthchas* all point to a landscape in which feudal concepts were shallow-rooted, and their impact had not yet overwhelmed or erased the institutional character of pre-feudal tenures and obligations. Indeed, there is a case for arguing that the territorialisation of rights and burdens may have developed from two different directions, with some assessments being derived from the pressure to territorialise early military levies, fiscal dues, skats and Crown rents, and others being derived from the need to territorialise the discharge of obligations like *cuid-oidhche*.[87] We cannot rule out the possibility that the first stages of territorialising them may extend back deep into the medieval period. Yet despite the Gaelic and Norse origins of assessments in the Hebrides, and despite the deep-rootedness of their metrological bases, we have no reason for supposing that they became 'land' as opposed to house assessments until much later. Even then, the Scottish Crown found it necessary to introduce an Old and later, a New Extent to frame or emplace its own fiscal demands.

Further light on the problem is shed by comparing assessments with the actual pattern of townships. One of the most striking features about early assessments is not just their patterning, but how they relate to individual townships. Frequently, one finds standard units of assessment, like the widely used assessment of two-and-a-half merklands in Ardnamurchan or four merklands in Kintyre, covering not one but a pair or small cluster of townships. Given their shared liability for rent, such townships must have been under constant pressure to share resources together. The only conclusion that we can reach from such a situation is that such townships and their shared assessment were brought together late in the physical life of the townships involved. For comparison, we might note what Geddes had to say about townships on Lewis. Looking at how the large townships which lie along its north-west coast (i.e. Bragar, Arnol) were entered in a rental that was drawn up soon after the Seaforth estate was confiscated following the 1715 rebellion, he drew attention to the way in which the tenants in some townships were grouped into small clusters. Europie, at the northern tip of Lewis, for instance, is recorded in the rental as held by 19 tenants, with two groups of eight and two tenants listed together and paying £15 Scots each, a group of six listed together and paying £20 Scots each, a pair listed together as paying £30 Scots each and a single tenant listed separately and paying £40 Scots.[88] He suggested that far from having a unified or integrated structure, these townships may have comprised small groups who farmed separate portions of the township.[89] In fact, when we look at an early nineteenth-century estate plan for the area, and even at the first-edition 6-inch OS map, townships like Bragar (see Figure 1.3) appear visibly sub-divided into different concentrations of settlement, some of which have their own name.[90] Geddes's paper may help us unravel the form of other early rentals in which tenants appear arranged into distinct sub-groups.[91] In such cases, the township assessment appears to have been thrown around not one but a number of small discrete groups of tenants and a number of small dispersed sites of settlement, so that the framework of assessment simply represents an extra layer of organisation and definition to a pattern of tenure and settlement that was both more detailed and older than the framework of assessment embracing it. Of course, we cannot rule out the further possibility that the imposition of a unitary assessment may have encouraged greater nucleation and co-ordination in the ordering of the township and its farming practice *in toto*, providing a more dispersed or dis-aggregated system with a greater degree of unity than it had hitherto possessed.

I have dwelt at some length on these matters because they affect how we read the nature of farming townships when they first come into detailed view over the sixteenth century. Far from dealing with communities whose tenurial structure was extremely deep-rooted, we may be faced with town-ships whose organisational form was relatively youthful or recently insti-tutionalised when we first see them c.1500, possessing structures that had only evolved with the slow spread of feudal ideas and the fairly late attempt to impose regular rents or to make townships liable for Crown dues.[92] A case for seeing their runrig systems of layout as equally youthful has also been argued from field evidence, with some townships bearing signs of a pre-runrig landscape consisting of enclosed fields and a more loosely dispersed form of settlement.[93] The possibility exists, therefore, that far from being archaic, the formation of runrig communities or farming townships may have come about fairly late in the region's history, being a product of late medieval responses to the growing territorialisation of renders and obligations. Arguably, the imposition of feudal assessments on townships prescribed tenant behaviour. Whatever factors we invoke to explain the formation of open field systems – the use of joint ploughing, population growth, shortage of critical resources like pasture, risk aversion – the assessed framework of a township had the critical effect of ring-fencing solutions, forcing landholders to seek solutions that set their interests one against the other. Certainly, once landholders faced a system in which rent was apportioned per unit of assessment, then those burdened under the same township framework of assessment had every incentive to work together so as to equalise the gains as well as the burdens of rent.

THE TENURIAL BASIS OF HIGHLAND AND HEBRIDEAN TOWNSHIPS

When we examine the character of west Highland and Hebridean tenures through available rentals and estate surveys for the sixteenth–eighteenth centuries, it is immediately clear that the organising feature of those townships held by more than one tenant was the way in which holdings were treated as shares in the corporate resources of the township. Generally speaking, these shares were expressed in one of two ways, either in units of the township assessment, such as so-many pennylands, merklands, maillands and their fractions, or as aliquot shares. In many rentals, the interchangeability between these two systems of share definition is transparent. On Harris, for instance, most townships were set in terms of pennylands or fractions of a pennyland, but amongst such entries were others which expressed shares in direct terms. Thus, a 1703 rental set the Northtown of Pabbay, a three-pennyland, amongst the five tenants in terms of their pennyland fractions, whilst the four pennyland of Ensay was set to over 20 tenants in pennyland fractions, many holding farthings and clittigges (=half farthings), whereas the adjacent two pennyland township of Lingay was set to the two tenants, Alexr. McGillichallum and Rorie McMurthie vic Neill, each 'ye halfe yrof'.[94] The later 1754 rental for Harris shows the same side-by-side use of these two forms of entry, with the six pennylands of the Kirktown of Pabbay being let in sixths, with two tenants having a sixth each, another tenant having two-sixths, and another four tenants sharing two-sixths 'equally among them'. The one-pennyland of Scalpay meanwhile was divided simply into a farthingland and three farthingland.[95] The same mix of forms occurs in the 1754 rentals for other parts of the MacLeod estate on Skye. The pennyland of Torse in Duirinish, for example, was set to seven tenants, one having a farthingland and the other six being grouped into pairs, each of which shared a farthingland 'equally'.[96] Alongside such entries were others which recorded tenants as having a half or third each, such as those for Vattin and Ramasaig.

That assessments, or their sub-fractions, were deemed interchangeable with those entries allocating aliquot shares of a township to tenants could of course have been deduced from the way some sources represent each land unit as carrying a proportionate share of rent. More revealing are the clues as to how such shares were interpreted. Both rentals and tacks across the region make it clear that land-unit shares were meant to be 'equal'. Rentals refer to shares being held 'equally' or 'by equal proprtions': thus the 1754 rental for Harris notes Raa and Paible on Taransay as held 'equally' by their tenants, whilst Meikle Scarista was held by its eight tenants 'by equal portions'.[97] Though some list the pennyland sub-divisions in detail, many tacks for the Macdonald estate adopted the simple solution of setting a township to a group of tenants and then declaring that they were to hold it 'equally betwixt them'.[98] Again some complex tacks combined both methods, such as that which set Killivaxter to five tenants in terms of their pennyland shares, Peannuchkiter to two tenants in terms of penny land shares, Feaoll to two tenants in terms of pennyland shares, but Quirtolan and Peanvickvannan each to two tenants, each 'Equally betwixt them'.[99] Tacks for other estates enlarge on the equality involved, describing shares as 'just and equal'. The 1769 tack for Ramasaig, on the western side of the Duirinish peninsula, set 'the just and equal half of the Three pennyland Town and Lands of Ramsaig' to Neill Mackinnon.[100] The same terms were used to describe the quarters and thirds set to tenants in late eighteenth-century tacks for Lochalsh and Kintail.[101] It presumably had the same meaning as the phrase 'share and share alike' which occurs in early nineteenth-century Sutherland tacks for townships like Baddydaroch and Lochbeannoch in Assynt.[102] It underlines the point made earlier that what really mattered about feudal land assessments, and why their introduction mattered, was because they not only prescribed the total interests of a township but set the proportionate interests of each tenant one against the other. Before they could begin to farm, tenants had to clarify their respective interests, to set them apart on the ground. That is why such a tenure had a determinate role in the shaping of the runrig township.

In comparison with their open-field counterparts in other parts of Europe, Highland and Hebridean runrig was a very imperfect form of open field. Though a mid-eighteenth-century plan of townships on Tiree, along with plans for some of the late surviving runrig townships that have been documented for islands like the Uists, show surprisingly regular field layouts, with regularly-shaped fields sub-divided into regularly-shaped strips, these were not typical of runrig layouts generally.[103] In the majority of runrig townships, field units were small and irregular in shape, and highly variable in terms of surface quality, making their equal sub-division between tenants extremely difficult, especially where more than a handful were involved.[104] The small size of many arable fields or plots in the western Highlands and Islands, their variety of shape and disposition, coupled with the size of the holdings, meant that the degree of fractionation involved could be extreme, with corn 'being sown in diminutive patches' as Pennant described arable on Rhum.[105] When we confront such conditions, we are again forced to question whether it represents a longstanding system, one with ample time to adapt to local circumstances, or whether it is better seen as a late adaptation of a system to circumstances for which it was peculiarly ill-suited.

For contemporaries, one of the hallmarks of Highland runrig was the practice of re-allocating strips between landholders on a short-term basis, with many having particular strips only for the duration of a single growing season. There is no doubt that this was certainly a feature of west Highland and Hebridean runrig. The 1771 survey for Tiree talked about tenants dividing 'their portions yearly by Lot'.[106] It was a feature that John Blackadder noted about runrig on Skye and North Uist in his survey of 1799-1800. On the former, he reported that land in parishes like Slate was still held under runrig and that 'no one person occupied the same spot He held at last breaking', whilst in the case of the latter, runrig involved 'changing the possession yearly'.[107] A later survey of the Skye portion of the Macdonald estate compiled in 1811, just before many of its runrig townships were swept away, repeated Blackadder's point, saying that the island's 'club farms' were held under the 'worst system of runrig, which is that of changing their crofts from one year to another'.[108] On the mainland, a survey of Ardnamurchan in the 1840s referred to 'the absurd system of runrig, or alternate annual changing of the whole arable land of the farm among the different occupants of these joint holdings'.[109] For some early writers, this was diagnostic of runrig's early origins, since it captured what they saw as a tribal or communistic concern for equality between holdings, establishing it not only through the scattering of strips but also by re-stating the equality time and time again. 'Like all ancient and barbarous customs', wrote the 8th Duke of Argyll, annual reallocation 'was clung to most tenaciously'.[110]

In fact, a simpler explanation is more likely. In most cases, reallocation was bound up with the fact that holdings or shares were held at will or on a year-to-year basis, especially those holding land from a tacksman. It was more commonplace in the west Highlands and Hebrides simply because many agreements involving the smaller tenants were annual affairs. This point was made a by a number of contemporaries but none made it more bluntly than Dr Samuel Johnson. Reflecting on a visit to Coll about how many tacksmen and landowners gave no lease to their tenants, he exclaimed to Boswell that he thought it wrong for tacksmen and landowners 'to keep them [=tenants] in a perpetual wretched dependence on his will. It is a man's duty', he wrote, 'to extend comfort and security among as many people as he can. He should not wish to have his tenants mere Ephemerae – mere beings of an hour'.[111] Yet his description of tenants as 'mere beings of an hour' is surely capped by the tenant who described himself simply as 'an instant tenant'.[112] Of course, inextricably linked to the temporariness that permeated many west Highland and Hebridean tenures was the fact that in parts of the region, the precise layout of arable shifted on a regular basis, especially under Hebridean systems of cropping which made some reallocation essential for purely agrarian reasons (see Chapter 7).

Far from supporting a case for seeing runrig as an archaic form of open-field, the practice of regular annual reallocation can be used to sustain an opposite argument. To restate an earlier point, what is striking about descriptions of how reallocation was practised is the fact that it was designed, after ploughing and sowing, to give each tenant specific strips of land, which could then be weeded, manured and eventually harvested as private property for the season, albeit property that was highly fragmented. In other words, it was hardly a system suffused with the spirit of a 'primitive communism' that some have attached to it. If it had developed out of such a spirit, then it had clearly abandoned some cherished notions. Indeed, one is inclined to ask why, given the equality of rent per unit of land assessment, tenants did not simply farm in common and then divide the product as they did the rent. In the circumstances, an equally plausible interpretation is that runrig incorporated earlier notions about private property or severalty into its very constitution, hence its curious compromise between managing some resources and activities together, but allowing each tenant to feel associated with particular strips, albeit just for the growing season.

I have tried to show that the farming township reflected the influence of a range of different factors. Far from being structured in a fixed and timeless way, we need to see its organisation in more flexible terms. This is not to deny that we may be dealing with an old landscape, one whose core areas of settlement had long been occupied and farmed. However, when we focus down on the farming township, an institution that some see as embodying this archaism of form, its different sources of order appear to interlock with each other in a loose, even *ad hoc* sort of way. Thus, whilst some townships appear to be mechanically stamped out with the same assessment rating (i.e. five pennylands, or two-and-a-half merklands), with each individual township apparently bearing a standard allocation of rights and obligations, others appear deliberately grouped into twos and threes under the same rating of assessment. Likewise, whilst some individual townships appear labelled as a tirunga or as having a 20-pennyland assessment, and others are rated as a half or quarter of a tirunga or as having a ten- or five-pennyland assessment, we find still other townships whose division into halves and quarters was part of their internal organisation. Further, the internal organisation of some townships around shares (halves, quarters, thirds, etc.) appears as a relatively seamless aspect of their organisation, apportioning the amount of land held and the amount of rent paid, and perhaps linking tenants to particular ploughteams or horsegangs, but not altering the fact that the tenants involved farmed the land through a co-ordinated scheme of husbandry. However, in other instances, the internal divisions into halves and quarters appears more tangible and more divisive. In large townships especially, we cannot rule out the possibility that tenants grouped around these halves, quarters or thirds may have farmed their shares in a more discrete way, so that, as Geddes postulated for Lewis, what was entered in a rental as a single township was really a grouping of sub-townships, perhaps managing its gross grazing rights through a single township herd but farming the scattered patches of arable as if they were a cluster of discrete, sub-townships. In effect, whether an estate chose to see the shares or portions of a standard unit of assessment like a tirunga or five-pennyland as internal shares of a single township, as 'internal' shares of a loosely integrated set of sub-townships, or as the basis for a cluster of wholly separate, discrete townships (i.e. Kerehusegar, Tiree) may have been a relatively minor organisational decision, one that could be implemented easily and just as easily reversed. Furthermore, the customary form adopted by rentals may afford few clues as to what solution was actually in force.

NOTES

1. The phrase 'window on the Iron age' is adapted from the title of Jackson, *The Oldest Irish Tradition: A Window on the Iron Age.*

2. NLS, Sutherland Papers, DEP313/1047, Loch's Report on Reay Country 1829. Visiting the region in 1811–12, Macculloch wrote that if alone, the Highland cottage was 'a shapeless pile of stones and turf' and 'if congregated into a town', it 'looks like a heap of dunghills or peat-stacks', Macculloch, *Western Highlands and Islands*, iii, p. 14. I have developed this analogy between the human and physical landscapes further in Dodgshon, 'Deconstructing highland landscapes', unpublished.

3. Grant, *Social and Economic Development of Scotland*, p. 108; Uhlig, 'Old hamlets with infield and outfield systems in western and central Europe'. Amongst the most articulate of those who saw the clachan and its runrig or rundale system of farming in Celtic areas as archaic was Evans, 'The Atlantic ends of Europe'; Evans, *The Personality of Ireland*, p. 61. Evans actually hints at a pre-Celtic origin, but his dating relies on the dating of lazy-bed type ridges, not infields or rundale.

4. NLS, ADV 29.1.1, vol. vii, Copy of the last discharge of Sir James Campbell to the Tennents of Ardnamurchan 1725.

5. SRO, Forfeited Estates, E656/2/2, Rentall of Sir Donald McDonald's Estate in Sky, c.1718.

6. Gaskell, *Morvern Transformed*, pp. 124–5.

7. Cregeen, 'Tacksmen and their successors', pp. 93–144. See also Macinnes, *Clanship, Commerce and the House of Stuart, 1603–1788*, p. 145.

8. McKerral, 'The tacksman and his holding', p. 22. See also Macinnes, 'Crown, clans and fine', p. 36.

9. IC/AP, Bundle 746, The Haill Landis of the Lordship of Kintyr wt ye Tennentis and Inhabitantis names wt ye haill number of cattle ky and horses, 1636.

10. Cawdor Castle, Cawdor Papers, Bundle 721, Rent of Ilay for the Years 1703, 1704, 1705 and 1707.

11. IC/AP, Box 2531, Rental of Tiry, what it payed in the year: 52 and in all years thereafter, 1675.

12. This apparent increase in tenant numbers per township would, of course, help explain why Duncan Forbes found the island's soils exhausted and why the estate regarded the island as over-populated or as having too many 'super-numeries'; see Cregeen, *Argyll Estate Instructions*, p. 1.

13. DC/MDP, 2/487/12 Ane account of yt Rorie Campbell ... of the rents of the Harries at Martinmas 1687.

14. Ibid.

15. Quite apart from the effects which King William's lean years, 1696–1703, may have had on the island, it was also badly affected by the great sand blows of 1697. Rentals, such as ibid., 2/487/15 the Rental of ye Land of Mack Leod his pairt of Harish 1698, refer to townships like Kirktown in Pabbay now having a reduced pennyland rating. A later 1724 rental, 2/487/19, talks about 'the yearly pay of the Isle of Pabbay being once Sixteen pennie Land now only Ten pennies'. A comparison between the 1680, 1698 and 1703 rental illustrates the shifts in occupancy taking place. Between 1680 and 1698, the number of tenants in the Kirktown of Pabbay fell from 11 to 8. Between 1698 and 1703, the number fell from 8 to 7, whilst only 3, or possibly 4, were left in possession by 1703. See ibid., 2/487/9, The Rental of ye Hareis as set 1680; 2/487/15, Rental of ye Laird of Mac Leod.. 1698; 2/487/18 Rentall of Macleod's Lands ... 1703.

16. Ibid., 2/485/2, Arrangements for the Sett of Glenelg, mid-18th century.

17. Ibid., 2/482/2, Rental of Harris (lists tacks granted from 1769 onwards).

18. Ibid., 2/487/13, The Accompt of Dond. Campbell of ye rents of Hareis, 1688.
19. Ibid., 2/485/6, Rental of Skye Estate, 1683.
20. Ibid., 2/485/7, Rental of Skye estate, 1684; ibid., 2/485/9, Rental of Skye estate, 1685; ibid., 2/485/7–8, 'Rests of Crope yeare', 1684/5.
21. Ibid., 2/484/10, The Rents of the Lands of Sky for the cropt 1686.
22. Ibid., 2/485/26/3, Judiciall Rentals of the Baronies of Durinish, Waternish, Bracadale and Minginish, 1724. See also ibid., 2/493/1, Judiciall Rental of the Barronie of Waternish, 30 July 1724, which confirms that 2/485/26/3 was wrongly dated as 1664.
23. Ibid., 2/493/6, Rentall of the Barrony of Waternish, crop 1754; ibid., 2/493/8, Rentall of the Barony of Waternish, crop 1754.
24. Ibid., 2/485/55, Rental of the Estate of MacLeod, 1789.
25. Ibid., 2/485/35/1, Scheme Rental and Augmentation 1768.
26. SRO, Forfeited Estates, E7746/73, Report on the Judicial rental of Cromarty estate, 1755.
27. The main exception to this statement was Islay, with some tenants having control over clusters of townships down into the eighteenth century.
28. Macinnes, 'Civil wars, inter-regnum and Scottish Gaeldom', pp. 63–4.
29. IC/AP, N.E. 11, 1543–1610, The rentall of the haill landis and sowmes yairone pasturit within ye parochin of Inchaild, 1609; Ibid., Bundle 746, The Haill Landis of the Lordship of Kintyr wt ye Tennentis and Inhabitantis names wt ye haill number of cattle ky and horses, c.1636.
30. DC/MDP, 4/295, Report on Tacksmen, 1769.
31. Ibid., 4/294, Letter, 1769.
32. IC/AP, 251, Rentall of Tiry, what it payed in the year: 52 and in all years thereafter, 1675.
33. Ibid., Box 2531, Memorandum of ye Rentall Tirie, 1662.
34. Good descriptions of pre-clearance crofts in Lochtayside are provided by McArthur (ed.), *Survey of Lochtayside 1769*, xxxvi–xxxviii, pp. 60 and 96–7.
35. SRO, Campbell of Barcaldine Muniments, GD170/420/1/4, rental of Lesmore, etc, Glenure, 1757.
36. SRO, Breadalbane Muniments, GD112/9/1/3/48, Calculation of the value of farms in Netherlorne drawn for sowing and holdings, 1730. Altogether, this list details the number of families occupying 25 townships and breaks them down into tenants and cottars. 17 had cottars, averaging 2.58 each.
37. Data for Tiree has been drawn from IC/AP, V65, Number of Inhabitants in the Island of Tiree, with the Holding Sowing and Increase of Each farm, 1768, James Turnbull.
38. Murray of Stanhope, *True Interest*, appendix.
39. Ibid.; NLS, ADV 29.1.1, vol. vii, Copy of the last discharge of Sir James Campbell to the Tennents of Ardnamurchan 1725.
40. Dunvegan Castle. MacLeod of Dunvegan Papers, 4/252/1, List of those of the Parishes of Duirinish, Waternish and Arnibost who were not in the rebellion, 1746.
41. Ibid.
42. NLS, Map of Harris the Property of Alexander Hume, Surveyed by William Bald, 1804–5.
43. DC/MDP, 380/30, Sale Details for Glenelg, 1823.
44. SRO, Breadalbane Muniments, GD112/9/5/17/7 The sett of Lord Neil's Lands for the year of God, 1667.
45. SRO, Campbell of Duntroon Muniments, GD116/1/142, Tack for two horsegang of Oib and others, 1706.
46. See, for example, Lamont, 'Old land denominations', part i, pp. 196–9; ibid., part ii, pp. 88–90.

47. IC/AP, RHP8826/1, A General Description of the Island of Tiriy, by James Turnbull, 1768; Ibid., V65, Remarks on the Island of Tiree, 1771.

48. SRO, Breadalbane Muniments, GD112/12/1/2/14, Proposals for the Set and Improvements of Netherlorn 1785. See ibid., GD112/14/12/7, Lord Breadalbane's Querys, with answers and observations thereto, by His Lordships Chamberlain in Argyleshire, 1783, which talks about the 'Arable land divided annually, after sowing, into ridges or less proportions, & lots cast for them'.

49. Carmichael's description of Hebridean townships was first published in Skene, *Celtic Scotland*, iii, pp. 378–93. A full version was published as ' Grazing and agrestic customs of the outer Hebrides', pp. 40–54, 144–8, 254–62 and 358–75.

50. A good illustration is the rental of Ardnamurchan in SRO, Breadalbane Muniments, GD112/10/1/4/68, Copy Rule Regulations. Breadalbane papers also contain rentals which carefully list the merklands of each township even though no obvious use appears to be made of them.

51. Easson, 'Ouncelands and pennylands', p. 3.

52. SRO, Forfeited Estates, E746/166, Report Ninian Jeffreys Factor of Coygach with regard to the Sowming of the different Farms on that Barrony. Jeffreys wrote that 'the practice of the best farmers on this Coast is to ascertain the value of the farm by the number of Milk Cows it can maintain thro' the year'.

53. This was a common approach simply because the number of stock that could be roumed also determined the amount of manure that was available to sustain arable.

54. For comment on this aspect, see Dodgshon, 'Law and landscape in early Scotland', pp. 127–45.

55. Lewis, for instance, is described as equalling 'ffyftein davoch' in a 1663 document, SRO, Breadalbane Muniments, GD112/128/23/2, Copy Tack of the teinds of Lewes, 1663.

56. SRO, Fraser Mackintosh Collection, GD128/11/1, Rental of Mackintosh estate, 1701, refers to the Davoch of Moy.

57. Glenelg is described in terms of davachs in a 1583 charter, see Innes and Buchan (eds), *Origines Parochiales Scotiae*, appendix, p. 829.

58. Ibid., ii, p. 692.

59. See Bangor-Jones, 'Ouncelands and pennylands', p. 22.

60. Easson, 'Ouncelands and pennylands', p. 10. Apart from Harris, I would not add any new areas of use to Easson's map. However, pennylands were used more extensively on Skye and the Uists than her map would suggest.

61. IC/AP, Box 2531, memorandum anent Tirie, c.1680, reports each tirunga on Tiree as equalling 20 pennylands. However, pennylands were not used in any of its rental to set land on the island.

62. DC/MDP, 2/492/1–2, Rental of Sleat, 1741 and 1743; CDC/MP, GD221/4284, Tacks 1759–1777.

63. SRO, Clanranald Papers, GD201/1/351/6, Rent of Ballivanich, 1756, which refers to the townships as 'five pennys Double land'. See also Easson, 'Ouncelands and pennylands', p. 4.

64. Relevant to this is the observation by Johnson that farmers on Skye distinguished between 'long land' and 'short land', which he presented as a distinction betwen land that was ploughed and land that was spaded. See Johnson, *Journey to the Western Islands of Scotland*, p. 79.

65. To judge by its assessments in terms of merklands and pennylands, the former were treated as equal to two pennylands in both Ardnamurchan and Morvern. By comparison, IC/AP, Bundle 1009, Letter by John Campbell, 28 Feb. 1758, which said that 'over all the Isle of Mull lands are not described by marks but by pennies – Now a penny land in that Island is reckoned equal to a mark'.

66. Skene, *Celtic Scotland*, iii, pp. 428–40.

67. McNeill (ed.), *ERS, xvii, AD 1537–1542*, pp. 611–50.

68. Ibid., pp. 625–33. Most of the Breadalbane rentals used merklands to set land until the eighteenth century. Good examples are provided by SRO, Breadalbane Muniments, GD112/9/43, Rental of the Estate of Breadalbane 1736.

69. Ibid., GD112/10/1/4/68, Copy Rules and Regulations Agreed between James Riddell Esq. and Donald Campbell, 1774, includes lists of townships and their pennyland assessments in Ardnamurchan and Sunart. For Morvern, see Gaskell, *Morvern Transformed*, pp. 124–5.

70. IC/AP, 2531, Memorandum Anent Tirie.

71. Elsewhere, the term mail is used as a standard term for rent, e.g. SRO, Breadalbane Muniments, GD112/9/22, Victual payable to Lord Neill Campbell out of his lands of Loyng, Seil and Nether Lorne, 1667, which refers to the 'mails' paid by each townships in terms of food rents.

72. SRO, Clanranald Papers, GD201/1/351/10, Certified Acct. of the Valued Rent of the Isle of Canna.

73. McKerral, 'Ancient denominations of agricultural land'; McKerral, 'Lesser land and administrative divisions in Celtic Scotland'.

74. Lamont, 'Old land denominations', part i, pp. 183–203.

75. Ibid., p. 187.

76. Ibid., p. 187.

77. Ibid., pp. 190–1.

78. Ibid., pp. 187 and 189–90; ibid., part ii, p. 92.

79. Ibid., pp. 184–5 and 187.

80. Townships in Ardnamurchan and Sunart, for instance, are assessed in the Crown rentals for 1541 in terms of merklands, but in late estate rentals in terms of pennylands. See McNeill (ed.), *ERS, xvii, AD 1537–1542*, pp. 624–5; NLS, ADV 29.1.1 vol. vii, Murray Papers, Abstract of the Rentall of the Barrony of Ardnamurchinn and Sunart, 1723.

81. SRO, Breadalbane Muniments, GD112/10/1/4/68, Copy Rules and Regulations Agreed upon betwixt James Riddell Esq. and Donald Campbell, 1774.

82. IC/AP, 2531, Memorandum Anent Tirie.

83. A fuller review of these points can be found in Dodgshon, 'Scottish Farming Townships', in press.

84. Lamont, 'Old land denominations', part i, p. 190. In his later 'The Islay charter of 1408' paper, Lamont does, in fact, go much further in conceding that in adjusting the old Irish system based on 'cowlands' to the merkland evaluation introduced in or after 1266, there was 'an alteration of farm boundaries to produce Mark and Half- marklands', p. 182. Interestingly, he also admits the possibility that the introduction of a Norse ship impost based on 20 pennies in areas like Skye may have 'profoundly affected the already existing sub-division into farms and crofts', pp. 177–8.

85. Easson, 'Ouncelands and pennylands', p. 9.

86. For a discussion of the early medieval territorialisation of rights as a wider issue, see Dodgshon, *The European Past*, chapter 5.

87. The comments made by Thompson, 'Ouncelands and pennylands in Orkney and Shetland', p. 29, are relevant here.

88. SRO, Forfeited Estates, E655/1/2, Judiciall Rental or Account of the Reall Estate of William late Earl of Seaforth 1718.

89. Geddes, 'Conjoint tenants and tacksmen on the isle of Lewis, 1715–1726'.

90. I have discussed this further in Dodgshon, 'West Highland and Hebridean settlement', pp. 424–8.

91. Other examples of tenants being grouped according to their rent liability are provided by SRO, Forfeited Estates, E656/1, The Account of the Reall Estate which belonged to Sir Donald Macdonald late of Sleat in North Uist, 1718.

92. Barrow, 'The Highlands in the lifetime of Robert the Bruce', pp. 382–3.
93. Dodgshon, 'West Highland and Hebridean landscapes'; Dodgshon, 'Rethinking Highland field systems'.
94. DC/MDP, 2/487/18, Rentall of MacLeods Land in the Harries, 1703.
95. Ibid., 2/487/28, Rentall of the Barony of Harris, Crop, 1754.
96. Ibid., 2/490/14, Rental of the Barony of Duirinish, 1754.
97. Ibid., 2/487/28, Rental of the Barony of Harris, Crop, 1754.
98. E.g. CDC/MP, GD221/4277/6/2, Tack for 1734 for Glasphen; GD221/42775/2, Tack for Couliscard, 1734.
99. E.g. ibid., 4277/5/3 Tack for Killivaxter, Peinmuchkiter, Feoll, Quirtolan and Peanvichvannan, 1734.
100. DC/MDP, 2/61, Tack between Normand MacLeod and Neill Mackinnon, 1769.
101. SRO, Seaforth Papers, GD46/1/213, Old Leases 1781–1795.
102. NLS, Sutherland Papers, DEP313/1000, Expired Leases for Assynt, 1812.
103. Moisley, 'Some Hebridean field systems, pp. 29, 31 and 33.
104. If one reconstructs the layout of early townships, either through field work or early cartographic data, it is difficult to see how such highly irregular field units could be divided equally between tenants through runrig. Indeed, the immediate question that arises is why such townships did not attempt at some point to regularise such fields, to equalise the length of each strip, so as to ease the many and recurrent problems that must have arisen over re-allocation, especially if townships were long established. Where one can still see the strips or rigs into which such fields are divided, it is clear that many rigs were so unequal that the allocation process must have been riddled with dispute.
105. Pennant, *Tour* i, p. 278.
106. IC/AP, V65, Remarks on the Island of Tiry, 1771 by Alexr. Campbell, Chamberlain of Tiree.
107. SRO, RH2/8/24, John Blackadder's Description and Valuation of Lord Macdonald's Estates of Sky and North Uist, 1799 and 1800.
108. CDC/MP, GD221/116, Report Relating to the Value and Division of Lord Macdonald's Estate in Skye, John Blackadder, 24 December 1811.
109. SRO, AF49/2B, Book of Survey/Ardnamurchan, 1840s, compiled by Thomas Anderson.
110. Argyll, *Crofts and Farms in the Hebrides*, p. 7.
111. Boswell, *The Journal of a Tour to the Hebrides*, p. 294.
112. This term was used by John McCoil vic Inish, a tenant in Smearsary, to describe himself during the compilation of a 1718 rental for Moydart; see SRO, Clanranald Papers, GD201/1257/1, Rental of the Estate of Moydart, 1718.

7 The Township Economy

In the final analysis, all that has been discussed so far depended on the success or failure of the township economy, and the ability of those who worked the soil both to support themselves and to generate a surplus. Looked at closely, the township economy poses a range of questions for us. First, there is the straightforward matter of farm accounting, establishing the types of crop grown and stock reared, and their relative importance within the township economy. Second, there is the question of what mattered most amongst the basket of goods produced by townships. Were township economies organised to produce subsistence, a surplus, or both? What did subsistence consist of in terms of farm output? What was produced as surplus? What effect did the shift away from chiefly patterns of consumption have on the nature and use of this surplus? When and why did tenants become engaged in marketing?

When we look at the existing literature, there already is a strong debate over some of these questions in the context of the eighteenth and early nineteenth centuries, but relatively little in the context of the sixteenth and seventeenth centuries. To a large degree, this lack of debate in the context of the sixteenth and seventeenth centuries reflects the paucity of documentary material. Yet whilst accepting its severe limitations, the documentation that is available does afford some insight into the kinds of question posed above. In particular, it provides us with a foundation, admittedly a restricted one, for measuring change in the long term. Instead of a static, timeless pattern of cropping and stock management, one in which what we see in the eighteenth century is projected backwards and made to speak for earlier centuries, we are faced with a fairly complex pattern of adjustment in farm practice. Given the impact which the shift away from chiefly patterns of need and consumption must have had on township economies, we could hardly have expected

159

otherwise. This particular shift, though, needs to be seen as part of a much wider pattern of change, as phases of population growth, land pressure and new market trends brought about new and conflicting conditions of farm production.

Altogether, I propose to break the discussion down into three parts. First, I want to collate the scattered data available for reconstructing township economies over the sixteenth century. In this first section, I want to concentrate on the broader issues, establishing the types and amount of crop grown and the kind of livestock kept. Second, I want to bring this perspective forward by looking at how such patterns may have changed from the sixteenth century down to the mid-eighteenth century. Third, I want to draw on the much greater array of material that becomes available by the mid-late eighteenth century to establish the character of the township economy in the decades immediately prior to the spread of sheep farming and the creation of crofting townships.

THE SIXTEENTH-CENTURY TOWNSHIP ECONOMY

The starting point for any analysis of the township economy over the sixteenth century must be the Crown rentals available for the first half of the century.[1] Their value as indicators of the township economy stems from the formally structured character of townships. As explained in the last chapter, townships covered by the Crown rentals bore standardised assessment ratings. Thus, in areas like Ardnamurchan and Sunart as well as on islands like Colonsay and Islay, the majority of townships were rated as two-and-a-half merklands each. In addition, and as already noted in Chapter 3, within each area or on each island, such townships mostly paid a standard rent. Admittedly, there were some differences between areas and islands over what each merkland paid between and within them, and some townships carried surcharges of malt and marts, but generally speaking, there appears to have been a standard rent per merkland within each district. This uniformity of both merkland rating and rent burden, together with the relationship between them, has a bearing on what we can say about the township economy. This is because when we are permitted to see it in detail, there appears to be an intended link between, on the one hand, the amount of land sown and the number of cattle soumed within a township and, on the other, its assessment rating. Of course, this would be a logical link given that townships paid a rent proportionate to their assessment rating. In effect, the townships covered by the Crown rentals were probably bound within an institutionalised matrix of relations, one that brought their assessment, sowing and stocking, levels of output and rent burden together. Patently, such a matrix would have considerable significance for how we interpret the sixteenth-century township economy. It would mean that the economy of townships across the south-west Highlands and Islands or the area covered by the Crown rentals would have been been scaled and structured in a fixed and regimented way, with townships in each district or on each island having a set amount of sowing (=arable) and sowming (=stocking) as well as the same amount of rent liability. Such a remarkably ordered landscape may have been relatively youthful, a product of the recent assessment known as New Extent and one superimposed on what had been a more varied pattern of exploitation; and we cannot be certain whether tenants responded in an equally regimented way. However, as estates shifted into cash rents and, more critically, as they began to levy economic rents that were more sensitive to the individual resource mix of townships, any apparent order would have been gradually undermined.

Beyond this overall uniformity as regards the scale of cropping and stocking, we can draw two other broad conclusions from sixteenth-century rentals. The first is that township economies were clearly mixed in a broadly based way. This is shown not only by the range of produce and stock owed as rent, but also by the way in which the victual payments that lie at the core of sixteenth-century rents involved equal payments of meal and cheese. In some instances, their payment is given as simply so many stones of victuals, and then qualified as half meal and half cheese.[2] For areas with only limited possibilities for arable, like Ardnamurchan and Sunart, this emphasis on a balanced township economy would have effectively forced a significant arable economy. In origin, the presence of this significant arable sector even in rugged mountainous areas was due as much to the pressure of socio-political needs as to the more immediate demands of a township's own subsistence needs. However, what we cannot do is to take the balance between meal, bere and malt payments or between marts and sheep payments that are evident in the Crown rentals and translate them into a township economy whose actual cropping and stocking matched them proportionately. As I argued in Chapter 3, the chiefly economy was probably selective in what it abstracted from the peasant economy. It was not simply an enlarged version of it. Each had different priorities, with bere (or malt) and marts forming the mainstay of the one and oat meal and cheese of the other.

A second conclusion that can be drawn from Crown rentals concerns evident differences in output. Rents per merkland appear standardised within each area or island, but not between them. Each merkland in areas like Ardnamurchan, Sunart, and Morvern owed less meal and cheese than those on Islay and Colonsay or in Kintyre.[3] Townships on Tiree bore the greatest burden, each merkland paying just under seven bolls of bere and seven stones of meal,[4] though the 1588 rental for the lands of Iona Abbey suggests that one or two townships in the Ross of Mull also paid high levels of meal as rent.[5] Such differences may reflect deep-rooted differences in levels of exploitation, a by-product of chiefly ambitions. Equally plausible though, is that more was being extracted as surplus because more was produced as surplus. In other words, the difference levels of rent reflect logical differences in output between areas like Morvern and Tiree. Certainly, when Tiree's high levels of rent per merkland are set beside its traditional description as *terra ethica* or its description in the late sixteenth century report on the Hebrides as McConnell's girnel and as 'all teillit land, and na gurs but ley land',[6] it is easy to see its differences as based on the greater output of its arable. Local differences in output probably account for other differences manifest in the Crown rentals. It might explain, for instance, why all townships in Sunart paid marts but only a handful of townships in Ardnamurchan did so. Later stocking figures show Sunart had more cattle per merkland or pennyland than Ardnamurchan, so that there may be a simple resource-based explanation for such differences. However, given that those townships in Ardnamurchan that were burdened with marts were not necessarily those that were best endowed with pasture resources, there may have been other factors at work.[7]

The types of township covered by late sixteenth-century rentals for Campbell of Glenorchy's estate are all inland townships, mostly in Glenorchy and Breadalbane. Most were more suited to stock production than to arable. However, as with townships elsewhere, what is immediately apparent from even the earliest rentals is that whilst more were suited to stock, most were organised to produce enough meal for subsistence and to pay some grain as rent. To judge from those entries which record how much seed was provided under steelbow, the greater proportion of arable was cropped with oats.[8] However, a significant number of townships in the earlier 1582 and 1594 rentals also cropped bere. Though some townships seem to have paid a high proportion of their victuals in bere, such as Innerdoquhart and Craiginescar, most paid only small amounts.[9] Further, when we put together the amount sown and the amount paid in as rent, where this is possible, most of the bere crop appears to have been uplifted as rent. Again, as on Tiree, the bere crop appears almost as a crop for the estate. Compared with townships on Tiree, though, the bere acreage was significantly smaller than that under oats.

Turning to the livestock sector, the 1582 and 1594 rentals enable us to reconstruct stocking levels for cattle and, in some townships, sheep, but not for horses or goats. The data on 'kye' is particularly comprehensive, with information on the different types of stock being recorded, including how many were 'calfit kye', how many were moved in as new stock and how many were put to the bull. The rentals were interested in such matters because they were mostly estate stock. Under the steelbow system, they were managed on the estate's behalf by the tenants. We have no way of knowing exactly how many constituted the tenant's portion of the herd, or whether the tenant's gain lay in their part-share of the butter and cheese produced together with all the manure. However, scattered references to stock which belonged to the tenant 'himself' plus the fact that townships were required to pay marts confirms that tenants owned some of the stock.[10] The fact remains, though, that the scale of stocking levels present, and the obvious signs of an estate movement of stock between townships, can be taken as reflecting the needs and organisation of an estate economy as much as the township economy. By comparison with the numbers of cattle, only small numbers of sheep are mentioned. In all probability, most of the sheep would belong to the tenants themselves and are not mentioned in the rental lists. As with the differences noted between the bere and oat crop, cattle may well have been regarded as an item primarily of the chiefly economy and sheep as an item of the tenant economy.

In addition to the data on stock, the 1582 and 1594 rentals also confirm the importance of livestock produce to the township economy. Most townships produced and paid small token amounts of fresh and salted butter, and quite substantial amounts of cheese. With a commitment to paying nine stones of cheese 'owt of ilk cuppill of new calfit kye' and as many as ten or more 'calfit kye', cheese payments could be substantial. The four tenants holding Calleloquhane, for instance, had 25 'new calfit kye', and therefore a liability for over 108 stones of cheese between them.[11] Clearly, if we add their own needs, the township must have had a very sizeable output of cheese.

PATTERNS OF CHANGE: CASE STUDIES

By the seventeenth century, data for cropping and stocking becomes more widely available and more direct in character. For a number of areas, we can build up a broad picture of how township economies may have changed from the sixteenth century down to the mid-eighteenth century. In a few cases, the comparison provided is a simple one between two sets of data, neither of which is wholly consistent with the other. In other cases, though, we can build a more detailed and robust comparison, one that enables us to monitor change more closely.

For Ardnamurchan and Sunart, we can draw an indirect comparison between the data provided by the 1541 Crown rental and that provided by Murray of Stanhope's 1727 survey.[12] Though one is concerned wholly with rents and the other with a mix of stocking levels, cash rents, teinds, and payments in kind made under the heading of what it calls meat duty and presents, the two sources allow some comparison. Working on the assumption that one merkland equals two pennylands, no significant change appears to have taken place between the merkland assessment of townships given in the 1541 Crown rental and the pennylands uses in the Murray survey, or indeed in a 1755 rental for the estate.[13] Further, at both dates, the framework of assessments still played a part in determining the liabilities or rights of each township, being used to set the level of rent in the Crown rental and to determine stocking levels, meat duties, presents and teinds in the other. In terms of stocking, the 1727 survey suggests that townships in Ardnamurchan had a souming rate fixed according to their pennyland assessment, with most having an average of just over 13 cattle and 18 sheep per pennyland. Though there appears more variation, most also had, on average, three horses per pennyland. Sunart townships had on average slightly more cattle and sheep per pennyland, at 20, and slightly more horses, at 3.5 per pennyland. The higher ratings for Sunart townships suggest that the differences evident from the 1541 rental, with all Sunart township paying marts but only select Ardnamurchan townships doing so, were probably based on real stocking differences. Just as cheese was paid in proportion to the number of merklands in the 1541 rental, so also do we find the cheese and butter paid as 'meat duty' and the cheese and butter paid as presents in the 1727 list proportioned to the number of pennylands, the cheese being a stone per pennyland and the butter a quarter per pennyland in both areas.

Unfortunately, the 1727 survey provides no data on arable, so no direct comparison can be made with the volume of meal payments recorded in the 1541 rental. It does, however, provide a statement of how much each township paid as teind and, when used in conjunction with a 1723 rental[14] which lists some payments of meal, can yield some clues as to the role of the arable sector. Though there are small variations, all townships appear to have paid a standard amount of teind per pennyland. If we work on the assumptions that teind was one tenth of the total crop and that yields were about threefold on seed, then each pennyland must have had about 1.3 bolls of sowing. For comparison, the same assumption applied to the 1541 pay-ments in meal suggests that each merkland paid 1.6 bolls of meal, or 0.8 per pennyland. To convert meal into grain, we need to multiply by a factor of about 1.5–2.0, giving about 1.2–1.6 bolls of sowing per pennyland. The 1723 rental assigns each Ardnamurchan township a small amount of meal duty, which was presumably oat meal. There is no mention of the small amounts of bere paid in the 1541 rental. The meal duty was clearly apportioned on the basis of one stone and a quart for each pennyland, suggesting that pennyland assessments were still seen as indicative of a township's arable resources or at least its sowing.[15] Despite their greater burden of grain pay-ments in 1541, including payments of malt, the 1723 rental suggests that townships in Sunart were no longer burdened with any meal duty, a factor which would have afforded greater flexibility to its township economies. By 1723, though, farm production in Sunart must have been affected by the fairly sizeable local demand generated by the large community of miners who lived around the Strontian area.[16]

Altogether, detailed data is available for Islay in 1541, 1614, 1686, 1722 and 1733.[17] That for 1686 and 1733 lists only the converted rents of each townships, but that for 1614 and 1722 provides enough data to shed light on township economies. When compared to the 1541 rental, the 1614 rental shows no basic change in what each township produced. Such stasis may give a false picture, for in the previous year tenants on Islay petitioned the King over the extra exactions that had been introduced by Sir Ranald Macdonald, who held the lease for a short while before.[18] Yet the exactions at the heart of the complaint were unrelated to the dues and renders listed in the island's rentals. In a sense, the very nature of the petition makes it clear that whilst tacksmen on the island had a vested interest in enlarging the gap between what they collected in and what they paid out, this was not easily achieved when the core of rents were still paid in kind and set in a customary form. Sir Ranald was clearly trying to think around the package of traditional payments, rather than tinkering with them.

The 1722 rental enables us to look at actual patterns of cropping and stocking.[19] As with the 1686 rental, the substantial payments formerly made in the form of meal, marts and cheese had been converted into cash, with only minor payments or presents like butter, wedders, geese and hens still specified and paid in kind. However, the rental does specify levels of both cropping and stocking for each township, so that we can assess how township economies may have altered since the 1541 rental. The most important conclusion to be drawn from the 1722 data is that whilst there had clearly been structural changes in the disposition or grouping of townships and their assessment rating, with far fewer signs of the two-and-a-half-merkland township that was meant to be the norm back in the sixteenth century, nevertheless, there still appears to have been a broad if not determinate link between the assessment rating of townships and what they were supposed to sow and stock. Thus, we find townships with identical assessments, such Toradill and Taycarmagan, recorded as having identical patterns of cropping and sowing. These townships were both rated as 33/4d lands, or two-and-a-half merklands, and each was soumed at 40 cows, 16 horses and 80 sheep, whilst each had 30 bolls of corn or oat sowing and 8 bolls of bere.[20] Yet nearby townships like Kilbryd and Nether Lyrine were both rated as 16/8d lands, though the former had soums for 30 cows, 16 horses and 60 sheep and sowing for 24 bolls of corn and 4 of bere, whilst the latter had soums for 40 cows, 12 horses and 80 sheep, and sowing for 30 bolls of corn or oats and 4 of bere.[21] However, by way of a cautionary note, a gloss to the 1722 rental adds that 'some times they sow in most touns more than is got down as convenience and improvement can allow these inhabitants'.[22] Clearly, the traditional framework of assessments had started to become redundant by 1722, at least in some townships.

The 1722 rental makes it clear that township economies also had a dimension of activity that earlier sources may have concealed from view. It confirms what the late sixteenth-century report on the Hebrides discloses, that most townships grew bere, albeit not in large quantities (Figure 7.1). Calculated per township rather than per entry, the amount varied from just over four in Killarow and Kilmeny parish to over five bolls per township in Kildalton. All three districts or parishes also sowed a similar amount of oats, from just under to just over 30 bolls per township. The gloss to the rental also adds that the inhabitants sowed peas, rye, potatoes 'as they think fit, or thair convenience can allow them'.[23] Legislation had long encouraged the cropping of peas, whilst rye was valued as a source of thatch though its cultivation was waning in most parts of the Hebrides by the mid-eighteenth century.[24] The reference to potatoes in the 1722 rental is the earliest for the region, but it is likely that they were still treated as a crop of the kailyard rather than the field.[25] As regards stocking (see Figure 7.1), the 1722 rental only provides

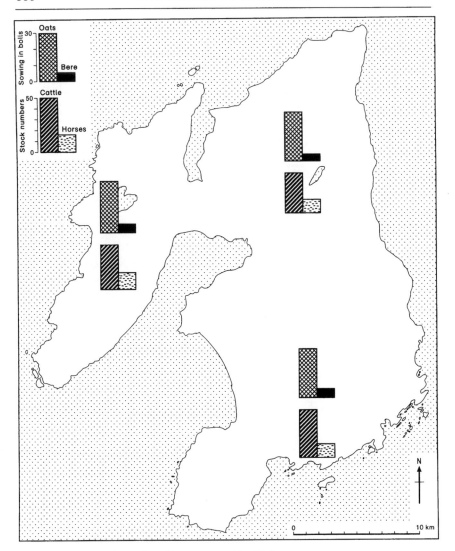

FIGURE 7.1. Islay: sowing and stocking per township, 1722
Source: Smith (ed.), *The Book of Islay*, appendix iii.

data on horses and cattle, with no reference to sheep. In both cases, the average number per township was comparable to other southern Hebridean islands, with horses averaging betwen 12 and 15 per township and cattle between 29 and 40. These overall averages hide the fact that some tenants or tacksmen were responsible for township clusters and may have farmed one or two in their own hands. However, though some of these clusters carried between 60 and 100 horses *in toto*, they still fitted in with the general island average of 8 horses for every 20 bolls of sowing. In other words, despite the number involved, most are likely to have been working rather than breeding horses. As regards cattle, one or two of these township clusters, such as that based around Losset, Octamore, Leack and Killchomman, carried between c.200 and 300 cows, raising the possibility that some Islay tacksmen may have been dealing heavily in the cattle-droving trade by the early eighteenth century.

As already noted in Chapter 3, Tiree possesses a good sequence of rental data and relevant commentary. We are provided with the basis for a detailed comparative analysis of the township economy on Tiree at four different dates: 1541, 1652, 1680 and 1768.[26] Mention has already been made of what the 1541 Crown rental can tell us about the township economy. The value of rentals for 1652 and 1680 lies in the way they record not just the rent of each township, but provide data on actual rates of sowing and souming. This is supplemented by commentatories that explain the principles by which the rent of each tirunga and merkland are calculated, and the amount which each was, in principle, allowed to sow and stock.[27] Together, the various sources enable us to grasp not only the relationship that existed between the different forms of assessment on the island, and the relationship which they had to rents, but also, the relationship which they had to the levels of sowing and stocking in each township. From them, we can reconstruct the most detailed picture available of a Hebridean island during the seventeenth century.

The cornerstone for the analysis lies in a 1652 rental. This rental assesses most townships according to whether they were a tirunga or a quarterland. In addition to listing their rent, it also lists their souming and stocking. The latter appear to have been determined by the assessment rating of a township, with each tirunga having 48 bolls sowing of corn or oats and 24 bolls sowing of bere, that is, one boll of oats and a half boll of bere per each mail land, whilst its souming rate was fixed at 144 soums, made up of both horses and cows, or two soums for each boll of sowing.[28] Though there are a few townships where these rates are not observed,[29] there are enough references to the fact that it was the set or perceived rate for a tirunga for us to assume that it had once been the standard rate in all townships. Indeed, part of the very title of the document says that it defines what a tirunga 'is meant to susteine'.[30] Given that 48 mail-lands equalled the tirunga, there appears a simple principle at work, with each mail-land sowing one boll of oats and one half boll of barley.[31] In other words, when seen in terms of sowing and stocking, the mail-land may have been a unit of farming capacity, one that transformed the large and ostensibly fiscal character of the tirunga into what a person could actually sow and stock. The assumption that the 2:1 ratio of oats:barley in sowing was built in to the assessment rating of the island would in fact be consistent with descriptions of Hebridean cropping that present it as based on a regime of two years of oats and one year of bere.

The 1652 data enables us to map Tiree's township economy in direct terms (see Figure 7.2). As noted above, the standard assumption made by the rental was that each tirunga had 48 bolls sowing of oats and 24 bolls

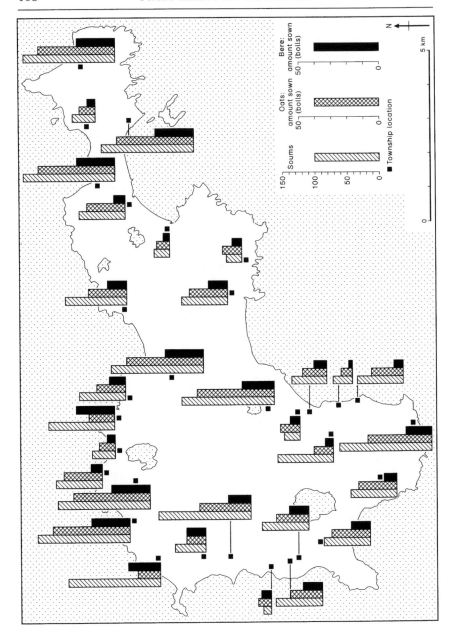

FIGURE 7.2. Tiree, 1652
Source: IC/AP, Box 251, rentall of Tiry, what it payded in :52 and all all years thereafter, compiled 1675.

TABLE 7.1. Tiree: comparison of rents, output and surpluses, 1541–1768

Crop	Sown	Gross yield	Rent	Surplus
1541: Oats (bolls)	480	1056	132	924
1541: Bere (bolls)	480	1680	840	840
1662: Oats (bolls)	480	1056	266	790
1662: Bere (bolls)	480	1680	532	1148
1680: Oats (bolls)	766	1685	238	1447
1680: Bere (bolls)	408	1428	347	1071
1768: Oats (bolls)	507	1115	0	1115
1768: Bere (bolls)	547	1914	0	1914

Sources: McNeill, *ERS, xvii, AD 1537–1542*, pp. 647–8; Argyll Papers, Inveraray Castle, Memorandum of the Rentall of Tiree, 1662; ibid., 3531, Rental of Tirie, 1680; ibid., V65, List of Inhabitants … 1768.

sowing of bere. In actuality, only 766 bolls of oats were sown out of the set sowing rate of 960 bolls, whilst only 408 bolls of bere were sown out of a set total rate of 480 bolls.[32] Given that the output of oats tended to be about one third less than that of bere, the actual difference between the two crops in terms of the amount harvested would have been less. However, this does not alter the fact that both crops were being sown at a rate that was less than that set for each tirunga. One possibility is that this reflects changes in the demands of the chiefly economy after the Statutes of Iona (1609). As the rental for 1652 also reveals, food rents by then had fallen by a third compared to their 1541 level, 33⅓ bolls as opposed to 48 bolls per tirunga (see Table 7.1). Having more of their meal and malt left in their own hands, tenants may have adjusted cropping downwards in response. More significantly, the reduction in sowing and rent would have left them with more bere in hand simply because the reduction in sowing was less than the reduction in the amount of bere paid as rent.[33] As regards stock, the 1652 rental is less informative. As with the c.1680 commentary on Tiree rents, it lists a generalised soum covering cows, horses and sheep of 144 soums per tirunga, that is, two soums for each boll sown. Though the 1652 rental was meant to specify the pattern of rents in MacLean's time and that of 1680 the position after the earl of Argyll had taken control, the basic structure of the township economy as disclosed by the 1680 rental is similar to that detailed in the 1652 rental.[34]

By the time of the 1768 survey, further significant changes had taken place (see Figure 7.3). Though a few townships, like Balewilline and Kenoway, still preserved the allocation of 144 soums to a tirunga, actual patterns of cropping had shifted to a more individual balance across the various townships. What now stands out is that the cropping of oats had fallen away still further to only 507 bolls compared with the actual sowing rate of 766 bolls in 1652. The survey also disclosed that 48 bolls of rye were sown on the island, but the amount was in decline owing to its excessive demands on the soil. By comparison, there had been a significant increase in the amount of

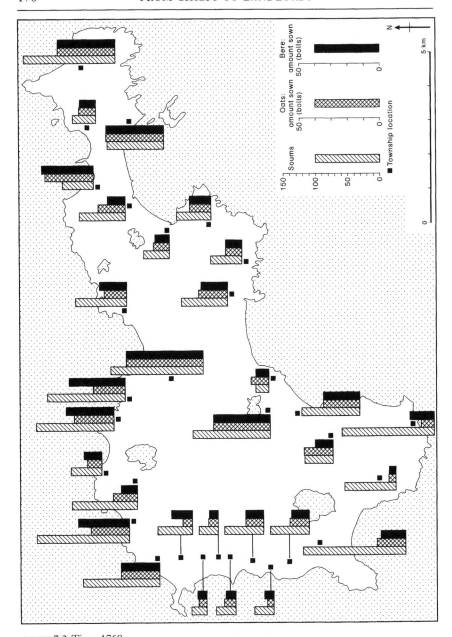

FIGURE 7.3. Tiree, 1768
Source: IC/AP, V65, Number of Inhabitants in the Island of Tiree with the Holding, Sowing and Increase of Each Farm, 1768, James Turnbull: SRO, RHP8826/2. Originally published in Dodgshon, 'Strategies of farming in the western Highlands and Islands', p. 685.

bere sown from an actual sowing rate of 408 bolls in 1652 and 1680 to one of 547 bolls in 1768.[35] They had, said one visitor to the island in 1788, 'an excessive fondness for raising Barley'.[36] Clearly, the increase in bere provided some compensation for the decline of oats, but overall, tenants were still sowing less in 1768 than they were in 1652 and 1680, or 1102 bolls compared with 1174 in 1652 and 1680.

In his 1737 report on Tiree, Duncan Forbes of Culloden painted a picture of soil exhaustion, with declining yields and a greater-than-normal abundance of weeds.[37] His report may shed some light on why arable appears to have contracted slightly, but it cannot provide the complete answer. We also need to understand how tenants responded not simply to changes in the composition of rent but to its conversion into a cash payment, a process largely complete by 1768. In 1541, tenants must have paid by far the greater proportion of their bere crop as rent. By c.1652 and 1680, the amount paid appears to have been moderated by at least one third. By 1768, all meal and bere rents had become payments in cash.[38] This means that tenants had their entire bere crop for their own use, a crop that was now being sown in greater quantities. They responded to this new opportunity in two ways. First, they consumed it as barley bread. Whereas people on adjacent islands like Coll ate oat bread, Tiree's inhabitants were noted at the start of the eighteenth century as eating barley bread.[39] In effect, as bere ceased to be uplifted in rent, the inhabitants of Tiree appear to have colonised their bere acreage for subsistence. Of course, the inhabitants still had to find a substitute so as to make up their cash rents. Stock were certainly one item produced and sold, though it is worth noting that all townships still maintained souming rates that were the same as those recorded in the 1652 and 1680 rentals (144 per tirunga or 3 per mail lands), or a little lower.[40] However, a second response was the conversion of bere into whisky, with over 50 distilleries on the island by 1768, an average of over 1½ per township.[41]

Detailed information on cropping and stocking is also available for 77 townships in Mull, scattered across Torosay, Aros, Morenish and western Ross. As with Tiree, a range of documentation was generated when the earl of Argyll took possession of MacLean of Duart's lands in the 1670s. One particular survey detailed how the estate had been set in 1662, and provides systematic data on both stocking and sowing (see Figure 7.4). Altogether, it covers Torosay, Aros, Morenish and the Ross of Mull, listing information for 74 townships in all. In terms of sowing, it suggests an overall average of 17.8 bolls of oats per township, with townships in Ross averaging 15 bolls and those in Aros, over 21 bolls. Approximately one half also sowed bere, but only in small quantities of between 0.5 and 2 bolls. When such sowing data is compared with the level of meal and malt extracted from Mull townships according to the late sixteenth century report on the Hebrides, it suggests that the amount of bere sown may have fallen significantly. As regards cattle, the 1662 rental suggests that cattle and sheep were kept in equal numbers, townships having an overall average per township for both cattle and sheep

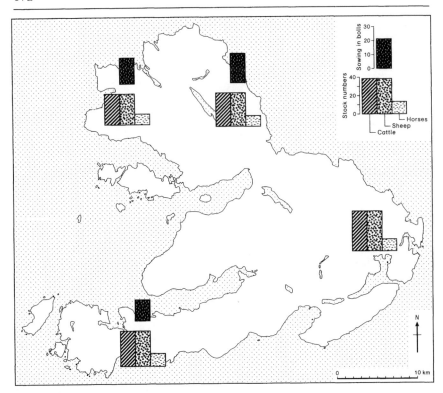

FIGURE 7.4. Mull: sowing and stocking per township, 1662
Source: IC/AP, N.E.11, 1650–1669, Accounts and Rentals, Rentall of Mclaines lands, Mull, 1662.

of 37.5 each. Townships in Torosay, the core of MacLean's estate, had the larger herds and flocks, with an average of just over 42 cattle and sheep per township, whilst those in Morenish had the smallest, with just over 33 cattle and sheep per township. Of course, seen in terms of soum rating, this amounted to a far higher rate for cattle than for sheep. Given the amount of sowing involved, a feature of these Mull townships is the fairly high average number of horses per township, or 12.5. The numbers in some townships suggest that we need to look beyond the basic need for plough horses and horses for carting. For example in Sron, where 24 were reported, horse breeding may well have been a small part of the township economy.[42]

The MacLaine of Lochbuie estate also compiled souming lists for its townships. A list compiled in 1743 for 33 townships in the east of Mull suggests that average cattle numbers there were as high as 64.4.[43] Sheep had a slightly higher average per township of 64.8, whilst horses averaged 15.3 per township. These are significantly higher averages than those recorded in the 1662 rental for similar townships elsewhere on the island and raise the possibility that stocking levels may have increased by the mid-eighteenth century.

Two of the earliest and most detailed stocking lists are available for mainland parts of Argyll during the early seventeenth century, one dating from 1609 covering mid and northern parts of the county and the other, compiled c.1636, covering townships in Kintyre. As indicators of the live-stock sector of the township economy, their value is enhanced by the fact that they break stock down between tenants, sub-tenants and other occupiers. In doing so, they enable us to glimpse some of the differentials that existed within the farming community. The 1609 listing for parts of mid and north Argyll covers 120 different townships.[44] Altogether, they contained an average of 43.9 cattle, 18.4 sheep, just over 6 horses and just over 6 goats each, though the figures for sheep and goats need a small upward adjustment to allow for those entries which record only their value not their number. When broken down between occupiers, they suggest only modest personal holdings of stock, with each listed occupier having an average of 11.2 cattle, 4.8 sheep, 1.5 horses and 1.5 goats. Such gross averages, though, hide the differentials that were already present between tenants by 1609. When we look at individual holdings of livestock, it is clear that some individuals had accumulated sizeable herds and flocks. If we take holdings of cattle as the prime indicator, quite a number of occupiers had more than three times the overall average for the area. Furthermore, it is striking that some of the largest individual stock holdings, involving herds of over 50 cattle, were in the hands of individuals who were recorded as the sole occupier of a township. Clearly, the idea of a commercially driven township economy was already being established by the early seventeenth century.

In the case of Kintyre, the c.1636 list gives data on cattle and horses for 114 townships.[45] If we take cattle, the prime stock of value, the average number per township was 45.3 animals. The average number of cattle per tenant was only 11.4, though the dominant tenant in each township had an average of 21.4 animals. The 1609 data for mid and north Argyll does not enable us to calculate how many cattle were held by the dominant tenant, but its figures for the average number of cattle per township and per occupier are similar to those for Kintyre. Altogether, there were relatively few Kintyre townships in which any one occupier had more than three times the average number of cattle for the entire area. The largest cattle farmers tended to be those tenants or tacksmen who held an entire township on their own, though that said, the person with the largest herd of cattle, or 96 animals, was actually one of ten tenants in the township of Kildavie. In terms of horses, townships had an average of 14.1 animals, significantly more than in the mid and north Argyll list. The average per tenant was 3.5 animals, enough to contribute to a plough team and for carting. The larger or dominant tenant in each town-ship possessed 6.3 horses, enough to maintain a full ploughteam. Overall, the number of horses both per township and per occupier are significantly greater than the corresponding figures for mid and north Argyll, a sign perhaps not just of the greater role played by arable in Kintyre, but of the area's greater interest in horse breeding.

A reconstruction of both cropping and stocking over the seventeenth and eighteenth centuries is also possible for various parts of the Breadalbane estate. As with the rentals for 1582 and 1594 discussed earlier, a number of the estate's rentals for the seventeenth and eighteenth centuries contain quite detailed information on cropping and stocking. Because of the estate's use of steelbow tenure, some rentals list the amount of oats and bere provided as seed, as well as that paid as rent. Supplementing this data are a number of souming lists available from the early seventeenth century onwards which detail the stock carried by townships, enabling us to monitor change in stock balance across a century and a half. Altogether, the following discussion has been based on sowing and stocking data from rentals for 1600, 1620, 1629, 1667, 1669–78, 1688, 1697, 1717–20, 1736, and 1780–1,[46] supplemented by souming lists for c.1600–30, 1730 and 1780–1[47] and the Lochtayside survey of 1769.[48]

Compared to those available for 1582 and 1594, many more townships are covered by these later rentals. If we set the data for those townships recorded in the 1582 and 1594 rentals alongside that available for 1620, little change appears to have taken place. From a cropping point of view, they appear to have cropped the same amount in 1620 as they had in 1582 and 1594.[49] Clearly, there were no short-term fluxes in this respect. Even comparing the data on cattle shows a broad stability in the numbers and age balance of the herd, suggesting that the size and age balance of the herds listed in both sets of rentals were part of a regular scheme of management. A rental shortly after, for 1629, extends the coverage, embracing other townships in Glenorchy, the Braes of Lorne and parishes like Ballivoydan. Again what stands out is the presence of arable everywhere, with significant amounts of bere being cropped even in Glenorchy though we are not dealing with anything like the scale of arable present on islands like Tiree and Islay, simply 10–20 bolls of sowing at the most.[50] An undated document entitled 'The Soums of Glenorchy in Sir Duncan's Time', and probably dating from the early seventeenth century,[51] provides a valuable insight into the livestock sector of these townships (see Figure 7.5). This is one of the earliest indications of stock balance available for the region. Though each township's merkland assessment is listed alongside their soums, there is no simple or uniform relation between it and the township's souming rate. Townships with similar merkland ratings appear to have different souming rates. However, as with later evidence, the list does confirm that each township's soum was seen as a balanced or structured affair, with a defined mix of cattle, sheep, horses and goats. In most cases, the number of 'great cows wt their two year olds', equalled the number of sheep and goats, with the average number of cows across the 42 townships listed being 50.7, that of sheep being 49.9 and that of goats, 47.3. The average number of horses per township was nine, or enough for a ploughteam and for general cartage. Of course, despite the equivalence between cattle, sheep and goats, the grazing needs of cattle would have amounted to by far the greater claim on pasture resources. The

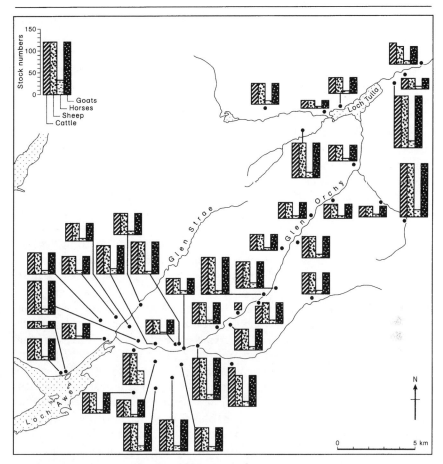

FIGURE 7.5. Glenorchy: stocking, early seventeenth century
Source: SRO, Breadalbane Muniments, GD112/12/1/2/1, The Soums of Glenorchy in Sir Duncan's Time. Dating this survey is difficult as Sir Duncan was chief for 48 years! On the assumption that the list was that current during the latter part of his chieftainship, we can assume that the list dates to the early seventeenth century.

entry for Ardtalle comfirms that a soum was defined as the grazing needs of a 'great cow wt their two year olds', with a horse or mare being defined as two soums, and five sheep or goats as one, weightings that probably applied to all townships.[52] Seen in terms of their soum weighting, cattle comprised about 57.5 per cent of grazing needs within each township, horses about 20.5 per cent , sheep just over 11 per cent and goats just under 11 per cent. When we bring the evidence for cropping and stocking together, it again suggests broadly-based rather than specialised township economies.

A detailed rental of 1667 for the Netherlorne portion of the Breadalbane enables us to see the economy of townships that had much larger arable sectors.[53] Further, it enables us to see how estate policy could affect actual patterns of cropping. The estate clearly saw these townships as major producers of grain. If what they paid or owed in victuals reflected what they sowed,[54] then these townships cropped much more bere than those further inland. On average, bere formed about 15–20 per cent of the victual rent but there were some instances, such as with the township of Auchnasaul, in which tenants actually paid marginally more bere than oat meal.[55] In these townships, there must have been a far closer balance between oats and bere on the ground even allowing for the greater yields provided by bere and for the possibility that estates uplifted a higher proportion of the crop. More interestingly, the fact that the estate still collected in this bere without converting it into cash meant that tenants in Netherlorne would still have been locked into a cropping regime determined by their rent bundle.

An opportunity to look at patterns of cropping and stocking in Netherlorne in more detail is provided by a detailed listing of sowing and souming compiled in 1730.[56] The survey is preceded by a long discussion of how rents should be computed. It effectively argues for a move away from the rigid formulae of early rentals to one in which the individual resources of each township were evaluated in their own terms, hence its tabulation of what was hitherto sown and stocked, together with what was owed as rent. When analysed (see Figure 7.6), it confirms that by the standards of the region, these Netherlorne townships had substantial arable sectors. In all cases, the amount of sowing in oats, or corn, greatly exceeded that of bere, with each of the 34 townships in the list sowing an average of just over 44 bolls of oats compared to only 3.8 bolls of bere. As regards stock (see Figure 7.7), a few townships maintained an exact balance between the numbers of cattle and sheep, but the general pattern was for herds and flocks to be unequal in size. Furthermore, the average number of sheep kept per township (62.8) was higher than the average number of cattle (52.9). As one would expect of an area with a significant arable sector, the number of horses per township (10.7) was more than sufficient to maintain a horsegang or ploughteam. A further feature about Netherlorne (1730) is that there was no straightforward link between how much stock was carried by a township and the amount of oats sown by it. However, some of those with the greatest discrepancy between the two, having small acreages but large stock populations, were former shielings like Leckich and Penifour.

The most important conclusion revealed by the 1730 Netherlorne survey, though, is that when we compare it with earlier stocking lists and with earlier rentals that provide data on steelbow sowing, like that for 1667,[57] it appears possible that townships were now both sowing and stocking more. However, a cautionary note needs to be made about the possible increase in sowing. It is based on a comparison between the 1730 sowing data and that provided as seed under steelbow tenure in the 1667 rental. As already noted, a problem with steelbow is that whilst it was meant to establish a tenant's capacity to farm, and therefore must have carried notions of what the township's capacity was deemed to be, it may not have been entirely restrictive. Tenants may have been able to add their own sowing, so that we may be faced with

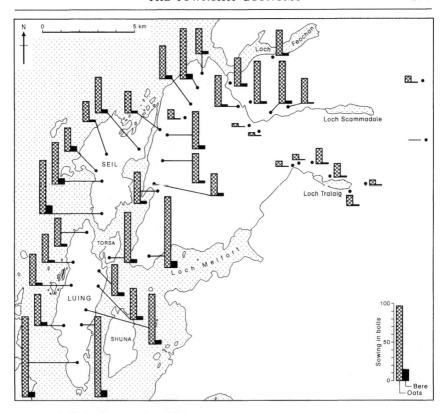

FIGURE 7.6. Netherlorne: sowing, 1730
Source: SRO, Breadalbane Muniments, GD112/9/1/3/43, Calculation of the value of the farms of Netherlorne – drawn from sowing and holdings 1730.

two interlocked economies, the steelbow economy funded by the landowner and an expansion beyond this basic economy funded by the tenant. In other words, tenants may already have been sowing more than is labelled as steelbow seed in the 1667 rental.

No contemporary survey of sowing rates exists for other parts of the Breadalbane estate, but a 1727 survey does provide the stocking rates in other areas.[58] It is noteworthy for its striking local variations in how townships were stocked. These variations are simple. Townships in areas like Strathfillan, Lochdochart, Auchlyne and what it calls 'Macnab's lands' around Kinell all had stock populations based on cattle, sheep and horses. However townships in Glendochart, Auchmore, Clochrane, Artallanaig, the East End of Lochtay, Lawers, Crannich and Glenlochay were all reported as having soums of cattle and horses only, suggesting that they may have shifted their livestock sector towards a concentration on cattle (see Figure 7.8). Given its proximity to Lowland markets, the Loch Tay area was clearly maximising its locational advantage.

In the case of Glenorchy, we can actually set stocking data for this period,

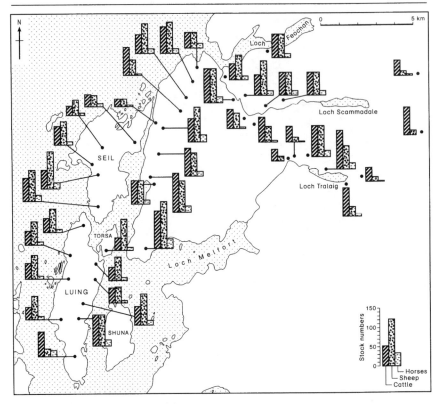

FIGURE 7.7. Netherlorne: stocking, 1730
Source: SRO, Breadalbane Muniments, GD112/9/1/3/43, Calculation of the value of the farms of Netherlorne – drawn from sowing and holdings 1730.

1730, beside that for the early seventeenth century. By 1730, overall cattle numbers per township averaged 53.3 and sheep numbers averaged 54.1 (see Figure 7.9). Yet though the average number of cattle and sheep had risen compared to the early seventeenth century, the absence of soumed goats in the 1730 list meant total stocking levels had fallen in most townships by then (see Figure 7.10). The 1730 data also provides sowing data for Glenorchy. From it, we can see that all townships, even on the southern edge of Rannoch, cropped oats and, in some cases, small amounts of bere (see Figure 7.11).

THE TOWNSHIP ECONOMY IN THE LATE EIGHTEENTH AND EARLY NINETEENTH CENTURIES

By the mid-eighteenth century, rental and survey data become available on a more extensive scale and for a wider variety of estates. So too do commentaries, both published and in manuscript. Using such data, it becomes possible to take an overview of the region, drawing out some of its broad

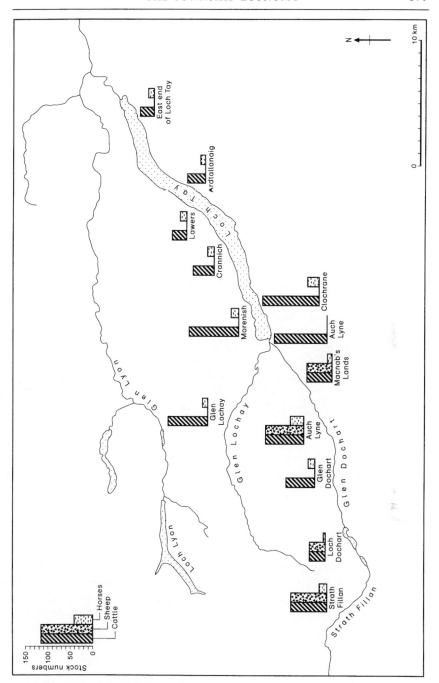

FIGURE 7.8. Breadalbane: stocking, 1727
Source: SRO, Breadalbane Muniments, GD112/9/43, Rental of the estate of Breadalbane 1736, contains section entitled 'Comprisement of the Soums of each merk land in Breadalbane By Skillfull Birlawmen in the year 1727'.

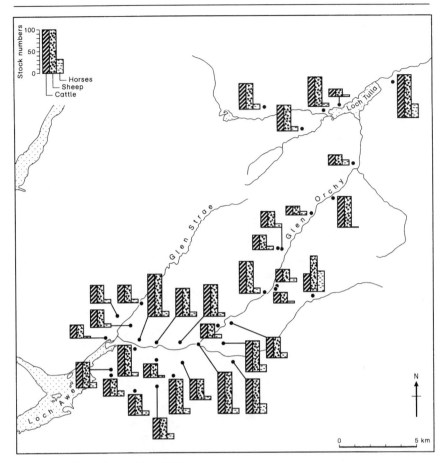

FIGURE 7.9. Glenorchy: stocking, 1730
Source: SRO, Breadalbane Muniments, GD112/16/12/3/1, Rentall of Glenorchy Shewing the
present Rent ... Holdings and Sowings, 1730.

variations and common strands. Of course, given what has already been said
about estates like Breadalbane and Tiree, we cannot expect to be dealing with
a static pattern. Adjustments and responses to a variety of new pressures and
opportunities are likely to have been taking place everywhere, even before
the clearances for sheep and before the re-organisation of townships into
crofting townships.

  If we take the southern and south-west Highlands first, data for the closing
decades of the eighteenth century enable us to continue the analysis of
adjustments on Campbell of Glenorchy's Breadalbane estate. A detailed
survey of cropping and stocking was drawn up for Lochtayside in 1769 and
for the entire estate in 1780–1. If we take the 1769 survey first (see Figures
7.12 and 13), three significant conclusions stand out. The first is that when
we compare their sowing rates for oats with those specified under steelbow

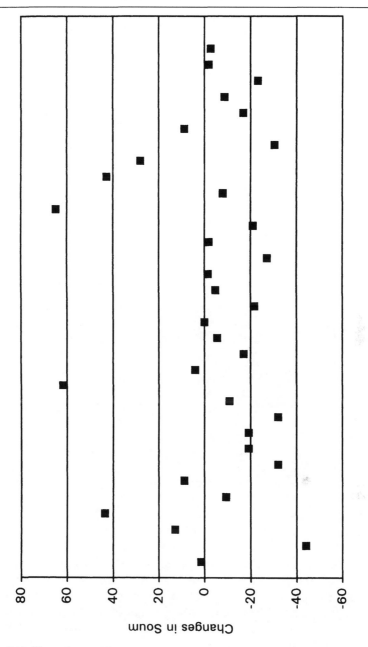

FIGURE 7.10. Glenorchy: stocking changes, early seventeenth century–1730 (based on weighted soums)
Sources: SRO, Breadalbane Muniments, GD112/12/1/2/1, The Soums of Glenorchy in Sir Duncan's Time; ibid., GD112/16/12/3/1, Rentall of Glenorchy Shewing the present Rent ... Holdings and Sowings, 1730.

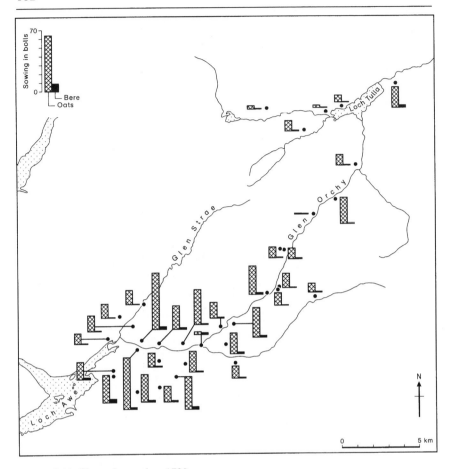

FIGURE 7.11. Glenorchy: sowing, 1730
Source: SRO, Breadalbane Muniments, GD112/16/12/3/1, Rentall of Glenorchy Shewing the present Rent ... Holdings and Sowings, 1730.

tenure in earlier rentals, such as those for 1600 and 1620, there are again apparent signs of an increase in the amount of arable being sown during the intervening 150 years, with townships now averaging over 20 bolls sowing of oats. Second, there also appears to have been an increase in the cropping of bere, with townships averaging 5 bolls of sowing each, perhaps as a response to the growing activity of local brewsters and distillers.[59] Third, and in some ways the most interesting, when we compare the Lochtayside stocking rates given in the 1727 survey with those of the 1769 survey, significant new shifts appear to have taken place. The concentration of soums on cattle and horses had disappeared by 1769, with most townships now having significant numbers of sheep (average 95.2) and some even having goats (average 26.5). In case it is argued that the earlier survey could not have included sheep, all the Lochtayside townships listed in it had columns for sheep but no figures were

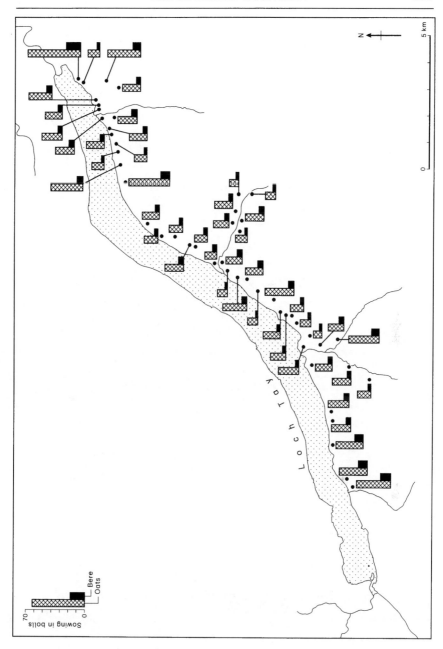

FIGURE 7.12. Lochtayside: cropping, 1769
Source: McArthur (ed.), Survey of Lochtayside 1769, pp. 75–207.

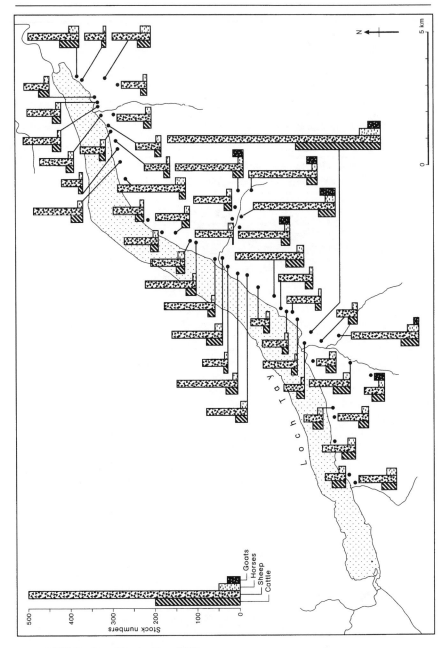

FIGURE 7.13. Lochtayside: stocking, 1769
Source: McArthur (ed.), *Survey of Lochtayside 1769*, pp. 75–207.

recorded. Moreover, when we actually compare stocking rates in the two surveys, it is clear that not only have sheep appeared in the 1769 survey, but that cattle numbers have been reduced and reduced significantly, the township average now being only 24.4. Clearly, one appears to have been substituted for the other. In effect, tenants in these townships, most of which were still held in runrig, may have been anticipating the market trend that was eventually to bring their system to an end.

The 1780–1 survey is easily the largest and most comprehensive of all the surveys available, with information on the cropping, stocking and landholding of all the townships making up the Perthshire portion of the estate.[60] Overall, it confirms the sort of cropping levels apparent in the more restricted 1769 Lochtayside survey, with each township sowing 19 bolls of oats and 4.5 bolls of bere. However, it also shows an average of 2.1 bolls of potatoes now being sown, with some townships sowing more than enough for subsistence. Apart from the appearance of potatoes, the most significant feature of the township economy appears to have been the continued decline of cattle and the corresponding increase of sheep, with cattle now averaging 21.9 animals per township and sheep 137. As already noted in regard to the 1769 survey, this increased stocking of sheep took place within the context of runrig townships. However, so long as they carried multiple tenants, such township were caught in a dilemma, with the need for a sizeable subsistence sector limiting how much wintering was available for stock and severely constraining the year-round stocking levels of the township. Ultimately, specialisation in sheep required a reduction in subsistence arable. In fact, the Breadalbane estate had taken some steps in this direction before the close of the eighteenth century. In the late 1780s, it set townships in Glenorchy to fewer tenants, who responded by greatly expanding the size of their sheep herds.[61]

By comparison, western coastal townships on the Breadalbane estate display more variation in their township economies. Some of those controlled by the wealthier tacksmen had shifted into specialised cattle production by the late seventeenth century, so that any later shift into sheep would have been a smooth process. However, estates like Breadalbane regarded its western or coastal townships in Netherlorne and those on inshore islands like Luing and Seil as 'corn country'. Though such townships kept stock for manure and for meeting some of their cash needs, their economy was driven more by what arable could produce. The estate was partly responsible for this. Townships on Luing, for instance, still paid 260 bolls of meal and 41 bolls of bere as rent down to 1785, when crop failure persuaded the estate to take its converted value.[62] With fairly sizeable farm populations, to produce such surpluses on top of subsistence needs must have kept the economies of such townships committed to what came out of their arable sector.

Other holdings in the area, such as Campbell of Glenure's townships in Netherlorne and on Lismore, were in a similar position. In addition to subsistence needs, they paid substantial grain payments down to the 1750s and 60s.[63] A manuscript of 1774 gives a rare glimpse of the actual cropping and stocking of a township on the estate, that of Acharn. Its four tenants sowed 64 bolls of oats and 13 bolls of bere, plus what was sown by the three crofts in the township. Of the c.192 bolls of oats which must have been harvested, it paid 24 bolls in meal as rent, leaving a very healthy surplus for subsistence and for marketing. Of the c.45–52 bolls of bere which it must have harvested, 24 were paid as rent. Presumably, part if not all of its bere surplus may have gone to the changehouse present in the township. Its stocking was clearly limited by the amount of arable present, with 40 cows held by the tenants and 10 by the crofts. No mention is made of the working horses that must have been present, but each cow was matched by a sheep. In total, such stocking could hardly have been enough for manuring arable.[64] A similar concentration on arable was still apparent on the Campbell of Sanda estate in south Argyll. Survey data recorded in rentals for the second half of the eighteenth century show townships still had a very high percentage of arable (i.e. North Machrerioch, Achadadice, Blasthill, Acharua and Eden). The rentals give no indication of what they did with this arable, rents being accounted in money except for what were called 'casualities', but to judge from the 30 bolls of meal paid as rent by the estate's mill, a payment based on multures, a great deal of grain must have still been produced on the estate.[65]

When Archibald Menzies carried out a tour of the southern Hebrides and adjacent mainland areas like Kintyre for the Forfeited Estates commissioners in 1768, he drew a similar distinction between that already noted for the Breadalbane estate, with cattle farms on the higher ground and corn farms of the lower ground. He reported the former as selling over 2000 cattle annually,[66] whilst other sources suggest that the corn farms marketed large quantities of meal and bere, much of the latter being distilled.[67] In fact, detailed cropping and stocking data compiled for 17 of the Duke of Argyll's Kintyre townships in the 1770s suggest that the distinction between upper and lower farms was still muted rather than sharp, with townships having a broadly based farm economy. From this data, we can see that all townships were sowing large quantities of oats (averaging 51.5 bolls per township), modest amounts of bere (8 bolls per township) and significant amounts of potatoes (15.1 bolls per township). All had stocks of black cattle and horses, with an average of 45.4 soums per township.[68] According to Menzies, bere began the cropping cycle, receiving all the available manure, followed by oats for two years, though in a visit made the year after Menzies, an advisor for the estate, John Burrel, suggested that the introduction of potatoes as well as peas and beans had started to displace bere, at least as a subsistence crop.[69] Like other regions that depended on manure, Kintyre appears to have been caught between the needs of its arable and livestock sectors, with complaints about its arable being starved of manure[70] and its cattle being starved of adequate grass, especially summer grass.[71]

When we move north along the western seaboard, townships had to cope with more difficult rugged conditions. Those in Ardnamurchan typify the sort of township economy we find in these areas by the late eighteenth and early nineteenth centuries. According to a survey of 1807, the surviving run-rig townships still had sizeable arable sectors despite the physical problems of the area. In most cases, though, arable was only maintained at this level by the use of the spade for much of it consisted of 'small and detached pieces'.[72] This effort to bring land into cultivation was driven by the simple fact that they were 'oppress'd with too many small tenants'.[73] Yet though such townships must have been organised primarily to provide subsistence, there are hints that some late changes in stocking were made in response both to the increase in arable and to market shifts. If we take the 1727 survey data and compare it with data available for the 1830s, when a fair number of its townships were still organised on a runrig basis, the number of horses appears to have been reduced significantly, presumably because more was now spaded and holding sizes made the use of the plough uneconomic. Generally, the number of cattle appears to have fallen, but the number of sheep had increased.[74] A note in the 1807 survey suggests that tenants had started the shift from black cattle to sheep fairly late.[75] As on the Breadalbane estate, this shift involved runrig townships that were clearly following market trends and not simply those townships which had been cleared for sheep by then.

Further north, the Knoydart or Barrisdale estate formed what was argu-ably the most rugged environment for human settlement to be found on the western coast. Despite its ecological problems, its township economy was still organised around the small acreage of arable maintained by each township. Detailed surveys for 1755 and 1771 shed light on this economy (see Figure 7.14). Cropping was based on oats and potatoes, the latter being a fairly recent introduction. Most townships had no more than a few bolls of sowing, but they did have vast acreages of hill ground, albeit beyond a very steep and hazardous ridge for those townships lying alongside Loch Nevis that caused them an annual loss of stock by 'bone break'.[76] Most of the hill pasture, though, was poor quality. When we analyse their stock balance, a number of distinct features emerge. The most striking is the fairly large numbers of horses maintained, 463 in total for barely 70 acres of arable. Given there was only one plough on the estate, few could have been used for ploughing. Most must have been for local cartage, or for sale through markets like Inverness. In relation to the small amounts of arable, cattle numbers were surprisingly high, possibly because the area relied heavily on the sale of cheese and butter for its cash rents.[77] All townships, except two, carried herds of both sheep and goats, the herds of the latter being amongst the largest per township in the region. Finally, Barrisdale was one of a number of areas[78] whose grain output was insufficient to satisfy local needs (see Table 7.2). Its sales of butter and cheese were used to buy in extra grain.[79] By 1771, an overall increase in arable plus the greater use and yield of potatoes must also have provided some relief.[80] However, local townships also derived a substantial part of their diet from local fishing.[81]

Northwards beyond Barrisdale, lie a number of other difficult areas.

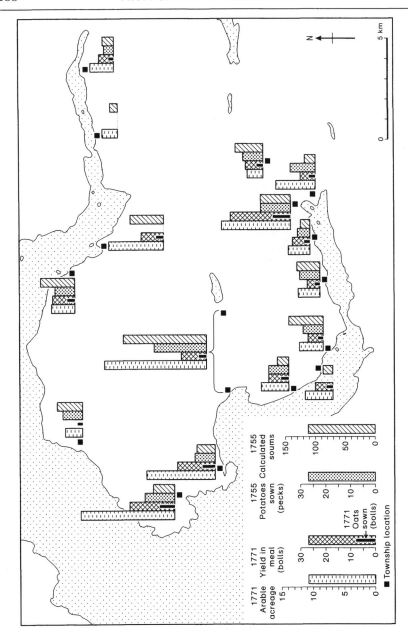

FIGURE 7.14. Barrisdale, 1755–71
Notes: Livestock data has been extracted from a 1755 survey and cropping data from a 1771 survey. A combination of both surveys has been used because the 1755 data provides detailed stocking figures and arable acreages but not the amount sown or produced. The 1771 survey, meanwhile, provides detailed figures on the amount sown and the meal produced per township but its stocking data is incomplete.
Sources: Wills (ed.) *Statistics*, pp. 4–5: SRO, Forfeited Estates, E729/3 States of Various Farms 1755; ibid., E741, Forfeited Estates 1745 – Barrisdale Reports Concerning Farms 1771.

TABLE 7.2. Barrisdale township budgets

| Meal (bolls) | | Cattle | | |
Produced	Bought	Maintained	Sold	Lost
9	3	30	5	2
9	3	30	5	2
18	10	48	8	0
15	6	30	6	0
10	4	36	8	0
8	1.66	28	5	5
7	4	20	0	0
6	5	45	6	1
5	1.25	31	3	0
7	0	20	3	0
24	22.5	105	16	6
7	10	55	10	2
6	6	12	6	1.5

Sources: SRO, Forfeited Estates, E741, Forfeited estates 1745 – Barrisdale – Reports Concerning Farms 1771.

Evidence for estates like Glenelg and Coigach shows townships that were similar in character to those of Ardnamurchan, with relatively small arable sectors but fairly extensive acreages of hill pasture. In character, their combination of oats and barley cropping coupled with balanced herds and flocks[82] suggests only modest changes in the township economy were in progress when detailed evidence brings them into view during the 1750s, 60s and 70s. In Coigach, a 'good deal' of potatoes were already being cropped by 1750s and most of the rent burden appears to have been shifted onto live-stock, with cattle, horse, sheep, goats, butter and cheese all being marketed.[83] In the case of Glenelg, major social upheavals took place in the early 1770s, when tenants responded to rent rises and falling prices by leaving some townships en masse, such as the five tenants in Cullendown who 'All went in a body to America'.[84] In the end, the removal of traditional township forms came slowly to Glenelg. When the estate was put up for sale in 1823, some townships were still held as 'club farms' alongside others which had switched to single tenancy and to a greater involvement in stock production.[85]

Further north, this sort of differentiation occurred much earlier on the Assynt portion of the Sutherland estate. When Home's survey was completed in 1774, townships on the estate were already divided by the estate into two types, coastal and inland. This distinction was 'a fundamental fact in the agriculture of Assynt'.[86] Coastal townships were heavily settled, having some of the largest tenant numbers per township in the region. Though having modest arable resources, they depended on arable supplemented by fishing for their survival.[87] By contrast, the inland townships were held by single tenants or tacksmen and committed to specialist cattle production.[88] As Bangor-Jones observed, the droving trade in this part of the region can be traced back to the mid-seventeenth century, and involved both large and small tenants. However, in the long term, it benefited the larger tenant most. It is in this context that we should see the differentiation of inland cattle farms from heavily settled coastal townships on Assynt, with tacksmen and the larger tenants on the former working to enlarge their specialist interest in cattle production from at least the 1730s onwards.[89]

Moving westwards, we can divide the inner Hebrides into two broad zones. In the North, Skye must have experienced some change over the early eighteenth century, for tenants on both the MacLeod of Dunvegan and Macdonald Estates were paying a significant part of their rents in cash by the early eighteenth century and so must have had some flexibility over cropping and over how they balanced their rent burden between crop and stock. A significant number of townships appear to have taken what we can call the maximum subsistence option, using the grain no longer paid as rent to expand their subsistence economy to its limits and shifting the burden of rent wholly on to the sale of cattle. When surveying the Macdonald estate in 1799, Blackadder wrote that the prevailing idea was that every township should have enough tillage to support itself in grain without resorting to the market and that the grazing and yearly cast of cattle should pay the rent, though he added that they also kept sheep and goats.[90] Where he describes cropping, it was based on oats and potatoes, the introduction of the latter having largely supplanted the local cropping of bere. Echoing Adam Smith, he portrayed every family in the country as 'a kind of independent Colony of itself, They turn up what part of the Soil is necessary to support them with Meal and Potatoes, take their own Fish, Manufacture and make the most of their own Cloth and Husbandry utensils. Their cows supply them in summer with Butter, and Milk, after which a few of them are sold to pay for the small spot on which they live'.[91] Even in his 1811 report, Blackadder gives the impression that most townships were still runrig townships, or 'club farms'.[92] Yet rentals make it clear that both the Macdonald and MacLeod of Dunvegan estates also contained some townships held by tacksmen that were largely farmed by them using the labour of cottars. The MacLeod of Dunvegan estate especially appears to have observed a distinction between townships set 'in tenandry' and those set to tacksmen from the early eighteenth century.[93] It may well be that those set to tacksmen had developed a more specialised pastoral element to their economy even by then, supplying larger numbers of cattle to the droves that moved stock south. Indeed, we need to allow for the possibility that the distinction which estates like the MacLeod of Dunvegan estate drew between crofting townships and sheep farms during the late eighteenth and early nineteenth centuries may have been pre-figured in the landholding character of townships as far back as the early eighteenth century if not earlier.

Of the inner Hebridean islands, Mull is the most difficult to categorise. The 1743 rental for the Lochbuie estate shows that whilst the estate still gathered in livestock produce, including wedders, veal and horse corn as rent, all traces of meal or bere payments in kind had disappeared.[94] Mention was made earlier of a souming list of 1753 which suggests that townships carried good stock levels, including equal numbers of cattle and sheep and more than enough horses to maintain tillage. The principle behind souming was that every pennyland should have a right to soum and roum 64 cows, with an equal number of sheep. As regards horses, most townships appear to have stocked them at a rate equal to about a quarter of their cow numbers.[95] Even allowing for the fact that some townships were large and complex in tenurial terms, they were undoubtedly well stocked when compared with townships elsewhere in Argyllshire. On the face of it, Mull townships may have followed the sort of strategy evident in Glenorchy and Breadalbane, with fairly sizeable levels of arable still being maintained for subsistence but with townships becoming more involved in the marketing of stock over the second half of the eighteenth century. Indeed, souming lists for 1790–91 and for 1800 give the impression that the estate was actually trying to reduce pressure on grazings by issuing stronger regulations over souming levels.[96] In fact, compared with the 1753 stocking data, the actual number of stock carried by some townships, such as Rossall, appears to have increased significantly.[97] Despite the fact that one township, Tapull,[98] was banned from substituting cattle for sheep in its soums, it was sheep numbers that appear to have increased most when we compare the 1790–91 and 1800 lists. In fact, even when Walker visited Mull back in 1764, he noted the particular importance which farmers there already attached to sheep. The greater value of sheep compared with elsewhere helped to 'render Sheep Farming more lucrative and inviting than the Grazing of Black cattle'.[99] All the signs are that as in Breadalbane, some farmers on Mull exploited the new opportunities opening up for sheep farming even whilst townships were still held on a runrig basis.[100]

As Storrie has shown, Islay was experiencing a wide range of change by the second half of the eighteenth century, with tenant numbers being reduced and the layout of some townships undergoing structural reorganisation into more efficient forms as early as the 1750s and 60s and the island already on the way to being a model of change.[101] More than in other parts of the region, the traditional township was already disappearing by the third quarter of the eighteenth century. Indeed, whereas other parts of the Hebrides still impressed by their excess of tenant numbers during the second half of the eighteenth century, Islay impressed some contemporary commentators as being 'different from the rest of the Islands' because its townships did not appear to have such problems.[102] Its rich pasture grounds, especially in the north-east of the island, already provided the basis for a thriving commercial cattle sector by the time of the 1722 rental. As on the mainland, there are signs that some tacksmen were already dealing in specialised cattle production by then. To judge from the number of cattle reported as exported from the island each year in Walker's account of the island (1764), this specialisation continued into the second half of the eighteenth century.[103]

As regards cropping, oats were by far the major crop on the island. In the 1722 rental, it accounted for over 85 per cent of all grains sown. Even allowing for the higher yields of grains such as bere, oats was the most dominant crop. Commenting on these figures, Storrie has expressed surprise at the comparatively low figures for the amount of bere sown.[104] Given cropping regimes on the island, at least those described later in the 1760s, one might have expected to see larger amounts of bere being sown.[105] She suggests that we can expect the growth of the whisky industry to have generated more, not less, demand for bere. Yet we also need to keep in mind that even by the 1760s, only a few decades after their first appearance in the Hebrides, Islay was growing and exporting large amounts of potatoes, a crop which often substituted for bere in the early stages of its diffusion.[106]

Thanks to the meticulous and sustained way in which John Burrel recorded change, one of the best documented Hebridean islands in the context of the late eighteenth century is Arran.[107] A list drawn up in 1770 details the cattle, sheep, horses, and sowing in all 87 townships on the island.[108] A number of points stand out from the list. The first is the fairly high stocking levels for cattle and sheep, the former averaging 49.2 animals per township and the latter 119.8 per township (see Figure 7.15). In all probability, the high number of sheep reflects an early response to the growing market for them. When Archibald Menzies visited the island in 1764, though, he commented on what he saw as a tendency to overstock.[109] Burrel possibly agreed, for shortly after the 1770 list was drawn up, he introduced new souming rates that restricted stocking in a number of townships.[110] A second feature of Arran's township economy is the modest numbers of horses per township, or 6.5, though the averages were almost double that on some of the more fertile townships in the south of the island. A third feature, one no doubt linked to Menzies's stricture that Arran farmers made little effort to keep wintering ground for stock, is the fairly substantial amounts of grain that were sown on the island, with townships sowing an average of 31.5 bolls of grain (see Figure 7.16). Even by 1770, though, subsistence was being extended by potatoes, with townships planting an average of 5.9 bolls. Altogether, this represents a significant arable sector when compared with other Hebridean islands like Mull.

In the Outer Hebrides, Lewis and Harris shared similar township economies. Although having some large townships, with sizeable arable sectors, when we compare the number of tenants involved with the amount of arable, it is clear that the amount of arable per family had become restricted, especially if we take into account the amount that was broken by rock outcrops or poorly drained. More than in other parts of the Hebrides, tenants on Lewis and Harris were locked into subsistence economies, cropping heavily with oats and small amounts of bere but with potatoes being adopted on an extensive scale over the second half of the eighteenth century.[111] No souming lists are available for the late eighteenth century. However, one drawn up in 1824 for Lewis is particularly revealing. Whether seen at the level

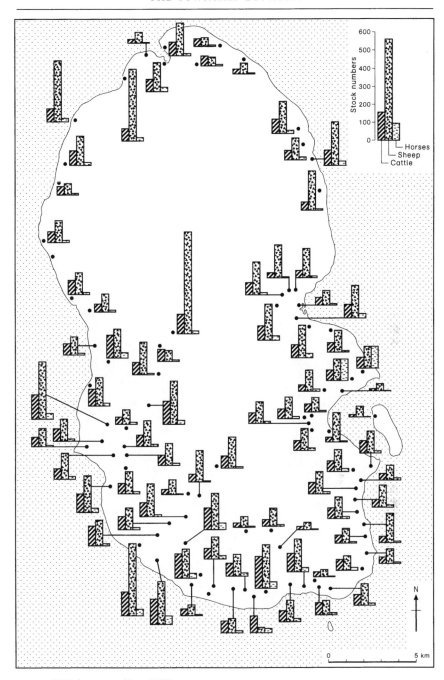

FIGURE 7.15. Arran: stocking, 1770
Source: Brodick, Arran Estate Office, John Burrel, vol. i, 1766–1773, pp. 144–6.

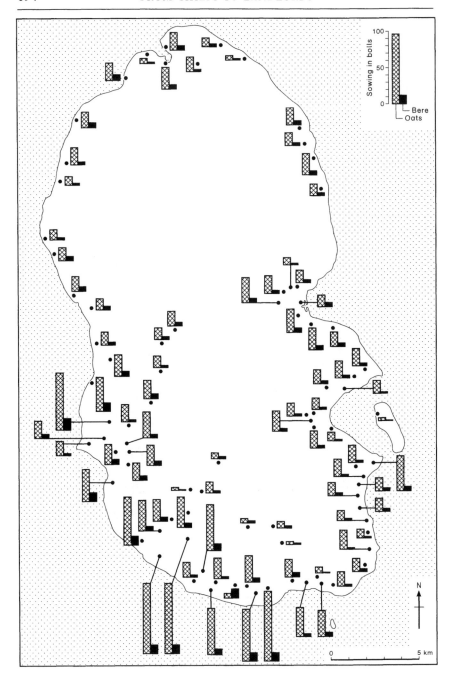

FIGURE 7.16. Arran: cropping, 1770
Source: Brodick, Arran Estate Office, John Burrel, vol. i, 1766–1773, pp. 144–6.

of the township or the level of the tenant, only small numbers of stock (cattle, sheep and horses) were involved.[112] As with other parts of the Hebrides, Lewis farmers probably traded off the grass needed to support larger stock numbers against an increase in arable, substituting seaweed for the manure lost or now no longer available. More so than in other areas, they maximised arable at the expense of stock. The estate seems to have gone along with this strategy. When we read through estate documentation for the late eighteenth century, there are few signs of any debate over sheep replacing people.[113]

Any review of Harris really needs to be divided into two parts. Its mainland townships stand comparison with those of Lewis, with arable sectors that were broken by rock outcrops and poor drainage. If we take the figures provided by the survey prepared in 1772, the mainland townships carried the greater proportion of Harris' population (68.3 per cent) but the lesser proportion of arable (31 per cent).[114] Despite this adverse balance, cropping was still based on oats and bere, with a small and declining acreage of rye.[115] The failure of the survey to mention potatoes suggests that either land pressure was not yet critical or that they were not yet a significant field crop as opposed to a garden crop. In fact, its mainland townships were still bound to make modest payments of meal as rent as late as the 1750s.[116] By comparison, the islands were better endowed with arable, despite the problems which sand blows had caused. Bernera still had over 1000 acres of arable and Pabbay over 400 acres. Despite this contraction, the township of Kirktown, or Kirkibost, owed 56 bolls of victuals which the estate augmented by 10 bolls in 1754, whilst Lingay and Northtown was bound to pay 16 bolls.[117] With this tradition of such large payments, plus their own subsistence needs, there can be no question that these townships were organised first and foremost to produce grain. Arguably, the use of seaweed as manure would have enabled them to cultivate far more than in a system dependent solely on manure.

In many ways, islands like Pabbay and Bernera have much in common with the Uists, with the mixture of sand and peat creating flat, workable and fertile soils. Blackadder's report in 1799 suggests that North Uist still cropped significant amounts of bere as well as oats and rye. Indeed, whereas other areas used a cropping cycle of two years oats and one bere, townships in North Uist cropped two years bere and then one year oats.[118] When we look at stocking levels, what stands out, as for other parts of the Uists, is the importance of horses. The explanation lies in their heavy use of horses for ploughing and for carting seaweed both for kelp and manure.[119] Though stock were sold, they reportedly covered only one third of the rent, the rest presumably coming from kelp.[120] Without the incentive to rear cattle or sheep on a greater scale, North Uist farmers preferred to maximise the resources needed for arable or kelp production.

The traditional image of the township economy depicts it as organised around time-honoured routines of husbandry, one that experienced little change prior to when the clearance of some townships for sheep and the re-organisation of others into crofting townships brought it to an abrupt end. As I have tried to show, there is a case for arguing that the township economy was experiencing adjustment and change from at least the early seventeenth century onwards. The typical township economy prior to this point was a mixed economy devoted to providing all-round subsistence both for the tenants themselves and for the chiefly household, one that as a consequence had a significant arable sector and which carried a balanced range of stock and poultry. From this baseline, we can detect a range of adjustments along two broad pathways of change. First, as the demands of chiefly households declined, a more commercial sector emerged, one geared to the marketing of cattle, grain and malt. The marketing of cattle involved most parts of the region by the mid-seventeenth century, the Hebrides no less than the mainland. Macinnes has suggested that by the 1670s herds of over 400 cattle were being droved out of the region on a regular basis. However, 'droves in excess of 1000 head of cattle became a noted feature of the Highland economy from the 1680s', once Falkirk market had been established as a collection and transhipment point and as demand from the English market increased.[121] The marketing of grain and malt was more selective, drawing on surpluses only from the more fertile areas, such as the eastern side of the Cromartie and Sutherland estates or areas like Kintyre. The role of landowners was instrumental as regards the early marketing of stock and grain. When faced with huge inflows of stock and grain to their bow and girnal houses, but a growing range of legislative checks on how they might consume them via displays of conspicuous consumption, chiefs logically turned to the marketplace. Whether through the demonstration effect provided by these estate-led strategies of marketing, or through a policy of wadsetting, feuing or setting townships to 'gentlemen' , there had slowly emerged a range of townships in many areas that were held by small landowners or by a single or dominant tenant and which – by the late seventeenth century – relied on a township economy that was increasingly being energised by market demands, either for cattle or for grain. In terms of the capital which they committed to farming and in terms of outlook, this new breed of Highland farmer provided a wholly new sector of Highland farming, one whose township structure was to provide an easy but crucial testing ground for sheep during the third quarter of the eighteenth century.

The second pathway of change involved those townships that were burdened with excess numbers even by the mid-seventeenth century, either because they were set directly to a cluster of multiple tenants or because their tacksmen sub-let them in this way. For these townships, margins of production were drawn more tightly so that their economies became driven more and more by subsistence needs. Further, as numbers increased, such townships not only increased their arable but, as I will discuss at greater length in the following chapter, they increasingly resorted to a range of strategies that enabled them to intensify arable output at the expense of stock. Such townships faced a dilemma. As their rent was converted to cash, they were able to shift its burden from arable to pasture by marketing livestock, especially cattle, thereby releasing more arable output for consumption. However, their arable was expanded at the expense of winter pasture and meadow, whilst what pasture remained was degraded by the cutting of turf. Put simply, whilst they played an expanding economic role in generating the cash needed by the township economy, livestock played a reduced agrarian role as a source of manure: this shift away from the integration of arable and pasture was especially evident in the Hebrides or where seaweed was abundant. The potential conflict which it produced within the economy of such townships was to become a critical source of complaint by the mid-eighteenth century when surveyors highlighted what they saw as a gross neglect of the region's most marketable commodity, namely, livestock.

NOTES

1. Burnett (ed.), *ERS, xii, AD1502–07*, pp. 698–709; McNeill (ed.), *ERS, xvii, AD1537–1542*, pp. 624–5.
2. For example, the 1505 rental for South Kintyre provides instances in which the total victual rent for a township is declared in terms of its weight in stones and then broken down between how many stones of meal and how many stones of cheese, see Burnett (ed.), *ERS, xii, AD1502–07*, pp. 698–709
3. McNeill (ed.), *ERS, xvii, AD1537–1542*, pp. 611–13 and 515–20, shows that townships in Ardnamurchan and Sunart paid 10 stones of meal/cheese per merkland; Islay, Kintyre, Colonsay and Aros (Mull), 12 stones, and Tiree, 8 bolls of meal and bere.
4. McNeill (ed.), *ERS, xvii, AD1537–1542*, p. 650.
5. Gregory and Skene (eds), *Collectanea de Rebus Albanicis*, pp. 161–71.
6. Skene, *Celtic Scotland*, iii, p. 437. The report talks about the amount of rent paid as 'sa great of victuall, buttir, cheis, mairtis, wedderis and other customes, that it is uncertain to the inhabitants thairof quhat thai should pay'.
7. A 1727 survey of Ardnamurchan and Sunart suggests that townships like Bourblaige, with 750 acres of arable and grass, paid marts whilst a township like Laga, with over 4000 acres, paid no marts. However, the precise ecology of townships may be important here, for Blourblaige had access to the productive pastures that skirted Ben Hiant. See Murray of Stanhope, *True Interest*, appendix on 'Anatomie of Ardnamurchan and Sunard'.
8. Innes (ed.), *The Black Book of Taymouth*, pp. 268–99. To judge from those entries which record how much seed was provided under steelbow, the greater proportion of arable on the Breadalbane estate at this point was cropped with oats, most townships cropping between 5 and 20 bolls.
9. Ibid., pp. 268–95, shows a number of townships in the 1582 and 1594 rentals also cropped bere, but in most cases, it amounted to only one or two bolls.
10. Ibid., pp. 274 and 276. However, scattered references to stock which were in the tenant's 'awin hand' plus the fact that townships were required to pay marts confirms that tenants owned some of the stock.
11. Ibid., pp. 268–9.
12. McNeill (ed.), *ERS, xvii, AD1537–1542*, pp. 624–5; Murray of Stanhope, *True Interest*, appendix.
13. The 1727 survey gives the pennyland assessment of Ardnamurchan as 160 pennylands. The individual assessments of each township are the same as in the

1756 rental, see SRO, Campbell of Barcaldine Papers, GD170/420/2, Rental of the estate of Ardnamurchan, 1756.

14. NLS, ADV 29.1.1, vol. vii Murray Papers, Abstract of the Rentall of the Barrony of Ardnamurchin and Sunart, 1723. which lists some payments of meal, can yield some clues as to the role of the arable sector.

15. Ibid. By comparison, the payment of teinds in the 1727 survey shows a more variable link to pennylands, though some townships do pay a similar amount for similar ratings.

16. NLS, ADV 31.6.6 No. of Examinable Persons in Sv. Parts of the Highlands 1741, suggests that there were already 200 miners in the Sunart area by 1741.

17. Islay rentals for 1614, 1686, 1722 and 1733 are provided by Smith (ed.), *The Book of Islay*, appendix a.

18. Gregory and Skene (eds.), *Collectanea de Rebus Albanicis*, p. 160; Masson (ed.), *RPC, x, AD1613–1616*, 'Book of the isles', pp. 13–14.

19. Smith (ed.), *The Book of Islay*, pp. 521–43.

20. Ibid., p. 525.

21. Ibid., p. 525.

22. Ibid., p. 521.

23. Ibid., p. 521.

24. References to the decline of rye as a crop on Harris and North Uist occur in McKay (ed.), *Walker's Report on the Hebrides*, pp. 55 and 65. In both cases, the reason given was its exhausting effect on the soil.

25. Smith (ed.), *The Book of Islay*, p. 521.

26. McNeill (ed.), *ERS, xvii, AD1537–1542*, pp. 614–15; IC/AP, Bundle 251, Rental of Tiry, what it payed in the year :52 and in all years thereafter compiled 1675; ibid., Box 2531, Rentall of Tirie, 1680; ibid., V65, Number of Inhabitants on the island of Tiree with the Holding, Sowing and Increase of Each Farm, 1768.

27. Ibid., Box 2531, Memorandum anent Tirie, c.1680; Bundle 494, letter 1 June 1681, Dealing with Tiree rental.

28. Ibid., Bundle 251, Rental of Tiry, what it payed in the year :52 and in all years thereafter compiled 1675. It should be noted that writing in 1883, the duke argued that each *mail* equalled four soums, or 192 per tirunga; see Argyll, *Crofts and Farms in the Hebrides*, p. 8. In origin, though, it probably represented a levy or tax in grain; see Lamont, 'The Islay charter of 1408', p. 178.

29. Ibid., V65, Number of Inhabitants on the island of Tiree with the Holding, Sowing and Increase of Each Farm, 1768.

30. Ibid., Bundle 251, Rental of Tiry, what it payed in the year :52 and in all years thereafter compiled 1675.

31. Ibid., V65, Number of Inhabitants on the island of Tiree with the Holding, Sowing and Increase of Each Farm, 1768.

32. Ibid., Bundle 251, Rental of Tiry, what it payed in the year :52 and in all years thereafter compiled 1675.

33. Ibid., Box 2531, Memorandum anent Tirie, c.1680.

34. Ibid., Box 2531, Rentall of Tirie, 1680.

35. RHP 8826/2, A General description of the Island of Tiriy, Surveyed in 1768 by James Turnbull.

36. IC/AP, Observations on Tirie by Minister McColl, 4 July 1788.

37. Ibid., V65, Duncan Forbes of Culloden's Letter concerning the Duke of Argyll's estates in Tiree, Morvern and Mull, 24 Sept. 1737 (reprinted *Report of the Commissioners of Inquiry*, appendix, pp. 389–92).

38. Ibid., Bound Rental Volumes, Tiree, 1740, records most townships on Tiree as still making quite substantial payments of bere and meal. Kennoway, for instance, still paid 21 bolls of bere and 21 bolls of meal. Ibid., Argyll papers,

V65, Number of Inhabitants on the island of Tiree with the Holding, Sowing and Increase of Each Farm, 1768.

39. Martin, *Western Islands*, p. 271.
40. IC/AP, V65, Number of Inhabitants on the island of Tiree with the Holding, Sowing and Increase of Each Farm, 1768.
41. Ibid., RHP 8826/2 A General Description of the Island of Tiriy. Surveyed in 1768 by James Turnbull.
42. Bred horses were certainly a significant export from Mull in the eighteenth century. According to Walker, 500 were exported from the island each year in the 1760s; see McKay (ed.), *Walker's Report on the Hebrides*, p. 155.
43. SRO, MacLaine of Lochbuie, 174/736, List of Soums allow'd for Lochbuys estate for preceding and succeeding years 1743.
44. IC/AP, N.E.11, vol. 1543–1610, The Rentall of the haill landis and sowmes gudis ... within the parochin of Inchaild, etc., 9 October 1609.
45. Ibid., Bundle 746, The Haill Lands of the Lordship of Kintyr therof c.1636.
46. SRO, Breadalbane Muniments, GD112/9/7, Rental 1600; GD112/9/9, Rental 1620; GD112/9/3/3/1, Rental 1629; GD112/9/5/17/7, Rental 1667; GD112/9/24, Rental 1669–78; GD112/112/9/3/3/3, Rental 1688; GD112/9/3/3/7, Rental 1697; GD112/9/40, Rental 1717–20; GD112/9/43 and 44, Rentals 1736; GD112/9/54, Rental 1780–1.
47. Ibid., GD12/12/1/2/1, The Soums of Glenorchy in Sir Duncan's Time; Ibid., GD112/9/43, Rental of the Estate of Breadalbane 1736, including 'Comprisement of the Soumes of each Merk Lands in Breadalbane By Skillfull Birlawmen in the Year 1727'; Ibid., GD112/9/1/3/48, Calculation of the value of farms in Netherlorne drawn up for sowing and holdings, 1730; GD112/9/54, Rental of the Earl of Breadalbane's estate in Perthshire from crop 1780.
48. McArthur (ed.), *Survey of Lochtayside*, pp. 75–207.
49. Innes (ed.), *The Black Book of Taymouth*, pp. 265–99; SRO, Breadalbane Muniments, GD112/9/9, Rental 1620.
50. Ibid., GD112/9/3/3/1, Coppie of the Rentall of the Lands of Glenorchy, 1629.
51. Ibid., GD112/12/1/2/1, The Soums of Glenorchy in Sir Duncan's Time.
52. Ibid., GD112/9/1/3/48, Calculation of the value of farms in Netherlorne drawn up for sowing and holdings, 1730.
53. Ibid., GD112/9/5/17/7, The Sett of Lord Neills Lands for the Year of God 1667.
54. This has, in fact, support from a later 1688 rental for these townships which suggests that in the case of townships held by steelbow, every boll of sowing in grain was balanced by the same number in 'steilbow'; ibid., GD112/9/3/3/3, The Earle of Breadalbane's Rentall in Argyll, 1688.
55. Ibid., GD112/9/5/17/7, The Sett of Lord Neills Lands for the Year of God 1667.
56. Ibid., GD112/9/1/3/48, Calculation of the value of farms in Netherlorne drawn up for sowing and holdings, 1730.
57. Ibid., GD112/9/5/17/7, The Sett of Lord Neills Lands for the Year of God 1667.
58. Ibid., GD112/9/43, Rental of the Estate of Breadalbane 1736, including 'Comprisement of the Soumes of each Merk Lands in Breadalbane By Skillfull Birlawmen in the Year 1727'.
59. Ibid., GD112/9/44, Rentall of the earl of Breadalbane's Estate in Perthshire, 1736 provides an early indication of how estates were sanctioning official brewseats, such as the croft ale house at Tayinlone in Easter Ardnewage, the malt barn and two brewseats in Wester Ardewnage, the Brewseat and malt kiln at Killin and the brewseat at Carwhin.
60. Ibid., GD112/9/54, Rental of the Earl of Breadalbane's estate in Perthshire from crop 1780. The calculations given in the text are based on 187 townships but exclude all farms referred to as a croft.
61. Ibid., GD112/14/12/7/8, Lord Breadalbane's Querys, 1783.

62. Ibid., GD112/9/3/3/20, Rental of the Earl of Breadalbane's Estate in Argyle-shire, 1795.

63. SRO, Campbell of Barcaldine Papers, GD170/420/1/6, Rental of Portcharran, 1758. See also, GD170/420/1/1, Rentall of Glenure's Lands in Lismore, 1753.

64. Ibid., GD170/420/1/15, Rental of Achuoran, 1774.

65. SRO, Campbell of Sanda, GD92/173, Rental Book of Sanda's Lands, 1748–1784, especially Rental of the estate of Sanda, 1781.

66. SRO, Forfeited Papers, E729/9/1, Journal of Archibald Menzies, general Inspector, 1768.

67. Mention has already been made of the duke of Argyll's claim that many of his tenants in Kintyre were distilling whisky illegally, see IC/AP, Bundle 2530, Instructions His Grace the Duke of Argyll to David Campbell his Chamberlain in Kintyre, 1761.

68. IC/AP, Bundle 1953, Lists of sowming and sowing, Kintyre, 1770s.

69. SRO, Forfeited Papers, E729/9/1 Journal of Archibald Menzies, 1768; IC/AP, Bundle 208, Journall by Mr. Burrell in Kintyre, 1769.

70. Ibid., Bundle 2530, Instructions His Grace the Duke of Argyll to David Campbell, 1761.

71. SRO, Forfeited Papers, E729/9/1 Journal of Archibald Menzies, 1768.

72. SRO, AF49/2A, Valuation of the Estate of Ardnamurchan, 1807.

73. Ibid.

74. SRO, AF49/2B.

75. Ibid., Notes compiled by Thos. Anderson c.1840. The figures provided by Anderson show sheep dominant by c.1840.

76. SRO, Forfeited Estates, E788/42, report on the Estates of Barrisdale and Kinlochmoidart c.1755.

77. Ibid.

78. See also SRO, Breadalbane Muniments, GD112/16/13/4/1–2, Copy report by Alexr. McNab concerning the Glengarry estate, 1769 which describes Knoidart as 'serving itself' but other parts as not.

79. SRO, Forfeited Estates, E788/42, Report on the Estates of Barrisdale and Kinlochmoidart, c.1755.

80. The 1755 survey describe potatoes as 'much attended to by them'; ibid. and E729/3, States of Various Farms, 1755.

81. A 1771 survey described local farmers as deriving 'great support' from herring, curing as many fish as will serve them for three-quarters of the year; see ibid., E741, Barrisdale – Reports concerning farms, 1771.

82. Ibid., E729/1, Report from Captain John Forbes, 1755; E746/151, General Report on the Estate of Cromarty.

83. Ibid., E746/151, General report on estate of Cromarty.

84. DC/MDP, 2/105/1–2, Statement of Tenants in Glenelg, 1776.

85. Ibid., 380/30, Advertisement of Sales of estate of Glenelg, 1823 (also SRO RHP23075/3).

86. Adam (ed.), Home's Survey of Assynt, p. xliv. The general contrast between coastal and inland townships is discussed ibid., pp. xliv–liii and Bangor-Jones, 'The clearances in Assynt'. Home's survey, and the contrast between interior and coastal farms, is splendidly mapped in Simms, 'Geographical interpretation of historical sources; Simms, Assynt, see maps in folder.

87. For specific comment on coastal townships, see Adam (ed.), Home's Survey of Assynt, pp. 11, 14–15, 17, 19, 29, 42 and 49; OSA, xvi (1795), p. 193.

88. For comment on the tacksmen of inland townships, see Adam (ed.), Home's Survey of Assynt, pp. 35–8.

89. Comment on the development of grazing farms in Assynt over the eighteenth century is provided by Bangor–Jones, 'The clearances in Assynt', pp. 2–3. His

forthcoming 'Society and Economy', an essay on Strathnaver, in press, also provides valuable comment on the development of cattle droving.

90. SRO, RH2/8/24, John Blackadder's Description and Valuation of Lord Macdonald's Estates in Sky and North Uist, 1799 and 1800, pp. 3, 14–17.

91. Ibid., pp. 107–8.

92. CDC/MP, GD221/116, Report Relating to the Value and Division of Lord Macdonald's Estate in Skye, made by John Blackadder, 1811.

93. DC/MDP, 2/485/26/3 Judiciall rental.

94. SRO, MacLaine of Lochbuie Papers. GD174/715, Rentall of the Estate of Lochbuie, 1753.

95. Ibid., GD174/736, List of the Soums allow'd for Lochbuys Estate for preceeding and succeeding years, 1753.

96. See, for example, ibid., GD174/856/2 Souming of Ardmeanach. Agreement by tenants reducing their soums to the number stated, 1791.

97. Ibid., GD174/856/10, Glenbyre and other farms. Souming for Kinlochbuy 1800'.

98. Ibid., GD174/856/2, Souming of Ardmeanach, 1790–1.

99. McKay (ed.), *Walker's Report on the Hebrides*, p. 157.

100. Ibid., p. 160.

101. Storrie, *Islay: Biography of an Island*, pp. 68–71 and 75–90.

102. SRO, Forfeited Estate, E729/9/1, Journal of Archibald Menzies, General Inspector 1768. Menzies put its exceptionalism down to the way in which the migration of many of its younger men and women to Ireland eased the pressure on land. The case for this migration, a loss more 'detrimental than any caused by disease', was also made by Walker; see McKay (ed.), *Walker's Report on the Hebrides*, p. 97. See also Storrie's case for its exceptionalism; Storrie, 'Islay: a Hebridean exception', pp. 87–108.

103. McKay (ed.), *Walker's Report on the Hebrides*, p. 100.

104. Storrie, *Islay: Biography of an Island*, p. 68.

105. Cropping regimes are detailed in SRO, Forfeited Estate, E729/9/1, Journal of Archibald Menzeis, General Inspector, 1768.

106. McKay (ed.), *Walker's Report on the Hebrides*, pp. 101–2.

107. Brodick, Arran Estate Office Records, Burrell, Arran Journal, 2 vols, 1766–1773 and 1776–1782.

108. Ibid., vol. 1, pp. 31ff.

109. SRO, Forfeited Estates, E729/9/1, Journal of Archibald Menzeis, General Inspector, 1768.

110. Brodick, Arran Estate Office Records, Burrel, Arran Journal, 2 vols, 1766–1773 and 1776–1782.

111. McKay (ed.), *Walker's Report on the Hebrides*, p. 55; DC/MDP, 1/466/24, Description of Harris, 29 Feb. 1772; *OSA*, xix, 266; ibid., X, p. 354; Shaw, *The Northern and Western Islands of Scotland*, p. 95.

112. SRO, Seaforth Papers, GD46/17/63, Number of cattle and horses in the district of Barvas, 1824.

113. A memorandum written in 1820 offered draconian solutions. It talked about how the population of Lewis should be 'disposed of', reducing the population from 12000 to 2000, the latter employed as shepherds, fishermen or kelpers; see ibid., GD46/17/55, Volume of Papers, letters, etc., October 1820, Observations after examining the north part of Lewis.

114. Based on DC/MDP, 1/466/24, Description of Harris, 1772; 1/466/22, Contents of the Mainland of Harris and Adjacent Islands, 1772.

115. McKay (ed.), *Walker's Report on the Hebrides*, p. 55.

116. DC/MDP, 2/487/31, Rental of Harris, 1754).

117. Ibid., 2/487/28, Rentall of the Barrony of Harris, 1754.

118. CDC/MP, RH2/8/24, John Blackadder's Description and Valuation of Lord Macdonald's Estates in Sky and North Uist, 1799 and 1800.

119. McKay (ed.), *Walker's Report on the Hebrides*, p. 209. See also comments in SRO, GD403 Mackenzie Muniments, Report of the Value of North Uist, by John Blackadder, 1811; Shaw, *The Northern and Western Islands*, p. 117.

120. SRO, RH2/8/24, John Blackadder's Description and Valuation of Lord Macdonald's Estates of Sky and North Uist, 1799 and 1800. John Blackadder, ibid., thought that the 'grazing of so many useless Horses on every one of the farms will make an equal loss or discount on the profits which ought to arise from the Grass, amounting altogether to no less than the sum of 800 pounds, equal to one third of the present rent of the whole island'. Shaw documents an instance of horse breeding for North Uist; *The Northern and Western Islands*, p. 117.

121. Macinnes, 'Civil wars, inter-regnum and Scottish Gaeldom', pp. 63–4. See also Whyte, *Agriculture and Society*, p. 240.

8   The Farming Township: Its Strategies and Constraints

In this chapter, I want to look at the strategies of farming though which communities exploited the resources at their disposal. The character of west Highland and Hebridean farming townships, with their localised pockets of fertile soil backed by vast quantities of hill ground, created a complex web of opportunities and challenges for them. If we are to understand how they responded to these opportunities and challenges, we need to consider three dimensions of the problem. First, we need to examine the prevailing types of field economy and the systems of crop and stock husbandry used to sustain output. Embedded in these themes are fundamental questions about how arable and non-arable were integrated and whether the needs of one had priority over the other. Second, we need to consider the social context of production. In the Introduction, I said that communities faced a slope of opportunity costs. I put it in these terms because the difference between what could be cultivated and what could not was not simply about ecology or ground conditions. It was also about the social needs of a community and their capacity, through changes in labour input or demand, to steepen or lower the slope of opportunity costs. Third, having outlined the agro-ecological and social dynamics of prevailing strategies, we need to understand their potential constraints and dysfunctions when seen as a part of a growing and evolving system of husbandry.

THE HIGHLAND TOWNSHIP AND ITS FIELD ECONOMY

Though it is possible for arable to be maintained in cultivation for long periods without manure,[1] ecological conditions in the western Highlands and Islands would have worked against such a low-input system. Fertile soils were limited in distribution. More serious, heavy leaching meant Highland and

Hebridean soils needed regular inputs of nutrients if they were to maintain output. Though this was more acute on the sandy soils of some Hebridean townships, the problem was not confined to such soils. Compounding the problem further was the fact that the acidity of many Highland and Hebridean soils inhibited the uptake of key nutrients. Under these circumstances, cultivation in the western Highlands and Islands needed to be based on systems of husbandry that sustained nutrient levels on a regular basis. Not without very good reason did Donald Monro, Archdeacon of the Isles, continually refer to arable in the region as 'manurit land'.[2]

Other than some form of shifting cultivation, the simplest solution to the problem of maintaining nutrient flow was to add winter livestock manure. Stock would be housed in a byre over winter and their manure stored in readiness for applying it to arable in spring. There is every reason to believe that this was the root strategy adopted by all Highland and Hebridean townships. In its established form, such systems would have consisted of an arable sector surrounded by a head dyke or ring garth, with cattle paths leading from the pasture beyond the dyke through or round the arable to the settlement core and its byres or kailyards. To supplement winter feed and to maximise manure, we can also expect such systems to have been widely associated with the use of meadows that were either cut for hay or grazed, at least initially.

By the time Highland and Hebridean field systems come into view during the eighteenth century, they appear divided between two broad types: one based on infield–outfield cropping and the other on a grass–arable system of cropping (see Figure 8.1). The former can be documented for much of the southern and south-western Highlands, and some parts of the western Highlands and Islands. Detailed descriptions are provided by a variety of surveys. Archibald Menzies provided detailed description of its practice across parts of the south-western Highlands and Islands. In Kintyre, he wrote, their 'corn farms are divided into Infield & Outfield Cropeing of infield is 1st Barley to which they give 2 spring plowings 2nd and 3rd Year Oats which gets one plowing then begin Barley etc, etc. Their Outfield is five years Oats five years rested and the Cattle & sheep folded upon it before Breaking up'.[3] Further north, in Netherlorne, Menzies found a similar system, with the 'Cropeing of Infield is Barley – Oats – Oats – Barley 1 year rested To the Ground design'd for Barly they give a Plowing the beginning of Winter a second in spring and immediately before sowing turn it over with a spade which they call brogging The dung they put on after brogging some after sowing, They give one Plowing to their Oats'. Outfield was divided into six breaks or fields, 'of which 3 plow'd 3 rested, They tath their Outfield before breaking up, some near the Coast sand and take one Crope Barly 2 oats'.[4] A description of its practice on Luing drawn up in 1798 by Robert Robertson talked about local infield–outfield system being described in terms of an infield or wintertown and an outfield. In all the townships on the island, he wrote, 'Infield croft ground or what they call wintertown is divided into Three divisions one sown

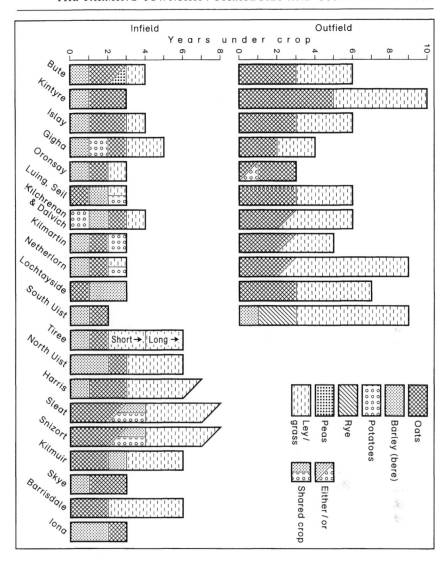

FIGURE 8.1. Cropping regimes in the western Highlands and Islands
Sources: SRO, E729/9/1: SRO E741: SRO RH2/8/24: RHP972/5: SRO RHP8826/2: *Walker's Report on the Hebrides,* pp. 55, 77, 207 and 210: *OSA,* x, pp. 354, 462: xi, p. 300: xiv, pp. 141, 159, 303: xvi, pp. 186–7: xix, p. 266. Originally published in Dodgshon, 'Strategies of farming in the western Highlands and Islands', p. 687.

with oats one with Barley and one is Ley a third of which is planted with Potatoes Outfield or Tath ground are divided into Three Divisions: one of these broke up for Oats after what they call tathing their cattle upon it, and taking Two crops of Oats off, without any more manure then let it out for Two or Three years carrying a scanty crop of grass till they are over the other Two divisions so this means the Tathing goes round in a rotation'.[5] The basic features of these descriptions are repeated in surveys for other areas.[6]

Arguably, the key organising feature of such systems is how they used available manure. Infield, or wintertown, was that part of the township where stock were kept over autumn and winter, feeding on the harvest stubble, and what townships described as their winterings, or sheltered green pasture within the head-dyke. This sheltered green pasture would also include meadow land, either cut for hay or grazed. Extant surveys suggest many mainland townships, as well as some of the Hebridean islands, maintained small amounts of meadow. The 1769 survey of townships along the south side of Lochtayside, for instance, had an average of 8.56 acres of meadow each.[7] According to a survey of 1809, Luing had 987 acres of arable and only 23 acres of meadow.[8] Its use, though, was not universal. Whilst hay was reportedly cut in coastal areas like Glenelg[9] and Assynt,[10] it was said to be neglected as a winter feed in Barrisdale[11] and Coigach.[12] In the case of Barrisdale, though, the evidence is conflicting. A survey of 1755 reported over 100 acres 'in hay'[13] but a written commentary accompanying the survey noted that 'no Hay made on this Estate'.[14] On Arran, a survey of 1772 shows only 20 townships out of the 99 on the island had meadow, with the island's 10284 acres of arable being supported by only 144 acres of meadow.[15]

A further supplement to winter feed was provided by woodland. Early eighteenth-century references exist to the Irish farmers who had leases for the townships of Drumliart, Kinchrakine, and Park of Ardlatle in Glenorchy[16] and who had licence to cut timber on the Breadalbane estate using the cover of the latter to cut 'Birtch, Aller, and oyr Timber at pleasure for horse graith'.[17] References to such deliberate harvesting of tree fodder, though, are rare. More usually, stock simply grazed in woodland, eating young firs, the leaves and branch shoots of birch and oak and, in the case of goats, stripping bark.[18] Initially, the grazing value of woodland must have been accepted as within the bounds of accepted custom so long as tenants left timber 'hanging and standing' at the end of their tack or occupation.[19] We find an abundance of references to the grazing of woodland by the eighteenth century simply because many landowners now saw other more valuable uses for timber than having it damaged by stock. Many now compelled tenants to enclose the woods present in their townships, preventing stock from getting access to them,[20] and took steps to ban the most difficult and destructive of animals when it came to woodland, namely, goats.[21] References to wood 'being much destroyed & peeled by goats', though, are still common in mid-to-late eighteenth-century management papers.[22] The problem of goats aside, the enclosure of woodland over the eighteenth century must have 'hurt the farm considerably' as it did Lower Kinchrackine in Glenorchy in the 1780s.[23]

As a system of cropping, infield arable could not be expanded indefinitely. Quite apart from the fact that the extent of infield was initially limited by a township's assessment or by what it could sow, there were problems over sustaining a sufficient supply of winter manure. The very land that was needed for wintering stock, particularly sheltered pasture and meadow, was the very land into which infield arable was expanded. In short, if infield arable was subjected to sustained growth, a point would have been reached at which the needs of arable and those of stock would have conflicted. If tenants forced the issue, the outcome would have been a reduced supply of winter manure being spread across a larger arable acreage. Once this constraint was reached, townships faced two possible ways forward. First, they could exploit the summer waste of manure, or that produced by cattle, horses and sheep when they grazed the hill pastures. This could be done by tathing, or folding stock on part of the land outside of the head dyke that surrounded infield. As Robertson's description of townships on Luing makes clear, tathing could only take place before cultivation not during it. This meant that once a part of the newly colonised outfield had been tathed and brought into cultivation, the tathfold had to be moved to a new section thereby setting in motion a shifting pattern of cultivation. To confuse it with early forms of shifting cultivation as some have done is to miss the role which tathing played in preparing outfield land and its critical effect on the cycle of cropping.[24]

An alternative way of expanding output whilst maintaining nutrient flow to arable was by exploiting the extensive resources that most townships had access to in the form of their non-arable sector. In mainland areas especially, peat and turf gathered from hill pastures were both used as manures along with roof thatch. The transfer of peat soil or any sort of soil from beyond the head dyke was a direct and immediate solution.[25] The addition of turf was a less direct process. Widely used for wall and dyke construction and for layering on roofs, it was afterwards composted and added to arable, the delay in its use being beneficial given the relatively slow breakdown of the nutrients locked up in turf. The scale of its use is shown by the extent to which dykes were reported as built of turf, or turf and stone,[26] and by the number of bailie or barony court proceedings which contain acts banning the cutting of turf either from green grass or from land within the head-dyke.[27] Such practices suggest that some Highland farmers were placing the needs of their arable above that of their stock, sacrificing their ability to maintain the one in order to sustain or expand the output of the other. The scale of the sacrifice is hinted at by a commentator who argued that the flaughter spade used for turfing had done more damage than the Act of Union![28]

In terms of the crop rotations used, mainland descriptions suggest that infield was cropped two years with oats and one with barley, whilst outfield was cropped solely for barley (see Figure 8.1). However, two changes to this staple rotation are evident by the mid-to-late eighteenth century. First, potatoes were introduced, initially at the expense of bere but later at the expense of oats.[29] Second, in his tour of the Hebrides for the Forfeited Estates commissioners, Menzies refers to the use of a ley break on infields in the south-western Highlands and Islands, including mainland areas like Kintyre.[30] We cannot equate ley exactly with fallow, for it was simply land abandoned to grass without any attempt to weed. However, where a ley break did exist within a three- or four-break system, the differences from a so-called two- or three-field system could only have been marginal. Certainly, there is no way that any infield system in the western Highlands and Islands could be regarded as a one-field system, given their sub-division into different cropping breaks.

As Figure 8.1 shows, when we turn to look at field systems in some of the western isles, we find what can be called grass–arable systems. These involved the division of all arable into two or three sectors, with one part cropped for two or three years then abandoned to grass, whilst a new sector was brought into cultivation and cropped in the same manner. During the full cropping cycle, the different sectors would be shifted between grass and arable, and back to grass again. Despite its outward appearances though, we must resist the temptation to see this as a surviving form of shifting cultivation, the most primitive type of cropping. What matters is the fact that under such a system, arable was manured before cultivation. Further, when we compare some grass–arable systems, they actually involved a higher proportion of arable in cultivation at any one moment than many infield–outfield systems.

Rather than trying to hide such a system beneath a veil of archaism, the real challenge is to explain why these Hebridean communities adopted such a system in preference to a conventional infield–outfield system. Two possibilities need to be considered. The first is that it was bound up with the problems of assessment. A case has been made out for seeing infield–outfield systems in Lowland areas as based on the distinction between what was assessed and what was non-assessed land, or between what was considered arable and burdened with rent and what represented common waste. The structuring effect of assessments on township layouts derived from the fact that assessments were 'meithed and marched', that is, given a specific orientation and limiting definition on the ground.[31] As already argued in Chapter 6, not only did the feudalisation of tenures develop late in the western Highlands and Islands, but also, the broken, discontinuous and shifting nature of arable created obstacles for any attempt to turn assessments into finite blocks of arable that were precisely fixed and defined on the ground. Whilst having frameworks of assessment, and whilst having a ring-dyke around arable, many Hebridean townships are more likely to have been limited through the amount of grain which they could sow rather than the acreage which they could crop. Lacking any hard-and-fast distinction between what was infield and what was outfield, Hebridean townships may have had greater freedom over how they responded to growth.[32]

An alternative interpretation requires us to concentrate on the fact that many Hebridean townships relied more on applications of seaweed than livestock manure to maintain nutrient flow. On Tiree, where cropping was organised on the basis of two years in crop, two years grass, it was said to account for three-quarters of all the manure used.[33] On Coll, it was said to be the only manure used.[34] It was also used extensively throughout the Long Island.[35] As a manure, seaweed provided a good source of key nutrients but its effects were more transient than livestock manure. In a report on Tiree, its effects were limited to a year.[36] If used in preference to the stock manure, it would not have been so easy to maintain the constant cropping of infield on the basis of applications once every three or four years. Its application to arable every two or three years, with land then rested under ley or grass for two or three years may have been seen as the solution to this problem.

On the positive side, the substitution of seaweed for livestock manure may have enabled some communities with abundant supplies of seaweed and the labour to apply it, to break free from the constraints on expansion that were set by the relatively finite supply of manure. A feature about those islands which used seaweed, and one which a number of commentators drew attention to, is that stock wintered outdoors and little use was made of meadow. Surveying the island in 1768, Turnbull said that they 'were never in use to House their cattle in Winter'.[37] As Walker put it, having 'neither stables nor cow houses, they collect no dung.[38] The same was true of Coll[39] and, according to a report of 1677–88, Lewis.[40] Of course, it also needs to be noted that in comparison with many mainland townships, the milder Hebridean winters enabled stock to be outwintered with less risk. Linked to this outwintering of stock is the fact that some Hebridean islands made little use of hay or meadows. Despite his frequent references to husbandry, Martin Martin makes only a passing reference to the cutting of hay.[41] Detailed surveys of Harris (1771)[42] and Skye (1799)[43] record townships as having no meadow or very small amounts. When Walker first visited the Hebrides in the 1760s, he suggested that the use of hay was only just being introduced in the Outer Hebrides but he dated its adoption on Skye to a few decades earlier, or the 1730s.[44] His general assessment was endorsed by Turnbull's survey of Tiree (1768). 'The people', he reported, 'were never in use to house their cattle in winter, or to make any hay till within these 14 or 15 years'.[45] By the time Turnbull compiled his survey, there were 293 acres of meadow but he does not make it clear whether this was the actual area of grazed or cut meadow or the amount of land which he felt could be used as meadow.

This neglect of hay in the Hebrides, at least before the 1730s, could of course be explained by the presence in many townships of the outer isles and on islands like Tiree, Coll, and Colonsay, of machair, a sand-based pasture that was rich in calcium. In the milder, if no less stormy, climate of the western isles, machair provided townships with a very productive grassland, as well as one that provided an earlier and later growth of grass. Its use could have substituted for hay. Seen alongside the pasture that formed on arable when not under crop, it must have provided communities with reasonably good reserves of winter feed. The main problem with its use, though, is that any pressure exerted on it would have exacerbated the tendency of machair to erode easily. With some of the largest arable acreages in the region, the temptation to over-stock machair must have very real by the eighteenth century. In the circumstances, the use of seaweed provided an escape from such pressures.

Of course, seaweed had an alternative use by the mid-eighteenth century. For landlords and tenants alike, it could be made into kelp and sold for cash. As landlords asserted more and more control over seaweed, distinguishing more carefully between what could be used for kelp and what could be used as manure, many tenants must have found their supplies squeezed.[46] By the 1730s and 40s, the conflict over its use may have precipitated the adjustment mentioned by Walker and Turnbull, with farmers in parts of the Hebrides starting to supplement what seaweed they could still get with a greater use of hay. Adopting a hay-making strategy and thereby maximising their use of animal feed, would have enabled them to intensify their production of winter manure and to compensate for any problems that were emerging over the use of seaweed.

It will be clear from what has been said that infield–outfield and grass–arable systems used livestock in different ways. Indeed, there were differences in how they valued stock. These differences are apparent from their differences in stocking balance (see Table 8.1). Infield–outfield systems had a very prescribed need for stocking with horses. Being the most demanding stock in terms of feed, and rated in most cases as a double soum, their main use was for working arable. The extensive use of the spade or caschrom would have moderated this need. Any need for packhorses to carry cheese and butter to market or for carrying peat and turf, though, would have increased it. The surprisingly high numbers of horses kept by tenants in Barrisdale, an area in which only one plough was used, can best be explained by the difficulties of moving peat and turf from its high pasture grounds, and the large quantities of cheese and butter marketed in burghs like Inverness.[47] One or two mainland townships, though, kept large numbers clearly because they were breeding them. A rental of Glenorchy townships, for instance, shows townships like Auchlader and Arivean kept far more than one would expect given their fairly limited sowing rates. In all probability, they were being bred for sale.[48] Even the very earliest of the Breadalbane estate rentals, or those for the late sixteenth century, show that horses were moved around the Breadalbane estate as part of its steelbow system of tenure so we can expect some townships to have acted as suppliers.[49]

The main type of stock kept on infield–outfield townships, and therefore their main source of manure, was that of cattle. Where sources specify which animals were housed over winter, and therefore, which animals provided the main source of manure for arable, they invariably name cattle, though horses too were generally housed.[50] Many townships traditionally kept as many sheep as cows. In terms of their weighting within souming systems, though,

TABLE 8.1. Stock balance based on importance of particular stock as a percentage of total soum

Area	Cattle	Horses	Sheep	Goats
Slisgarrow Barony 1755	42	35	13	10
Kinloch Barony 1755	17	13	62	8
Breadalbane 1727	63	36	1	0
Breadalbane 1780	31	32	37	0
Glenorchy 1730	61	27	12	0
Netherlorne 1730	56	30	14	0
Braes of Lorne 1730	67	20	13	0
Ardnamurchan 1727	62	29	9	0
Sunart 1727	67	23	10	0
Barrisdale 1755	62	18	10	10
Coigach 1755	55	30	9	6
Assynt	69	13	14	4
Islay 1722	46	29	25	0
Arran 1770	57	15	28	0
Mull 1753	60	28	12	0
Rhum 1794	44	37	19	0
Kilmuir 1794	76	15	8	1
Tiree 1768	38	59	3	0
Barra 1794	33	50	17	0
S. Uist 1794	51	26	23	0
N. Uist 1794	32	52	16	0
Harris 1794	32	56	12	0
Barvas 1794	49	39	12	0

Note: The calculation has been based on soum weightings of one cow and five sheep equalling one soum, and a horse equalling two.
Sources: Except for Ardnamurchan and Sunart, which is based on a 1723 survey, figures used are for 1760s–90s. Data has been drawn from SRO, Forfeited Papers, E729/9/1: Murray of Stanhope, *True Interest*; Wills *Statistics*, pp. 4–8: *OSA*, x, p. 368, p. 411, xiii, p. 294, 306, xiv, p. 200: xix, p. 266. In the case of North Uist, the total for cattle has been calculated using the annual number sold per annum. In the case of Harris, the proportion of sheep has been estimated using the Outer Hebridean average.

sheep were seen as a much smaller claim on grazing resources. By the late seventeenth century, this numerical balance had begun to alter as some tenants began to specialise in cattle and as others exploited the role of cattle as a currency within the estate economy.

When we turn to grass–arable systems in the Hebrides, the main feature of their stocking balance is the relatively large number of horses which they carried, especially in the Outer Hebrides and on inner Hebridean islands like Tiree (see Table 8.1). In some cases, such as on Harris, North Uist and Tiree, they appear as a major demand on grazing resources if we standardise the souming rate for horses at twice that for cows. The explanation was simple. As Turnbull put it in his survey of Tiree (1768), the 'reason of their keeping so many, is owing to the number they use in manuring their Ground with Sea

Ware'.[51] However, in the case of Tiree, the fact that extensive use was made of the plough also contributed to the local demand for horses. This is made clear in a report on the island which Minister McColl sent to the Duke of Argyll in 1788. 'When on one farm', he wrote, six or eight ploughs are thus set agoing, and five or six score horses with creels sent to rise sea ware off the shore, besides some idle mares & followers, such a farm takes many hands & horses'.[52] Yet in some ways more revealing of the role played by horses in carting seaweed is James Boswell's reference to the large number of horses on the adjacent island of Coll, an island whose arable was almost entirely dug with the spade or caschrom.[53] As an island, Harris had a similar character to Coll, with extensive use made of seaweed, as well as the spade and caschrom, so its high proportion of horses need not surprise us.

Though there was less interest in managing them for their manure, all the islands maintained good numbers of cattle, their weighted souming rate making them either the major demand on grazing resources or a demand at least equal to that of horses everywhere, except on Harris, North Uist and Tiree. Though most Hebridean islands must have been actively supplying cattle to mainland droves by the mid-seventeenth century, there are no signs that specialisation was starting to shape stocking balances by then. In those instances where we can actually compute the number of sheep, most townships appear to have maintained equal numbers with cows though their differences in souming rate, with each cow plus followers equalling five or – in the case of the small native Hebridean breed – ten sheep plus followers, meant that sheep were seen as requiring far less support.

FARMING TOWNSHIPS AND LABOUR STRATEGIES

Late eighteenth- and early nineteenth-century estate commentators and surveys treated many parts of the western Highlands and Islands as over-populated. The duke of Argyll himself described Tiree as being 'over-peopled'.[54] Even in the early nineteenth century, the Lochtayside portion of the Breadalbane estate, an area not normally associated with excess numbers, was seen as suffering from a 'crowded state of the population' due to 'a mistaken feeling of compassion to the small farmers'.[55] In an analysis of holding size, Gray tried to put this overcrowding in a statistical form. He suggested that many tenants were trying to maintain their families and servants on less than 12 acres of arable even by the middle decades of the eighteenth century, and that by the late eighteenth century, following the spread of potatoes, the amount of arable per family had fallen to below 2½ acres (1 ha) 'in the more crowded lands of the north and west'.[56] Arguably, the problem may have been compounded by the tendency of some estates to distinguish between townships held by only one or two tenants, and worked by cottars, and others in which sub-letting and sub-division was allowed to develop unchecked. The question of holding size per tenant has a bearing on the strategies of husbandry that could be adopted in a township. When we survey both the manuscript and published sources on the husbandry techniques that prevailed in the western Highlands and Islands over the eighteenth century, what stands out is their universal stress on the backwardness of techniques. Typical is the comment in a 1799 report on Skye which referred to local farmers as having 'an obstinate bigotry' in wanting to continue 'in the antedeluvian stile of their forefathers'.[57] Similar sentiments were expressed in a report on Tiree in 1801, with ordinary farmers being described as having a 'stubborn attachment to old customs'.[58] Equally pertinent are the references to their labour-consumptiveness, with many aspects of husbandry involving 'arduous labour'[59] and 'much tediousness and expense'.[60] For Macculloch, the amount of labour invested in cultivation made the landscape 'almost Chinese'.[61]

A prime target of such comments was the extensive use of the spade and caschrom to cultivate land. Late eighteenth- and early nineteenth-century surveys provide detailed information on the balance between land that was ploughed and land that was dug. Some of the more fertile islands, such as Tiree, were still entirely ploughed, though many of the ploughs used were small, light ploughs with a single stilt called *cromnagads*.[62] However, there were other islands as well as mainland districts where the two were balanced more equally. Bald's 1807 survey of Ardnamurchan and Sunart, for instance, recorded 1588 out of Ardnamurchan's 3484 acres of arable, or 47.6 per cent, as dug whilst in Sunart, 1012 out of 1727 acres, or 58.8 per cent, were so prepared.[63] Even in Ardnamurchan though, there were individual townships in which more was dug than ploughed.[64]

In still other areas, by far the greater proportion of land was prepared with the spade and caschrom. On Harris, 5115 acres out of the 6958 acres that were classed as arable were reportedly dug with the spade in an 1804–5 survey. Like so much spaded arable, much of it was interjected with pasture. Particularly noteworthy about Harris are the large acreages spaded on islands like Pabbay, Ensay and Bernera.[65] A similar proportion was dug with the spade on Coll. A survey of what was known as the Two Ends of Coll belonging to the duke of Argyll described the townships of Bowest as entirely spaded as was 'the greater part of the Arable corn ground in this island'.[66] As on Harris, much of this spaded land would have included the 1674 acres of 'rocky arable', as opposed to what was just 'arable' (1859 acres), that existed on the island when it was surveyed in 1794.[67] In fact, according to the *Old Statistical Account*, Coll had only 30 working ploughs, or one for every 118 acres, whilst Tiree had 160 ploughs, or one for every 51 acres of arable.[68] Evidence for mainland areas like Barrisdale, Coigach and Assynt also suggests that by the greatest proportion of arable was prepared with the spade and caschrom.[69]

A common reaction to this widespread use of the spade and caschrom was that it represented a primitive trait or survival. Such an assertion ignores a number of vital features about the circumstances of their use. The first is the fact that the spade and caschrom were used most extensively on difficult, marginal ground. Indeed, there is a sense in which we should reverse the chronology of their use and say that with the spade and caschrom, many communities were able to extend cultivation out over marginal ground, or ground that was too stony, wet or steep for use with the plough. Though the spade and caschrom could be used with a system of broad asymmetrical rigs, their common use was with the narrow lazy-bed, a form of rig that had a number of benefits. It enabled soil to be deepened where it was otherwise too thin and stony. It improved drainage, and facilitated the movement of nutrients within the soil. When used in conjunction with the potato over the eighteenth century, a crop that not only gave a food yield more than twice that of grain and which tolerated soil acidity better even than black oats, the husbandry of spade or caschrom/lazy-beds/potatoes provided a highly successful means of extending cultivation onto marginal ground.[70] Once we see them in these terms, it follows that the spade and caschrom would have become more widely used as townships found cause to extend cultivation onto such land. Obviously, there were circumstances in which the pressure to cultivate such land must have existed early on. It is difficult, for example, to see how most of the townships in Barrisdale could have been cultivated from their outset except by use of the spade or caschrom. Donald Monro's references to arable on smaller islands like Taransay being 'delvit with spaidis, except sa mekle as ane hors pleuch will teill' as early as 1549[71] are probably best explained in these terms. Monro mentions arable being dug as well as ploughed on Harris, but makes no mention of spaded land on Lewis. This is surprising for when Martin Martin visited the island barely a century later, he was struck by how 'industrious' the natives were because they 'undergo a great Fatigue by digging the Ground with Spades'.[72]

Compared with the plough, the spade and the caschrom also had the advantage of providing a yield bonus. Estimates put that gained by use of the spade at about 25 per cent more than that yielded by ploughing and that of the caschrom at about 33 per cent more.[73] Clearly, for communities hard pressed for subsistence, such yield bonuses would have been attractive especially when combined with the fact that it could involve land that was not ordinarily cultivated by the plough. However, there was a further, less obvious bonus in using the spade and caschrom when compared to the plough. The latter generated substantial feed costs in maintaining plough-teams. By switching to the spade and caschrom, townships saved on these costs, enabling more pasture to be devoted to cattle or more arable to be devoted to the demands of human consumption. In other words, the spade and cachrom offered gains through factor substitution.

The question of maintenance costs needs to be seen against trends in holding size. Any increase in population or tenant numbers would inevitably have reduced holding sizes per tenant. To a degree, any such reduction could be offset by an expansion of arable. Though the evidence is not abundant, the small handful of estates that did carry out two successive surveys of arable prior to the spread of crofting and the clearances suggest that increases in arable were taking place over the mid-to-late eighteenth century.[74] Indeed, there are mid-eighteenth century tacks which bound tenants to increase arable.[75] However, whatever the gains made by an expansion of arable, the fact remains that many townships had average holding sizes by the end of the century that would have made the use of a plough unattractive. Estimates about how much land a plough could sustain vary according to the type of plough used, but even the small light plough of the Hebrides appears to have needed at least 20 acres of arable to be economic, plus the pasture and horse-feed needed for the maintenance of a ploughteam. Sharing a plough was obviously a possible solution but townships squeezed by a growth of numbers must have increasingly counted the price in terms of the subsistence needed to maintain plough horses. Clearly, even without taking into consideration the harsh fact that the arable of many west Highland and Hebridean townships now embraced marginal land to which the plough was unsuited, some communities must have had sound reasons for extending their use of the spade and caschrom at the expense of the plough, reasons that had nothing to do with cultural survivals or conservatism.

Of course, the spade and caschrom also had costs. In terms of labour, they were far more expensive than the plough. When the first surveyors, all improvers and marketeers to a man, were set loose on west Highland and Hebridean estates, they viewed the comparative labour costs of the spade/caschrom and plough with horror. Blackadder's survey of Skye and North Uist provides us with a breakdown of these costs. After noting that the 'plough is seldom used, as it requires so many men and Horses (four Men and four Horses)', he went on to propose that a new plough with two good horses and one ploughman could do as much work as an existing Hebridean plough with four horses and four or five men and as much as 12 men with a caschrom.[76] Clearly, on this basis, land prepared with the caschrom required three times as much labour as land prepared with the Hebridean plough. The problem for Blackadder and other surveyors is that they viewed the problem in terms of how tenants could minimise production costs so as to maxmise market gains. By contrast, many tenants, especially those in multiple-tenant townships, were concerned to maximise output, *at whatever cost*. As population rose and holding size fell, means and needs would have come together for them, with tenants having both the labour and the incentive to adopt more labour-intensive strategies. Once we bring these various points together, that is, the greater suitability of the spade and caschrom on marginal ground, their yield bonus compared to the plough, and their greater feasibility on smaller holdings, and once we set them beside the fact that many tenants were concerned to maximise output rather than to reduce labour costs, we can better understand why the spade and caschrom were used. Rather than seeing their use as an instance of long-term cultural survival, it would be more realistic to see them as having a cyclical relationship to the plough. As population rose, the advantages of using the spade and caschrom would have increased. As population fell, the reverse would have been true.

We can apply the same argument to other aspects of west Highland and Hebridean husbandry. Methods of harvesting and preparing grain were seen as particularly consumptive of labour. The sickle was widely used. In addition, many communities resorted to the simple technique of pulling the grain up at the root by hand, particularly the bere harvest. Not surprisingly, those from outside the region saw this as indicative of its role as a refuge for primitive practices, a form of harvesting which, for Duncan Forbes of Culloden, had been used 'since the beginning of time'.[77] Some years after Culloden's 1737 report on the Argyll estate, the Duke moved to ban the practice, at least as regards bere, through estate management instructions issued in 1750.[78] Over a decade later, though, in 1771, a survey of Tiree still found tenants practising the 'very hurtfull Custom in regard to manageing their Bear harvest – when the Crope is ripe, in place of cuting it, they pull every stalk from the Root, leaving the Surface in the same situation, as it had been potched by swine'.[79] Similar regulations against pulling 'up the roots of any corn, oats, or bear, or any other white crop' were incorporated in Articles of set for Lewis issued around 1790.[80] Despite this hint of the practice being used to harvest all grains, most references to it suggest it was primarily used to harvest bere.[81]

Once harvested, prevailing techniques of preparing grain could be equally demanding on labour and, in the eyes of would-be improvers, equally primitive. A particularly important part of grain preparation in the region given its cold, wet autumns was that of drying the harvested grain. Three methods were used. One particular practice that incurred much condemnation was that of graddaning, whereby the grain and chaff/staw were separated, and the grain dried by taking handfuls of the harvested crop and holding it over a fire, then shaking out the grain as the chaff and surrounding straw burnt away. Though the meal produced by such a method was dark, even black in colour, it was deemed wholesome. The degree to which we can document the practice of graddaning suggests that it was widespread throughout the west and north-west Highlands and Islands. However, it was being banned on an equally widespread scale by the mid-eighteenth century as landowners and their advisers became more sensitive about the way in which it destroyed part of the straw value of crop. The Argyll estate banned its use 'absolutely' in Morvern in 1733[82] and on Tiree in 1750.[83] The MacLeod of Dunvegan Estate banished its use throughout western and north-western Skye in 1735.[84] When the Macdonald estate extended the ban to its estates in north-east, east and southern Skye,[85] it effectively became banished altogether from Skye, a ban reaffirmed by Justices of the Peace for the Island in 1788.[86] It could not have been an effective ban, though, for the 'execrable practice' was still being noted in Sleat in 1799.[87]

What may have been a derivative of graddaning once the latter had been banned involved threshing the grain then placing it in a pot and heating it over a fire to dry the grain. This was known as *uirearadh* and was common in Skye. Like graddaning, it was a method that could be used to produce bread quickly.[88] A third method, one that was pressed on tenants by land-owners was the use of the kiln. When the MacLeod of Dunvegan estate banished the practice of graddaning in 1735, it accompanied the ban by an insistence that all meal paid as rent should be kiln dried.[89] By the 1790s, the *Old Statistical Account* report on Harris was able to record that all townships there had acquired kilns.[90]

Once dried, grain was ground either by the conventional water mill, the horizontal mill or the quern. There are important scalar differences between these different forms of grinding corn. In the more fertile parts of the western Highland and Islands, the large 'vertical' water mill, with its obligations of thirlage, was a longstanding feature of the landscape, with many districts having at least one. As soon as rentals for these areas become available, they record the presence of such mills and the holdings attached to them, whilst other forms of documentation record the many disputes that invariably surrounded them.[91] The large 'vertical' water mills, though, were not universal. Many areas along the western seaboard and out on the islands had only scattered examples. Ardnamurchan, for instance, had only one vertical mill, though Sunart, with a smaller overall arable acreage, had three.[92] In some cases, where vertical mills were few or scattered, they could be supplemented by a small township-based horizontal mill. Kilninian parish in Mull was said to have five conventional water mills supported by three smaller horizontal mills.[93]

However, in the more remote parts of the western seaboard and more generally in the Hebrides, grain was prepared with the small hand-quern. If the vertical mill served a district or group of townships, and the horizontal mill a township or large holding, the quern was the implement used by the individual tenant. It was particularly suited to townships that did not possess a suitable or adequate fall of water and whose output was too small to sustain the cost of taking grain to what might be a distant mill and paying multures. In Coigach, for instance, a horizontal or ladle mill was used at the then small township of Ullapool, but elsewhere only the quern was used.[94] A survey of townships in Barrisdale in 1771 also reported the quern as the standard means of grinding corn.[95] Apart from one tacksman using a 'small' mill, presumably a horizontal mill, tenants used the quern throughout Harris.[96] Even on Tiree, most tenants appeared to have used the quern down to the 1760s and 70s.[97] Like the spade and caschrom and like the use of the sickle, what struck surveyors and other commentators on the region about the use of the quern was how much labour was involved. Turnbull makes this clear in his 1768 report on Tiree. An 'expensive and troublesome method', he declared, which occupies the time of of two and sometimes three women 'at once'. By it, 'so much of their Time is taken up, that it must greatly retard them from other industry'.[98] Using his own calculations for the total output of Tiree and for the amount of grain ground per day by two women with a quern (or three firlots of oats or six pecks of bere), we can estimate the total annual labour consumed as around that of 200 women, about one third of all those on the island, for three months each year. For comparison, Pennant estimated that on Rhum, where all grain was prepared with the quern, it took two pairs of hands four hours to grind a single bushel of corn,[99] a rate marginally more productive than that for Tiree.

However tempting it is to account for the use of practices like the spade/caschrom, the sickle, graddaning and the quern in terms of cultural survivals, we cannot ignore the fact that, like the use of additional manures like turf and seaweed, they all demanded huge inputs of labour. Once we move back beyond the heavier populations of the mid-to-late eighteenth century, and reverse the trend towards smaller holdings in place by then, it is difficult to see how such heavy inputs of labour could have been sustained. Further, as a group of techniques, they were all particularly suited to a distinct ecology of production, one in which subsistence was at a premium and in which the opportunity costs of cultivating difficult marginal land were low. Again, such ecologies become less not more important as we push our perspective back in time. The point which I am working towards is that instead of seeing such practices as survivals, there is a stronger case for seeing them as responses or strategies that may have been phased in step with fluxes in population pressure, phases of low population pressure being associated with greater use of extensive strategies and phases of heavy population pressure being based on more labour-intensive strategies. Some areas of settlement, especially on the smaller more marginal islands that enabled clans to plant new cadet branches but not much else, may have had ecologies that suited labour-intensive strategies like the spade and quern all the time. From such niches, their practice may have spread more widely when population growth made out the case for their use elsewhere.

HIGHLAND AND HEBRIDEAN FARMING: ITS CRISES AND THRESHOLDS

In this final section, I want to draw together the threads of a theme that I have touched on in a number of chapters, namely, the crises and thresholds of resource use which west Highland and Hebridean communities had to overcome in order to ensure their ongoing survival. Whether we see these crises as induced by climatic extremes or by excess numbers, they required solutions. Both could trigger short- and long-term shifts in the critical balance between food surpluses and food deficits, creating potential disequilibria that could threaten the very existence of a community.

We can best understand the nature of these crises and thresholds by first trying to define the balance between surplus and deficit more precisely. By the eighteenth century, fairly good data becomes available for yields, or returns on seed. The regional data has been summarised in Figure 8.2. As can be seen, by the mid–late eighteenth century, there were many areas in which the average yields for oats varied from a return on seed of around 2.5× to about 3.5×, with one or two of the smaller Hebridean islands like Iona and

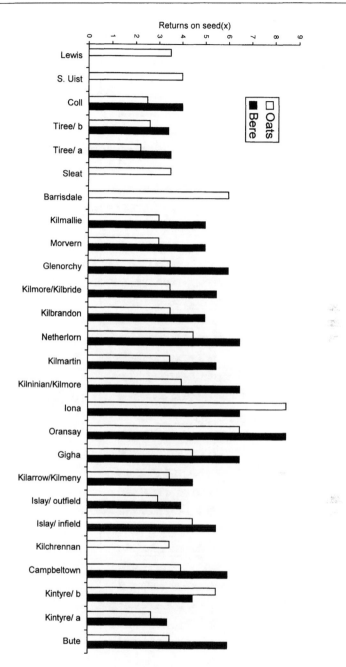

FIGURE 8.2. Crop yields in the western Highlands and Islands, late eighteenth–early nineteenth century

Sources: SRO, Forfeited Estates, E729/9/1: ibid., E741: ibid., E788/42: IC/AP, V65, Number of Inhabitants ... With the Holding, Sowing and Increase of Each Farm, 1768: *OSA*, x, pp. 270 395–6: xi, p. 299: xiii, p. 330: xiv, pp. 141 and 159.

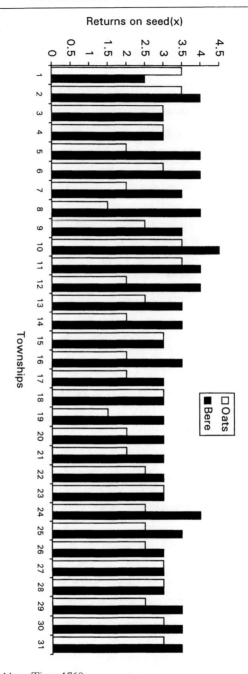

FIGURE 8.3. Crop yields on Tiree, 1760s
Source: IC/AP, V65, Number of Inhabitants … with the Holding, Sowing and Increase of Each
farm, 1768.

Oronsay boasting yields of around 8× and mainland areas like Barrisdale and South Kintyre having yields of 6× or more. Generally, returns on seed for bere were higher, with average output in most areas ranging from around 3.5× up to 6× or more, though some commentators made claims for exceptional local yields of over 10×.[100] What stands out from Figure 8.2 is that there were many large and well populated areas of the region whose returns on seed were in the lower part of these ranges for oats and bere.[101] Indeed, in the case of oats, the basic subsistence crop for many of these areas, average output must have been barely sufficient once we take out what was needed for seed and what, until the early eighteenth century, was paid as part of their rent. Bere offered better margins of return, but it was usually grown in more limited amounts and received most of the winter manure.

We can probe closer into the data on yields by looking at areas for which data is available on a township by township basis. That for Tiree and Barrisdale make for a revealing comparison. Tiree was long regarded as one of the most fertile of the Hebridean islands. By the time of Culloden's survey in 1737, though, communities on the island were clearly facing severe problems of production. Yields were falling and arable was infested with weeds,[102] though this was a common feature of Highland and Hebridean arable.[103] Subsequent surveys suggest the problem lay in over-production, with Tiree townships both overstocking and overcropping. Whatever nutrients were transferred via seaweed and thatch was patently insufficient to make good the deficit. Clearly prompted by continuing concern over this problem, James Turnbull was commissioned to carry out a detailed survey of yields over a four-year period in the mid-1760s. Arguably, his figures provide us with the most detailed and reliable analyses of yield that we have for traditional west Highland or Hebridean systems, figures that avoid the tendency of some estimates to overstate output by focusing on the best-practice holdings whose yields are likely to be better documented and to present farming in an 'improving' light. When we examine the Tiree data (see Figure 8.3), it suggests that Culloden's concerns were well founded. Overall, if returns for all townships are averaged, then those for oats average out at 2.6× and those for bere at 3.4×. More realistically, if we set the entire seed sown on the island against the entire recorded output, it suggests an average return for oats of only 2.2× and for bere of 3.5×. There can be no question that such yields placed Tiree communities in a marginal position. Variations brought about by normal fluctuations in weather patterns could easily erode such slender margins. To compound matters, any subsequent growth of population would have stressed the balance between arable and pasture further, reducing nutrient flow to a still greater degree. In fact, the island's population grew substantially over the remaining decades of the eighteenth century, from 1676 in 1769 to 2776 in 1802, or a 66 per cent increase.[104]

Arable on Tiree was largely prepared with the plough. By contrast, the more limited arable of Barrisdale was almost entirely dug with the spade and caschrom. The data for its townships is available only in terms of how much

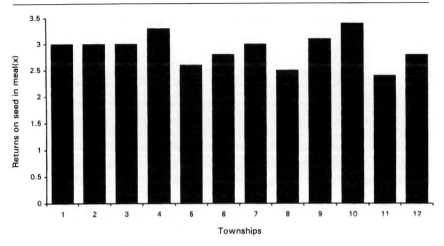

FIGURE 8.4. Crop yields in Barrisdale, 1771
Source: SRO, Forfeited Estates, E741, Forfeited Estates 1745 – Barrisdale Reports Concerning
Farms 1771.

yield of meal was returned by the seed used. As can be seen from Figure 8.4,
all its townships had a return of around about 3 bolls of oat meal for every
boll of seed. To compare this with the figures for Tiree, we need to allow for
a loss in the grinding of grain. Once we do this, the Barrisdale data suggests
a return on seed of about 4.5 to 5×. This is noticeably higher than the figures
for Tiree, a difference that can be explained by the extensive use of the spade
and caschrom in Barrisdale and by the fact that because the amount of arable
per township was far smaller in Barrisdale than on Tiree, inputs of labour are
likely to have been far higher, acre for acre.

With such low average yields in an area of sharp climatic variability and
recurrent hazards, some security could be achieved through more diversified
cropping strategies. Though surveys generally record only oats and bere as
the staple crops, some go beyond field crops and make it clear that the farm
production of field crops were supplemented by the produce of the kailyard.
Given the relative shelter of the kailyard, the vegetables produced in it may
have offered a limited protection against the failure of field crops.[105] Initially,
potatoes too would have been a crop of the kailyard. By the mid-eighteenth
century, though, they were being widely adopted as a field crop.[106] With a
significantly higher yield than grains, a greater tolerance of wet conditions,
and a food value that was significantly greater than grain per acre, they
offered greater security of subsistence against poor seasons. In time though,
the very scale of dependence on them, combined with outbreaks of blight,
made them a source of equal risk.[107]

Arable, of course, was only part of a township's resources of subsistence.
Communities could also survive on livestock, livestock produce, poultry and
fish. Proportioning the importance of these and other sources of food is

difficult largely because reliance on them varied locally. Much value was attached to cheese and butter but there is a case for arguing that meat, especially beef, had only a limited place in the diet of some Highland and Hebridean townships.[108] The same reservations cannot be made of poultry, which were consumed in quantity on all holdings. Fish were also a part of regular diets, especially along the coast. Commentaries on the role of fish, though, are equivocal. Some talk about the region's neglect of fishing.[109] What they had in mind was the lack of local involvement in largescale buss fishing along the west coast. Most of the busses that dominated the herring fishery were either Dutch or manned by Clydesiders, with the latter concentrating particularly on fishing the lochs that fret the west coast like Loch Broom.[110] It was not until the British Fisheries Society began to provide boats and to build curing stations and harbour facilities around new villages like Ullapool and Tobermory in the 1780s that local communities could claim an interest in this type of largescale commercial fishing.[111] However, the delayed response to such opportunities does not mean that communities ignored the possibilities of fishing altogether. There are ample signs that fish were caught and consumed as a vital part of local diets. Coastal communities in Assynt and Barrisdale, for instance, extended their subsistence base with fish, though significantly these were communities with small average-holding sizes.[112] In a few cases, estates collected fish in as rent, a practice that hints at the existence of a more specialised approach by some tenants.[113] By the 1770s and 80s, a number of estates, such as the Argyll[114] and Sutherland estates,[115] began to see fishing as a basis for estate reorganisation, with some townships either being classified or planned out *de novo* as fishing townships. In effect, holding sizes were kept small so that tenants were forced to supplement both their diet and cash needs by fishing.

In many ways, the real survival problem for west Highland and Hebridean townships was not so much the problem of short-term fluxes in output brought on by poor seasons or storms but the challenge of long-term expansion and how they coped with the way it tilted the balance between crop and stock. The idea that crop and stock were balanced was a fundamental principle behind the traditional organisation of many townships and one embodied in the notion that a township's assessment was linked to the number of animals which it could roum and soum. Whilst the number of stock a township could roum and soum over winter may seem to place a priority on a township's capacity to support stock, it was really just another way of acknowledging that the amount of stock kept by a township over winter determined the level of manure which it could apply to arable in spring and, therefore, the amount of arable which it could maintain. However, to reduce it solely to a matter of how much manure could be produced is too simplistic. There was another reason why the winter stocking capacity of townships was a critical factor. Many highland and Hebridean townships had access to vast quantities of summer grazings. However, under traditional forms of management, these hill grazings would have been undergrazed.

TABLE 8.2. Cattle:sowing ratios

Breadalbane 1780	3
Lochtayside 1769	2.92
Glenorchy 1730	3.71
Lorne 1730	1.8
Arran 1770	2.73
Islay 1722	1.89
Mull 1662	3.9
Tiree 1680	2.12
Tiree 1768	2.31

Sources: SRO, Breadalbane Muniments, GD112/ 9/54, Rental of Earl of Breadalbane's Estate in Perthshire, 1780–81; SRO, Breadalbane Muniments, GD112/16/12/3/1, Rentall of Glenorchy Shewing the present Rent ... Holdings and Sowings, 1730; ibid., GD112/9/1/3/43, Calculation of the value of the farms of Netherlorne – drawn from sowing and holdings 1730; McArthur (ed.), *Survey of Lochtayside 1769*, pp. 75–207; Brodick, Arran Estate Office Records, John Burrel's Arran Journal, vol. 1, 1766–1773, pp. 144–46; IC/AP, N.E.11, 1650–1669, Accounts and Rentals, Rentall of Mclaines lands, Mull, 1662; ibid., V65, Contents of the Different Farms of Tiree, by James Turnbull, 1768; ibid., 3531, Rental of Tirie, 1680; Smith (ed.), *The Book of Islay*, appendix iii.

Indeed, there is a case for arguing that they were increasingly undergrazed. The basic problem at issue here is that the average township could not winter the same number of stock as it could summer. If available winter feed was limited, then it acted as a constraint on what townships could maintain throughout the year.

If we are to grasp why summer grazings may have been increasingly under-grazed, and winter grazings correspondingly over-grazed, then we need to appreciate how the relationship between arable and pasture was supportive yet antagonistic. The stock that could be kept in winter main-tained arable. Table 8.2 shows the kind of relationship that existed on a number of estates between how much was sown in terms of oats and the number of cattle kept. Clearly, local factors, not least the use of seaweed as a manure, could vary the relationship. Yet whilst the number of stock kept over winter had a bearing on how much arable was cultivated, the existence of any arable actually worked against the support of livestock because it was created and expanded at the expense of the very land used as sheltered winter pasture and meadow. In any manure-based system of farming, the flow of nutrients from pasture to arable, via stock manure, is at an optimum when their respective balance or ratio, arable to pasture, is in the order of 20:80.[116] As the proportion of arable increases, the flow of nutrients and therefore, output or yields, falls away, becoming critical when their ratio is 50:50. This means that any sustained increase in arable beyond about 20 per cent of available land brought diminishing returns in terms of output, as com-munities fell into a nutrient-flow trap.[117] At first sight, such a trap, with all its implications for subsistence, would appear to have little relevance to a region like the western Highland and Islands, given that even to close its modern peak of population, or in c.1800, it did not have more than 9 per cent of its land under crop. The problem lay in the amount of land available as winter pasture. If we take survey data covering the period from mid-eighteenth to the early nineteenth century, and calculate the relationship between arable and what could be counted as winter pasture ('green' pasture, machair and meadow), then the balance between arable and pasture becomes far more critical (see Figure 8.5). If dependent on nutrients transferred via stock alone, many townships would have faced a crisis of output once arable approached these levels of intensity.

The ease with which farming townships could fall into a nutrient-flow trap forms an essential backcloth to the diverse strategies being employed by the eighteenth century. Faced with a decline in nutrient flow from their pastures and meadows, farming townships could escape the impending crisis by exploiting a wider range of resources from their extensive non-arable sector. Outfield was a particularly significant change of strategy because it used the otherwise wasted manure produced by stock over summer on the grazings that lay beyond the head dyke, or inner dyke as it now became. The extensive use of manurial supplements, like turf, peat, seaweed and shell-sand, also provided a logical escape route, enabling townships to stretch arable beyond the limits set by their available livestock manure. Other labour-demanding solutions included techniques such as the use of the spade and caschrom in conjunction with lazy beds. Both the spade and caschrom increased yields compared to the plough, due to the way in which they improved the cycling of nutrients and, therefore, were a rational strategy in an agro-ecological environment that was increasingly nutrient-poor.[118] Equally, as pressure on grazing resources mounted, we can expect greater pressure on sensitive eco-systems like machair and greater use of supplements like woodland. To repeat a point made earlier, throwing a blanket classification over these various strategies as ongoing primitive or archaic traits misses the vital point that together, they provided solutions to circumstances that were historically specific. In all probability, the use of some may have cycled in step with fluxes in population and land pressure, with need and means moving in step with each other. We can certainly vouch for their extensive use in the eighteenth century but it remains equally possible that they may have been used extensively during other possible phases of population growth and land pressure, such as the twelfth and thirteenth centuries, but may have been less important when such pressure eased.

Taking an overview of Highland and Hebridean farming systems as they appear by the late eighteenth century, what is most striking is the inner conflict that existed between the needs of the arable sector and those of the livestock sector. For a large body of the population, what appears to have mattered most, what was given priority, were the needs of the arable sector. The traditional integration of crop and stock within a relationship of mutual support was being stressed if it had not broken down. The extent to which vital pasture resources were ploughed up or turfed provides ample proof of how arable output was being valued ahead of livestock needs. Such a

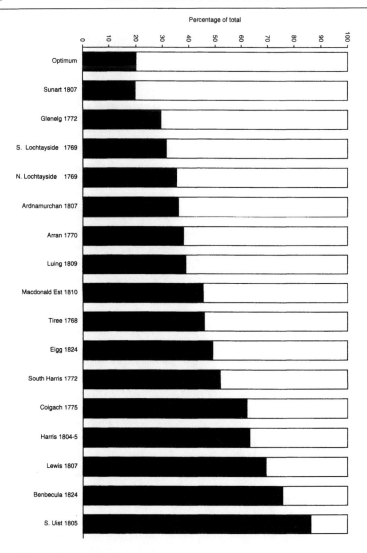

FIGURE 8.5. Arable:pasture ratios
Sources: DC/MDP, 1/380/29(RHP23075/2), Glenelg Survey; ibid., 1/466/22 Contents of the
Mainland of Harris and Adjacent Islands 1772; McArthur(ed.), *Survey of Lochtayside*; Brodick,
Arran Estate Office, John Burrel's Journal, part i, 1766–1773, pp. 178–80; SRO, Seaforth Papers
GD46/17/46, Contents of the Island of Lewis, Extracted from Mr. Chapman's Books of the
Plans of Lewis, 1817; SRO, RHP 1039, Plan of the Island of Benbecula, 1805; NLS, Survey of
South Uist by William Bald, 1805; SRO RHP 5990/1–4 Eastern Part of the Island of Skye, 1810,
surveyed by John Bell; SRO, Clanranald Papers GD201/5/1235/1, Particulars of Sale – Egg,
Canna and Sanday, 1824; SRO, RHP 3368, Plan of the Island of Coll, 1794, Surveyed by
George Langlands; IC/AP, V65, Contents of the Different Farms of Tiree, by James Turnbull,
1768; SRO, RHP 72 Ardnamurchan and Sunart, the Property of Sir James Riddell, 1806 and
AF49/1 Survey of Ardnamurchan and Sunart; SRO, Forfeited Estates, E741 Barrisdale –
Reports Concerning Farms 1771, by William Morison; SRO, Forfeited Estates, E746/189, Plans
of Farms of Coigach, 1775, by William Morison; NLS Sutherland Papers, 313/3583; Adam
(ed.), *Home's Survey of Assynt*, 1774; *NSA*, xiv, p. 210.

prioritisation, though, faced new and conflicting circumstances by the mid-eighteenth century. Though stock may now have provided only a proportion of the nutrients needed by arable, and though they took second place behind arable in any competing claim on resources, they had a growing economic value within the farm economy, providing even small farmers with the money needed for rents that were increasingly converted into cash. Further, some of the better-endowed farmers were now exploring strategies that placed the maintenance of stock ahead of the heavy demands traditionally made by the needs of human subsistence, and doing so to great effect and profit. In the final, concluding chapter, I want to explore these tensions further and to show how they manifest a fundamental divergence of attitude between the smaller west Highland and Hebridean farmer on the one hand, and the landowners and larger tenants on the other, a divergence that provides a foundation for understanding the radical changes that were already starting to sweep across the region by the end of the eighteenth century.

NOTES

1. Catt, 'Longterm consequences of using artificial and organic fertiliser'.
2. E.g. Munro, *Monro's Western Isles*, pp. 68–9.
3. SRO, Forfeited Estates, E729/9/1, Journal of Archibald Menzies, General Inspector, 1768.
4. Ibid.
5. SRO, RHP 972/5 Agricultural Survey of Netherlorn by Robert Robertson.
6. Published descriptions occur in *OSA*, x, pp. 354, 462; xi, pp. 141, 159, 303; xvi, pp. 186–7; xix, p. 266.
7. McArthur (ed.), *Survey of Lochtayside 1769*, pp. 75–207. For comparison, townships on the north side of Lochtayside averaged 4.71 acres of meadow each.
8. SRO, Breadalbane Muniments, GD112/14/13/9, Acreages for Luing, 1809.
9. DC/MDP, 380/28, Plan of Glenelg (also SRO, RHP23075/1).
10. *OSA*, xvi, p. 185.
11. SRO, Forfeited Estates, E746/151. General Report on the Estate of Cromartie, ND.
12. Ibid., E729/1, Report from Captain John Forbes, 1755.
13. SRO, Forfeited Estates, E788/42, Forfeited Estates. Report on estates of Barrisdale and Kinlochmoidart c.1755.
14. Ibid., E741, Forfeited Estates 1745, Barrisdale: Reports Concerning Farms.
15. Brodick, Arran Records Estates Office, Rental of Arran, 1772.
16. SRO, Breadalbane Muniments, GD112/16/13/3, Rentall of Glenorchy showing the Present Rent, 1730.
17. Ibid., GD112/16/10/2/1 Instructions to James Campbell and his Report on Glenorchy, 1728.
18. See, for example, ibid., GD112/16/10/2/12–13, Report of the Situation of Lord Breadalbane's Woods in Argyllshire by John Campbell, 1783; GD112/16/10/2/20, Survey of Woods and Plantations, 1792.
19. Ibid., GD112/16/4/3/44, Letter ex James Campbell, Inveraray, 10 August 1799.
20. Ibid., GD112/16/102/11 Report of State of Lord Breadalbane's Woods in Argyleshire, 1786, which lists a total of 2030 acres of woodland but only 150 acres as not already enclosed.

21. Instances of goats being banned are provided by SRO, MacLaine of Lochbuie Muniments, GD174/827, Interrogatorys to be put to the Tenants, 1782; IC/AP, Bundle 663, Instructions by His Grace the Duke of Argyll & Greenwich to Mr Campbell of Airds, 1733.
22. See, for example, SRO, Breadalbane Muniments, GD112/16/10/2/23–4, Reports by Dougall McPherson, 1793 and 1795.
23. Ibid., GD112/9/3/3/14, Rental of Earl of Breadalbane Estate in 1788.
24. See, for example, Uhlig, 'Old hamlets with infield and outfield', p. 305. Uhlig's paper is still well worth reading despite its assumptions about outfield.
25. Evidence for the transfer of 'blackearth and peat dust … manure' on Harris is provided by OSA, x, p. 351.
26. References to turf or stone-and-turf dykes occur in a range of sources, such as SRO, Forfeited Estates, E746/189, Plans of farms of Coigach, 1775. By the late eighteenth and early nineteenth centuries, though, most references were concerned with preventing such dykes from being built; see, for example, SRO, AF49/2A, Valuation of the Estate of Ardnamurchan and Sunart, 1807; Armadale House, GD221/4289/2, Lease of Balliloch and Sponish, South Uist, 1822.
27. Despite the references to its practice in the western Highlands, the main area of use and damage appears to have been the eastern Highlands, at least to judge from the Act of Parliament passed against the cutting of turf in 1685, APS, viii, pp. 494–5.
28. Cameron, 'Ancient farming customs in Scotland', p. 298.
29. Examples of potatoes being used to extend arable onto waste or muir is provided by DC/MDP, 2/9, Tack for Sandaigg, 1744.
30. SRO, Forfeited Estate, E729/9/1, Journal of Archibald Menzies, General Inspector, 1768.
31. This point is discussed further in Dodgshon, 'The nature and development of infield–outfield', pp. 1–23.
32. There is a relevant note in Turnbull's survey of Tiree. He uses an infield–outfield distinction in classifying what was good and poor arable but admits that local farmers did not use such a distinction themselves; SRO, RHP8826/2, A General Description of the Island of Tiry, Surveyed 1768 by James Turnbull.
33. McKay (ed.), Walker's Report on the Hebrides, p. 185; IC/AP, V65, Observations of Tiriy by Minister McColl, 1788.
34. SRO, RHP8826/2, A General Description of the Island of Tiry, surveyed 1768 by James Turnbull includes discussion of the Two Ends of Coll held by the Duke of Argyll.
35. Mckay (ed.), Walker's Report on the Hebrides, p. 77; SRO, RH2/8/24, John Blackadder's Description and Valuation of Lord Macdonald's Estates of Sky and North Uist, 1799 and 1800. See also OSA, xiii, pp. 293, 305, 330.
36. IC/AP, V65, Observations of Tiriy by Minister McColl, 1788 who said its effects were 'soon exhausted and produces only one crop'. See also Fenton, The Shape of the Past 2, pp. 48–82.
37. SRO, RHP8826/2, A General Description of the Island of Tiry, Surveyed 1768 by James Turnbull.
38. McKay (ed.), Walker's Report on the Hebrides, p. 185.
39. Boswell, The Journal of a Tour to the Hebrides, p. 289.
40. Macfarlane (ed.), Geographical Collections, ii, p. 212.
41. Martin, Western Islands, p. 337.
42. DC/MDP, 1/466/22, Survey of Harris, 1771.
43. SRO, RH2/8/24, John Blackadder's Description and Valuation of Lord Macdonald's Estates of Sky and North Uist, 1799 and 1800.
44. McKay (ed.), Walker's Report on the Hebrides, pp. 78 and 208.

45. SRO, RHP8826/2, A General Description of the Island of Tiry, surveyed 1768 by James Turnbull.
46. Typical of the restrictions on kelp are those contained in SRO, Seaforth Papers, GD46/17, vol. 80, List of tenants on Lewis, which binds tenants to ' use all diligence in preserving the annual crop of kelp ware within our respective districts from being cut destroyed or used for any purpose except for kelp'.
47. A good illustration of butter and cheese sales is provided by those sold out of Coigach, SRO, Forfeited Estates, E746/151, Report on the Estate of Cromary, section on Coigach barony.
48. SRO, Breadalbane Muniments, GD112/16/13/3/1, Rentall of Glenorchy, 1730. Tenants in Coigach also appear to have bred horses for sale.
49. Innes (ed.), *The Black Book of Taymouth*, pp. 298–9.
50. Examples are provided by *OSA*, x, p. 215.
51. SRO, RHP8826/2, A General Description of the Island of Tiry, surveyed 1768 by James Turnbull.
52. Inveraray Castle, Argyll Papers, V65, Observations on Tirie, Minister McColl, 1788.
53. Boswell, *Journal of a Tour to the Hebrides*, pp. 156 and 289. For information on the fact that Coll arable was dug, see IC/AP (also SRO), RHP8826/2, A General Description of the Island of Tiry, surveyed by James Turnbull, 1768. Boswell also notes the large number of horses on Raasay, *Journal of a Tour to the Hebrides*, p. 156.
54. The term 'supernumeries' was used by the Duke of Argyll in regard to what he saw as the excess numbers on Tiree during the late eighteenth century; see Cregeen (ed.), *Argyll Estate Instructions*, p. 1ff.
55. SRO, Breadalbane Muniments, GD112/14/13/1/2, Undated and Untitled Report on Breadalbane Estate (presumed c.1820).
56. Gray, *The Highland Economy 1750–1850*, pp. 30 and 240–1.
57. CDC/MP, GD221/4440/1, Observations on an Expedition to the Island of Sky, 1799.
58. Argyll, *Crofts and Farms in the Hebrides*, p. 14.
59. *OSA*, x, p. 353.
60. SRO, Forfeited Estates, E741 Barrisdale – Reports Concerning Farming, 1771.
61. Macculloch, *Western Highlands and Islands*, iii, draws the comparison with China in two places, pp. 94 and 118.
62. McKay (ed.), *Walker's Report on the Hebrides*, p. 181; SRO, RHP8826/2, General Description of the Island of Tiry, surveyed by James Turnbull, 1768.
63. SRO, AF49/2A, Valuation of the Estate of Ardnamurchan and Sunart, By Alexr. Low, 1807.
64. Townships like Bourblaige and Ormsaigbeg both had significantly more spaded arable, than ploughed arable, SRO, RHP72; AF49/2A, Valuation of the Estate of Ardnamurchan and Sunart, Alex. Low, 1807.
65. NLS, Map of Harris, surveyed by William Bald, 1804–5.
66. SRO, RHP8826/2, A General Description of the Island of Tiry, surveyed by James Turnbull, 1768.
67. RHP3368, Plan of the Island of Coll by George Langlands, 1794. Langlands distinguished between 'arable' (1859 acres) and 'rocky arable' (1674 acres).
68. *OSA*, x, pp. 393 and 411. It should be noted that these figures for arable represent the total amount of land worked during any cropping cycle as arable, not necessarily the annual acreage under arable.
69. SRO, Forfeited Estates, E788/42, Reports on the Estates of Barrisdale and Kinlochmoidart, c.1755; ibid.,E741, Report of the Contents Measures and Estimate Rents of the Annexed Estate of Barrisdale, 1771; ibid., E746/180

Plans of Farms of Coigach, 1775; Adam (ed.), *Home's Survey of Assynt*, p. 42; *OSA*, xvi, p. 185.

70. It is worth noting that in its source area of South America, the potato was grown using a hand-spade very similar to the caschrom and in ridges similar to the lazy bed. Geographers, especially, have mapped these raised field systems and have analysed their contribution to the more efficient cycling of nutrients and moisture. See, for example, Smith, Denevan and Hamilton, 'Ancient ridged fields in the region of Lake Titicaca', pp. 353–67.

71. Munro, *Monro's Western isles of Scotland*, p. 80. It is surprising that despite many references to land being delved, Monro never mentions the caschrom as opposed to the spade.

72. Martin, *Western Islands*, p. 3; Munro, *Monro's Western Isles of Scotland*, pp. 86–7. See also McKay (ed.), *Walker's Report on the Hebrides*, pp. 42–3.

73. Examples are provided by ibid., p. 211.

74. Examples of such an increase can be documented for parts of Skye and Harris. In the case of Skye, a comparison of data from Stobie's survey of 1766 with Bell's survey of 1811 for Portree parish shows an increase of 806 acres to 1379 acres, though one or two townships actually recorded a small decrease; see CDC/MP, GD221/5612/6, Macdonald Estate Acreages in Plans of 1766, 1811 and 1877. In the case of Harris, a 1772 survey records 5047 acres of arable whilst an 1804–5 survey records 8767 acres, see DC/MDP, 1/466/22, Contents of the Mainland of Harris and Adjacent Islands, 1772; NLS, Map of Harris, by William Bald, 1804–5.

75. SRO, Seaforth Papers, GD46/1/212, Old Leases 1765–1781, Tack for all and haill lands of Meikle Salachy (Lochalsh); NLS, Sutherland Papers, DEP313/3160, Tacks of Earl William other than Assynt, 1757–66, no. 6 Tack all and whole Toun and Lands of Farrbrask, Swordly and Kirktown.

76. SRO, RH2/8/24, John Blackadder's Description and Valuation of Lord Macdonald's Estates of Sky and North Uist, 1799 and 1800.

77. IC/AP, V65, Duncan Forbes of Culloden's Letter concerning the Duke of Argyll's Estates in Tiree, Morvern and Mull, 24 Sept. 1737 (reprinted in the *Report of the Crofters Commissioners of Inquiry*, appendix A, p. 392).

78. IC/AP, V65 Instructions for the Chamberlain of Tyrie, 23 Oct. 1750.

79. Ibid., V65 Remarks on the Island of Tirii, 1771 [Probably by Alexander Campbell, Chamberlain of Kintyre].

80. SRO, Seaforth papers, GD46/1/278 Articles of Sett for Lewis, c.1790.

81. See, for example, McKay (ed.), *Walker's Report on the Hebrides*, p. 43; Mitchell, 'James Robertson's tour'.

82. IC/AP, Bundle 663, Instructions by His Grace the Duke of Argyll and Grenwich to Mr. Campbell of Airds, factor of Morvern, 17 Feb. 1733.

83. Ibid., V65, Instructions of the Chamberlain of Tyrie, 25 Oct. 1750.

84. DC/MDP, Section 2/8, Acts of Court, 29 April 1735, Conditions for Tacksmen.

85. CDC/MP, GD221/3695/4, Memorandm. ND (probably 1730s); McKay (ed.), *Walker's Report on the Hebrides*, p. 209. Walker also noted its practice on Lewis; ibid., p. 43. To the south-east, Pennant reported its use on Rhum; Pennant, *Tour*, i, pp. 280–1.

86. SRO, Mackenzie Papers, GD401/40/1–2, Meeting of the Justices of the Peace for Skye, 1788.

87. CDC/MP, GD221/4440/1, Observations on an Expedition to the Island of Skye, 1799. See also *OSA*, xvi, 1795, 228.

88. *NSA*, xiv, p. 284.

89. DC/MDP, Section 2/8, Acts of Court, 29 April 1735, Conditions for Tacksmen.

90. *OSA*, x, p. 356.

91. Indicative of the attitude which many people had towards millers was that

written in a complaint against Robert Mackay, tenant and miller at Knockarthur on the Sutherland estate. Tenants complained of the 'disgrause' that 'he had no skill or notion of the mill, or of manageing the miln only greed', NLS, Sutherland papers, DEP313/982/37, Petition by tenants of Knockarthur, 1788.

92. Murray of Stanhope, *True Interest*.
93. *OSA*, xiv, p. 149.
94. SRO, Forfeited Estates, E729/1, Report from Captain John Forbes, Factor upon the Annexed Estates of Lovat and Cromartie, 1755; E746/151, General Report on the Estate of Cromartie; E746/79/9, Letters from Coigach, 1756–82.
95. E788/42, Report on the Estate of Barrisdale and Kinlochmoidart, c.1755.
96. *OSA*, x, p. 356.
97. SRO, RHP8826/2, General Description of Tirii, 1768; IC/AP,V65, Remarks on the Island of Tirii, 1771.
98. SRO, RHP8826/2, General Description of Tirii, 1768.
99. Pennant, *Tour*, i, p. 281.
100. See, for example, *OSA*, x, p. 354; DC/MDP, Advertisement for sale of Harris, 1775.
101. These figures are comparable with those published in the Macneil Report of 1851; see Devine, *The Great Highland Potato Famine*, p. 14.
102. Forbes of Culloden, letter printed in the *Report of the Commissioners of Inquiry concerning the Duke of Argyll's estate in Tiree, Morvern and Mull*, 24 Sept. 1737, pp. 389–92.
103. McKay (ed.), *Walker's Report on the Hebrides*, p. 76 comments on the range of weeds to be found in South and North Uist. Equally interesting is Macculloch's comment 'I have had the patience to count the ears of barley in a field ... and that there were scarcely six in a square yard; the remainder of the crop consisting of Holcus avenaceous', Macculloch, *Western Highlands and Islands*, iii, p. 213.
104. Argyll, *Crofts and Farms in the Hebrides*, p. 13.
105. Archibald Menzies' comments on what was grown in Colonsay kailyards are relevant here, the range including artichokes and sunflowers; SRO, Forfeited Papers, E729/9/1, Journal of Archibald Menzies, General Inspector, 1768.
106. Walker notes seeing fields of 10–15 acres of potatoes, all in lazy beds, by the time of his visit to Islay in 1764; McKay (ed.), *Walker's Report on the Hebrides*, p. 101.
107. Devine, *The Great Highland Potato Famine*, especially pp. 33–6.
108. The important work by Gibson and Smout on the history of Scottish diet between the sixteenth and eighteenth centuries is relevant here. Talking about the country at large, they note that whilst most of the late medieval and early-modern evidence favours a diet that was based as much on meat as on grain, the eighteenth-century evidence suggests a shift to a diet that was more exclusively grain- or meal-based. See Gibson and Smout, 'Scottish food and Scottish history', pp. 59–84, but especially pp. 71–3 where they talk about a 'vast change' in Highland diets towards one based on meal and, later still, potatoes. See also Gibson and Smout, *Prices, Food and Wages in Scotland*, especially pp. 226–9.
109. An early reference to the neglect or under-use of fishing around the Hebridean isles is provided by Skene, *Celtic Scotland*, iii, p. 430. See also Martin, *Western Islands*, pp. 340–49, though he does confirm that Stornoway was still used as a base for fishing, p. 347. However, writing in the 1760s, Walker makes it clear that the Stornoway fishermen had only just tried buss fishing, using a single boat, and leaves the reader with the impression that the Hebridean involvement in largescale local fishing was still all about potential, estimating that the 500–750 barrels of herring produced per year on Lewis (mostly at Stornoway) could be raised to 20,000 barrels with proper investment; McKay (ed.),

Walker's Report on the Hebrides, pp. 44–5. Of course, the failure of the Fife Adventurers in Lewis would have affected attitudes towards a local fishing industry; see Mackenzie, *History of the Outer Hebrides*, pp. 290–328; Lang (ed.), *The Highlands of Scotland in 1750*, p. 33.

110. Youngson, *After the Forty-Five*, pp. 106–7.

111. Knox, *Discourse on the Expediency of Establishing Fishing Stations or Small Towns in the Highlands of Scotland*, pp. 32–4, recommended 40 fishing stations along the west coast. All were to be planned, with 16 houses each and a range of relevant craftsmen (boat builders, coopers, netmakers, weavers, chandlers, etc). See also Beaufoy, *Substance of the Speech of Henry Beaufoy*, pp. 33–7, 52–3, 57. On p. 71, he expounded a principle that landlords were already acting upon, arguing that 'care must be taken that the quantity of land assigned to each houses be not so great as to induce the inhabitants to become bad farmers, rather than good fishermen'.

112. Discussion of the role of fishing in Assynt and Barrisdale can be found in SRO, Forfeited Estates, E741/Forfeited Estates 1745 – Barrisdale Reports Concerning Farms, 1771, which talks about the 'great Support' to local townships provided by herring, and how 'They cure as many fish for their families as will serve them ¾ of the year'.

113. Early references to fish being collected in as rent occur in IC/AP, N.E.11 1615–31, Accounts and Rentals, Rental for townships in Argyll, 1617–18, including from the 'Water of Awe'. Fish were also collected in as rent on the Breadalbane estate from the tenants of Pollfern, SRO, Breadalbane Muniments, GD112/9/40, Rental 1717–20, and 'green herring' from tenants beside Lochbroom on the Coigach estate, see Cromartie Papers, GD305/1/163/133. In a 1755 report on the Coigach estate, it was said that tenants became 'a little reduced in their Circumstances by the Herring Fishing not succeeding so well' towards 1740; SRO, Forfeited estates papers, E746/73, Report on the Judiciall rental of Cromartie estate, 1755. See also Smith, *Jacobite Estates of the Forty-Five*, p. 159; Gray, *The Highland Economy*, p. 116.

114. Cregeen (ed.), *Argyll Estate Instructions*, pp. xxx–xxxi.

115. A good illustration of the growing use of fishing as a supplement to both the subsistence and cash needs of the smaller tenants is provided by Adam (ed.), *Home's Survey of Assynt*, p. xlviii. The same townships recur in NLS, DEP313/1000, Expired Leases for Assynt, 1812, tack to Donald Macdonald, 1802, for Clashnessie, Achnacarron, Culkein, Achnacorre, Balchladich, Store and Clachtoll, which set the lands 'not for his own natural possession' but for the sub-tenants under him 'who are to be employed in the fishery, or manufacture', the former being based on herring and cod fishing. Contemporary leases (DEP313/2151, State of the Tacks and Rents upon the Sutherland Estate, 1826) show townships like Clachtoll (31 tenants) Clashnessy (26 tenants), Store (19 tenants) and Culkein/Achnacarron (25 tenants) were well-settled townships, but made up of smallholders. To the north, in Caithness, Donaldson, *Caithness in the Eighteenth Century*, p. 118, provides examples for Sir John Sinclair's Ulbster estate.

116. Shiels, 'Improving soil productivity in the pre-fertiliser era', pp. 71–2.

117. Dodgshon, 'Budgeting for survival', pp. 83–93.

118. Dodgshon and Olsson, 'Productivity and nutrient use in eighteenth-century Scottish Highland townships', pp. 39–51.

9 The Western Highlands and Islands on the Eve of the Clearances

I have tried in this book to show how the chiefly systems of socio-political control and behaviour that still characterised the western Highlands and Islands in the sixteenth century, and whose needs shaped the character of farm production, gradually decomposed into a system dominated by the relations between landlords and tenants and by a conflict between the former's interest in raising the marketable product of land and the interest of many of the latter, especially the middling-to-lesser tenants, in the basic needs of subsistence. These changes underpinned a diverse array of adjustments that had already brought a fair degree of change to the region by the time the clearances and the creation of crofting townships initiated a sharper break with the past from the late eighteenth century onwards. Whatever else we conclude, we cannot assume that the region was suddenly disturbed from a timelessness of order by the far-reaching institutional changes that swept the region from the late eighteenth century onwards.

As I outlined in Chapters 2 to 4, there is a case for arguing that chiefly systems formed an integrated system of socio-political and economic order, one in which the different parts of the system shared the same goals even though their inputs and benefits differed. As the system decayed, the interests of chiefs and those of the majority of their tenants diverged, so that by the end of the period under review there is a strong case for saying that they conflicted. Forced as much by changing political realities and government pressure as by circumstances, chiefs slowly donned the mantle of landlords and became increasingly concerned with how their estate income could be maximised through the capitalisation of all estate resources and by marketing what could be produced to advantage. More and more, would-be landlords saw the key to solvency in the introduction of specialised stock production, first cattle then, by the mid-eighteenth century onwards, sheep. For the majority of their clansmen, meanwhile, subsistence and survival became the over-riding goal of their township economy. Previously, it had been second-ary, albeit in a token sense, to the material support of the chief. Furthermore, whereas their township economy had been bolstered by its position within the wider chiefly economy, and the support which it could expect in times of crisis, the decay of the latter and its values meant that they were left to evolve strategies of survival that were more sufficient in themselves. In time, this meant prioritising arable output at the expense of stock. Yes, the latter were a source of cash rents, but for the ordinary farmer, if not for the aspiring and increasingly commercialised tacksman, marketing stock was about a trade in use rather than exchange values, or what Postan called householding, that is, taking produce to market in order to obtain what the household economy was deficient in as regards basic needs.[1] For most ordinary farmers, marketing was not yet about profit, for their basic inputs were not costed that way. As one writer put it in a more recent debate about crofter values, 'time is not money in the Gaelic value-system, and money is anyway not necessarily the most desirable acquisition'.[2] By way of a conclusion, I want to review how this divergence came about, the differences in attitude and values which it engendered, and its consequences for change.

HIGHLAND PRODUCTION AND THE MARKETING OF PRODUCE

Without question, one of the most powerful solvents of chiefly systems of behaviour was the effect which legislation and the actions of central govern-ment had on the economic management of estates. There were two ways in which these helped to redirect the management of estates. First, they forced chiefs to levy more regular rents, curbing the irregular uptake of renders in the form of hospitality and sorning. Second, and more critical, by reducing the incidence of feuding and excessive feasting, and by reducing the size of chiefly households, the Crown effectively removed the basis on which food rents were gathered in for in-house consumption. Chiefs still found them-selves with large quantities of rents in kind but now faced a change in how such rents could be used. Two possibilities existed. They could market pro-duce themselves or they could convert such renders into cash rents.

The first of these managerial strategies was a step that chiefs were well placed to make, for the sheer quantity of rents in kind which some gathered in would have made it easier for them to organise the marketing of produce. The very fact that the cost of assembling grain or stock was borne by tenants meant that chiefs also had lower transaction costs. Some landowners were particularly jealous of this advantage.[3] Furthermore, the scale at which they could operate would have made it easier to negotiate contracts with par-ticular merchants and drovers, again lowering transaction costs. When a family dispute arose between the wife of the late Lord Strathnaver and the new Lord Strathnaver over what money she had received from the sale of the

estate's annual uptake of grain rents in 1719, she had reportedly sold 948
bolls of bere out of the estate's total uptake of 1749 bolls to Baillie William
Frazer, a merchant in Inverness. Another Inverness merchant was sold 250
bolls and a merchant at Uphat, 150 bolls.[4] Such tied contracts involving large
quantities of produce were probably a feature of chiefly interactions or deals
with the marketplace from the moment they first began to redirect their food
rents to it. Though lucrative, chiefly attempts to market grain were largely
confined to fertile areas around the eastern and southern edges of the Highlands, where access to nearby markets gave them some advantage.[5] However,
more fertile pockets in areas that were not so well placed, like Netherlorne,
were also involved in the grain trade.[6] As explained in Chapter 5, some landowners continued to uplift these grain payments in kind from the more fertile
parts of their estates down to the late eighteenth century. Indeed, when
viewed across the seventeenth and eighteenth centuries, landowners appear
to have dominated the grain trade in so far as it penetrated into the Highland
region.

Highland chiefs were also instrumental in establishing the foundations
for the cattle-droving trade. Even under chiefly systems of socio-political
control, chiefs had cause to maintain farms, or bowhouses, at which the cattle
paid in as marts were kept or stored. When change forced a rethink of the
values traditionally attached to cattle, these bowhouses would have been
ready-made centres for the co-ordinated marketing of stock as market
demand gathered pace over the seventeenth century. It could also be the case
that the success of such bowhouses provided a role-model for the specialised
cattle farms that had started to develop in the hands of the wealthier tacksmen and tenants by the end of the seventeenth century. Significantly, areas
which appear to have turned to more specialised cattle production by the
early eighteenth century, such as Argyll and wester Ross, had estates in which
bowhouses had long operated as collecting centres for the gathering in of
stock paid by tenants as rent.

Chiefs who responded to changing circumstances by converting rents in
kind into cash rents did not find it a straightforward solution. Many tenants
were simply not in a position to sell produce so as to raise the necessary cash.
Quite apart from the poor quality of much of the grain involved, the distances
involved surcharged many west Highland and Hebridean townships with
heavy costs of transport when it came to marketing relatively small quantities
of grain themselves. It is not surprising, therefore, that the conversion of
grain rents went through a long transitional phase, with landowners exercising flexibility over whether rents were paid in cash or kind. Even where
rents were being recorded in cash, it is clear that tenants were still able to have
marketable produce like cattle set against their rent liability. Nor is it surprising that many tenants in the more remote townships of the Hebrides saw
the conversion of bere into whisky as the best way of marketing surplus grain,
for it raised the value of what was being transported by processing it. However, the pressure to convert to cash also produced a response that took many

tenants down a cul-de-sac from which it became difficult to extricate themselves. In those townships which did not produce significant grain surpluses, tenants shifted the rent burden away from a broad range of produce onto livestock, especially cattle. The shift initially benefited tenants by moving the burden of rent onto their large and under-utilised non-arable sector, allowing them to maximise the subsistence value of their arable sector. If we assume that tenants had previously paid one third of their grain as rent and used one third as seed, then what was left as subsistence, or for turning into malt and whisky, was doubled for they now kept two-thirds. Clearly, this would have had a profound effect on the capacity of townships, enabling more people to subsist on arable without any need for an increase in its extent. To sustain such a shift, though, tenants were forced to market stock. In so far as many tenants would have seen this in terms of use rather than exchange values, it would not have involved or signalled a change in basic attitudes. However, when seen within the framework of the peasant economy, the needs of arable and pasture would now have become opposed rather than mutually supportive and compatible.

The more the region was drawn into marketing, the more these basic problems were brought to the fore. In the long term, any system of production geared to the market was forced to maximise regional advantage, to constantly reduce costs so as to compete. If landowners increasingly behaved as landlords, then the invisible hand of the market had a part in the process. Increasingly, the region was no longer structured within its own values, but had to accept that it suffered market disadvantages, including the sheer isolation of many of its westerly and north-westerly communities. When the earl of Seaforth agreed to collect the Bishop's third from Lewis for the Bishop of the Isles in 1663, the bishop stipulated that the cash equivalent had to be delivered to his house in Glasgow 'without duie defalcation or modification in respect of the distance of ye place'.[7] Such perceptions of distances in the region and the insistence that they had to be absorbed as part of the costs of living in the area must have very much par for the times by the second half of the seventeenth century, when stock and crop were starting to flow freely out of it. Quite apart from any notions of natural advantage, stock were always going to be preferred to grain in any system of marketing from the more remote areas simply because they walked – and swam in the case of islands like Mull – to market.[8] By the early nineteenth century, such attitudes had matured into a very insightful appreciation of how ease of movement mattered in relation to what could be marketed. In a report on the Breadalbane estate, written around the late 1820s when the possibilities of steam navigation along the west coast first became apparent, one commentator actually talked in von Thünen terms about the disadvantages of the region. Around every large town, he wrote, there was 'a circle of monopoly of a certain extent, which enjoys a monopoly against that town'. Thus vegetables wanted in Glasgow, he went on, could only be produced within a five-mile circle, whilst fresh eggs, milk, fresh butter, and fowls could only be produced within 12 miles. Calves, lambs, etc. 'can be brought much further'. Under such conditions, the 'western isles were entirely outside these circles of monopoly'. But now, however, transport improvements, notably the introduction of steam navigation, had redrawn the circles so that the region could compete.[9]

CHIEFS AND THE CASH ECONOMY

Estates of account, in which income and expenditure were set against each other, brought their own problems to Highland and Hebridean land-owners. Though many received increasing amounts of cash as rent over the sixteenth–eighteenth centuries, the fact is that many struggled to remain solvent once their debts were properly accounted. Shaw has documented the extent to which many leading families, such as the MacLeod of Dunvegan and the Seaforth Mackenzies, were in difficulties even by the early seventeenth century.[10] Part of the problem was the amount of potential estate income intercepted and consumed by tacksmen. Though originally intended to spread income socially and to root the clan securely, such a system became more of a burden than an advantage to landowners as they were forced more and more to operate in a world in which production costs mattered. A further problem was that landowners also became increasing consumers in a world that needed cash rather than endlessly recycled social credit. The Statutes of Iona (1609) had forced chiefs to educate their sons in the Lowlands. This ensured that subsequent chiefs acquired tastes and habits which required profit and regular cash flows, often at a rate which their estates could not sustain. Their castles were rebuilt or extended and fitted with finer and finer furnishings and new art forms. Lifestyles changed, with more time being spent away from their estates, and more being spent on the temptations of cities like Edinburgh and London. When, in 1828, the earl of Breadalbane penned some thoughts on how his estate should be improved from London, his chamberlain noted that 'whether what he projects in a coffee house in London can be executed in Luing or Lesmore I cannot say'.[11] His comment captured some of the problems that now burdened such estates.

There were also deep-seated problems with the organisation of their estates that affected income. In the long term, the income of many Highland estates was seriously compromised by the way chiefs or landowners had wadset or feued what, *in cumulo*, were large and lucrative portions of their estate. What seemed a solution to passing cash flow problems became in time a serious loss of estate income. Though some managed to levy a 'superplus' rent, surcharging feuars and wadsetters with extra payments for their holdings, this was not a widespread solution.[12] A further problem was that many Highland and Hebridean estates entered the eighteenth century with large areas of land set to tacksmen. The favourable conditions on which many of these were set land did not stop them from squeezing the rents of those beneath them, effectively creaming off more rental income from the estate.

To compound matters still further, tacksmen themselves were notorious 'ill-payers' of rent, so that estates did not always collect in the rents with which tacksmen were actually burdened.[13] Given these problems, it is not surprising that many landowners and their advisers saw the removal of tacksmen as a first step towards putting their estate finances on a more secure footing, though relatively few were quick to follow the Argyll estate's early example of setting land in open auction.[14] Indeed, notwithstanding the example set by the Argyll estate, references to the exactions of tacksmen continue down into the second half of the eighteenth century.[15] Yet despite the cash-flow problems posed by the tacksmen system, there is a good case for arguing that what really crippled estates was the custom of granting rebates and rests to all tenants, not just tacksmen, during recurrent crises. One estimate put the frequency at which estates rebated all rents at about one year in five.[16] A precise scaling of the problem is provided by figures available for estate income during and immediately after a major subsistence crisis like King William's lean years, 1696–1703. Figures for the Campbell of Cawdor estate on Islay show how the financial problem continued on after the end of the crisis itself, as the estate struggled to find tenants and as those willing to take on tacks struggled to recover the capital needed to farm. In the parish of Killarow alone, the estate was left with arrears of £1587.19s. 5⅝d out of a total rent of £2484 1s 1⅖d for the period 1703–07.[17]

The dilemma in which estates found themselves, even by the late seventeenth century, is shown by the way in which they responded to these problems. Though faced with an irregular and uncertain estate income, most took steps to augment rents further by the closing decades of the seventeenth century. The effect was to steer their customary commitments as chiefs and traditional landowners into collision with the growing pressures for them to behave as landlords. If the spur was the prospect of indebtedness, the opportunity which they seized upon was that provided by the growing profitability of the cattle trade. Introducing rent increases, though, was not straightforward. The initially rigid structure of Highland and Hebridean rents made increases or augmentations difficult to implement. The very fact that they were itemised separately as 'augmentations' helps make this point. The scale of the increases is well shown by those estates for which detailed data is available, such as Kintyre and Coigach (Table 9.1). As elsewhere, such increases acted as a lever for change. The pressure which this introduced into the township economy inevitably led to complaints among tenants, especially when production crises made it difficult to pay rents at any level, such as after the poor harvests of 1771 and 1783.[18] In fact, in the balance of debate, many contemporary commentators favoured the side of the farmer arguing that landowners had done little to sustain such increases by investment. They start at the wrong end, said Pennant when told about the 'rage' for increasing rents in Lochaber in the 1760s, squeezing the bag before helping farmers to fill it.[19]

Many of these endemic problems of income were apparent on the Macdonald estates in Skye. A memorial on the poor financial health of the

TABLE 9.1. Sample rent increases, late seventeenth to mid-eighteenth centuries

Coigach (merks)		Kintyre (pounds)	
1678	2125	1672	20813
1689	2455	1692	23020
1701	1905	1711	28568
1725	7107		
1740	6140		

Sources: IC/AP, Bundle 2530, Instructions His Grace the Duke of Argyll To David Campbell his Chamberlain of Kintyre 1761; SRO, Cromartie Papers, GD305/1/63, Rentals 1612–1824.

estate drawn up in 1733 outlined how they affected estate income. In its exposé of the estate's problems, it could easily have been drawn up for other estates. It mentioned how wadsetters had the best farms and held them on lucrative terms. Rent abatements, non-payments of rent, and eases of the casualties were commonplace, whilst rents were not being properly set or defined by written tacks. No doubt following the example of their chief, Skye tacksmen were accused of spending more 'on a fine suit or Silk Gown than will answer the masters' Rent, tho' their Stock does not exceed 2000 or 3000 mks'.[20]

CHIEFS INTO LANDLORDS

Acting together, the growing importance of marketing in the estate economy of the western Highlands and Islands, combined with the financial pressures that were already squeezing many landowners hard by the late seventeenth century, slowly brought about a profound change in attitude. Landowners began to think more and more as – to use Macinnes' phrase – 'commercial landlords',[21] concerned with maximising the gross income of their estates. Informed and cajoled by a battery of advisers and improvers who descended on the region, and by family lawyers who gave their written counsel from afar, they took steps to make their estates viable.[22]

We can see this most clearly through the way in which estate resources were increasingly capitalised, especially over the eighteenth century. Surveyors, mostly of Lowland extraction, were brought in to establish a more exact inventory and valuation of what estates comprised, with rents being generated for the first time on the basis of what a farm actually possessed rather than imposed through coarse-scaled assessment ratings.[23] Valuable resources like woodland were taken out of the farm economy and reassigned to the estate economy. Rights of wood-leave, allowing tenants use of timber for basic farming needs (plough timbers, roof couples, door),[24] along with the grazing of woodland by stock, were extremely closely defined and increasingly specified as to amount and cost.[25] This was a particularly acute problem for the Hebridean islands which had long relied on having rights of woodleave in adjacent mainland areas.[26] Estates began to enclose woodland

and to devise a range of lucrative agreements with contractors to cut bark and timber. The Breadalbane estate woodlands in Glenorchy and Lochaweside, for instance, were contracted to the Lorne Furnace Company in 1754, the agreement allowing timber to be cut on a twenty-five-year cycle.[27] When the Lochbuie estate contracted to allow the Bonawe Iron Works to exploit 'growing woods oak ash and all others of Planting Excepted on the said Estate' on Mull in 1756, the agreement also covered the harvesting of bark. It also included the working of coal on the farm of Knock owned by the duke of Argyll.[28]

The aggressive way in which Hebridean estates moved, via tack agreements, to restrict tenant use of seaweed suitable for kelp can also be seen as an attempt to capitalise estates.[29] Also revealing was the way in which estates began building new mills so as to exploit, via mill rents, their share of the profit generated by multures in areas which could not have paid multures before. The diverse array of casualties formerly paid by all townships were converted into cash, even in townships where their payment in kind appears to have long been in default. Likewise, old and neglected renders were converted into cash, such as so-called 'bygones', a collective name for obligations like those of hunting and hosting that were abolished by an act of George I in 1717.[30] Having to pay for 'bygones', as well as for casualties and woodleave, was an issue when the tenants of Toyer petitioned the earl of Breadalbane in 1722 for an ease of payment at a time when money was scarce.[31]

Ultimately though, the prime way in which estates worked to capitalise their resources, and thereby to raise their income, was through the specialisation of township or farm economies on livestock, first cattle, and later, sheep. As market demand pushed the price of stock up, the economic choice confronting estates became increasingly stark. Admittedly, many initially believed that the choice was between people and cattle, not between people and sheep. Campbell of Knockbuy was one of the pioneers of specialised cattle production in Argyll over the 1720s and 1730s, so it is no surprise that he can be found arguing the case for the spread of black cattle production. Sheep, he suggested, faced too many risks, especially from foxes.[32] Yet even as late as the 1780s, the earl of Breadalbane himself was asking his Argyllshire chamberlain to distinguish between those farms 'proper for the purpose of raising and grasing black cattle & what for raising grain'. In the same note, though, his chamberlain, John Campbell, drew his attention to the profound change which had just taken place in Glenorchy. From 'almost every farm in that Country having a considerable Stock of black cattle and sowing a great number of bolls of different grain, the whole to a triffle, is now turned under sheep, and no Tenant of any considerable stock can tell within some hundreds what he has upon his farm.[33]

Campbell's words capture the nature and extent of the change that was to sweep over many townships as they were cleared for sheep. The strategy seized upon by estates was simple if socially destructive. By reducing the

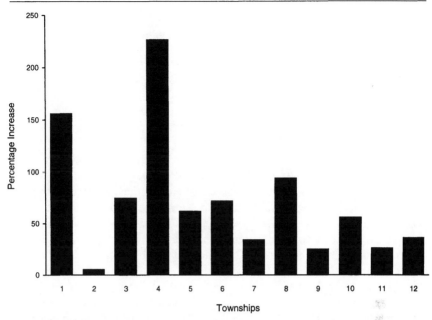

FIGURE 9.1. Post-clearance increases in stock levels
Sources: SRO, Breadalbane Muniments, GD112/16/12/3/1, Rentall of Glenorchy Shewing the present Rent ... Holdings and Sowings, 1730; ibid., GD112/9/3/3/30, Schemed rental of lands belonging to Lord Breadalbane in Glenorchy, Lochowside, 1799.

tenant numbers present in runrig townships, and converting their subsistence arable into winter feed for sheep, they were able to realise the summer potential of available hill grazings. In fact, because of the capital involved in stocking sheep farms, many continued to be held by two or three tenants until well into the nineteenth century.[34] Furthermore, and not unconnected with the previous point, many townships continued to be self-sufficient so that the full benefit of devoting arable to winter stock feed was not immediate.[35] However, despite these qualifications, stock levels increased dramatically. Where we can actually compute the numbers involved, such as for parts of Glenorchy and Lochtayside, the scalar increases involved were considerable (see Figure 9.1). So were the increases in rent that brought about the switch to sheep. In a short essay on the impact of sheep farming on the higher ground of Ross-shire, one farmer suggested that farms, 'when let of sufficient extent for a sheep-walk, bring three, four, or five times more rent than formerly'. He acknowledged that some will see this as against the interests of the country because of its removal of 'many of the aborigines of the soil' but went on to say that 'others argue, with greater justice, that whatever system brings the Highest rent must eventually promote the real good of the community'.[36] Readers of the *Farmers Magazine* who were not convinced by such logic were later subjected to the persuasions of another writer who claimed that sheep had raised rents on the Sutherland estate ten-fold.[37] For cash-strapped estates, the switch to sheep must have seemed compelling, one that offered traditional landowning families the chance of holding on to their estates at a time when a rising tide of bankruptcies was forcing many to relinquish their control.[38] Yet where we can actually glimpse the thinking of traditional landowners, it suggests that some responded to the detached and calculating advice of their advisers and to the imperatives of the marketplace with a some degree of reluctance. When faced with the dilemma on the Macdonald estate on Skye in 1802, for example, Lord Macdonald replied that he did 'not wish to dismiss great numbers of his tenants'.[39] Indeed, as late as 1829, the then Lord Macdonald was said to have 'been in the practice of allowing abatements on his Estates indiscriminately to all Tenants without distinction'.[40] We find similar sentiments held by the earl of Breadalbane. Despite advice to the effect that his estate carried too many people, and that he had been slow to respond to new opportunities,[41] the earl's response was equivocal. He accepted the rationalisation of Netherlorne reluctantly,[42] but he and his forbears were criticised by their advisers for feeling 'indifferent to what [was] passing around them, or did not wish to increase their revenues by dispossessing the families who resided upon their property ... or to a kindly, but I presume to a mistaken Feeling of compassion to the small farmers'.[43] We find a similar difference of perspective between adviser and landlord in a letter written to the earl of Seaforth about Lewis in 1800. After suggesting that the entire population of Lewis could be reduced to 120 shepherds plus their families and those living from kelp and fishing, the author of the unsigned report acknowledged that 'the proprietor may not be disposed to break the strong ties of affection which unite ten thousand people, to the place of their nativity'.[44]

There is a case for arguing that the mixed feelings which some traditional landowners had towards change may have shaped the management strategies which they implemented over the second half of the eighteenth and early nineteenth centuries. Certainly, the dual approach taken by many estates, with some townships being reorganised into crofting townships and others being cleared for sheep, suggests that their policies were designed to accommodate different expectations. There is also a case for supposing that such a dual approach may have been deep-rooted in the minds of landowners. As I explained in the previous chapter, estates like MacLeod of Dunvegan's estate on Skye and the Argyll estate appear to have drawn a deliberate and considered distinction between townships held in tenandry and those held by tacksmen as early as the late seventeenth century. Once we appreciate how some of the latter appear to have been organised as holdings worked by the labour of cottars or smallholders, we can see how fundamentally different such a distinction may have been for the estate. Sustained over the eighteenth century, it may have provided a well-established foundation for the distinction between those townships which estates re-organised into crofts and those cleared for sheep farming though, in the event, the clearances went beyond those townships previously farmed by a dominant tenant or tacksman. The situation in areas like Assynt by the mid-eighteenth century suggests that it was possible, even before the appearance of largescale commercial sheep farming, for estates to reorganise structurally in a way that the led directly into the changes of the late eighteenth and early nineteenth centuries. Of course, there were areas which showed no such anticipation. As with the interior or continental parts of the Breadalbane estate, like Glenorchy, what stood out about the Strathnaver portion of the Sutherland estate is that it does not appear to have experienced any preparatory changes, so that when faced with the opportunities of sheep farming, it required a fairly sudden and dramatic restructuring of townships.[45] In time though, the increasing number of traditional landowners who went bankrupt over the eighteenth and early nineteenth centuries, and the sale of their estates to bankers, merchants and industrialists from the south, brought an even more abrupt change, one which applied an even more unbridled form of landlordism. Many of the more brutalised instances of township clearance or relocation stemmed from the new values introduced by such adventitious landowners.

KINSMEN INTO CROFTERS

We cannot begin to understand conditions in the western Highlands and Islands by the late eighteenth and early nineteenth centuries if we ignore how the interests of landowners and their lesser tenants had progressively diverged over the preceeding century or so. By the late eighteenth and early nineteenth centuries, these differences were irreconcilable. As landowners increasingly saw the commercial exploitation of stock as the foundation for a more secure estate income, the great mass of their tenants and cottars saw the intensification of arable as their prime goal for survival. Many lesser and middling tenants, those holding a fraction of a township, such as a third, quarter, sixth or less, plus the now innumerable cottars, had become boxed in by a relentless series of choices which the growth of numbers had led them towards if not actually forced onto them. Possibly as many as six distinct strategies were adopted at different times, strategies whose combined effect was to transform their domestic and township economies into high-energy, high-input arable systems: labour-intensive systems of cultivation using the spade and caschrom; the development of outfield systems exploiting the stock manure produced over summer; adoption of manurial supplements like seaweed, turf and peat; the transfer of rent from a generalised package of rents in kind that included substantial grain payments to a narrow cattle-generated cash rent; the processing of bere into malt and even whisky; and the adoption of the potato. At least five of these strategies enabled communities to produce more in the way of subsistence. However, once dependent on them to maintain a particular level of subsistence, it was well-nigh impossible for communities to abandon them without numbers being reduced. Indeed, without the radical changes that subsequently occurred, it might be ques-

tioned whether some of the larger, more settled runrig townships in the far
west could have maintained their viability at such high levels of intensity.

The position of livestock within the economy of these runrig townships
requires careful definition. When we consider the views of surveyors and
commentators who visited the region over the eighteenth century, they con-
vey the impression that the prime product of farming even for runrig townships was that of cattle and dairy produce. Report after report states that the
main product of farming was cattle.[46] If we rely solely on their judgement,
traditional townships would be seen as organised first and foremost around
livestock production with the needs of arable having a lesser, supporting role.
Such an impression, though, would be misleading. What these surveyors
and commentators were really concerned with is what could be sold off the
farm. In a rural economy penetrated by markets, the farm enterprise is what
generates profit by off-the-farm sales. In this respect, their judgement does
not mislead.

By the eighteenth century, tenants across the region relied on sales of
cattle, cheese and butter to raise the increasing quantities of cash needed for
rents. As I tried to explain in Chapter 7, the live cattle trade for many tenants
probably developed around that organised by landowners who, when faced
with changes in the chiefly economy, began to market more and more of their
surplus, including cattle. In most cases, the droves were organised at a district
level, so that drovers would have found it easy to switch from a system of
droves assembled by landowners to one assembled directly from tenants.
Indeed, in practice, the difference between the two forms may have been
without meaning. Yet despite their involvement in marketing, the vast
majority of farmers in the region still organised their farm economy to
produce livelihood and subsistence rather profit. Marketing for them was
about use values or householding, with the cash raised being used to cover
their cash rents, or to buy in more subsistence, but no more. In a world of
tight margins and recurrent crises, what really mattered was subsistence.

It is a simple question of perspective. In the mind of surveyors and
commentators, what mattered was the marketable off-the-farm surplus. In
the mind of the ordinary farmer, it was the consumable on-the-farm surplus.
The difference of perspective captures the dilemma of the ordinary peasant
economy by the late eighteenth century. To achieve the former, arable
cropping had to take second place to the needs of livestock. To achieve the
latter, livestock had to take second place to the needs of arable. Of course, in
a 'sustainable' system of traditional farming, the two were integrated in a
mutually supportive way. Yet no analysis of traditional farming in the western
Highlands and Islands as it had developed by the late eighteenth century
could support such a conclusion about it. Arable had been expanded at the
expense of critical winterings or feed for stock and, in many townships, had
become dependent on extra-manurial supplements, some of which included
turf from summer pastures, to maintain arable output. Stories of stock being
poorly fed and being carried from the byre to the fields in spring reflect the

imbalance which prevailed between the two sectors.[47] In the most extreme cases, we might even say that communities were freeloading on their non-arable sector and running the risk of creating permanent environmental damage. Inevitably, such an imbalance created conflict within the township economy. More seriously, it created conflict within the estate economy, setting the needs of many of its tenants against the needs of the estate. It is this conflict at the heart of the estate economy that defines the core problem for the region by the late eighteenth century.

Given the huge social cost of the changes which eventually transformed this situation, it might be asked whether alternative solutions were available. What if an imaginary Smallholders Commission of 1784 as opposed to a Crofters Commission of 1884 had given more security to tenants, would it have led to a different path of change? Much revolves around the question of whether traditional farming on the eve of change was sustainable. Taking a critical view, it might be argued that farming had become too focused, too narrowly dependent on crops like potatoes and on high labour inputs. Its capacity to cope with crises was correspondingly reduced. Certainly, without a framework of estate support, its reaction to the famines which periodically afflicted the region, before and after the potato, might have been more disastrous.[48] Given the environmental damage that could be caused by traditional practices, there might have been other constraints on its sustainability. Possibly, a more freehold system might not have been able to control the pressure created by practices like the turfing of pastures, or the over-stocking of hill pastures. With so much low-value grazing, Highland communities might have fallen foul of the dilemma about all commons, with what belongs to everyone being valued by no one. Such scenarios, though, ignore what has been the persistent theme of this book, and that is, that far from being preserved like some archaic form held timeless in aspic, Highland and Hebridean communities displayed a remarkable responsiveness and capacity for adjustment over the sixteenth to eighteenth centuries. Arguably, they could have continued to be responsive even had the clearances or crofting not changed the nature of the problem.

NOTES

1. Postan, *The Medieval Economy and Society*, p. 198.
2. Whitaker, 'Some traditional techniques in modern Scottish farming', p. 164.
3. SRO, Campbell of Barcaldine Muniments, GD170/1629/58/1, Letter Taymouth, 23 Feb. 1697, has the note by the earl about grain deliveries which says 'I am told it has been caried here on my tenants horses as if it were myne, yet it is a great abuse to you & of me, for I do not allow you to be bagage men to any body but myself'.
4. NLS, Sutherland Papers, DEP313/923, Misc. Management Papers 1712–28, Memorial for Messrs. Alexander Gordon factor for William Lord Strathnaver, 1727.
5. The flow of grain from the northern Highlands by the early to mid-seventeenth century, especially from Caithness and Easter Ross, was especially significant,

with some estates constructing specialised port facilities, including warehouses for grain storage. The warehouses at Staxigo were reported to hold 4000 bolls of oats and 4000 bolls of barley. See Donaldson, *Caithness in the Eighteenth Century*, p. 157. To judge from Brand's figures, these warehouses alone would have handled half the grain exported from Caithness; see Brand, *Brief Description of Orkney, Zetland, Pightland-Firth and Caithness*, p. 225. See also Richards and Clough, *Cromartie*, pp. 42–3; Whyte, *Agriculture and Society*, pp. 223–34.

6. We have fewer clues as to how Breadalbane regularly disposed of the grain rents which he gathered in from areas like Netherlorne, other than references to the sale of meal to the garrison at Fort William in the 1690s; see SRO, Campbell of Barcaldine Muniments, GD170/62943, Letter, 5 November 1694.

7. SRO, Fraser Mackintosh Collection, GD128/23/2, Copy Tack of the Teinds of the Lewes etc by the Bishop of the Isles to Kenneth Earl of Seaforth, 1663. The continuing perceptions of distance are well shown by the way a tenant brought in to Strowan during the mid-eighteenth century by the Forefeited Estates Commissioners, a Mr Rattray, was reported to be 'arranging to leave the district on account of his distance from markets and the expense of carriage', Millar (ed.), *Forfeited Estates Papers*, p. 252.

8. Haldane, *The Drove Roads of Scotland*, pp. 85–9.

9. SRO, Breadalbane Muniments, GD112/14/13/1, Report on the Breadalbane Estate, ND. As regards the date of the report, it refers to the *recent* introduction of the steam service from Glasgow along the west coast. The first steam service to Mull was introduced in 1821; see Gray, *The Highland Economy 1750–1850*, p. 175. This would make the report almost contemporaneous with von Thünen's *Der isolierte Staat* whose concepts it shares.

10. Shaw, *The Northern and Western Islands*, pp. 43–6. See also Devine, *The Great Highland Potato Famine*, pp. 85–7; Macinnes, 'Crown, clans and fine', pp. 45–6.

11. SRO, Campbell of Barcaldine Muniments, GD170/817, Letter, 22 Nov. 1828.

12. Good examples of a superplus rent being paid by wadsetters and feuars are provided by SRO, Breadalbane Muniments, GD112/9/40, Rental of Braes of Lorne, 1718; ibid., GD112/16/13/3/1, Rental of Glenorchy, 1730.

13. A memorial for Lord Strathnaver, drawn up in 1727, spoke for many estates when it talked about 'making good the Rents of the Gentry, who generally speaking are the most backward in paying, so that they having no court or Authority to apply to, The Rents are on that account exceedingly ill-paid', NLS, Sutherland Papers, DEP313/923, memorial for Messrs Alexander Gordon factor for William Lord Strathnaver, 1727.

14. Cregeen, 'Tacksmen and their successors', p. 116.

15. The onoing presence of tacksmen is well shown by the fact that some of the most severe criticism of them was that made by travellers like Dr Johnson, who visited the region in the 1760s. See, for example, Johnson, *Journey to the Western Islands of Scotland*, pp. 86–7.

16. *Burt's Letters from the North of Scotland*, ii, pp. 155–6.

17. Cawdor Castle, Cawdor Papers, Bundle 721, Rent of Ilay for the Years 1703, 1704, 1705, 1706 and 1707.

18. A good illustration of this is provided by the rests or rebates issue by the MacLeod of Dunvegan estate for the crisis of 1771–2; see DC/MDP, 2/485/44, Rental of MacLeods lands in Skye and Harris 1771; ibid., 4/306/3/ Letter, Alexr. Morison, 18 March 1771. See also SRO, Macdonald of Sanda Muniments, GD92/173, Rental Book for Sanda's Lands, 1748–1752, rental for 1773; Johnson, *Journey to the Western Islands of Scotland*, p. 137. For extensive comments on the poor seasons of the early 1780s, see *PP*, 1846, xxxvii, 'Documents relative to the distress in Scotland in 1783'.

19. Pennant, *Tour 1769*, p. 228.

20. CDC/MP, GD221/3695/2, Memorial on the Abuses in the Present Management of Macdonalds Estate, 1733.
21. Macinnes, *Clanship, Commerce and the House of Stuart, 1603–1788*, pp. 221–8.
22. CDC/MP, GD221/3695/2, memorial on the Abuses in the Present Management of Macdonalds estate, 1733, provides a good illustration of how the inputs to the management of Highland estates began to change by the first half of the eighteenth century.
23. Virtually all the great Highland and Hebridean estates were surveyed during the eighteenth century, but especially between the 1760s and 90s. The earliest survey, but one that did not involve a cartographic survey, was Sir Alexander Stanhope's survey of Ardnamurchan and Sunart. It is clear from a letter which he wrote to Lord Hardwicke, though, that Stanhope felt that a detailed topographic survey, as well as an inventory of all resources, should be made of areas like Argyll, see Murray of Stanhope, *True Interest*, appendix, letter to Lord Hardwicke (1740).
24. An indication of just how scarce timber was in parts of the western Highlands and Islands is provided by the way tenants were allowed to remove critical items of house timber, such as roof couples and doors, at the end of their lease. A note on the duke of Argyll's possessions on Coll, or the 'two ends of Coll', talked about it being 'customary in that part of the Country to carry off timber' from houses, IC/AP, Minutes of proceedings in the Duke of Argyll's Business, Sept. and Oct. 1747. See also NLS, DEP313/3326, Lease register for the Reay Estate, 1797–1815 and Dodgshon, 'West Highland and Hebridean settlement', pp. 422–3.
25. As well as a growing amount of evidence restricting tenants' use of woodland, particularly for grazing by goats and sheep, one also finds evidence of traditional rights of woodleave being costed. Good instances of quoted prices for plough beams and roof couples can be found in DC/MDP, 2/500, Mr. Nicol's Report on the Value of the Woods of Glenelg, May, 1778, with 'Cupel Trees Manufactured Sold the Tennants' at 12/- per dozen and ploughbeams at 4/- per dozen, different prices prevailing when they were sold off the estate. Evidence for the introduction of a 'rate per use' instead of woodleave for house timbers and the like so as to curb the malpractices of the latter are noted in SRO, Breadalbane Muniments, GD112/11/1/14, Petition for the Tennents of Toyer, etc, 1722; Ibid., GD112/16/102/13, Extension of Report of Lord Breadalbane's Woods in Argyllshire by John Campbell, 1783. The taking of such timbers also figures in local court proceedings; see SRO, Clanranald Papers, GD201/1/227A, Minutes of Baron Court at Borrodill Arrisaig, 1739; SRO, Mackenzie Muniments, GD403,40/1–2 Meeting of the Justices of the Peace for Skye, 1788.
26. For instance, MacLeod of Dunvegan's woods in Glenelg were divided between 'Sky Harries and Glenelg'; DC/MDP, 2/500, Letter concerning woods at Glenelg, 27 April 1778. Their planned sale in 1778 recommended that this arrangement should be abandoned. Likewise, part of the woods at Dignish was reserved to supply the needs of tenants on Luing and Seil for 'house timber'; SRO, Breadalbane Muniments, GD112/16/10/2/12, Report on the situation of Lord Breadalbane's Woods in Argyllshire by John Campbell, 1783. The earl's tenants on Lismoir had woodleave in Kingarloch; ibid., GD112/16/10/2/1, Report James Campbell, 1728. Tenants on Tiree had wood leave in Morvern, IC/AP, Bundle 663, Instructions ... Morvern 17 Feb. 1733.
27. SRO, Breadalbane Muniments, GD112/16/10/2/11, Report of State of Lord Breadalbane's woods in Argyleshire 1786, reports that 1850 acres out of 2030 acres of firwoods was in the hands of the Lorne Furnace Company.
28. SRO, MacLaine of Lochbuie Papers, GD174/737, Copy Contract betwixt Colin Campbell of Carwhin and Nathanial Taylor, 1756.

29. A good illustration of the controls on kelp are provided by SRO, Seaforth Papers, GD46/1/278, Articles of sett, ND but probably early nineteenth century.

30. See, for example, SRO, Campbell of Barcaldine Muniments, GD170/420/1/13, Scheme of Glenure's Composition to the Duke of Argyll on his Entry 1767.

31. SRO, Breadalbane Muniments, GD112/11/1/1/14, Petition for the Tennents of Toyer, etc, 1722.

32. SRO, Campbell of Stonefield Papers, GD14/17, Mr. Campbell of Knockbuy's Epistle about Encouraging Manufacturing in Argyllshire, 1744.

33. SRO, Breadalbane Muniments, GD112/14/12/7, Lord Breadalbane's Querys, with answers & observations thereto by His Lordships Chamberlain in Argyllshire, 1783.

34. Good examples are provided by Glenorchy. Despite its shift in sheep in the late 1780s, its farms were still shared between two or three tenants down into the early nineteenth century.

35. Ibid., GD112/16/13/4/9, Report relative to sundry farms belonging to the earl of Breadalbane, by Robert Reid, 1810 provides good illustration of extent to which 'sheep' farms were still cropping grain for subsistence and even for sale, with a number reporting grain surpluses.

36. *Farmer's Magazine*, iv, p. 108.

37. *Farmer's Magazine*, iv, p. 51.

38. A good illustration of the turnover in land is provided by Gaskell's study of Morvern in *Morvern Transformed*.

39. CDC/MP, GD221/4190/13.

40. Ibid., GD221/5913, Report on Lord Macdonald's Estate on Skye, 1829.

41. See, for example, SRO, Breadalbane Muniments, GD112/12/1/5, Letter by John Campbell, 1795.

42. Ibid., GD112/12/1/2/14, Proposals for the Set and Improvements of Netherlorn, 1785.

43. Ibid., GD112/14/13/1, Report on the Breadalbane Estate ND.

44. SRO, Seaforth Papers, GD46/17/55, Volume of Letters, October, 1800.

45. The issue of Stathnaver is well dealt with in Richards, *A History of the Highland Clearances*, pp. 284–313. See also Fairhurst, 'The surveys for the Sutherland clearances'.

46. A survey of Harris in 1772, for instance, declared 'the staple commodity of the country' to be cattle, DC/MDP, 1/382, Copy of Correspondence betwixt A.B. and Mr. Fraser regarding the Sale of Harris, 6 Jan. 1772, whilst an 1825 sale description of Ulva said that even the 'smaller tenants live Cheifly by the rearing of cattle' though it went on, the 'oysters of Ulva are still more celebrated'; SRO, MacLaine of Lochbuie Papers, GD174/1087/1 Particulars of the Estate of Ulva, 1825.

47. Typical of the complaints about the poor stock condition of many Highland stock, especially those held by smaller tenants, is well shown by a tack agreement relating to East Loch, 1795, states that 'most of the Farms of Arran are burdened with too many Horses, Black Cattle, and Sheep, which by being ill fed, and ill attended to, are of small value'; see Brodick Castle, Arran Estate Papers, Printed tack agreement relating to East Loch, 1795.

48. In fact, by the time of the Highland potato famine in the 1840s, most commentators seem to favour a limited role for landlords whilst allowing for exceptions like MacLeod of Dunvegan. See, for example, Hunter, *The Making of the Crofting Community*, pp. 50–72, though Devine, *The Great Highland Potato Famine*, pp. 83–105 allows them a greater role.

Bibliography

MANUSCRIPT SOURCES

Scottish Record Office, Edinburgh

Forfeited Estates Papers, 1715 and 1745
GD14 Campbell of Stonefield Papers
GD46 Seaforth Papers
GD50 John MacGregor Collection
GD64 Campbell of Jura Papers
GD72 Macdonald of Sanda Muniments
GD112 Breadalbane Muniments
GD116 Campbell of Duntroon Muniments
GD128 Fraser Mackintosh Collection
GD170 Campbell of Barcaldine Muniments
GD174 MacLaine of Lochbuie
GD201 Clanranald Papers
GD305 Cromartie Papers
GD403 Mackenzie Papers
GD437 MacNeill of Taynish and Campbell of Danna papers

National Library of Scotland, Edinburgh

Murray Papers
Sutherland Papers

Inveraray Castle, Inveraray, Argyll

Argyll Papers

Dunvegan Castle, Dunvegan, Skye

MacLeod of Dunvegan Papers

Clan Donald Centre, Armadale House, Skye

Lord Macdonald Papers

Cawdor Castle
Campbell of Cawdor Muniments

Arran Estate Office, Brodick, Arran
Arran Papers

Brymor Jones Library, Hull University
Sir Ian Macdonald of Sleat Papers

PRINTED CONTEMPORARY SOURCES

Acts of Parliament of Scotland, 12 vols. Edinburgh, 1814–75.

Adam, R. J. (ed.), *Home's Survey of Assynt*, Scottish Historical Society, 3rd series, vol. lii. Edinburgh, 1960.

Beaufoy, H., *Substance of the Speech of Henry Beaufoy*. London: privately printed, 1788.

Boswell, J., *The Journal of a Tour to the Hebrides*. London: J. M. Dent, 1909 edition.

Brand, J., *Brief Description of Orkney, Zetland, Pightland-Firth and Caithness*, first published 1701, edited by W. Brown. Edinburgh: W. Brown, 1883.

Brown, P. H., *Register of the Privy Council of Scotland, vii, 1905–6*. Edinburgh: HM Register House, 1915.

Burnett, G. (ed.), *Exchequer Rolls of Scotland, xii, 1502–1507*. Edinburgh: HM Register House, 1889.

Burt's Letters from a Gentleman in the North of Scotland to His Friend in London, first published 1754, edited by R. Jamieson. Edinburgh: W. Paterson, 1876.

Cregeen, E. (ed.), *Argyll Estate Instructions (Mull, Morvern, Tiree), 1771–1805*, Scottish History Society, 4th series, 2 vols. Edinburgh, 1964.

Garnett, T., *Observations on a Tour through the Highlands and Part of the Western Isles of Scotland*, 2 vols. London: T. Cadell, 1799.

Gregory, D. and W. F. Skene (eds), *Collectanea de Rebus Albanicis*, Iona Club. Edinburgh, 1847.

HMC, *Third Report of the Royal Commission on Historical Manuscripts*. London, 1872.

Innes, C. (ed.), *The Black Book of Taymouth, With Papers from the Breadalbane Charter Room*, Bannatyne Club. Edinburgh, 1855.

Innes, C. (ed.), *The Book of the Thanes of Cawdor. A Series of Papers selected from the Charter Room at Cawdor 1236–1742*, Spalding Club. Edinburgh, 1859.

Innes, C. and J. E. Buchan (eds), *Origines Parochiales Scotiae*, Bannatyne club, 2 vols. Edinburgh, 1851–5.

Johnson, S., *Journey to the Western Islands of Scotland*, edited by M. Lascelles. New Haven: Yale University Press, 1971.

Knox, J., *Discourse on the Expediency of Establishing Fishing Stations or Small Towns in the Highlands of Scotland*. London: privately printed, 1786.

Lang, A. (ed.), *The Highlands of Scotland in 1750 From MS 104 in King's Library, BM*. Edinburgh: W. Blackwood, 1898.

McArthur, M. M. (ed.), *Survey of Lochtayside 1769*, Scottish History Society, 3rd series, vol. xxvii. Edinburgh, 1936.

Macculloch, J. R., *The Western Highlands and Islands of Scotland*, 4 vols. London: Longmans, 1824.

Macdonald, J., *General View of the Agriculture of the Hebrides, or Western Isles of Scotland*. Edinburgh: privately printed for R. Phillips, 1811.

Macfarlane, W. (ed.), *Geographical Collections Relating to Scotland Made by W. Macfarlane*, Scottish History Society, 1st series, vols li–liii, 3 vols. Edinburgh, 1906–8.

McKay, M .M. (ed.), *Rev. Dr. John Walker's Report on the Hebrides of 1764 and 1771*. Edinburgh: John Donald, 1980.

MacLeod, R. C. (ed.), *The Book of Dunvegan 1340–1920*, Spalding Club, 2 vols. Aberdeen, 1938–9.

McNeill, G. P. (ed.), *Exchequer Rolls of Scotland, xvii, 1537–1542*. Edinburgh: HM Register House, 1897.

Macphail, J. R. N. (ed.), *Highland Papers*, i, Scottish History Society, 2nd series, vol. 5. Edinburgh, 1910–11.

Macphail, J. R. N. (ed.), *Highland Papers*, ii, Scottish History Society, 2nd series, vol. 12. Edinburgh, 1914–15.

Macphail, J. R. N. (ed.), *Highland Papers*, iii, Scottish History Society, 2nd series, vol. 20. Edinburgh, 1918–19.

Macphail, J. R. N. (ed.), *Highland Papers*, iv, Scottish History Society, 3rd series, vol. 22. Edinburgh, 1932–3.

Martin, M., *A Description of the Western Islands of Scotland*, 2nd edition, 1716. Edinburgh: Mercat Press, 1981.

Masson, D. (ed.), *Register of the Privy Council of Scotland, vi, 1599–1604*. Edinburgh: HM Register House, 1884.

Masson, D. (ed.), *Register of the Privy Council of Scotland, viii, 1607–1610*. Edinburgh: HM Register House, 1887.

Masson, D. (ed.), *Register of the Privy Council of Scotland, ix, 1610–1613*. Edinburgh: HM Register House, 1889.

Masson, D. (ed.), *Register of the Privy Council of Scotland, x, 1613–1616*. Edinburgh: HM Register House, 1891.

Millar, A. (ed.), *A Selection of Scottish Forfeited Estates Papers 1715–1745*, Scottish History Society, 1st series, vol. lvii. Edinburgh, 1909.

Mitchell, A., 'James Robertson's tour through some of the western islands, etc, of Scotland in 1768', *Proc. Society of Antiquities of Scotland* xxxii (1897–8), pp. 14–15.

Munro, R.W. (ed.), *Monro's Western Isles of Scotland and the Geneaologies of the Clans 1549*. Edinburgh: Oliver and Boyd, 1961.

Murray of Stanhope, Sir Alexander, *The True Interest of Great Britain, Ireland and Our Plantations*, including 'Anatomie of Ardnamoruchan and Swinard'. London: privately printed, 1740.

The Old Statistical Account of Scotland, 21 vols. Edinburgh, 1791–99.

Pennant, T., *Tour in Scotland and a Voyage to the Hebrides 1772*, 2 vols. Chester: John Monk, 1772.

Pennant, T., *A Tour in Scotland 1769*. London: Benjamin White, 1776 edition.

Report of the Commissioners of Inquiry into the Conditions of the Crofters and Cottars in the Highlands and Islands. pp. XXXII–XXXIX. London, 1884.

Smith, A., *An Inquiry into the Nature and Causes of the Wealth of Nations*, ed. E. Cannan. London: Methuen, 1930 edition.

Smith, G. G. (ed.), *The Book of Islay*. Glasgow: privately printed, 1895.

Walker, J., *Economical History of the Hebrides and the Highlands of Scotland*, 2 vols. Edinburgh: University Press, 1808.

Wills, V. (ed.), *Reports on the Annexed Estates 1755–1769*. Edinburgh: Scottish Record Office, 1973.

Wills, V. (ed.), *Statistics of the Annexed Estates 1755–56*. Edinburgh: Scottish Record Office, 1973.

SECONDARY SOURCES

Adam, M. I., 'The Highland emigration of 1770', *Scottish Historical Review* xvi (1919), pp. 280–93.

Adam, M. I., 'The causes of the Highland emigrations of 1783–1803, *Scottish Historical Review* xvii (1920), pp. 73–89.

Andersen, S., 'Norse settlement in the Hebrides: what happened to the natives and what happened to the Norse immigrants', in I. Wood and N. Lund (eds), *People and Places in Northern Europe 500–1600; Essays in Honour of Peter Hayes Sawyer*. Woodbridge: Boydell, 1991, pp. 131–47.

Argyll, duke of, *Crofts and Farms in the Hebrides being an Account of the Management of an Island Estate for 130 Years*. Edinburgh: David Douglas, 2nd edition, 1883.

Armit, I., 'Broch landscapes in the Western Isles', *Scottish Archaeological Review* 5 (1988), pp. 78–86.

Armit, I. (ed.), *Beyond the Brochs: The Later Iron Age in Atlantic Scotland*. Edinburgh: Edinburgh University Press, 1990.

Armit, I., *The Later Prehistory of the Western Isles of Scotland*, BAR Reports, British series, no. 221. Oxford, 1992.

Armit, I., *The Archaeology of Skye and the Western Isles*. Edinburgh: Edinburgh University Press, 1996.

Bangor-Jones, M., 'The clearances in Assynt', paper presented to annual conference of Institute of British Geographers. Edinburgh, 1983, 14 pp.

Bangor-Jones, M., 'Ouncelands and pennylands in Sutherland and Caithness', in L. J. Macgregor and B. E. Crawford (eds), *Ouncelands and Pennylands*, St John's House papers, no. 3. St Andrews: University of St Andrews, 1987, pp. 13–23.

Bangor-Jones, M. 'Mackenzie families of the barony of Lochbroom', in J. R. Baldwin (ed.), *People and Settlement in North-West Ross*. Aberdeen: Scottish Society for Northern Studies, 1994, pp. 79–117.

Bangor-Jones, M., 'Society and Economy', forthcoming in a volume on Strathnaver.

Bannerman, J., 'The Lordship of the Isles', in J. Brown (ed.), *Scottish Society in the Fifteenth Century*. London: Edward Arnold, 1977, pp. 209–40.

Barrow, G. W. S., 'The Highlands in the lifetime of Robert the Bruce', in G. W. S. Barrow, *The Kingdom of the Scots. Government, Church and Society from the Eleventh to the Fourteenth Century*. London: Edward Arnold, 1973, pp. 362–83.

Barrow, G. W. S., 'The sources for the history of the Highlands in the middle ages', in L. MacLean (ed.), *The Middle Ages in the Highlands*. Inverness: Inverness Field Club, 1981, pp. 11–22.

Barrow, G. W. S., 'The lost Gaidhealtachd of medieval Scotland', in L. Gillies (ed.), *Gaelic and Scotland Alba Agus A'Ghaidhlig*. Edinburgh: Edinburgh University Press, 1989, pp. 67–88.

Barrow, G. W. S., *The Anglo-Norman Era in Scottish History*. Oxford: Clarendon Press, 1980.

Bil, A., *The Shieling 1600–1840. The Case of the Central Scottish Highlands*. Edinburgh: John Donald, 1990.

Bradley, R., *The Social Foundations of Prehistoric Britain*. London: Longman, 1984.

Brown, J. M. (ed.), *Scottish Society in the Fifteenth Century*. London: Edward Arnold, 1977.

Brown, K. M., *Bloodfeud in Scotland 1573–1625. Violence, Justice and Politics in Early Modern Society*. Edinburgh: John Donald, 1986.

Caird, J. B., *Park: A Geographical Study of a Lewis Crofting District*. Nottingham: Geographical Field Group, 1958.

Caird, J. B., 'The creation of crofts and new settlement patterns in the Highlands

and Islands of Scotland', *Scottish Geographical Magazine* 103 (1987), pp.
    67–75.

Caird, J. B. and H. A. Moisley, 'The Outer Hebrides', in J. A. Steers (ed.), *Field
    Studies in the British Isles*. London: Nelson, pp. 374–90.

Cameron, A. C., 'Ancient farming customs in Scotland', *Trans. Highland and
    Agricultural Society of Scotland*, 4th series, v (1873), pp. 292–311.

Carmichael, A., 'Grazing and agrestic customs of the outer Hebrides', *The Celtic
    Review* x (1914–16), pp. 40–54, 144–8, 254–62 and 358–75.

Catt, J., 'Longterm consequences of using artificial and organic fertiliser: the
    Rothamsted experiments', in Foster and Smout (eds), *History of Soils and Field
    Systems*, pp. 119–34.

Charles-Edwards, T., *Early Irish and Welsh Kinship*. Oxford: Clarendon Press, 1993.

Coull, J. R., 'The isle of Tiree', *Scottish Geographical Magazine* lxxviii (1962), pp.
    17–32.

Cowan, E. J., 'Clanship, kinship and the Campbell acquisition of Islay', *Scottish
    Historical Review* lviii (1979), pp. 132–57.

Crawford, B. E., *Scandinavian Scotland*. Leicester: Leicester University Press, 1987.

Crawford, I. A., Contributions to a history of domestic settlement in North Uist',
    Scottish Studies ix (1965), pp. 34–63.

Crawford, I. A., 'The present state of settlement history in the west highlands and
    Islands', A. O'Connor and D. V. Clarke (eds), *From the Stone Age to the 'Forty-
    Five*. Edinburgh: John Donald, 1983, pp. 350–67.

Crawford, I. A., 'The Udal', *Current Archaeology* 147 (1996), pp. 84–94.

Cregeen, E., 'Tacksmen and their successors: a study of tenurial reorganisations in
    Mull, Morvern and Tiree in the early eighteenth century', *Scottish Studies* 13
    (1969), pp. 93–144.

Cregeen, E., 'The changing role of the house of Argyll and the Highlands', in I. M.
    Lewis (ed.), *History and Social Anthropology*, ASA monograph no. 7. London:
    Tavistock Publications, 1970, pp. 153–90.

Dalton, G. (ed.), *Primitive, Archaic and Modern Economies. Essays of Karl Polanyi*.
    Boston: Beacon Press, 1968.

Darling, F. *West Highland Survey*. Oxford: Oxford University Press, 1955.

Davidson, D. A. and I. A. Simpson, 'Deep top soil formation in Orkney', *Earth
    Surface Processes* 9 (1984), pp. 61–81.

Dawson, J. E. A., 'The origins of the Road to the Isles: trade, communications and
    Campbell power in early modern Scotland', in R. Mason and N. Macdougall
    (eds), *People and Power in Scotland. Essays in Honour of T. C. Smout*. Edinburgh:
    John Donald, 1992, pp. 74–103.

Devine, T., *The Great Highland Potato Famine: Hunger, Emigration and the Scottish
    Highlands in the Nineteenth Century*. Manchester: Manchester University Press,
    1988.

Devine, T., *Clanship to Crofter's War. The Social Transformation of the Scottish
    Highlands*. Manchester: Manchester University Press, 1994.

Dodgshon, R. A., 'The nature and development of infield–outfield in Scotland',
    Transactions, Institute of British Geographers 59 (1973), pp. 1–23.

Dodgshon, R. A., 'Law and landscape in early Scotland', in A. Harding (ed.),
    Lawmakers and Lawmaking in British History, Royal Historical Society's
    Studies in History series. London, 1980, pp. 127–45.

Dodgshon, R. A. 'Symbolic classification and the development of early Celtic
    landscape', in E. Lyle (ed.), *Duality*. Cosmos: Yearbook of Traditional
    Cosmology Society, Edinburgh, 1985, pp. 61–83.

Dodgshon, R. A., *The European Past. Social Evolution and Spatial Order*. London:
    Macmillan, 1987.

Dodgshon, R. A., 'The ecological basis of Highland peasant farming

1500–1800 AD', in H. H. Birks, H. J. B. Birks, P. E. Kaland and D. Moe (eds), *The Cultural Landscape: Past, Present and Future*. Cambridge: Cambridge University Press, 1988, pp. 139–51.

Dodgshon, R. A., 'Pretense of blude and place of thair duelling: the nature of Highland clans, 1500–1745', in R. A. Houston and I. D. Whyte (eds), *Scottish Society 1500–1800*. Cambridge: Cambridge University Press, 1989, pp. 169–98.

Dodgshon, R. A., 'Farming practice in the western Highlands and Islands before crofting: a study in cultural inertia or opportunity costs?', *Rural History* 3 (1993), pp. 173–89.

Dodgshon, R. A., 'West Highland and Hebridean landscapes: have they a history without runrig?', *Journal of Historical Geography* 19 (1993), pp. 383–98.

Dodgshon, R. A., 'Strategies of farming in the western Highlands and Islands of Scotland prior to crofting and the clearances', *Economic History Review* xlvi (1993), pp. 679–701.

Dodgshon, R. A., 'West Highland and Hebridean settlement prior to crofting and the clearances: a study in stability or change?', *Proceedings of the Society of Antiquaries of Scotland* 123 (1993), pp. 419–38.

Dodgshon, R. A., 'Rethinking Highland field systems', in Foster and Smout (eds), *The History of Soils and Field Systems*, pp. 53–65.

Dodgshon, R. A., 'Budgeting for survival: nutrient flow and traditional highland farming', ibid., pp. 83–93.

Dodgshon, R. A., 'Modelling chiefdoms in the Scottish highlands and islands prior to the '45', in B. Arnold and D. Blair Gibson (eds), *Celtic Chiefdom: Celtic State*. Cambridge: Cambridge University Press, 1995, pp. 99–109.

Dodgshon, R. A., 'Deconstructing highland landscapes', unpublished manuscript.

Dodgshon, R. A. and G. Olsson, 'Productivity and nutrient use in eighteenth century Scottish Highland townships', *Geografiska Annaler* 70B (1988), pp. 39–51.

Donaldson, J. E., *Caithness in the Eighteenth Century*. Edinburgh: The Moray Press, 1938.

Duffy, P., 'The territorial organisation of Gaelic landownership and its transformation in County Monaghan 1591–1640', *Irish Geography* 14 (1981), pp. 1–26.

Duncan, A. A. M. and A. L. Brown, 'Argyll and the isles in the earlier Middle Ages', *Proceedings of the Society of Antiquaries of Scotland* xc (1956–7), pp. 192–220.

Easson, A. R., 'Ouncelands and pennylands in the west Highlands of Scotland', in L. J. Macgregor and B. E. Crawford (eds), *Ouncelands and Pennylands*, St John's House papers no. 3. St Andrews: University of St Andrews, 1987, pp. 1–11.

Evans, E., 'The Atlantic ends of Europe', *Advancement of Science* 15 (1958), pp. 54–64.

Evans, E. E., *The Personality of Ireland: Habitat, Heritage and History*. Cambridge: Cambridge University Press, 1973.

Fairhurst, H., 'The surveys for the Sutherland clearances, 1813–1820', *Scottish Studies* viii (1964), pp. 1–18.

Fellows-Jensen, G., 'Viking settlement in the Northern and Western Isles: the place name evidence as seen from Denmark and the Danelaw', in A. Fenton and H. Pálsson (eds), *The Northern and Western Isles in the Viking Age*. Edinburgh: John Donald, 1984, pp. 148–68.

Fenton, A., *The Shape of the Past 2: Essays in Scottish Ethnology*. Edinburgh: John Donald, 1986.

Foster, S. and T. C. Smout (eds), *The History of Soils and Field Systems*. Aberdeen: Scottish Cultural Press, 1994.

Fox, R., *The Tory Islanders. A People of the Celtic Fringe*. Cambridge: Cambridge University Press, 1978.

Fox, R. G., 'Lineage cells and regional definition in complex societies', in C. A. Smith (ed.), *Regional Systems, vol. 11: Social Systems*. New York: Academic Press, 1976, pp. 95–121.

Gaskell, P. , *Morvern Transformed: A Highland Parish in the Nineteenth Century*. Cambridge: Cambridge University Press, 1968.

Geddes, A., 'Conjoint tenants and tacksmen on the isle of Lewis, 1715–26', *Economic History Review*, 2nd series 1 (1948–9), pp. 54–60.

Gibson, A. J. S. and T. C. Smout, 'Scottish food and Scottish history, 1500–1800', in R. A. B. Houston and I. D. Whyte (eds), *Scottish History 1500–1800*. Cambridge: Cambridge University Press, 1989, pp. 59–84.

Gibson, A. J. S. and T. C. Smout, *Prices, Food and Wages in Scotland 1550–1780*. Cambridge: Cambridge University Press, 1995.

Grant, A., *Independence and Nationhood: Scotland 1306–1469*. London: Edward Arnold, 1984.

Grant, A., 'Scotland's celtic fringe in the late middle ages: the Macdonald Lords of the Isles and the Kingdom of the Isles', in R. R. Davies (ed.), *The British Isles 1100–1500: Comparisons, Contrasts and Connections*. Edinburgh: John Donald, 1988, pp. 18–41.

Grant, I. F., *Social and Economic Development of Scotland*. Edinburgh: Oliver and Boyd, 1930.

Grant, I. F., *Highland Folk Ways*. London: Routledge and Kegan Paul, 1961.

Gray, M., 'Economic welfare and money income in the Highlands 1750–1850', *Scottish Journal of Political Economy* 11 (1955), pp. 47–63.

Gray, M., *The Highland Economy 1750–1850*. Edinburgh: Oliver and Boyd, 1957.

Haldane, A. R. B., *The Drove Roads of Scotland*. Edinburgh: Nelson, 1952.

Halstead, P. and J. O'Shea, 'A friend in need is a friend indeed: social storage and the origins of social ranking', in C. Renfrew and S. Shennan (eds), *Ranking, Resource and Exchange*, New directions in archaeology. Cambridge: Cambridge University Press, 1982, pp. 92–9.

Hunter, J., *The Making of the Crofting Community*. Edinburgh: John Donald, 1976.

Innes, C., *Lectures on Scotch Legal Antiquities*. Edinburgh: Edmonston and Douglas, 1872.

Jackson, A., *The Oldest Irish Tradition: A Window on the Iron Age*. Cambridge: Cambridge University Press, 1964.

Kirch, P. V., 'Polynesian prehistory: cultural adaptation in an island ecosystem', *American Scientist* 68 (1980), pp. 39–48.

Kirch, P. V., *The Evolution of Polynesian Chiefdoms*. Cambridge: Cambridge University Press, 1984.

Lamont, W. D., 'Old land denominations and "Old Extent"', *Scottish Studies*, part i, 1957, pp. 183–203, part ii, 1958, pp. 86–107.

Lamont, W. D., 'The Islay charter of 1408', *Proceedings of the Royal Irish Academy*, 60c (1959–60), pp. 163–87.

Leach, E. R., *Pul Eliya. A Village in Ceylon*. Cambridge: Cambridge University Press, 1961.

Leneman, L., *Living in Atholl 1675–1785*. Edinburgh: Edinburgh University Press, 1986.

Logan, J., *The Scottish Gael, or Celtic Manners, As Preserved Amongst the Highlanders*, 2 vols. Inverness: Hugh Mackenzie, 1876.

MacDonald, A. and A. MacDonald, *The Clan MacDonald*, 3 vols. Inverness: Northern Publishing Company, 1896–1904.

Macinnes, A. I., 'The impact of the civil wars and inter–regnum: Political disruption and social change within Scottish Gaeldom', in R. Mitchison and

P. Roebuck (eds), *Economy and Society in Scotland and Ireland 1500–1939*. Edinburgh: John Donald, 1988, pp. 58–69.

Macinnes, A. I., 'From clanship to commercial landlordism: landownership in Argyll from the seventeenth to the nineteenth century', *History and Computing* iii (1990), pp. 176–85.

Macinnes, A. I., 'Crown, clans and fine: the "Civilizing" of Scottish Gaeldom, 1587–1603', *Northern Scotland* 13 (1993), pp. 31–55.

Macinnes, A. I., *Clanship, Commerce and the House of Stuart, 1603–1788*. East Linton: Tuckwell Press, 1996.

MacKay, A., *The Book of MacKay*. Edinburgh: Norman MacLeod, 1906.

Mackenzie, A., *History of the Clan Mackenzie*. Inverness: A. and W. Mackenzie, 1879.

Mackenzie, W. C., *History of the Outer Hebrides*. Paisley: A. Gardner, 1903.

McKerral, A., 'Ancient denominations of agricultural land in eastern Scotland: a summary of recorded opinion', *Proceedings of the Society of Antiquaries of Scotland* lxxviii (1943–4), pp. 39–80.

McKerral, A., 'The tacksman and his holding in the south-west Highlands', *Scottish History Review* xxvi (1947), pp. 10–25.

McKerral, A., *Kintyre in the Seventeenth Century*. Edinburgh, 1948.

McKerral, A., 'Lesser land and administrative divisions in Celtic Scotland', *Proceedings of the Society of Antiquaries of Scotland* lxxxv (1950–1), pp. 52–64.

Macpherson, A. *Glimpses of Church and Social Life in the Highlands in Olden Times*. Edinburgh: W. Blackwood, 1893.

Macpherson, A. G., 'An old Highland genealogy and the evolution of a Scottish clan', *Scottish Studies* 10 (1966), pp. 1–42.

Macpherson, A. G., 'Migration fields in a traditional Highland community, 1350–1850', *Journal of Historical Geography* 10 (1984), pp. 1–14.

MacRae, A., *History of Clan MacRae*, Dingwall: A. M. Ross & Co., 1899.

Mair, L., *Primitive Government*. Harmondsworth: Penguin Books, 1962.

Mather, A. S., 'Pre-1745 land use and conservation in a Highland glen: an example from Glen Strathfarrar, north Inverness-shire', *Scottish Geographical Magazine* 86 (1970), pp. 159–69.

Moisley, H. A., *Uig: A Hebridean Parish*, parts i and ii. Nottingham: Geographical Field Group, 1961.

Moisley, H. A., 'Some Hebridean field systems', *Gwerin* 3 (1960), pp. 22–35.

Munro, J., 'The Lordship of the Isles', in L. MacLean (ed.), *The Middle Ages in the Highlands*. Inverness: Inverness Field Club, 1981, pp. 23–37,

Nicholson, R., *Scotland: The Later Middle Ages*, vol. ii, The Edinburgh History of Scotland. Edinburgh: Oliver and Boyd, 1974.

Nicolaisen, W. F. H., 'Norse settlement in the Northern and Western Isles', *Scottish Historical Review* xlviii (1969), pp. 6–17.

Offner, A., 'Between the gift and the market: the economy of regard', *Economic History Review* L (1997), pp. 450–76.

Parker Pearson, M., N. Sharples and J. A. Mulville, 'Brochs and iron age society: a reappraisal', *Antiquity*, 70 (1996), pp. 57–67.

Postan, M. M., *The Medieval Economy and Society: An Economic History of Britain 1100–1500*. London: Weidenfeld and Nicholson, 1973.

Richards, E., *A History of the Highland Clearances: Agrarian Transformations and the Evictions, 1746–1886*. London: Croom Helm, 1982.

Richards, E. and M. Clough, *Cromartie: Highland Life 1650–1914*. Aberdeen: Aberdeen University Press, 1989.

Sahlins, M., *Tribesmen*. Englewood Cliffs: Prentice Hall, 1968.

Sellar, W. D. H., 'Highland family origins – pedigree making and pedigree faking', in L. MacLean (ed.), *The Middle Ages in the Highlands*. Inverness: Inverness

Field Club, 1981, pp. 103–116.

Sellar, W. D. H., 'Celtic law and Scots law; survival and integration', *Scottish Studies* 29 (1989), pp. 1–27.

Shaw, F. J., *The Northern and Western Islands of Scotland: Their Economy and Society in the Seventeenth Century.* Edinburgh: John Donald, 1980.

Shiels, R. S., 'Improving soil productivity in the pre-fertiliser era', in B. M. S. Campbell and M. Overton (eds), *Land, Labour and Livestock. Historical Studies in European Agricultural Productivity.* Manchester: Manchester University Press, 1991, pp. 51–77.

Shipton, P. M., 'Strips and patches; a demographic dimension in some African land-holding and political systems', *Man* 19 (1984), pp. 613–34.

Simms, A., *Assynt. Die Kulturlandschaft Eines Keltischen Reliktgebietes im Nordwestschottischen Hochland,* Giessener Geographische Schriften, 16 (1969).

Simms, A., 'Geographical interpretations of historical sources: the highland parish of Assynt in Sutherland in the eighteenth century based on estate records and manuscript sources', *Recherches de Géographie Rurale. Hommage au Professor Frans Dussart.* Liège: Seminaire de Géographie de l'Université, 1979, pp. 337–55.

Simms, K., 'Guesting and feasting in Gaelic Ireland', *Journal of the Royal Society of Antiquaries of Ireland* 108 (1978), pp. 67–100.

Simpson, I. A., 'The chronology of anthropogenic soils in Orkney', *Scottish Geographical Magazine* 109 (1993), pp. 4–11.

Skene, W. F., *Celtic Scotland,* 3 vols. Edinburgh: Edmonston and Douglas, 1876–80.

Smith, A., *Jacobite Estates of the Forty-Five.* Edinburgh: John Donald, 1982.

Smith, C. T., W. M. Denevan and P. Hamilton, 'Ancient ridged fields in the region of Lake Titicaca', *Geographical Journal* 134 (1968), pp. 353–67.

Smout, T. C., 'Famine and Famine Relief in Scotland', in L. Cullen and T. C. Smout (eds), *Comparative Aspects of Scottish and Irish Economic and Social History, 1600–1900.* Edinburgh: John Donald, 1977, pp. 21–3.

Steer, K. A. and J. Bannerman, *Late Medieval Monumental Sculpture in the West Highlands.* Edinburgh: RCAMS, 1977.

Storrie, M. C., 'Islay: a Hebridean exception', *Geographical Review* 51 (1961), pp. 87–108.

Storrie, M. C., 'Landholdings and settlement evolution in west Highland Scotland', *Geografiska Annaler* 67b (1965), pp. 138–61.

Storrie, M. C., 'Landholding and population in Arran from the eighteenth century', *Scottish Studies* 11 (1967), pp. 49–74.

Storrie, M. C., *Islay: Biography of an Island.* Port Ellen: The Oa Press, 1981.

Thompson, W. P. L., 'Ouncelands and pennylands in Orkney and Shetland', in L. J. Macgregor and B. E. Crawford (eds), *Ouncelands and Pennylands,* St John's House papers no. 3, St Andrews: University of St Andrews, 1987, pp. 24–44.

Turnock, D., 'Crofting in Lochaber', *Scottish Studies* xii (1969), pp. 33–45.

Turnock, D., 'North Morar: the improving movement on a west highland estate', *Scottish Geographical Magazine* lxxxv (1969), pp. 17–30.

Uhlig, H., 'Old hamlets with infield and outfield systems in western and central Europe', *Geografiska Annaler* 43 (1961), pp. 285–312.

Whitaker, I., 'Some traditional techniques in modern Scottish farming', *Scottish Studies,* 3 (1959), pp. 163–88.

Whittington, G., 'The field systems of Scotland', in A. R. H. Baker and R. A. Butlin (eds), *Studies of Field Systems in the British Isles.* Cambridge: Cambridge University Press, 1973, pp. 530–79.

Whittington, G. and W. C. Ritchie, *Flandrian Environmental Evolution in North-East Benebecula and Southern Grimsay,* O'Dell Memorial Monograph no. 21. Aberdeen: University of Aberdeen, 1988.

Whyte, I. D., *Agriculture and Society in Seventeenth Century Scotland*. Edinburgh: John Donald, 1979.

Whyte, I. D., *Scotland Before the Industrial Revolution: An Economic and Social History c.1050–c.1750*. London: Longman, 1995.

Withers, C. W. J., *Gaelic Scotland: the Transformation of a Culture Region*. London: Routledge, 1988.

Wormald, J., 'Bloodfeud, kindred and government in early modern Scotland', *Past and Present* 87 (1980), pp. 54–97.

Wormald, J., *Lords and Men in Scotland: Bonds of Manrent 1442–1603*. Edinburgh: John Donald, 1985.

Young, M. W., *Fighting with Food: Leadership Values and Social Control in a Massim Society*. Cambridge: Cambridge University Press, 1971.

Youngson, A. J., *After the Forty-Five*. Edinburgh: Edinburgh University Press, 1973.

Index

EU Authorised Representative: Easy Access System Europe Mustamäe tee 5

0, 10621 Tallinn, Estonia gpsr.requests@easproject.com

Printed and bound by CPI Group (UK) Ltd, Croydon, CR0 4YY

16/04/2025

01846981-0001